TRUST ME

MICHAEL BINSTEIN
AND
CHARLES BOWDEN

TRUST ME

CHARLES KEATING
AND THE
MISSING BILLIONS

RANDOM HOUSE
New York

Grateful acknowledgment is made to the following for permission to reprint previously published material:

BUG MUSIC: Excerpt from "Don't Tell Me Nothing" written by Willie Dixon. Copyright © 1986 by Hoochie Coochie Music (BMI). Administered by Bug. International copyright secured. All rights reserved. Reprinted by permission.

CPP/BELWIN, INC.: Excerpt from "Pancho & Lefty" by Townes Van Zandt. Copyright © 1972, 1983 by Columbine Music, Inc. c/o EMI-U Catalog, Inc. World print rights controlled and administered by CPP/Belwin, Inc., 15800 N.W. 48th Avenue, PO Box 4340, Miami, Florida, 33014. Reprinted by permission.

HAMSTEIN PUBLISHING COMPANY, INC.: Excerpt from "Standing On the Edge of Love" written by Jerry L. Williams. Copyright © 1986 by Red Brazos Music, Inc., Urge Music, Careers-BMG Music Publishing, Inc. All rights reserved. International copyright secured. Reprinted by permission.

KING OF SPADES MUSIC: Excerpt from "Me and The Devil Blues" (take 1) by Robert Johnson. Copyright © 1978 by King of Spades Music. All rights reserved. Reprinted by permission.

Library of Congress Cataloging-in-Publication Data

Binstein, Michael.
Trust me : Charles Keating and the missing billions / Michael Binstein and Charles Bowden.
p. cm.
ISBN 0-679-41699-4
1. Lincoln Savings & Loan Association—Corrupt practices.
2. Savings and loan association failures—California.
3. Securities fraud—United States.
4. Keating, Charles H. I. Bowden, Charles. II. Title.
HG2626.I78B56 1993
364.1′68—dc20 [B] 92-56795

Book design by Charlotte Staub
Manufactured in the United States of America
24689753
First Edition

For Harold Binstein. The finest man I know.
And for Janice Binstein. The finest woman I know.

—Michael Binstein

For Charlie Keating. He played by the rules as he knew them.
And he played damned hard.
And for Ed Gray. When he finally got to where he wanted to be
in life,
he suddenly remembered where he'd come from and what he'd
come from.
And that made all the difference.
And for that old man who lost all his money in some ACC bonds
that went bad
and in his eighty-ninth year opened his veins in a bathtub
and then watched the blood seep from his arm
until he knew his life had left
his earthly body.
The rest of us, well, the hell with us. We're on our own lookout.

—Charles Bowden

> Q.: If there was one statement you could make to the public about Charles Keating, Jr., what would it be?
>
> Keating: I don't really know. I don't really know.
>
> —*Arizona Business Gazette,* February 27, 1984

Simply stated, the purpose of the fraudulent scheme and artifice was to enrich the Racketeering Defendants by: (1) attempting to realize extraordinary profits by gambling Lincoln's assets . . . ; (2) improperly diverting funds from Lincoln . . . through exorbitant salaries, bonuses, benefits, and the like.

> —Racketeering complaint filed against Charles
> H. Keating, Jr., and others, September 15, 1989

I am not Niagara Falls, I am a drop of water.

> —Charles Keating, Jr., November 21, 1989, private
> logs, listed as one of four points under
> Legal Note

> The Court: When was that? Was the call made after Friday, on Friday, or before Friday? You don't know?
>
> The Witness: Your Honor, Charles Keating calls four or five or six times a day when he's out of the office. I would guess—
>
> The Court: Not from Europe he doesn't, does he?
>
> The Witness: Yes, Your Honor.
>
> The Court: Even from Europe?
>
> The Witness: Charles Keating doesn't sleep. . . .
>
> —Testimony of Judy Wischer, president of
> American Continental Corporation, before Judge
> Stanley Sporkin, United States District Court,
> February 15, 1990, Washington, D.C. p. 2390

CONTENTS

PART ONE

DON'T
TELL ME
NOTHIN'

All my life you been doin' me wrong
Now I don't know how to get along.
But don't tell me nothin'
But don't tell me nothin'
But don't tell me nothin'.
I can see rock 'n' rollin' is good for me.

—Willie Dixon

He has talked for hours and hours, and still he does not tire. He was an executive with Lincoln Savings and Loan and then moved over to the parent company, American Continental Corporation. Now it is the spring of 1992, and all that is behind him—except for the long reach of the law. So far, he has beaten them. They have not touched him, not a bit. Oh, sure, he's had to sign agreements, make paybacks from all those good deals. And no one is paying him a couple of hundred thousand dollars a year now. But he is not criminally charged, he is not facing prison. And he is still young, he has a lot more tickets to ride, and this is plainly written in his eyes.

"Let me tell you about the government," he snaps. "It's not the way you think, not at all. Here's what they do: they call you in for questioning, and when you get there they're all waiting in a room. And then they haul out this kind of chart, and they say, 'Here's what we've got on you' and then they run down this chart, ping, ping, ping. And man, I mean to tell you, you look at that chart. And then they say, 'Maybe you can beat what we've got, but if you guess wrong, you're going to go to prison for X number of years.' Then they get into the fact that you can help them, you can help them build cases against others. Especially Charlie, that's the one they want. But, hey, they don't start asking you questions, this isn't like a conversation, no, no. Bullshit, if it's a conversation. They haul out this other damn chart, and man, it's long, and it's got all these points, all these incidents, issues and stuff. And they go down that chart, just boom, boom, and they say, 'What can you give us on this point? How about this other point? And that's all they want, just stuff on these exact moments. Not explanations, not general discussion, just this exact stuff. And I looked at it, and I thought, fuck them, they've got nothing on me. And I won. But it wasn't pleasant."

The man looks across his desk, his eyes hard now, all the easy *laughs gone. He looks and looks as if to say: that's your govern-ment, and they're no saints either.*

And it is impossible not to wonder, if you are honest with your-self and if you are alive and hungry, what you might have done if someone had offered to pay you a couple of hundred thousand dol-lars a year. And what you might have done if you'd been in the room with those federal lawyers and they hauled out those charts and read your future in instances of alleged criminal acts instead of in the stars.

Of course, that is what the man wants understood. Nothing is quite the way you might think until you have been there. He just glares across his desk as he lets this notion sink in.

THE
GOVERNMENT
MAN

Mike Manning is almost forty, and in some ways he is like Charlie
Keating and the people around Keating in this summer of 1989.
He faithfully attends the same Catholic church where many of
Charlie's current and former employees at American Continental
worship, and so he sees Keating's troops at Mass each week. He
is of the same heritage, a blend of Irish and German. He, like
Keating, is from that vague center of America, a son of that fabled
Middle America that has become an icon of presidents and their
handlers. He, too, once played sports—football and golf—and also
went on to become a lawyer. Likewise, he is a family man. And as
Phoenix bakes through June and July and August, he works out
of the offices on Camelback Road that up until April of 1989 were
part of the headquarters of the $6 billion American Continental
Corporation.

On April 13, 1989, ACC declared itself in Chapter 11, and the
next day federal authorities seized the corporation's key asset, Lincoln Savings and Loan, a federally insured bank, but the vault
seems to be at least a billion dollars short. That is where Manning
comes in—he does not work for ACC but is a fee attorney for the
federal government. His job is to find out where the money went.
He is a specialist in insurance and bank frauds, and just two days
earlier in a Kansas City courtroom he wrapped up a five-year case
against Mario Renda of New York, a fraud artist who has penetrated 153 financial institutions and put billions into play. The
case has been the education of Michael Manning: at first no one
believed the fraud was occurring, and even when Manning gath-

ered evidence many still did not believe. Renda had pioneered a new level of fraud, one utilizing wire transactions of money, widely separated banks and individuals who never knew one another: a crime invisible to all but the most observant and the most obsessed. For five years Manning had done nothing but the Renda case, and when he finished he had achieved a mastery of bank fraud. He worried that he would never find another opponent as brilliant as Renda. Before dealing with Renda's intricate financial world, Manning had always been a fan of Mafia movies. Now, after meeting real mobsters, his stomach is turned. For months he has been planning a relatively long family vacation as his reward. But seven days after Renda pleads guilty in Kansas, he is on a plane to enter a case concerning Lincoln Savings and Loan.

The FDIC, the government agency in charge of this little problem, the possibly billion-dollar-or-more default of Lincoln Savings and Loan, has hired him because he is one of the few lawyers in the country who might stand a prayer of sorting out the mess. The task is not simple. Manning can look out the window, across a narrow lane at the part of the building that houses ACC's skeleton staff, and see trucks pull up and drive away with bags of shredded documents. At times Keating and his entourage will suddenly sweep through the section of the complex that the government has seized (and posted with armed guards) like he still owns the place. He might suddenly stop, point to how someone has rearranged the furniture, and snicker at the peasantlike tastes of these federal clerks. Jesus, he hates disorder. Or he'll notice things—photos, calendars, what-all—that the government people have tacked on the walls and snort with contempt about what a herd of slobs the people of this country have to pay for. And then Keating will be gone like some angry god, leaving a searing vapor trail. His presence is a constant for the federal folks poring over the records of his busted empire. At times they are afraid to speak out loud—does he have the offices wired? And they take walks outside when serious conversations are necessary.

Phoenix itself, it seems to Mike Manning, is not exactly glad to see him and his colleagues. Charlie Keating, while loathed by many in the city for his heavy spending and his crusade against dirty movies, had poured almost a billion dollars into Arizona real estate. He was possibly the largest single source of capital in a state with slightly over three million people, and now the federal government has turned off this money faucet. One day that summer, he flies to the West Coast for work on the case and overhears two businessmen on the plane denouncing the regulators and the government for slandering this fine local entrepreneur, Charles H. Keating, Jr. He goes to Mass, and at that part of the ritual where each communicant must greet the person by his side, he turns to find an ACC employee who spurns his offer of fellowship. His wife and three children miss their home in the Washington, D.C., area and feel out of place in the hot Phoenix desert. One day his four-year-old daughter tells him that she wants to "go back to her own country."

Fifteen lawyers under him are working to build a case, and they are divided into SWAT teams to trace the various parts of the gigantic dying beast that is ACC. The federal government's investigators do not inspire confidence—one observer describes them as "guys who couldn't even tie their own shoelaces and now they are bumping up against a financial maze and they don't even have a clue as to what it is or how it operates. They almost apologize for even bothering a guy like Keating." Besides that, the government with all its money and power is handicapped in dealing with financial cases on the scale of Lincoln. It is simply not used to assigning to a single case the small army required to comb through Lincoln's records. A private fee attorney like Manning, oddly enough, has access to that kind of staff. Manning's employer, the Federal Deposit Insurance Corporation,* is skeptical of the allegations. Some FDIC officials feel there might be some merit in Keating's claim that he is being persecuted by a sister federal regulatory agency, the Federal Home Loan Bank Board, the government machine that supervises the nation's three thousand federally insured savings and loans and their trillion dollars' worth of deposits. Indeed, Manning himself, in searching through the wilderness of documents, stumbles upon bank board memoranda that track an almost secret war that has gone on for years between Charlie Keating and the federal bank regulators. When Manning files a preliminary finding with the FDIC and FHLBB in June 1989, there are those in the Washington office of the bank board who simply

---

*In August 1989, federal legislation (FIRREA, Financial Institutions Reform, Recovery, and Enforcement Act of 1989) creates the Resolution Trust Corporation, which supersedes the FDIC as Manning's employer.

don't buy it. He senses their distrust, their skepticism. So he goes back to work, back to an archive that overwhelms everyone who enters it.

This archive holds some of the surviving records of Charlie Keating's transactions: three million documents, a pile worthy of some Eastern European nation after a revolution. But Manning has tenacity. He hates to lose, and he believes whatever has happened is hidden in plain view in the endless stacks of papers. And he senses that this is a rare opportunity—the biggest banking failure in U.S. history, the biggest financial failure in the history of Arizona, and all of it the work of one man, Charles H. Keating, Jr. It takes just the briefest moment for Manning to realize he is not likely to come across such a man again.

Why would a man loan a hundred million dollars to another man whose net worth was minus $150,000? Why would a man spend tens of millions on a project in dying, if not clinically dead, downtown Detroit to finance something called the Hotel Pontchartrain? Why is a savings and loan based in southern California financing a 20 percent share of a bank run for Saudis in Europe? Why are tens of millions of dollars flowing out of an employee stock option plan? Why do strange Middle Eastern names like Jamal Radwan and Toufic Aboukhater pop up? Why are millions coursing toward such saintly names as Mother Teresa and Father Bruce Ritter? Why are there so damn many subsidiaries? And why do so many of the billions of dollars in deals seem to make little sense on paper or any money in the actual world? Just what has he stumbled into here?

He stares at a mountain of paper and learns a new language. He meets things with names like Crescent Hotel Group of Michigan (CHG/M) and then finds that one day CHG/M sells a hotel called Pontchartrain to something called Hotel Pontchartrain Limited Partnerships for the price of . . . for almost no real money at all, simply for assuming a $38 million debt and then paying a . . . let's see, paying something called a loan origination fee of $600,000. Plus kicking in $490,000 in cash. And then after this flutter in the bookkeeping ledger, CHG/M books $9.5 million in income. He cannot fathom just who these different entities are. When the lawyers under his command start interviewing ACC and Lincoln employees, they discover that the men and women often cannot give their job descriptions or name the particular subsidiary they work for. They are quick to answer only one question. Ask any of them who's their boss, and they look up with surprise and say, "Oh, I work for Charlie—we all work for Charlie."

So Manning sits and reads, day after day, week after week, month after month. He is a solid man, a football player who has gone a bit to flesh. His hair and mustache are neatly trimmed, his voice is soft and he laughs and smiles easily. But he is implacable, and his open, friendly face masks a fierce competitive drive. He does not play to lose. Even worse than losing is the sensation of being beaten, of having someone else conquer. In these ways he is very much like Charlie Keating. It is a hundred ten, a hundred fifteen in Phoenix, the city melts and lies limp under the desert sun. All those with a few bucks in their pockets flee to the beaches of the West Coast or elsewhere. God knows Keating does—he is in London, Paris, Switzerland, Germany, Monaco. Manning stays put.

Slowly, a useful line of argument emerges for Mike Manning. He has found the language, he has fashioned the plot that will enable him to create a kind of play in which Charlie Keating is the villain. This bit of legal theater pivots on very simple things, much as the Greek tragedies feed off elemental themes. One word: money. One direction: toward Charlie Keating. One tactic: a profusion of documents, corporations, individuals, financial instruments. It is all so simple, he thinks, once one gets the drift. What he is examining is an elaborate fraud—yes, dammit, that is the only accurate word, fraud. In fact, in Manning's entire legal career, Charlie Keating is the only individual he has come up against who has mastered every known form of bank fraud. The deals are not simply about making money but about moving money. And about booking profit. Biological life depends on energy flow, financial life depends on money flow. Just as green plants display many strategies in their efforts to capture sunlight, there are many ways a financial organism can structure a deal to capture money. But the need never ceases—when the financial sun is blocked for a long enough period of time, well, then comes the dying.

So Manning and his team sit down and write and write and write. By early September 1989, he has produced a typewritten document of 168 pages. This early draft of the RICO (Racketeering Influenced and Corrupt Organization) complaint seeks the return of $1.2 billion. Racketeering—the word conjures up images of

Al Capone or Charlie "Lucky" Luciano. Does it really fit Charlie
Keating, a family man who helps finance a high school for black
kids in Harlem? Manning knows that his belief in a giant fraud
perpetrated by highly paid, well-educated businesspeople will be
met with doubt. He knows he must present a clear narrative that
people can follow. It will not be enough to file a document that in-
dicts Charlie Keating; no, this time he must create pages that vin-
dicate his belief that illegal actions have taken place, that money
has not simply been lost in the hurly-burly of normal business,
but ripped off. In fact, not simply ripped off, and here is where he
realizes he really has to educate people, including his fellow members of the legal profession. God, this part drives him nuts. He'll
be at legal conferences, at those professional meetings, and other
attorneys will find out what he is working on, that Keating thing
that has been in all the newspapers, and they'll want to know,
well, where did Charlie stash the cash? They don't seem to realize
that isn't how it works, that there is no chest full of gold buried
in the yard, no big Zurich bank account with a couple of hundred
million slopping out of the drawer onto those antiseptic Swiss
floors. Hell, this is the twentieth century—what are they expecting,
Captain Kidd? Jesse James? And it is not about some pile of filthy
lucre busted out and hidden, it is about how money is spent, how
it flies from bank to bank, shell corporation to shell corporation,
nation to nation, flies at the speed of electronic impulses pulsing
through chips and wires, flies such distances and through so many
ports of call that almost never can anyone reconstruct its path and
connect its destination with its point of origin. Then this money is
all carefully recorded on the books, and those meticulous goddamn books attest that it is all legal and on the up-and-up. And
suddenly the damn money is gone, consumed, devoured, made
into things like salaries, securities, bonds, dinners, jet planes,
buildings, churches, films, charities, land, stocks, currency plays,
and on the books, on those endless computer printouts so orderly
and number rich, it is all recorded, accounted for—and gone. It all
looks confusing and complex and strange but vaguely legitimate,
though the feeling lingers that it is a parody of bookkeeping and
fiscal responsibility. Yet it looks legal, the documents have a reas-
suring feel to them, the stilted language of the bills of transmis-
sion rings with rectitude. What Manning is trying to explain are
acts that wear all the clothes of normal commerce, all the raiments

of the law. But not the intentions of legitimate business. There is
something so solid about the ornate designs on stock certificates,
the cumbersome caveats on bonds. So it is always difficult to get
people to make the move from such records to that chilling word:
fraud. Pulled off right in front of your eyes. A kind of rape, and
when you want to make sure you can beat those statutory
charges—ah, you say, she looked eighteen and not innocent—you
haul in a respected accounting firm to certify your books and a
huge law firm to go over the files for the regulators' review. And,
Mike Manning thinks, this happens every day, if you know how to
do it. It's a subtle, patient game. The accounting firms and those
big-league law firms seem seduced (well, it isn't that hard to lead
them when you lay down a trail of money), and before they know
it, they've crossed a line, committed themselves, in the rush of
serving the client and earning those wonderful fees, to acts recorded on memos and acts scribbled in the margins of sheets of paper, acts they will not want to have seen in the light of day, acts
they will not want to explain and answer for. And when you get
them to that point, then you own them. This is never discussed—
not if you do it right, not if you are patient and good at the game.
That is what Mike Manning wants people to understand, how corruption really works, how it goes down, how it is a silken game
pursued by well-heeled players who never mention any ugly words
while the action is going down. It is why he insists on this word—
fraud. And, of course, when it is all over, no one ever admits to
crossing the line, or that it exists.

He is at this moment less a lawyer than a kind of educator—hell,
more like a storyteller writing a novel with plot, characters, and
motives. Manning is going over the complaint yet one more time at
home over the weekend, a television is purring in the background.
It is tuned to CNN, and suddenly a broadcaster is talking about
the suit Manning is working on at that very moment, and then the
television screen fills with the actual front page of a working draft
of the document. Manning is stunned. Somehow, he thinks, the
invisible hand of Charlie Keating's world has reached into the tight
security of a federal suit and plucked out a preliminary copy of the
complaint. Of course, this does not make any sense—why would
Charlie Keating want to publicize his own coming indictment? But
he ticks off all the security measures he has instituted: the regular
sweeps of the office for possible bugs; the careful shredding of

work documents; the review of the janitorial service to make certain the people are trustworthy; the elaborate safeguards built into the office computer programs to ward off invaders—the kind of things, as it happens, Charlie Keating would regularly do. He has been on guard for months, ever since he and his staff discovered memos to Keating alerting him to the plans and thoughts of federal regulators and enforcement agencies. Manning hates playing on someone else's field, and for months he has felt he has had to do just that, stalk Charlie Keating in Phoenix, where it seems to Manning that everyone reports back to Keating. He has been warned by former Keating employees and business associates of Keating's passion for gathering intelligence by any means.

As CNN hums on with its report on the yet-to-be-filed complaint, Manning wonders if he has suffered some kind of Watergate-type break-in. Normally, the initial filing of a complaint is a cursory, legal shot across the bow. But Manning is no longer operating in a place where the word *normal* applies.

He has been to this place before, this world where the rules and beliefs of average people do not apply. Once when he was preparing the Renda case he was in a hotel working late at night to be sharp for a deposition the following morning. He called down for room service, and soon a properly uniformed hotel staffer rolled a cart with his dinner into his room. Later, after Renda's conviction, he discovered that substitutions had been made in the staff and the man who had brought him his meal was Renda's man checking up on how his work was progressing. How did he learn this? Renda later admitted it to a strike-force lawyer and the FBI.

Manning, like any good trial lawyer, sees himself as a kind of underdog. Charlie Keating—Christ, he's out there right now, and what in the hell is he up to? What might he do? Manning tells himself that he must not simply win in court. No, no, he must face down what he sees as a hostile state, he must confront an angry business community. And he must learn to live with an adversary—a guy who stands six foot five inches and practically sneers at the government, a guy who Manning now imagines is able to—goddammit!—come into his own home and look over his shoulder as he works. He can't get into Charlie Keating's house, which squats amid twenty-six walled acres of grass and trees, really a compound surrounded by the homes of his children. A kind of Hyannisport in the desert for a kind of Kennedy clan in the making.

He can't get at the various corporations, since on April 13, the night before the federal seizure, Keating and his people tucked them all away behind the security of a Chapter 11 filing. Charlie Keating knew they were coming for him. Somehow he had been tipped off, but months later Mike Manning and his squads of lawyers are still not sure just how.

Manning is in a war where everyone feels outnumbered. The people in the private sector being investigated by the authorities feel overwhelmed. It is, to be sure, a kind of permanent mental condition in the eighties, one so pervasive that even the federal government feels outgunned. There is more money circulating through the computer-driven financial world than anyone feels comfortable with. The high velocity of deals destroys any easy sense of security. The planet in some ways has become borderless; corporations and cartels rise above the bumbling actions of nations and drive these hoary entities—these governments with their flags and anthems—like invisible forces.

Business has become a kind of ghost in the machine of government. In 1980, the SEC interviews Michael Milken of Drexel Burnham Lambert about his bond-trading operation. The investigators typically pull down $25,000 or $30,000 per year, and now they discover they are stalking people who make millions a year. They ask Milken what his workday is like, and he tells them he has about two hundred telephone calls a day, often carrying on ten conversations at a crack. Ivan Boesky, the rising star of Wall Street, has three hundred buttons on his phone and an Orwellian intercom and video system trained on his brokers.

There is one other matter that bothers Manning, that actually offends him: greed. He totes up the salaries and payouts to Charlie Keating and his family members made during the five years they controlled Lincoln, and the number comes out around $34 million. He stares down at Charlie and Mary Elaine Keating's 1987 income tax return and sees over $5 million in income and almost no personal donations to charity. The millions given to Mother Teresa and Father Bruce Ritter flow from corporate coffers, and given the financial ruin of Lincoln, this means to Manning that Keating gave away other people's money. Manning hails from a kind of blue-collar world—athletic scholarships to get through college, taking a full load of classes, holding down two or three jobs at a time—and he hates greed. In fact, he worries that now that his income as a private attorney has slid into the six figures, his daughters will not have to work their way through college. And that this fact will somehow cheat them, make them less than they can be. Manning sees money as almost a by-product of his work—and he works all the time and is kind of embarrassed by his success. His personal heroes speak to something else in life: public service. When he looks at Charlie Keating's world—the corporate planes, the gold-plated fixtures, the lavish meals—he is disturbed. He prides himself on not being motivated by money, on not making decisions based on money, on not living for money. And now day after day as he plows through the documents he seems to be staring at almost a lust for money. He is at a loss for words, and so he does what he always does in a big case: he creates a lexicon, a new language. Then he insists that everyone under him use this lexicon. He will force people to understand, he thinks, by teaching them new words and phrases from a vocabulary he creates and controls. Terms like "upstreaming cash," "accommodation parties," "straw buyers," "sham transactions." And his very favorite: fraud. Again and again, he will use the word fraud until he makes it stick.

Mike Manning goes to Mass and still sees the people who work at ACC. He has at last begun to imagine a scenario that will describe the dimensions of what their boss has done. But there is one remaining task he must complete if he is to be a confident and successful civil prosecutor. He must ask and answer a different question: Who is Charlie Keating? There are many things he does not know as he works on his legal complaint against Keating, things like the fact that Charlie has sacks of coins delivered to his house, sometimes keeping $25,000 in small change at home. Why? Who knows why? He just does it.

You think you are starting to understand him if you are a Mike Manning obsessed with Keating's actions. And you patiently wade through his logs, his memos, his everything, wade up to your ass in minutiae: Who is he meeting that day at noon? What does that wire order for money signify? And no matter how hard you work, there are always these loose ends. They are everywhere, occurring every damn day you can find good records for, popping up every hour if you can bag some of those telephone logs. Charlie Keating does not seem to have a monomania—greed, sex, power—he seems to have manias. He is flying off in all directions, every day, all the time. It makes a guy feel uncomfortable with his case. Sure, you know in your guts you can nail him. But can you understand him? This is the kind of thing you wind up asking yourself, and you wonder what in the hell you have become, some kind of shrink?

... It is 8 A.M., August 23, 1989, and Charlie Keating meets with various staff at his $300 million Phoenician Hotel in Phoenix. He discusses doors for the lobby and how to keep the glass clean; he also wants to know about the schedule for cleaning the huge resort's various bars. He has questions about the establishment's bakeries, about its kitchens and the stewarding at the executive conference room. Then he moves on to taste the menu at the hotel's new Terrace restaurant. He is a fiend for detail. . . . Or it is September 5 and he flies with his wife and daughter and son-in-law and secretary to London. . . . Or it is September 8 and he flies with his family to Düsseldorf, Germany. . . . Or it is September 9 and he flies on to Medjugorje, Yugoslavia, and stays with the Sivric family in the small village where the Virgin has appeared repeatedly since 1981. For three days he lives in a small house with poor people, a house with dirt floors where the beds are straw, and for three days Charlie Keating prays to the Mother of Christ. . . . And then he flies on to Rome, and finally on the fourteenth day of September he arrives in Monaco and stays at the Hotel de Paris, Place du Casino, Monte Carlo. Here lives his good friend Toufic Aboukhater, a man with whom Charlie Keating has done many deals, a man who is close friends with the oil sheiks in Kuwait. . . . Or it is September 15 in Phoenix, Arizona, and Michael Manning files in court a $1.2 billion racketeering suit naming one Charles H. Keating, Jr. . . . It is September 25 when a plane takes off from a city in Brazil and Charlie Keating is seated in the first-class section. . . . He has been checking out the country, especially a spot stuffed with Germans who had fled there after World War II. When he calls his aide, Judy Wischer, she says, "Charlie, what are you doing there?" and he says, "Well, they can't extradite you from here" and then he laughs. . . .

Manning has hours and hours of videotape of Charlie Keating's world, footage shot to record his work in creating an empire. It is not simple stuff like board meetings or ribbon cuttings. It records scenes not regularly witnessed in U.S. corporations: Charlie walks into a room with a paper sack and rows of people sit facing him.

He reaches into the bag and tosses $30,000 worth of bills into the air. The green money floats slowly to the floor.

Then there is the old 1983 American Continental annual report. The cover is black, and Keating hates the report for a simple reason: the black glossy ink shows fingerprints. In the beginning of the booklet is a color photograph of Charlie at his desk, a glass Madonna glowing on the edge of his work space. As chairman of the board of ACC, he points out the future to his shareholders and reports that the future looks very, very good: "On September 30, 1983, the Company entered into a merger agreement with First Lincoln Financial Corporation . . . [which] owns Lincoln Savings and Loan Association. . . . This is a tremendous acquisition for the Company. . . . I trust if any of our services can benefit you that you will call upon us. 'Welcome Home.' "

The chairman of the board has a plain, open face, a comfortable look that sometimes comes to rest on the faces of old uncles. The chairman is not homely but not handsome, his clothes well tailored but not flashy. He is smiling almost shyly and wears metal-rimmed glasses, a blue shirt, and the regulation red power necktie of the eighties. A gold cuff link peeks out from the dark sleeve of his suit jacket, and a pen is poised in his right hand. All in all, he looks as plain and comfortable as an old shoe.

Everyone calls him Charlie. That's all. Just Charlie.

She is twenty-one in 1985, her blond hair framing a pert face, and she is short. Her bones are small and fine. She had started at American Continental Corporation a few months before and likes the money. The hours are long, long, long, but the money is good. So she has bought a BMW and started taking holidays on the beach in San Diego. One morning a manager she works under walks up to her and says the night before he'd been out drinking with some of Charlie's executives, and they'd all decided she is the perfect woman: since she is short and has a flat head, she can give a blow job and they can stack a six-pack of beer on her skull at the same time. And she gets so damn mad as he speaks.

There are other things like that. A guy in one of the divisions starts spreading the word that he is having an affair with her, and then a lot of guys started saying that. "And they were all so disgusting," she says with anger. "I never would have even gone with them." She'd be in a meeting and some guy she hardly knew would say, "Hey, how about last night? We had a great time, didn't we?"

And she'd say, "In your dreams, asshole."

She stays year after year. She says it is not really the money. Everyone at ACC mentions attractions besides the money. And hardly anyone seems to leave.

THE
COMPANY
MAN

Everyone fears the summer sun as the temperature climbs past
120°. The air is molten, and a kind of general amnesia spreads
over Phoenix like lava. There have been many such times of forgetfulness in the past few years. That's why people have been coming
here for decades, to forget, to invent, to escape real lives and real
records. The publisher of the state's major newspaper, Duke Tully,
had to resign a few years back when it was discovered that his distinguished combat career as a pilot in Vietnam—at cocktail parties
he liked to arrive in a colonel's uniform and launch into lengthy
descriptions of the sensation of having SAM missiles hurtling at
him like telephone poles—never happened. Local residents made a
few bucks peddling T-shirts that announced "I Flew with the
Duke." After that there is a successful drive to impeach the governor, fueled in part by his quirky defense of the word pickaninny as
an appropriate and polite term for describing black children. The
next governor falls off a bleacher at a public occasion, lands on
her head, and never seems quite the same again. The state's two
U.S. senators are investigated by their colleagues for possibly vio-
lating Senate ethics. The real estate economy, which in good part
is the sole economy of this boom-and-bust-driven state, has just
fallen dead on the desert floor.

No one really has ever wanted to remember in Arizona. Phoenix
was founded by three men who figured they could make a killing
after the Civil War selling hay to troopers stationed there to fight
the Apaches. One of the founders died in Yuma prison after rob-
bing the Wickenburg stage; the second wound up in a shack out

in the desert and drank himself to death; the third, true to the city's soul, invented a new life and cleaned up in real estate. The city itself is built on the vast agricultural ruins of a culture called Hohokam, a civilization that essentially died of thirst during some bad years toward the end of the thirteenth century. Now the city likes to name things after these earlier failed developers. The word *hohokam* comes from the language of a surviving desert tribe on the nearby Gila River and means "all used up," or "busted." A flat tire, for example, is hohokam.

Arizona has always appreciated the quick buck, the lucky strike. Mining literally invented the state, and the state has always been for sale. In the nineteenth century, the Southern Pacific Railroad is said to have shipped $25,000 to the governor so he could distribute it to the territorial legislature by way of buying the Yuma crossing of the Colorado. The governor is said to have returned $20,000 of the boodle, explaining he did not want to spoil the boys. Ned Warren, a real estate fraud artist in the 1960s, once noted that Arizona was the only place he had ever operated where politicians took the first offer. Here, collective amnesia is not an affliction but a way of life.* Phoenix lends itself to a kind of mental dozing. About two million people live in the valley, and yet they share a preoccupation with the question: what exactly is wrong with Phoenix? Why is it so—well—soulless, so boring? It is as if Phoenix were a miniature Los Angeles designed by Canadians.

A man is waiting for an appointment in this valley of forgetfulness. It will take months and months of talking for both his name

---

*An excellent short course in the manners and morals of Arizona and Phoenix is contained in Joseph Stedino's (with Dary Matera) *What's In It for Me? How an Ex-Wiseguy Exposed the Greed, Jealousy, and Lust That Drive Arizona Politics,* Harper-Collins, New York, 1992. In one passage recounting a secretly taped conversation between George Stragalas, a longtime Democratic pol, and Stedino, posing as a Mafia front seeking legalized gambling in the state, the following exchange takes place in the summer of 1990:

George Stragalas, as usual, was overflowing with sharp political insight. . . . "So [Keating] buys the Lincoln Savings in California and runs it like a personal bank account and legally did it. His mistake was that he starts selling bonds and stock of Continental Corporation out of Lincoln Savings which weren't secure. And his second mistake was he started selling to little old ladies . . . and it got so crazy. I mean, he hires his son, a million dollars a year salary . . . his nephew, $800,000. It gets crazy."

"Did he have the [Arizona] legislators in his pocket?" I asked.

"He had the entire state in his pocket! . . . If you wanted to do anything in this town, you had to be on Keating's good side. And he was ruthless. . . ." (p. 75)

and face to emerge. He is behaving normally for those who hail
from a very special world that until quite recently flourished in
Phoenix, that unique bailiwick once ruled by Charles H. Keating,
Jr. There is so much to consider, the man wants to explain: there
have been threats on his girlfriend's life; there are detectives sitting across from his home day and night, and he has no idea who
they are working for. Perhaps Charlie, perhaps his estranged wife,
perhaps some federal agency, perhaps the attorneys representing
bankrupted bondholders in a fistful of civil suits. When he goes
out in the morning to pick up the newspaper, someone he does not
know is standing there and snapping his photograph. There are
billions missing, talk is a dangerous thing. Money trails lead to
Panama, the Bahamas, the Middle East, Switzerland. Various lawsuits promise to tie up the man's livelihood for years and years.
He is functionally bankrupt.

The man lives in a pink house, but he did not know this fact until
his girlfriend told him. He is color-blind. He now feels he has been
blind in many other areas as well. His name is George J. Wischer—
Chip to everyone—and he is in his early forties. A long, broad scar
tracks across his stomach from an operation for ulcers. His body is
slowly coming back from some distant country that he is now struggling to remember. At one time his weight ballooned up to 260
pounds. For a time he was drinking heavily. When his body finally
gave out, he ended up in an alcohol rehabilitation program. He was
kept in isolation for nine days until they flushed his cells sufficiently
enough for him to enter formal alcohol therapy.

Chip Wischer sits waiting for a conversation he would prefer to
avoid. Tomaso's restaurant in Phoenix is quite nice but not lavish.
It is an eatery with polite waiters, fine tablecloths, a place where
he felt very comfortable in those golden days when he was a name.
He ran Insurance West, one of Keating's many subsidiaries, and he
made good money doing it—a salary of a quarter million a year
plus millions more in stock options, limited partnerships, and the
like. One day when he was on his way home from work, he impulsively pulled over at a Mercedes-Benz dealership and plopped
down $50,000 cash for a car as a surprise for his wife. Judy
Wischer also worked for Charlie Keating, as the president of the
company. She was paid $1.1 million a year and may have been the
highest-paid female executive in the United States. Charlie liked to
brag that she was, anyway. Now in the summer of 1990 the fed-

eral prosecutors are everywhere, now the buildings, bank accounts, and records have been seized, now the hotels are gone, the jets and fine restaurants are distant memories, now almost everyone he once knew intimately is standing in rubble. Tomaso's is one of the places left where he can go and savor what he once was. Chip Wischer is full of memories of a time when money did not matter, but he knows those days are over.

Finally, the person he is waiting for enters and orders a drink. Wischer listens, listens for almost an hour as this stranger, Michael Binstein, scrambles, floods the air with words, probes for some common ground where trust can be discovered and shared. Binstein has this belief that if he just never shuts up, Chip cannot leave, and if he cannot leave, eventually he will talk. Hell, it often works. But Chip does not speak, perhaps because of the ghosts. There are so many ghosts. Charlie still comes into this friendly Italian restaurant, sweeps in with an entourage, and no one understands how he pays for it all. The racketeering suit alone keeps growing like some cancerous cell and now is almost three hundred pages long, a kind of revised history of Charlie Keating and his corporations produced by Mike Manning and his colleagues. The government is now seeking to recover over $2 billion. Keating is almost a full-time resident of the courtroom, his holding company is bankrupt, and a criminal suit on behalf of bankrupt bondholders is scheduled to take place in Los Angeles, but it is just one of many, many suits. The IRS is sniffing around his records; so is the SEC. An eighty-nine-year-old man has written a note and then committed suicide because the bonds he bought from Charlie Keating are suddenly worthless.

Somehow Keating can face these matters and not be shattered. In the months just before the collapse, when Charlie was scrambling to sell his savings and loan and get out with a few shreds of his empire, a dentist in the Los Angeles area, a man who had given up as lost the $25,000 nest egg he had put into American Continental junk bonds, went on the radio and denounced Charles Keating, Jr. And what happened? Charlie Keating called him up and said, come out here to Phoenix and I'll show you that the bonds are a good investment and that this will all work out. And the man came out, and for a day Charlie and his staff ushered him around Phoenix showing him their projects and purring in his ear that these ventures were good and true.

Yet this same Charlie, a man who cares if a bondholder with a $25,000 stake thinks ill of him, will come into Tomaso's for lunch and order a $150 bottle of Dom Perignon for the making of a single cocktail and then let the rest of the bottle go flat and useless. He can do that because he is still the center, the leader, the boss. In his late sixties, he has the kind of power that people seem better able to experience than to explain. He is very confusing to many people. For example, they cannot figure out why Keating keeps coming to Tomaso's since he does not like Italian food.

Charlie Keating is obsessed, he will tell people he is obsessed. But people seldom listen. They always think his words are a screen, a disguise for his real intentions. That somewhere behind his smile and his hard blue eyes lurks a deeper meaning. That his gangly body with its big feet and big hands is a prop to trick them, that his relaxed manner, his casual, unaffected speech is all feigned, that anyone who has had control over billions of dollars lives in some splendid, dark, and hidden universe that he will never disclose to outsiders. But he does. He tells them what he thinks all the time, and one thing he thinks is that he is obsessed by one man, Carl Henry Lindner, Jr., who is a resident of Cincinnati, Ohio, just as Charlie was for decades. Lindner is a man from outside the establishment, a guy who clawed his way to power and wealth and yet remains a secret to almost everyone. The day back in 1983 when Charlie bought Lincoln Savings and Loan out in Los Angeles, he whipped out a copy of *Forbes* magazine with its annual list of the nation's richest and most powerful human beings and flipped open to the page where Carl Lindner, Jr.'s, name rode way up there near the top, and he stabbed with his finger at that position and told the startled man selling him the bank, "That's where I'm going to be."

It is dangerous to underestimate the hold Charlie has over people. There is a woman, Patricia Johnson, who was close to Charlie that last good year, a woman who was with him every day, and when things got bad, she was ruined and tossed aside by him like a used rag—no notice, no severance. For a year Johnson could not get a job. She had to go on unemployment, and finally her parents were buying the food for her and her three children. At first she would go around Phoenix with a letter of recommendation written by her but signed by Charlie Keating. Hardly anyone would even see her, and when she did finally get in to see one banker, he read the letter and ripped it up in her presence, warning her not to show a copy of it to anyone if she ever hoped to get a job. A year later, she starts talking to reporters. Charles Bowden meets her for a couple of long lunches, and everything seems to be going just fine. And then private detectives suddenly start hounding her neighbors and asking about her personal habits. Then Keating's lawyers are on her and having her deposed. They ask her how much money Bowden has given her to talk. And suddenly she will not talk, she will not answer the phone, and finally she emerges on the other side of the nation in a new life. And yet what she really fears is this one thing: if Charlie called and said, come back, said, I've got a job for you, she is afraid she would go back to him and back to the world that he invents and charges with energy. Few can name the head of General Motors or IBM, but everyone knows who Charlie Keating is.

As Wischer listens in the quiet Italian restaurant as this stranger, Binstein, makes his pitch, listens to yet one more reporter trying to pry open the affairs of a world that is so beyond them all, he can remember the force of this power very well. He is an intelligent, well-spoken man, but whenever outsiders ask him about his life at the company, he cannot seem to convey his experience in words. And when he listens to questions from other people—lawyers and the press, for example—he realizes that they haven't a clue. They inevitably start asking about crimes, and that is where they lose him. These interrogators seem to think that ACC was one big criminal conspiracy where everyone sat around plotting new heists. Also, outsiders cannot understand a key part of his reality: he cannot seem to forget Charlie Keating. And what is the most difficult part for him, he may never stop missing him. And the money.

Also, Chip Wischer has fears that he cannot really explain to people who have not been in his world and tasted what he has tasted. For example, he and his girlfriend always carry guns.

Finally, Michael Binstein is getting desperate. He's been sitting in this restaurant talking at a man who does not seem to be there, a man who seems lost in his own thoughts, imprisoned in memories. Binstein decides to take a chance, and he says to Wischer, "This man emasculated you. What do you owe him? Why do you have this loyalty?"

Wischer seems to stir.

"I want to talk about this shipwreck in your life," Binstein continues.

He and Wischer go home. They talk from 8 P.M. to 1:30 A.M., go over simple, safe things—dates, chronologies, the rough bones of this history. The things no one ever goes to jail for. When Keating's empire collapsed, Chip's wife, Judy, stayed with Keating—Charlie had a habit of hiring couples as if he sensed such employment with its twin paychecks slipped a golden noose around a family's neck. And after twenty years of marriage and two children, she initially sued for not a divorce but an annulment.

Chip sits there in his ranch-style home and sips a soft drink and thinks back to the good times and the hard times. A glass case against one wall holds old knives and artifacts from the 1860s because Wischer is a junkie on the period. He has a couple of shelves of books on the War Between the States. In college he majored in literature, thought about becoming a journalist. Before that he broke horses, worked farms, hunted avidly in the Kentucky hills. He still loves animals, and his home is almost a zoo—four horses, the dog, two pygmy goats, rabbits, a chicken. And yet for more than a decade he lived essentially cut off from the whole natural world that he always loved. The only connection he maintained with his good ol' boy roots was his collection of Corvettes, a garage full of hot American cars. Now they are gone, and he is left with a framed poster of Corvette models down through the decades.

Wischer has a memorandum from Charlie Keating in his files dated August 21, 1987, that captures part of his difficulty in explaining those years. The memo is about Casual Day, a Keating fetish, a tradition in his button-down company that demanded that on every Friday the employees not wear ties or suits but dress in sportswear or shorts or sexy dresses. Wischer's section of the company sold insurance and had to deal with the public every day, so he never allowed casual days for his staff, hence the memo:

TO: CHIP WISCHER

FROM: CHARLES H. KEATING, JR.

SUBJECT: CHAIN OF COMMAND

INSURANCE WEST IS A SUBSIDIARY OF AMERICAN CONTINENTAL CORPORA-
TION. I AM THE CHAIRMAN OF THE BOARD OF AMERICAN CONTINENTAL CORPO-

RATION. THUS I AM IN CHARGE OF IWI! MEMOS TO ALL EMPLOYEES WRITTEN
UNDER MY SIGNATURE INCLUDE *YOU* AND THE *EMPLOYEES OF IWI. YOU MUST
ACCEPT AND RESPECT* THIS CHAIN OF COMMAND.

IT HAS COME TO MY ATTENTION THAT YOU DO NOT ALLOW THE EMPLOYEES
IN SCOTTSDALE TO ENJOY CASUAL DAYS WHEN *I* DETERMINE CASUAL DAYS.
NOR DO YOU ALLOW EMPLOYEES TO WEAR SHORTS! YOU *WILL* FOLLOW MY IN-
STRUCTIONS TO THE LETTER, OR I WILL FIND SOMEONE WHO WILL!

A CASUAL DAY PER CHK IS A CASUAL DAY FOR ALL EMPLOYEES OF ACC!

Now, years later, when Wischer looks over the memo, what
bothers him is that he cannot tell if it is some prank sent through
the company as a joke or if it is an actual memo from Keating. The
ones Charlie constantly sent sounded just like this one.

It is very hard for anyone to unravel the events during the years
ACC soared above the nation's financial markets. Everything
seemed to happen very fast and all in a jumble. And no one ever
seemed really to have a handle on everything that was going on
. . . except possibly one person. Ten days after that odd memo
lands on Chip Wischer's desk in August 1987, another message
is sent through the corporate system by the man called Charlie
Keating. . . . Send $400,000 from something called the Crescent
Lending Corporation to the Hotel Pontchartrain . . . use the phone
and transfer money from . . . Valley National Bank, Phoenix, Arizona, to . . . Account No. 50-055-0798 at Bankers Trust Company
in the city of New York to . . . Account No. 104-1434 in the city
of Detroit at the National Bank of Detroit. And this is a single
strand in a single deal, a little footnote to tens of millions flowing
toward a building in Detroit. And there are so many other cities
and so many other buildings. . . .

It's getting toward one in the morning as Chip Wischer tries to
explain where he has been and what he has seen. Every solid little
record seems to turn into just another question. Is the memo a
fake? What is Account No. 50-055-0798? Just how many corporations, banks, accounts, partnerships, pieces of paper were there?

A few days later Chip Wischer decides to talk again, and this
time the meeting is in the Gold Room of the venerable Biltmore.
The silver is heavy, the tables far apart, the sounds muted, the
light low. It is 11:30 A.M. when Wischer begins to talk. He first
connected with Keating in the 1970s in Cincinnati when he was a
raw kid from the hills of Kentucky. Charlie made him and his wife

rich, and he wound up in Phoenix, running an entire division of the corporation, living in a fine home in Paradise Valley. His voice rises and falls as he speaks, much the way the talk of family members does after a funeral as the good times and bad times of a dead person are recalled. There will be a laugh, and then a little while later a tightening of the voice. His eyes are blue, his hair graying, his face so very open. He has reached that moment in his life when he wants to say things so that they will be robbed of their power over him and finally go away.

People at the company used to say, "A day with Charlie is like a day at Disneyland. You get a day pass, but at night you have to leave. And you know it will end." The end could come very suddenly. You might be told to report to one of the company planes at the airport and then discover that you had no seat. Charlie had changed his mind, snap, just like that. Or you would fly with Keating on a corporate jet to a meeting and then return to the airport only to be told that you were off the plane and to get home as best you could. Off the huge plane with its rare woods, the golden faucets in the lavatory, the bottles of champagne kept chilled in the galley. Locked out of Disneyland. There was another saying in Charlie's company: "Everything in this company is voted on, and the vote is always one to nothing."

Chip pauses and tries to find another way to explain the place. There was this Indian portrait, he continues. "Did you ever hear the story about the picture, the moving picture?" At ACC, no one was allowed to decorate his or her office; Charlie controlled every single image that hung on the walls. But there was this cheap poster of an American Indian chief, and pasted over the head was a photo of Charlie's face. This poster might suddenly pop up on your office wall—the lithographs, paintings, etchings, and sketches that hung everywhere were constantly being changed. Charlie and his wife would come down on weekends and just move things around without warning. Usually when the Indian portrait showed up in someone's office, he or she was fired shortly afterwards. "But," Chip explains, "it took a couple people being gone before we said, 'There's a correlation between the picture showing up and that person being gone.' And you'd call afraid and say to someone, 'I got the Indian. What's going on?'"

The snake was another bad omen. Once Chip and Charlie's son, Charles Keating III (commonly called C3), were out at the Keating ranch near Phoenix, and they sighted a rattlesnake under a trailer. The son ran and got a .357 magnum, and after a hail of bullets, he had managed to kill the snake, but not before he'd shot the tires off the trailer. Then the snake—frozen—started appearing in peoples' desk drawers, and people who found the snake in their drawers tended to get fired. Finally, it got stuffed.

Inspiration was another tool in Charlie's arsenal. Chip would be in a meeting with Keating and Keating would want him to do something involving insurance that Chip knew was impossible. Finally Charlie would get fed up with his reasons and say, "Go ahead and do this." Wischer would give in and try it, and "by God, it would work!" Keating hated people who told him things couldn't be done. That's why he liked hiring young people. "Conversely," Chip noticed, "ACC would sometimes hire guys in their fifties, and rarely did it work because these guys would say, 'Now, Charlie, you just don't understand this like I understand it.' And man, that's the last thing you want to tell him. You were gone."

But the main memory employees retain is that no one at ACC could ever maintain a sense of balance. Wischer remembers one corporate Christmas party back in 1985 at the Century Plaza Hotel in Los Angeles. There were a couple of thousand people there—the employees (and their families) of Lincoln Savings and Loan, a piece of Charlie's empire, the cash cow. Chip had flown in from Phoenix in the company Sabre Jet and had promptly retired to the hotel bar with some other executives. They hung out there for hours getting drunk. When the party began in the ballroom, they sat at special management tables where endless bottles of Dom Perignon magically appeared. His wife, Judy, was there, Charlie, C3, all the top players. "We started getting fucking crazy," Chip recalls, "loud, noisy, dancing around." Charlie had arranged for three bands, one playing country, one rock, and finally one for himself that played big band music. The usual antics occurred— Charlie breaking glasses or tossing rolls or impulsively giving some employee a bonus of five grand or ten grand or twenty grand.

Another executive who was at many such parties remembers Charlie's high spirits with fondness. "Charlie always had fun," he says. "Threw food. Handed out bonuses, too. He'd write somebody's name on a matchbook and say, hey, this guy has been working very hard—write down $10,000 on the matchbook, his initials, CHK, and then have his secretary take it over to the guy's table. You know a few bonuses like that go around, and then the wine drinking starts and people are having a pretty good time. Charlie knew how to stir up a crowd. He understood cash and the effect cash had on you. He loved to take control."

The Christmas party in 1985 was of a piece with all these celebrations. Charlie didn't care if his people got drunk, so long as they mingled and acted as if they were having a good time. And this was not difficult for most of them because of the money. The pay was high, the perks were everywhere, and the bonuses, well, they kept everyone on edge and eager. Charlie was in his usual form, giving out those impromptu bonuses, ogling the good-looking women, handing out watches to the tellers and clerks at the savings and loan branches, and launching into one of the inspirational "go get 'em" speeches he was famous for. Finally, around one or two in the morning, Chip and his wife, Judy, and C3 and some other executives went up to a suite. They called down to room service for more food and liquor and, out of the sight of their subordinates, really let down their hair. C3, in a moment of fine feelings, took off his shoes and threw them through the fourteenth-floor window. One of them almost brained the doorman, but some wads of money hushed that up.

The Sabre Jet is scheduled to take off at 7 A.M., and Chip and the other executives straggle out to the airport with massive hangovers. Charlie is already there and impatient that some people are late. When Chip arrives, Keating is on the phone and a violent thunderstorm is sweeping in toward the runway. Charlie doesn't care—the Sabre Jet is based on a military fighter and is the only corporate jet checked out for aerobatics. No reason to wait, nothing can tear the wings off this bird. So they all pile into the plane, and Chip winds up in a seat facing backwards, one right across from Keating. There is no space—Charlie is six feet five inches and Chip is over six feet and still three-quarters drunk. Keating has got the morning paper spread out on his knees, and he is screaming about the delay and demanding to know why in the hell they can't take off. His lean face and thin hatchet nose are in Wischer's face, and his breath is terrible. The pilots move the plane toward take-off, then stop, then begin again, then stop, while the black fists of clouds swing in closer. The storm cell has them worried. But Keating cannot take the damn delay, and he begins to thump Chip on the chest, leaning his face into Wischer's and denouncing him for something he has done, some deal, memo, decision. The details hardly matter: he is giving Chip the treatment, a taste of his famous rages. Wischer is sweating, he is sick from all that booze and vomit rises to his throat, and suddenly they take off and the plane lurches and bounces through the black, turbulent air. Chip looks into Charlie's red, angry face and thinks, "I'm going to throw up" and realizes that if he does his career will be over and the money will end. This last possibility is one he cannot face: trying to live without all that money. So he chokes down his vomit, lets Charlie's screams wash over him, ignores the finger thumping hard against his chest. And somehow he survives the flight back to Phoenix, and those paychecks keep coming.

It is now much later, he has been speaking for six hours. The lunchtime staff left the Biltmore hours ago and turned off the lights, and now the dinner crew is beginning to assemble. And still he talks.

He is sober now and can remember things. But somehow simply remembering is not always enough. For the prosecutors it is enough to abstract a kind of plot from 3 million pages of records and construct a motive that will lead to convictions on criminal charges or to the recovery of money on civil charges. For the accountants scurrying on all sides of the cases, it is enough to fashion a jumble of numbers that spell out either profit or loss using odd notions such as purchase accounting or capitalized interests, concepts the general public—being basically honest—doesn't even suspect exist. For the defendants it is enough to establish in the minds of the court a reasonable doubt about what they did and why they did it. But Wischer has pushed past this country of guilt and innocence. He wants to know what happened to him.

Charlie Keating is a byword now, a man decried in Congress, ridiculed on late night talk shows, a villain said to have helped wreck the economy of an entire nation.* He tells everyone that he has lost all of his money. And yet Charlie Keating is still operating, still moving through the world at this moment with his long stride

*For example, by the summer of 1990 when Joseph Stedino is running a government sting operation by posing as a Mafia figure and bribing local politicians wholesale, one of the bribed pols describes how they will remake his Mafioso image this way: "What you're gonna build up here, what I maintain you're gonna build up, you're essentially gonna be a nice Keating." (Stedino and Matera, *What's In It for Me?*, p. 75.)

and tall bearing, still eating at the best restaurants, still refusing to confess or plead for mercy or bow his head. Keating is in Chicago to confer with his lawyers for an upcoming trial. He stays at one of the city's four-star hotels, the Fairmont. When he comes out of the building he finds 250 demonstrators protesting a meeting of the National Abortion Federation that is being held in the same hotel. What does he do? He marches around with the demonstrators for a while.

Or he is in a Los Angeles courtroom to hear his attorneys poll one hundred potential jurors. Metal detectors screen all who enter the chamber, and the front row of spectator seats is kept vacant to isolate Keating from possible attackers. A few days before, a ninety-year-old woman had grabbed Charlie just outside the courtroom and yelled, "You took all my money."

Chip Wischer is trying to explain that it isn't so simple—an argument all of the people who have been around Charlie Keating make. They can't stand how everyone looks at them like they are criminals, like they did something that other folks would never, ever do. They can see it in reporters' eyes, hear it in their questions: Hooooooooow could you do that? Like they were goddamn SS guards or something, you know, people who were capable of and guilty of heinous acts. Child molesters, that kind of thing. Dammit, they were all—they *are* all—hardworking people, family people who studied hard in school and got good grades, went to church, believed in their wives and husbands, tried to make the world a better place, and you'd better know that, buster. See, everyone wants this easy way out, this way where you get to talk about THEM, the evil ones who did what no decent person ever would do. And it doesn't happen that way, no, no. What do you think? That everyone sat around plotting how to commit felonies? Or rip off money? That there were little secret vows—a nick of a knife on the finger and then you swore in blood? It doesn't happen that way. In fact, now that it's over, no one is quite sure just how it did happen.

It's a slow, creeping kind of thing, like a river barely rising and the thing driving that river is so far upstream you are only vaguely aware of why the river is rising, and half the time, honest to God, you don't even notice that it is rising. And then slowly the water comes up, and tongues of it begin to lap at the foundations of the building, at the foundations of your life, and you sorta notice it and toss down a few sandbags and you go back about your business, and God knows you've got a lot of that, it seems like all you ever do is work. And the damn river keeps rising, eating away the foundation, but hey, how can you keep track, there are all these deals on the table, decisions to be made (or better yet, decisions already made and the boss says, deal with them) and you bury yourself in your work—oh, sure, once in a while you catch sight of the big water and toss out some more sandbags, but this is really a detail, this is not what is on your mind—and you try so hard to make it work, hell, you're all pulling together, the company spirit feels great—it's us against them!—and this goes on not just hour after hour or day after day or month after month, that would be easy, anybody could probably handle that, but year after year. It seems like that's all you do. But there is never that minute, no, not really, when you sit down and stare at some set of facts and say, hey, we're committing a crime here. You don't even put such thoughts out of your mind—no time for that, no, not a spare second. You're so busy . . . just doing. And the river just keeps rising. And then—maybe you have to be there, taste the tension, feel the frenzy, see the stack of pink telephone messages, watch the clock march like it's on cocaine, and all you think of is, how can I get all this done?—and then you stop examining each and every little goddamn act and anything goes, anything. How do you explain that to people who never seem to taste that kind of life?

"What bothers me," Chip Wischer explains, "is simply this: am I supposed to believe that for twenty years I lived with a woman and for ten years I worked for a guy and that they were both crooks and I was too stupid to know it?"* He pauses after stating that problem, and his eyes harden. Whatever happened in those

---

*Chip Wischer is not the only one puzzled by what Keating's intentions were and were not. Congressman Henry Gonzalez, no friend of high-flying operators like Charlie Keating, stated at the Gonzalez hearings he chaired in November 1989: "The record suggests that Keating never made any secret of his plans. He left no doubt that he intended to push regulations to the limits and beyond, and to take on the high-risk ventures—everything from long-shot land developments to Ivan Boesky junk bond deals. Lincoln was the cash machine for Keating and American Continental Corporation—their own personal ATM. . . . The Memorandum of Understanding was much closer to a government license to gamble than it was to an enforceable regulatory action."

years, he will never believe that he was at a crime scene and did not grasp this fact.

"Let me tell you," he says, "about this wild and crazy ride I've been on."

They have all been waiting for this moment. They want to see him fall, and he knows it. It is April 10, 1992, and Charles H. Keating, Jr., faces sentencing on criminal charges in Los Angeles Superior Court. He is sixty-eight years old and surrounded by his wife, his son, his five daughters, their husbands, and some of his twenty-two grandchildren. He stands to address the bench before sentence is passed and says he is not a swindler, as charged and convicted, but a man who made quality investments and never bilked the bond holders who loaned him a quarter of a billion dollars, money that is all gone as he speaks this day. "Someday I hope I will be able to tell that story in full," he adds.

The judge is not swayed. He notes that Keating's bond salesmen wore T-shirts that said "Bond for Glory," and knowing his Woody Guthrie he points out the songwriter thought that more money is stolen with a fountain pen than with a sword. Keating gets ten years in prison—and must serve five years before being eligible for parole—plus a $250,000 fine. The bailiffs cross the room. Keating turns to his family and with his hands shaking passes them his cuff links and other valuables. His grandchildren start crying, and Keating looks down at them and says, "Just be brave. Don't worry about me. Everybody be calm."

They take the prisoner out to a white county van, maneuver his handcuffed and tall frame into a backseat. As the press cameras flash, Keating looks up and offers a broad smile. A few blocks away festers Los Angeles' skid row. The streets of skid row are clogged day and night with addicts seeking power and that special something to fill the emptiness within them. Some prefer booze, some drugs. At night, the climate changes from hopelessness into an even more forlorn country. The residents spread out on the sidewalks, perpendicular to the street, shoulder to shoulder, block after block after block. The street lights barely penetrate the shadows, the voices are the only sound, a low buzzing as if swarms of insects had settled in for the long black hours. A sprawled-out woman *hikes up her skirt and jabs a needle into her leg. Her thumb plunges down slowly on the syringe as the dreams begin. All this a few blocks away and many floors below where Charlie Keating spends his first night as a convict in the United States of America.*

For years he has donated $100,000 annually to the plight of the homeless, and now he can look out the slit window of his cell and see the fruits of his labor.

THE
MAN

He is waiting on May 20, 1988, and he is not good at waiting. He is the center of a $6 billion empire, and the center does not wait. His secretaries know this, they have all gotten the memo from his general counsel and corporate vice president Robert Kielty: when Charles H. Keating, Jr., requests a copy of a document, one does not just go to the copying machine, one runs to the machine and makes a copy and runs back. That's an official American Continental Corporation order. Speed is at the core of his life. In the past four years, he has spent almost $36 million on the care and feeding of three corporate jets plus his chopper. When the jets are in Phoenix, they rest in a special hangar that is so fine Keating sometimes uses it for corporate parties. The floor of the hangar is white and kept absolutely spotless. Things must always be clean. He will stop when inspecting a construction site, get a broom and dustpan, and stoop to clean up a pile of shavings left by some carpenter. When Keating wants to make a move, the planes take off. That is why he keeps nine pilots on his payroll plus a woman just to keep track of them. His pilots love him. The pay is high, and he buys them every gadget and technological toy they desire. His secretary keeps a bag packed by her desk ready for that command to jump into a plane and go to Los Angeles, New York, Washington, Florida, the Bahamas, London, Ireland, Paris, Monaco, Düsseldorf, Geneva, Yugoslavia. She is on call twenty-four hours a day. And when she is awake she is at Keating's side and she writes down everything he says in a notebook. She is his Boswell and she is always ready. But she never knows what is coming; no one does, perhaps not even Keating.

"What I wanted when I was growing up?" he reflects. "As I look back I've enjoyed everything I've ever done. Even the crises. I never had a game plan for tomorrow. I never thought I ought to be this or that. I was a lawyer because my father wanted me to be a lawyer. I was a Navy pilot because I thought that was great. I was a swimmer because people clapped when you won. I have thought about that often. I've really enjoyed it. Now if you sat me down and said, what would you rather be doing, I could think of alternatives. People are lucky to be born."

That is why he hates to wait. But today he is waiting for a very simple reason. On February 22, 1984, he assumed formal possession of a savings and loan named Lincoln in southern California. This kind of institution was then a totally unregulated new development of the Reagan years. That meant that Charlie Keating, thanks to federally insured deposits, could get access to almost any amount of money and the government would guarantee the folks who loaned it to him. And he could do with this money pretty much anything he wanted. When years later he was questioned by a reporter about the propriety of taking such insured money and plunking it into speculative investments like junk bonds, he flared back, "Ho, ho, ho, pal, I bought Lincoln, I paid fifty million dollars, of which I mostly owned, for Lincoln in an environment of total deregulation. . . . I didn't cause that to happen, I bought it when I did, and I was at that time permitted by law and regulation and still am to make the [speculative] investment."

Times changed, savings and loans started going belly-up, and Lincoln with its weird array of plunges into strange markets became almost a symbol of what was wrong in the eyes of worried federal regulators. Federal auditors found Keating in violation of reinstated rules on things like net worth and direct investment, plus things that had never been legal under deregulation, such as self-dealing. And for more than a year they've been trying to shut him down. "What we have," he thinks, "is two completely opposite philosophies. They may be right, I just don't see it that way. . . . You have to say one of two things, if they don't stop the industry from operating, an industry that accesses federally insured money, which is maybe what they ought to do. But as long

as they're going to continue to insure, then you've got to do something with that money that's profitable."

Early in May, the Federal Home Loan Bank Board, which over-
sees about three thousand savings and loans, met to discuss one
thrift in southern California that had captured their attention. It
was a singular meeting by many standards.

On the morning of May 5 the board sits down on the sixth floor
of the FHLBB building in Washington, D.C. Danny Wall, the
chairman, is there along with his two other board members and
various staff members. Technically, Lincoln is administered by the
board's branch bank in San Francisco, but personnel from that office are not at the meeting. This is highly unusual. They have been
tainted by a barrage of complaints from Charlie Keating and his
lawyers, complaints that the San Francisco office has a vendetta
against Lincoln and its owner, American Continental. Keating has
filed a fistful of lawsuits about this matter. What the board members hear in the staff reports is that Lincoln, like Charlie Keating
himself, is different. Darrel Dochow, a power in the FHLBB's bu-
reaucracy, walks a very thin line in this meeting. He is in his late
thirties, he is on the rise in a dangerous political climate, and he
is not eager to offend anyone. His boss, Danny Wall, has spent
most of his career on the Hill tending to the large, fragile egos of
U.S. senators, and he is not a man who makes a fuss or likes
those who do. In all his years of work in Washington, he has become noted for two things: wearing vests and favoring leather
boots with zippers up their sides. Dochow is careful in his choice
of words; he knows this world and he wants to stay in it. He puts
the situation this way: "Lincoln's profile, I don't think there is any
question among the analytical folk . . . that Lincoln is a more than
normal risk institution. Large land loans, . . . high-yield investments [junk bonds] . . . They have reaped their income consistently and quite profitably from these endeavors, primarily in what
I refer to as 'doing deals.' Mr. Keating has said that in his whole
life he has generated income from 'making one deal work after another deal. . . .' "

"Deal making" is a term that chills the hearts of federal bank
boards.

*   *   *

Deal making is at the core of Keating's being. Every human endeavor in his hands becomes a kind of deal. There is no clear line in his day between business and family, public life and private life. What are simple, limited things for others tend to become large and complex things in his hands. A family vacation can easily mutate into the movement of his private army. Keating does things like piling twenty family members into the jets (one for people who want to party, one for those who wish to sleep) and suddenly sweeping off to Italy to dine. Keating is building a huge resort in Phoenix, he thinks one of its restaurants should serve Italian cuisine, so he samples menus around the continent. He makes all the decisions in his corporation. He despises experts. He has fired a series of interior decorators and finally settled on his wife, Mary Elaine. Her task is to pick the furnishings for a $300 million hotel. After all, he has been living with her taste for four decades, and he thinks it's pretty good.

"I come in," he admits, "anywhere from three to six A.M. and work 'til seven or eight at night. But I'm constantly surrounded by my family. I'm very oriented to be with my family. My wife works here, the girls come in—all my life when my daughters call I pick up the phone no matter what. I work eighty to a hundred hours, and I know pretty much how many hours I'm working. I know there's only 168 hours in a week. I work pretty much every day. I'm not actually a workaholic in the sense that I would just as soon not be doing that. I'm in a difficult environment. I've always worked hard and long, but if somebody else ran this company, I wouldn't have any trouble walking away and not working. What would I do if I walked? The opportunities are legion. I might do some business. What's my pleasure? I like to be with people. I've traveled a lot, I'm very familiar with Europe. In a sense, I'm always on vacation. I like the people I do business with, I like what I'm doing. I have my family available—they're all mixed together."

The mix has gotten very complicated now that billions are in play.

This time, May 20, 1988, Keating has little choice but to wait. The final results of the May 5 meeting in Washington will be ratified and made known to him this day. His schedule begins very early. He usually rises at 3 or 4 A.M., swims a mile in his pool, and drives to the office on Camelback Road in Phoenix. Early callers are surprised to find the head of the corporation answering the phone in the largely empty building. Keating offhandedly explains his schedule as the result of a prostate condition and the irksome need to go to the bathroom. He has a history of being informal. Once a reporter noted that no one liked Charlie Keating. He did not like this statement, and in response he spent $1,783 on huge yellow buttons that said "I like Charlie Keating," which he handed out to visitors. He also ordered two special buttons that said "I am Charlie Keating." He cannot believe that people really dislike him. He does not see himself as an unlikable guy.

When he is criticized, he is quick to react. Once in the eighties, a Phoenix critic was constantly raking Keating over the coals. He just couldn't figure out why the guy seemed to hate him so. Finally he decided the man must be a homosexual; yes, that had to be it. So he called in his head of security, and he told him to hire somebody to check out this guy and find out if he was a homosexual. About a week later, Keating was in a meeting with one of his executives when his head of security broke in on them. He said, "Charlie, we've got a problem. The guy blew our cover." Keating was upset, he didn't need any more bad publicity, so he said, well, just pay the operative off and drop it. His head of security said, "Charlie, you don't understand, he *blew* our cover." Keating was horrified: he realized he had been an accomplice in a serious sin, a homosexual act. Keating fled the meeting and went straight to church so he could confess to a priest and have the weight of this sin lifted from his soul.

He is sixty-five years old, the father of six children, the head of dozens of interlocking companies that employ two thousand people, the gatekeeper of a cash flow of billions. He does not seem to tire. He cannot; he has too much money in play around the planet. He plans a city of 200,000 people on the edge of Phoenix, he gives Ivan Boesky a $100 million blank check for his various investment schemes, he swallows hundreds of millions of dollars of Mike Milken's junk bonds, he pours even more into raw Arizona land. He is building that $300 million resort in Phoenix, and has already built one rather expensive businessmen's hotel. He hires Arthur Young, a Big Eight accounting firm, to do his corporate audit for 1986 and 1987 and in working over his books the CPAs generate 200,000 pages of paperwork. It takes sixty or seventy accountants 30,000 hours just to examine his deals for 1987. He is making transactions so swiftly that the federal government cannot seem to find the proper documentation, and when it does find some scraps of paper from time to time, the auditors suspect the documents are backdated, basically frauds. He will show a visitor the room where the records are kept, the small room stuffed with files where the hated federal regulators camped for months as they combed his transactions, and a look of disgust will play across his face about the civil servant midgets trying to tell him what to do. Down the hall from this room of records stands a large bronze statue of an Indian with a tomahawk in hand-to-hand combat with a grizzly bear. His staff gave it to Keating to symbolize his feelings toward Paul Volcker, the head of the Federal Reserve system and the apostle of tight money supplies. Judy Wischer, the president of his holding company, American Continental Corporation, sums up the ACC worldview of regulators with one word: "faggots." He is a player, and a player keeps his money in play, always. Who has time for paperwork? When Charlie speaks of the regulators his lips grow thin and he suddenly looks like an angry old man. Then a new thought comes to his mind and he moves on like a hungry animal.

He is the product of the mid-twentieth-century Middle West. When he flies in one of his big corporate jets, he orders mashed potatoes and gravy and fried chicken. When he is in the fanciest restaurant, he always orders the same dessert, vanilla ice cream with chocolate syrup. When he is excited by being in a five-star establishment, he says, "Boy, this is really good, isn't it?" Or, "Hey, this is pretty neat. Isn't this neat?" If a phone rings when he is walking through the wilderness of desks in one of his corporations, he stops, patiently waits for the second ring, then picks it up. He is distressed by unshined shoes.

When young men on his staff travel with him, they wear out, yet he never stops moving. Even when he is supposedly resting, he never stops working. Consider May 13, 1987. He is at his $5 million estate in Florida soaking up some sun, but there are a few details to attend to. He tells his secretary to take notes: first he reviews a letter from a Suzanne Brown about an ACC project's removal of some telephone poles from behind her home and instructs one of his sons-in-law to get on the matter; he scrutinizes the minutes of a general staff meeting by one of his many subsidiaries; studies a French guide to hotels and restaurants in thirty-five nations and has it dispatched to an aide; looks for good ideas in a European hotel brochure; studies the menu of a restaurant in Germany for dishes to copy; has his son's banknote flipped to his best accountant; scans a stack of European magazines and has articles sent to an aide; dictates comments on an irrigation deal to an underling; dictates his thoughts on having a safe put into the company legal department; goes over a memo on notes receivable and gift taxes and dictates more thoughts; rips an article out of *The Wall Street Journal* on the fight by U.S. tobacco companies over liability suits and makes damn sure the company lawyers get copies; has a photo of his daughter mailed to her home in Phoenix; sends the daughter-in-law a shot of herself in the company chopper; absorbs a memo on Japanese banks; instructs his wife to review an invoice; issues a check for $25,000 and then dictates a letter concerning a yellow Mercedes to go with the money; reviews plans for a health spa in his new hotel; pays attention to a medical report on one of his daughters; runs through correspondence about a big hotel deal he has cooking in Detroit; checks over the résumé of someone looking for a job in purchasing; issues comments about one deal—loan #998806360. That still leaves time for examining a memo on occupancy rates at one of his hotels; going over the minutes of the board of directors' meeting at Kangaroo, Inc.; dictating a thank-you letter to the mayor of Detroit; cranking out a memo to one of his aides on that pesky subsidiary in the Bahamas; getting down his thoughts on a magazine article about one of his subsidiaries; checking and correcting an in-house biographical sketch of himself; making damn sure his head legal counsel sees that article on compensation in *American Banker;* looking over some new lighting designs for his upcoming resort; reviewing brochures from a hotel in Baden-Baden; and, of course, giving his thoughts on how public relations are being handled at one of his hotels in Phoenix. He keeps no record of his phone calls that day, but he is a compulsive caller—phones in all his cars and all his planes. He is notorious among his staff for calling them from his car as he is driving out of the parking lot.

He is a kind of pioneer in a new world where people make money not by making things but by doing deals, instant deals, compulsive deals, twenty-four-hour-a-day deals. They book profits and pay more attention to accountants than to production lines. He thinks what he is doing is simple patriotism. "This country," he will lecture again and again, "has got to cope with the Japanese economy and we're not and we're being swallowed alive, and yes, it is a regulatory problem. . . . It's a monumental problem. In my view, America will now lose the economic power it didn't lose in World War II. . . . Meanwhile, we're destructing our own financial system."

He is almost a missionary on this point. In May 1988, Ronald Reagan is approaching the end of his eight-year reign and the nation feels its honor and power have been restored. Charlie Keating knows better. He senses his nation is in a war for its survival. My God, doesn't anybody understand? Is it hopeless? "America's next president," he lectures, "may well be presiding over the worst disaster in the history of America. You've turned this nation from a great creditor nation to the world's greatest debtor. How are you going to get out of it? . . . There is no way out. Then what happens? We've got government officials reading off the Japanese for this and that—and they're probably right. But they're bellyaching with their masters. They're going to own the world, and there ain't going to be much we can do about it in our debilitated financial condition."

He hates the regulators, literally despises them as fossils hailing from the unusable past of American history. One of his executives remembers his attitude this way: "He always said I'm not going to grovel for those regulators. People would come in and tell him to grovel, that he had to deal with these guys. Charlie won't do it for anybody. There was a side of him where he could be so charming, but with people in power, regulators, he'd just say fuck 'em."

He is a gambler at heart, and a gambler always believes with every fiber of his being that he can beat the odds. Of course, as every gambler knows, the casinos survive because in the end every gambler is bucking the house and the house always wins in the long run. And that conflict is what makes for casinos and gamblers.

The FHLBB meeting in Washington, D.C., on May 5 is in some ways like the fable of the blind men examining an elephant. The federal employees have a stack of reports from their auditors that show that Keating's savings and loan does things like make loans of millions without checking out the person or the deal—indeed, sometimes the loan application is filed after the loan is made. They invest in things that the federal regulators view with some suspicion, like those hundreds of millions in junk bonds, like the $100

million given Ivan Boesky to play with. They make fifty-two development loans at one point without ever appraising the properties
in question. In fact, Lincoln runs for about two years without having any guidelines for the staff telling them how to make loans.
Then there are the matters of backdating documents and stuffing
files, two issues that have been referred to the Justice Department
for possible criminal prosecution. All in all, this is not Jimmy
Stewart in *It's a Wonderful Life*.

But Charlie Keating has them spooked with the force of his personality, with his connections in Congress, with his high ratings in
Forbes magazine. One federal regulator tries to express this fact to
the board: "Lincoln is being acknowledged as one of the highest-
performing institutions in the nation. . . . Another point I would
make about Mr. Keating is he is obviously very knowledgeable; he
is obviously uncomfortable in a regulated environment and for
him to change his modus operandi will be difficult, but he did appear sincere in wanting to do that. . . . I also believe that Keating
probably is the only one who can preserve a significant amount of
value for Lincoln. I believe that he is a—and he proved to us, he
is a very strong sales-oriented individual. . . ."

His mind moves very swiftly, so swiftly he frightens people. His
body is another instrument he uses for intimidation, a column of
flesh that manages to be gangly and toned at the same time. When
Keating enters a room he is at ease, his every gesture low key, and
yet he always seems coiled, ready to spring. He tells people that
his biggest regret in life is that he did not fire more people, and
then as he finishes saying this, he will smile like a leprechaun.
One veteran player in the Arizona real estate market explains very
simply why he refuses to do deals with Charlie Keating: "I'm
afraid my balls will wind up in his pocket."

A short way down the hall from his office is the glass room, a
chamber filled with computers and wired for satellite linkups,
across whose wall dances a row of clocks giving the time in
Zurich, London, New York, Chicago, and Phoenix. Computer
screens report the Dow Jones, Standard and Poor's 500, markets
in Eurodollars, deutsche marks, Swiss francs, pounds sterling,
yen, gold, and silver. This room and the computer system within
it are based on the work of a German named George Herrdum
who operates out of Düsseldorf and Switzerland and owns a firm

called GFTA. He has designed a market system telling players just how to play, and around ACC this system is called "the black box." Herrdum claims to have very powerful clients: General Motors, various Arab oil sheiks, and now Charlie Keating.

Charlie sits in his chair and watches the screens. Around him scurry his technicians, an almost priestly order of helpers who fulfill his every command. They work long days, and when they go home they wear beepers since global markets never sleep. Buy gold, sell silver, Keating will say. And then they will execute his decision. The room is not a normal brokerage office, it is a cockpit for one human being, Charles Keating, Jr., as he travels through the oceans of the world's money with a flick of the keys on a computer. The room is very quiet as he stares at the screens, and his face becomes very intense, wrinkled, and old. The eyes focus like hard jewels, the smile vanishes from his lips, and he seems like a man staring into an abyss. There are no meetings, no reports, no committees. There is just Charlie Keating very early in the morning in a glass room full of computers, a tall skinny man flipping money like a farmer turning over his manure pile.

He loves the tension of it. After all, he is a lifelong crapshooter. He even kept a craps table in his home in Cincinnati. Now he has one in Phoenix. Of all the casino games, craps is the one where the action is the fastest and where the losses can wipe a player out almost instantly. Charlie knows this well. He plays in Monte Carlo or in the London clubs with his Middle Eastern friends like Toufic Aboukhater, a money guy who represents the Kuwaitis in deals. That's what people don't understand about Charlie, that he is not simply a provincial savings and loan owner sitting in Phoenix, Arizona. He is global. He owns a good chunk of something called the Saudi-European Bank—a former president of France is on the board along with Charlie's friend former governor John Connally of Texas, a bunch of Middle East oil sheiks, and of course Keating or one of his aides. When Charlie hits the tables in Europe he plays big because he is with big people now. Sometimes he loses twenty-five grand in a night, or fifty or seventy-five grand, and he will have to wire home to ACC for a check to cover his losses. But by God he plays.

One of his key aides insists, "Anyone who ever tells you he understands Charlie Keating is either lying to you or making a mistake. He is the most complex, enigmatic human being you will

ever come across." Another person close to the family insists that
everyone is always trying to make him too complicated when he is
really simple. As he waits for the phone call on May 20 that will
tell him if the bank board has given him a new lease on life or left
him for dead, he can look up at a framed newspaper clipping on
the wall that demonstrates as well as anything Charlie Keating's
complex nature. The clipping is the obituary of a man named
Jimmy Schneider who had been a childhood classmate of Charlie's in Cincinnati. Schneider was an orphan—he used to sleep in
coal bins at night and then sell newspapers on the street. Charlie,
coming from a better home, would give Jimmy part of his school
lunch each day. And then Jimmy dropped out and Charlie lost
track of him. Years later when Charlie was a successful lawyer in
Cincinnati, he ran into Jimmy on the street. Schneider was now a
drunk, a cripple from polio, and a homeless person. Keating
started giving him a little money and using him as a runner on
various errands. He'd let him sleep on his office couch and kept
a wardrobe of clean clothes for him at his law offices. One of his
secretaries would take Jimmy aside every couple of days and tell
him that it was time to change his clothes. Sometimes Charlie
would send Jimmy on family chores, send him down to get the car
titles changed on the family fleet, things like that. When Jimmy
needed money, he'd come by Charlie's firm and get fifty bucks or
whatever he needed. When Jimmy would get busted for drunken-
ness, he'd call Charlie at 3 A.M. and Keating would go down and
bail him out. One day John Connally dropped by Charlie's office,
and someone took a snapshot of Charlie Keating and John
Connally and Jimmy Schneider. Finally, in the seventies, when
Charlie decided to move his family to Phoenix and try to make an
empire out of American Continental Corporation, he offered to
take Jimmy with him. But Schneider was getting up on sixty by
then and he was afraid to uproot himself. He came out to Phoenix
for a visit, but it just wasn't Cincinnati. He wanted his old bars,
his old pals, he wanted his routine of hitting a saloon first thing
in the morning for a shot and a beer. Still, he came to the corporation's going-away party at a fancy restaurant in downtown Cincinnati. Charlie wasn't there, Jimmy started drinking hard, and
then he had to go to the bathroom, which was at the bottom of a
long flight of stairs. He limped down the steps with his bad leg,
lost his balance, fell, and hit his head. Ten hours later he died of

a cerebral hemorrhage. Now as Charlie sits with his billions in Phoenix he looks at that clipping about Jimmy Schneider and the photograph.

At a glance, Charlie Keating is a successful, pontificating Republican business leader. But his moments of candor keep jarring this safe, conservative image. Once at dinner he is asked if he ever fears going broke. He pauses with a forkful of prime rib in his hand, that all-consuming absorption comes back, and he finally says, "All the time, every day. It's part of the problem of doing what we're doing. It's something that the press and the public doesn't appreciate. I come in with this hollow feeling in my stomach lots of times. We're not clipping coupons, we're not living off our old man's wealth. It's not a friendly situation."

On May 20, Charles Keating, Jr., does something he hates to do. He waits. Four years before when he bought that small federally insured savings and loan in southern California named Lincoln, the deal looked like a license to print money. He paid his $51 million, the money raised with $55 million of preferred stock sold by his friend Michael Milken. Lincoln had been a small operation focusing on home loans in its immediate neighborhood, an institution noted for its willingness to help finance minorities. The federal government essentially deregulated S&Ls in 1982. Then California followed with even more generous terms. Where the federal government's previous guarantee of deposits had required that the money go mainly for sound home loans, suddenly the S&Ls could invest the money in almost anything they desired. Two years before, the size of a deposit the government would insure had been raised from $40,000 to $100,000. The administration and the Congress had argued that these changes would solve the problems of the industry—losses resulting from competition with banks and from trying to make it with home loans. Basically, before deregulation savings and loans were borrowing money at 12 percent and legally forced to loan it at 10 percent. Between 1980 and 1983, 962 savings and loans out of the nation's 4,002 collapsed.

Keating saw the potential lurking under the rubric of deregulation. He hated rules and regulations, and now there were almost none. The first year he owned Lincoln the thrift made eleven home loans, four of them to Keating's employees. The rest of the money went into high-risk investments, things like junk bonds (eventually

$660 million), raw land (almost a billion dollars in Arizona alone), the gold and silver market, and so forth. In four years he paid members of his family $34 million in wages. And the money was very easy to acquire. The owner of a thrift simply called up a broker and bought deposits in federally insured $100,000 units ("jumbos"). By May 1988, Charles Keating had bought maybe $5 billion worth of deposits. In the world of savings and loans, these deposits (functionally debts that the thrift must pay back with interest) are considered assets. And when one has to pay back these loans, there is no problem; one simply buys more $100,000 units to meet the demand. Of course, it is slightly more complicated than that. The jumbos, "hot money" in the jargon of the trade, are short-term, expensive money, and while Charlie Keating dips into them, he focuses on building up a branch system that excells at bagging long-term deposits. Charlie Keating sleeps less and works harder and always, always looks for every edge in a deal. By early 1985, the federal regulators became alarmed at the vast growth of federally insured S&L deposits, and they cut back the amount that could go into risky direct investments to 10 percent. For three years Charles Keating has fought this change, spent tens of millions of dollars fighting it (his own estimate is $55 million), and through accounting techniques sought ways to avoid complying with it. He has given five United States senators $1.4 million to plead his case in Washington. He is in trouble; that is why he is waiting. As Charlie Keating sits in his office this May day, the federal government has begun to conclude that deregulation may result in a financial catastrophe that will cost it, say, $36 billion. Today, he will learn if the federal government will shut him down.

Rosemary Stewart has worked at the Federal Home Loan Bank Board for thirteen years. Chairmen come and go, but she has served under the last nine, and now at the May 5 meeting, she is director of the board's Office of Enforcement, the head cop, as it were. She wears her hair in a severe bun, she sits upright and rigid in her chair, she is very conscious of her duties and of her turf. She has risen in the federal civil service system and knows her rights. And as the head cop, she thinks the San Francisco office has failed to build a case against Lincoln and Charlie Keating. "[M]ost of this case is not regulations," she explains to the board. "Most of this has to be an unsafe or unsound practice charge, or many unsafe or unsound practice charges that the San Francisco Bank [office] believes lie here. However, the evidence to support that does not demonstrate losses, does not demonstrate abnormal risk, or loss, or damage, even anticipated, to Lincoln in a manner that we're confident we could prove."

There are a few moments of muttering and small questions after Ms. Stewart makes this point, and then Jordan Luke, chairman of the board's Enforcement Review Committee, finally has to add one little thought that has come to him after looking at Charlie Keating and his operation. "I am," he confesses, "left with a high level of discomfort about whether this institution is in fact profitable or is not. The phrase used by the San Francisco folks was that in some ways, they were prepared to allege, and I don't say that they can substantiate it or cannot, that Mr. Keating is engaged in a practice of doubling down, that is, as he loses his bets, he doubles them."

His life is very good, and he does not want to alter it. He is making a couple of million dollars a year. "What do you want me to say?" he asks. ". . . There's a lot of risk involved. Tomorrow I could be making zero. That's a lousy answer. You can sit here and holler it's too much or it's too little, but I don't know what to tell you. I think I'm worth more than a baseball star. I work a helluva lot harder, I don't have much time off. That's not a reason to get paid, though. The guys didn't get much time off when they built the pyramids, and all they got paid was the whip, right?"

He has a $2 million house in Phoenix, a $5 million house in Florida, another house in the Bahamas. He is a big spender. One night in February 1987, he sat down for dinner with four other people at Le Cirque in Manhattan, and when he finished dining the bill came to $2,495—of course, this included the $425 tip. Or he'll be in Los Angeles, realize he needs some new threads, and pop into Giorgio's on Rodeo Drive. He'll pick, oh, a number of items including eight suits for, say, $7,694.63, five sport jackets for $3,487.88, maybe six pairs of slacks for $1,693.35, and grab some shirts and ties for $1,874.41, and run up a tab of $19,025.35. Last year he paid himself in salary and benefits about $3.2 million, and he paid his family millions more. He loves to spend money. In the Bahamas, he lives in splendor among the islands' many poor blacks. He is known there for a standing offer he has made to his neighbors—he will pay any mother a hundred dollars if she will name her baby Charlie. He also keeps a company chopper ready to fly over to Florida when he feels like having a hamburger and milk shake brought to him. In two years, 1984 to 1986, Keating's corporations give $6 million to charity (although his private giving from his personal income is close to nothing). He has invested $200,000 in a film about a visitation of the Virgin in Medjugorje, Yugoslavia, and he flies there often to pray. His secretary keeps a cross in her desk, one given to Charlie by Mother Teresa, and this small crucifix contains a piece of the True Cross. Often when he has visitors, Charlie will yell for his secretary. She will run in with this holy relic and Charlie will show it off and smile. Of Mother Teresa, he will say, "We're good friends with that lady." She flies on his corporate jets, on his corporate helicopter. She is a living saint in his eyes, and he wants her grace to protect his family and his empire. Sometimes when things are bad, he will talk to her on the phone, and these calls will lift his spirits. He will walk into a meeting at his company and say solemnly, "Mother Teresa is praying for us." Charlie Keating likes to keep two things very close at hand: God and money. His simple desk hosts only two items: a large glass Madonna that watches over him as he works and a computer terminal that is linked with the world's money markets.

People just don't seem to understand, they seem to think his belief in God is some kind of ruse. It is not to him. Even the damn regulators can't understand. Take Father Bruce Ritter, the founder of Covenant House in New York. Every time Charlie Keating is in New York he tries to have dinner with Father Bruce. He has loaned him tens of millions of dollars, all to buy buildings and turn them into shelters so that the poor, the weak, the helpless can have a roof over their heads at night, have sanctuary from the evils lurking on the streets after dark. Keating does not like to speak of these matters, not at all. He will stand before portraits of the people he admires, someone like Mother Teresa, and he will be asked, how much money have you given her? And he will not answer or he will say, that is none of your business. These are not matters for the press, or for bragging, these things lie in another realm altogether. So when he is in New York he will have dinner with Father Bruce at Le Cirque or some other fine restaurant. Father Bruce will always act embarrassed to be dining in such fine surroundings when children are suffering on the street, and then he will launch into a speech about the horrors he has seen recently. The ACC people at the dinner will be horrified at the priest's tales and will secretly wish he would shut up so as not to ruin such a fine occasion. But Charlie will be moved, choked up by the wonderful work Father Bruce is doing. And afterward they will all pile into a Covenant House van and for the rest of the night they will cruise the bad streets trying to pick up kids, boys and girls out there selling their bodies for a warm place to sleep or some money for a little taste of drugs, try to pick these kids up and take them to a Covenant House shelter where they can be saved from temptation and ruin. He loans Father Ritter's group tens of millions of dollars to buy yet more buildings, to expand into yet more cities, and when the regulators question these loans, when these small minds from those lazy agencies in Washington demand to know what is the collateral—collateral when one is dealing with God?—his staff will shower them with clippings from magazines about all the good works Father Ritter and Covenant House are performing. When the regulators dismiss these materials, when they write, "the moral credentials of Covenant House and Father Ritter are not in issue, nor do they warrant special consideration or forbearance by this Office in reviewing Lincoln's lending activities," Keating can only wonder how these people were raised and what in God's name makes them tick. People sometimes ask him what he will do if he stumbles, if his financial machine falters and fails. And Charlie Keating will pause and say, well, maybe I'll go be a swimming coach, God knows I love that sport. Or maybe I'll go to India and work with Mother Teresa. People will hear these answers and not know quite what to make of them. They can't seem to get it. They just don't know.

He is alone, and he knows it. He is always alone no matter how many people he surrounds himself with. He feels this solitude, the danger in the air, and this feeling frightens him. "It's a bellyful to carry," he says. "It's risky, dangerous. There's the possibility of failure with it every day and every night. But in a way, it's a challenge, it's invigorating. There isn't any point in not being a player—you're here. It's not only the money, it's the disgrace: yourself, your manhood. I'm not sure I'd have a big problem with that; on the other hand I'm not sure I wouldn't."

People don't know, they just don't know what he has to deal with. Not just the deals, not just the federal regulators trying to

take him out, not just his six kids and the wife, not just the two
thousand employees, the deep drives in him to prove worthy of his
church, the deep feelings in him evoked by pornography. No, other
things. Back in August 1983 during the late hours of a hot evening, his dogs started barking outside his house in Phoenix. He
got his pistol (he keeps a trunk full of guns) and went out to investigate. He found a couple of intruders, faced them down, and
held them at gunpoint until the cops arrived. In September and
December 1985, he was trying to get some zonings through the
Phoenix city council and the hearings brought out that lunatic
fringe of environmentalists and the press jumped on ACC and then
boom! all kinds of company property was shot up, run over by
crazed drivers or just plain stolen. Christ, he had to post armed
guards at one development just to save it from these modern van-
dals. And then on February 6, 1986, at about 9:35 P.M., somebody
shot out the window of his office, his own executive office at ACC
right on the gold coast of Camelback Road in Phoenix. They
checked the size of the hole and pegged the caliber as a .32. Six
days later, at 7:14 P.M. somebody blasted the window again, and
this round looked to be a .32 also. Then on March 7, 1986, just
after midnight, somebody put three bullet holes into the front of
his son-in-law's eye clinic over on Fortieth Street. And, Christ, all
Charlie Keating is trying to do is run a business, give people some
work, help build up the country. His head of security is alarmed
by all this—naturally he has a squad of bodyguards and company
cops, how can anybody survive in this country without his own police force?—and suggests that recent columns in the newspaper
"were very inflammatory and designed to cast you and your associates and your company in the role of villains. They were intended
to incite the emotions of the reader as a David against the corporate Goliath." God knows, Charlie believes that statement is true.
The press, they just don't want to understand, they just can't comprehend what he is creating at ACC. And besides, as his head of
security reminds him, there is this unfinished business of Larry
Flynt, the publisher of *Hustler,* a cripple in a wheelchair since
someone gunned him down in the seventies. "He has indicated,"
his security chief continues, "that he blames you for his being
shot. Mr. Flynt is a wealthy man who is said to be unbalanced. No
one has ever been prosecuted for his shooting, but he has vowed
to spend all of his money to get the one that he believes had him

shot. All indications are that he believes that person to be you."
And then there is the matter of Keating's daughter, who was raped
back in Cincinnati—"Mr. Flynt is alleged to have claimed indirect
responsibility for the attack."* And if that isn't enough, there is
more. One of those countless vice presidents on a development
deal flipped a couple of million dollars back in May 1985 to a
company known to be owned by a family with "connections with
organized crime." And now the project manager is getting heavy
threats against himself and his family. The warning signs go on
and on, and that is what has the head of ACC security so spooked.
Look, he cautions, "Angry people can be dangerous."

Yes, angry people can be dangerous. There are times when
Keating will grow cautious and forbid his grown children, who all
live in houses near him, to leave the compound because he does
not feel it is safe. But as for giving in to his enemies, well, fuck
'em. Charlie Keating sometimes likes to walk home from work
alone—a habit that drives his security force crazy.

As he waits on May 20 for that phone call that will tell him his
fate, he is quite possibly the only person in his many corporations
who knows the real facts, because nothing happens in his world
without his okay and unless a person is constantly in his presence
one cannot possibly know what is going on. To begin with, he has
created a world much too complicated for the average person to
comprehend. American Continental is a corporation and Lincoln
Savings and Loan is one of its properties, but that hardly even
sketches the dimension of the universe that teems inside Charlie
Keating's head. In the beginning, back in February 1984 when he
assumed ownership of Lincoln, it was fairly simple: ACC owned
Lincoln and trailing in the wake of ACC was a cluster of subsid-
iaries with names like American Mortgage Company, Continental
American Securities, Inc., Continental Commercial Company, In-
surance West, Inc., and Provident Travel Services, Inc. Of course,
Lincoln brought a few subsidiaries in its own baggage that Charlie
now had to keep track of, outfits like Diversified Life Insurance
Company, First Lincoln Financial Services, Inc., Oxford Financial
Corporation, Reliable Title Company, Coast Construction Service
Corporation, and Provident Mortgage Corporation. But his deals

---

*To date, Flynt has neither denied nor acknowledged the allegations in the ACC
memo.

seem to breed more corporations, and by now, as Charlie sits and waits for that phone call in May 1988, no one in the business, possibly not even himself, can tick off all the subsidiaries: there are now American Continental Finance Corporation and American Continental Finance Corporation II, there are American Home Finance Corporation (AHFC) and AHFC II and AHFC III. There are Continental Home Finance Company, ACC Real Estate, AC Properties, Inc., AC Resources Corporation, Keating Homes, Inc., Medema Homes, Medema Continental Realty, AC Resources Limited Partnership I, AC Resources Limited Partnership II, Brooks Crossing Associates Limited Partnership, Dunlap Apartments, Inc., Park Drive Apartments, Inc., Tatum Place, Inc., there are AMCOR, LINFIN, Phoenician Commercial Properties, Inc., Phoenician Financial Corporation, Crescent Hotel Group, Crescent Hotel Group of Michigan, Inc. There are in fact fifty-four subsidiaries, perhaps even more. The various companies are like shoes that from time to time get lost under the bed. The federal auditors combing his books never found one in the Bahamas; they learned of its existence only because of an idle comment by an ACC employee. Nor were they aware of another subsidiary in the Netherlands Antilles. Or of one in Panama that swallowed up $50 million.

These are the playing cards in Charlie's world, places where he can push money in and out. No one in the company ever seems to object to his plans. The boards of the corporations are all packed with his employees, and they shuffle from one to the other so rapidly—the memberships of the boards often turn over two, three, four, or more times in a year—that the corporations have no real institutional memory and, an even nicer point, no one seems to sit on a board for a long enough stretch of time to be ever really legally responsible in a fiduciary sense. Charlie is charting the cartography of a new world that is driven by debt, but this does not really concern him. What he seeks is cash flow, the blood of life itself, and this constellation of corporations gives him blood. His operation is what is called an accounting-driven company. In a simpler era, business was about making something for a price and selling it for a higher price. Such primitive companies were called economically driven. They are dying or lying dead all around the American landscape as Keating sits and waits. They are fossils like steel companies, automobile companies, home-building companies. Charlie Keating has known for years, well ahead of most people, that this old business world was doomed and he understood the key to the new world: it is about booking profits. By this he means, and all those accountants mean—and Charlie has forty to fifty CPAs on his own company payroll—that a successful business follows accounting rules so that it can make its numbers grow. It discovers and invents gains with a pencil. Imagine a world that can ignore old verities like the law of gravity. Charlie Keating's corporations live in such a new world. Nor does he apologize for this. He boasts of it. After all, his company's colors are red, white, and blue, just like the flag.

In 1987 *Forbes* listed ACC as number twelve among all U.S. corporations in a survey of five-year earnings-per-share growth. Through 1986, Charlie's company had averaged a 43 percent return on equity for eight years. In 1984, he headed the fastest-growing public company in the United States. Under his leadership ACC posted net earnings of twenty, thirty, forty million dollars a year. He directly employed about two thousand Americans. But the federal auditors who swoop down to examine his books disagree with him. They see losses: pretax losses of $50 million in 1986, $43 million in 1987. In fact, when they scrutinize his many deals, they figure he is losing about $10 million a month.

Charlie and his key staff members like Judy Wischer denounce this old-fashioned way of doing accounting. They fight it tooth and nail, and they construct deals that they claim the federal government is too stupid and hidebound to understand. As Keating's financial life is being decided in Washington, D.C., what is at stake is a collision of cultures. Debt is the tool for survival now, and the rate of borrowing—by government, consumers, and corporations—has exploded. In 1977, these three groups had an indebtedness of $323 billion. By 1985, they were in hock to the tune of $7 trillion. But this was not seen as a problem by many players. Runaway inflation in the late seventies and early eighties meant that debt could constantly be serviced or paid down with ever cheaper dollars. In the lingo of the theater Americans call Wall Street, leverage (debt) was more valuable than equity (assets). And millions were playing by this logic. In 1945, the U.S. national debt stood at 119 percent of the gross national product (GNP). For decades the debt skidded down in ratio: 1960, 58 percent of the GNP; in 1969,

49 percent; in 1974, 35 percent. And then in 1975, the numbers turned, and by 1984 the national debt had risen back to 45 percent of the GNP. The stock market was stagnant, the home-building industry was all but dead because of inflation and high interest. Loaning money and earning interest on it was the best game in town. And borrowing money to bag corporations with and then dismembering the corporations to sell off the assets piecemeal was a new financial sport. Buying a bank was the best bet of all, because that's where the cash was kept. In 1979, 1,165 manufacturing companies and mining companies went belly-up. Wholesale goods suppliers saw 908 outfits go down, and 3,183 retail stores died along with 1,378 construction companies. But only ten banks failed. If there is a god in this new financial world, it is Michael Milken, who has financed the hostile takeovers and leveraged buyouts of major corporations with junk bonds and put billions of dollars into the hands of players like Charlie Keating. Drexel Burnham Lambert's in-house motto was, "Ready, Fire, Aim!" so Charlie Keating was not alone in his passion for debt or in his willingness to take risks. One deal among the hundreds illustrates the problem, helps sketch the clash of this new world with the old.

The object is the Deal; the problem lies in the rules. By January 1985, the federal regulators had severely restricted the ability of savings and loan operators like Charlie Keating to make direct investments (an equity position rather than a loan)—that is, their ability to take money right out of their federally insured savings and loans and plow it into anything they wanted to, regardless of the risk. By that date Lincoln was hundreds of millions of dollars over its new limit in direct investments. But Keating thought there was a legal way around this new rigmarole. This was the origin of the Hotel Pontchartrain deal, a maze so complex that federal regulators were still struggling to unravel it more than three years after it was launched into the stratosphere of U.S. finance.

On New Year's Eve 1984, while the rest of the nation was girding itself for a night of serious drinking, a subsidiary of Lincoln Savings and Loan called the Crescent Hotel Group of Michigan, Inc. (CHG/M) bought the Pontchartrain, a 422-unit hotel in downtown Detroit, for $19,500,000. Part of the inspiration for this deal was the fact that Henry Ford II was pouring millions into Detroit's downtown in an effort to bring back the dying urban core. Detroit had been losing 20,000 people a year since 1950, and the race riot of 1967 had served to hasten this march toward death—in the following decade 208,000 jobs, about one third of the total, fled Detroit. Under Ford's leadership Renaissance Center, a new downtown complex of towers, was launched, and the first phase was completed in 1977 at a cost of $350 million. Keating made a practice of piggybacking on deals led by what he saw as richer and wiser heads. As he explained to some reporters years later, "I'm not a, I've never thought of myself as being an able person to, you know, to see, generate an investment, so to speak. I'm more of a follower on that. It would be very exceptional for me to believe I could find, through my own devices, a good investment like that. I just couldn't, it wouldn't be something I'm strong at."

At the moment of his plunge into downtown Detroit real estate, the federal government has yet to restrict direct investments. But by March 31, 1985, when the next chess move in the Pontchartrain deal is made, direct investment has been all but strangled by new regulations. So this is what Keating and his colleagues do: they form Hotel Pontchartrain Limited Partnerships (HPLP), which is really Keating's family and executives at ACC. This new entity, HPLP, buys the hotel from CHG/M. Getting the money for this buy is easy. Lincoln loans money to one of its subsidiaries, Lincoln Commercial Properties (LCP), which in turn loans money to CHG/M, two notes to the tune of $38 million. HPLP then assumes these notes, in other words borrows $38 million from CHG/M in order to buy the hotel from CHG/M. What this means is that through a series of transactions $38 million of Lincoln money has been loaned to Charlie Keating, his family, and his fellow executives to buy a property. If Lincoln loaned the money directly to them, of course, this would be illegal as blatant self-dealing. If Lincoln put $38 million directly into the Detroit hotel, this would be illegal as direct investment rather than a loan.

On October 31, 1985, HPLP refinanced $8 million of the debt through a new note from Credit Lyonnais's Chicago branch. On January 1, 1986, CHG/M begins to make monthly advances of money to HPLP that by the end of the year total $10,446,055. This piggy bank is financed by having Lincoln make a $20 million loan to a subsidiary of Lincoln on December 2, 1986. There were some rough spots along the way. For example, an appraisal of the hotel in 1985 pegged its value at $37 million, less than the investment.

Keating and his colleagues needed an appraisal of at least $44 million to justify all the loans. So in December 1985, Judy Wischer called two American Continental employees into her office and told them she'd like them to get an appraisal for the Pontchartrain of $44 million or more. The two ACC employees found an appraiser who delivered an appraisal of $44.4 million, and shortly thereafter one got a new swimming pool for his house and the other bagged a new Porsche Carrerea Targa. And there were odd turns along the way, such as the moment in June 1986 when Lincoln and San Jacinto Savings and Loan in Dallas loaned each other $123 million on the same day, apparently in the hope that San Jacinto would as a kind of extra favor help service some of the debt on the Pontchartrain.

One of the problems with financing the Pontchartrain—besides the fact that the federal regulators thought it was illegal—was that the hotel consistently lost money and needed constant refinancing by shifting money from Lincoln into one of those fifty-four subsidiaries Keating had at his command and then getting the money from the subsidiary into the hands of HPLP to finance the hotel's steady operating losses. This was a direct benefit for Keating and his family and fellow executives, who were all nestled in the bosom of HPLP. But problems are not without their blessings. The losses of the Pontchartrain were designed to yield fine tax losses. Think of it this way: Keating and his family and executives bought the Pontchartrain with Lincoln's money and then each year got tax shelters. In 1985, Keating's personal tax losses from this one deal were $442,270; for 1986, they tallied $836,133; and for 1987 the losses blossomed to $925,491. These tax benefits were nothing to sneeze at if one were Charlie Keating because from 1985 to 1988, his salary ran to $6.8 million. Over a three-year period, the players in this deal together harvested $9,410,383 in tax benefits. And the problem of paying the debt on the hotel—well, that never really came up, since the boards of all these subsidiaries would periodically meet, refinance the notes, or simply restate them as ending with balloon payments to be paid in, say, 1997 or whenever. Essentially, in this case the rent never really came due. The only immediate product was the tax benefits.

A deal such as the Pontchartrain requires a lot of work, constant work. Consider the traffic necessary for just a few months of 1987: on January 2, Phoenician Financial Corporation (PFC, a subsidiary) pays the Hotel Pontchartrain $335,000; on February 3, PFC wires $380,023.21; on February 5, PFC ships $150,000; come March 2, PFC sends $500,000; then again on March 9, PFC wires $400,000; on June 12, PFC pays Crescent Lending Corporation (CLC), yet another subsidiary, $12,950,426.90; on June 30, PFC sends CLC another $402,889.12; and then CLC, newly enriched, begins pumping money into the Hotel Pontchartrain.

There is a cloud of documents to confuse everyone. There is a logic that baffles the uninitiated. There is complexity that causes the linear thinkers to lose their way. And there is genius in this deal and many others, and this genius is scored by an underlying simplicity. Cash flow is essential. Charlie Keating is a deal maker, and a deal maker must live to deal another day. Debt? A theory of bookkeepers, a hypothetical concept of small minds. Cash flow, credit, the roll and thunder of money are all that matters. If cash is available, anything, literally anything, is possible. With cash, even the Japanese can be kept at bay. Because with money one can buy things and with things one has power and with power one can rule rather than be ruled. So the deals come and the deals go, the subsidiaries proliferate, the notes, bonds, stocks, various financial instruments, they mutate. None of this really matters. Cash flow. Power. Deals. Tomorrow.

Against such a torrent of transactions, the federal government initially has rather limited troops. In 1984, when Keating bought Lincoln, there were 700 savings and loan examiners for 3,000 thrifts. This small group of folks was supposed to keep track of a $1 trillion industry. They were paid about $14,000 a year to start and if they made the grade might someday earn $25,000. Not surprisingly, the turnover rate was 25 percent a year. Against them stood Charlie Keating, his dozens of CPAs, his fifty-four subsidiaries, his billions of investments, and his mind, a mind capable of orchestrating the Hotel Pontchartrain deal. A mind that also kept books of sufficient caliber that finally the federal auditors could get a dim idea what he was doing in just this one deal of many deals. A mind that always insisted that the deal was legal. A mind that hailed from a new world, one he insisted would be the way of the future or there would be no future. Charlie Keating would tell anyone who asked him that fact, that belief.

He knew exactly what he was doing and did it every day, seven days a week.

* * *

Steven Hershkowitz has been FHLBB's man looking over Charlie Keating's love of junk bonds. He works under Ms. Stewart in the supervision wing of the outfit. He is not sure that Charlie Keating has done anything wrong except be a brilliant businessman. A year earlier in 1987, he had told another FHLBB employee who was studying Lincoln that he felt Charlie Keating and his empire were not a priority because they did not seem to be insolvent. His colleague looked at him speechlessly and then after a moment said, "Actually, Steve, we try to keep them from *going* insolvent." He tells the board frankly on May 5, that he is dazzled by what he has seen in the Lincoln operation. "It's hard to decide where to begin," he admits. Why, just yesterday he had popped into a colleague's office for just a minute and wound up spending forty-five minutes to an hour talking about just this single case.

"This is a very unusual case from an enforcement perspective," he continues. ". . . The documents we have been talking about are all traditional enforcement documents. But this is not a traditional regulatory case. The institution is not doing anything illegal; in fact, it is engaging in those types of transactions that have been contemplated by Congress and contemplated by this Board as the general direction that the industry might go in in order to increase its profits outside traditional business. . . . [T]his institution has management with a personal stake in the transactions and has been successful in turning real profits, not paper profits, in these kinds of transactions. . . ."

However, there is one little catch, he admits. And he has talked to federal regulators in San Francisco about this very point. Based on what he has seen, he thinks that if Lincoln continues to operate and plunge into "high-risk transactions," well, under that condition "it will, inevitably, fail."

He will be having lunch with Father Bruce in New York, scribble "$100,000 donation" on a matchbook, and flip it to the priest just to witness the expression on his face. He will be visiting a village in Ireland, meet some people, and fly the whole village back to Phoenix for a two-week vacation at his hotel. A girl in the mailroom will do something right, and he will give her a new Corvette. He will look out his window, see an employee walking past, turn to an aide, and say "Fire that person." It will be done, and

Charlie will never explain why the person was fired. It is always personal. Bob Brown had a job down in data processing. His wife baby-sat the kids of one of Charlie's key aides, they all went to the same church. Brown's real passion in life was old cars, not his job tending computers. Charlie's daughters Mary and Kathy were in charge of setting up one of the hotel gift shops and Brown was tapped to pick a cash register system with adequate data capacity. He selected one that turned out to be too small, and when Keating asked just who had made this mistake, his daughters told him. Brown was fired instantly, and it felt like an earthquake had toppled his world. The day he came to get his final paycheck, Keating was screaming in a meeting, the veins popping out of his neck, his fist pounding on a table. And Brown thought, maybe being fired isn't the worst thing that can happen.

His moods can vary, and there is never a warning. He will watch his computer screen, speak softly to his helpers in the glass room, and tens of millions of dollars will suddenly shift from one speculation to another. In his corporate domain, not only can no one put anything on the wall of an office without his permission, they can't leave anything on a desk top at night, either. Charlie Keating will not allow such untidiness. They are paid very well—it is common for secretaries to make $50,000 a year, and some make $100,000 a year. In 1988, seventeen of his executives will make more than $250,000, while five will top one million dollars. No one gets a set vacation. If a person has his or her job done, they can just take off for days or weeks. There are no regular hours. Nor is there an employee handbook. Charlie Keating works seven days a week, and he sets the pace. The security guards at ACC headquarters never get used to him showing up at 2 or 3 A.M. all ready for a day of hard work.

On or about January 29, 1988, as Charlie is in trench warfare with the federal regulators and constantly flying to Washington, he must still make space in his mind for shipping $110,000 from his subsidiary Crescent Lending Corporation to the Hotel Pontchartrain through an Arizona bank and a Detroit bank. Three days later, on February 1, he dispatches another $450,000 by the same route. On March 3, it is time for another $500,000; on April 4, $200,000 more, and on April 25, a bit more, $50,000. Keating's mind is a maze of numbers, and those around him do not often realize this burden that he carries.

No one can quite figure him out, and he knows this fact and relishes it. He personally hires the women who work around him. They are all young, mainly blond, often buxom. Outsiders call American Continental the Stepford Company. Keating does not like the way America is changing. He is against sloppy dress, filth, homosexuals. He hates cigarettes, and there is no smoking permitted. He is for the family, the clean cut, for the real America. And he wants ACC to speak for these values. Charlie Keating is keen on matters of sexual morality. Once he paid for medical care for a poor old black man in the Bahamas. He had the man flown to the United States for treatment, and then when he was healed he put him on a pension. The next year, Charlie had him hauled up to the States again for an examination and the doctor called Keating up and told him the old man had contracted syphilis. And Charlie flew into a rage. He said to the man, "I didn't get you fixed up so you could go down and screw every sheep in sight." He had the man injected with penicillin and never brought him stateside again. Keating hates filth and is the largest contributor in the United States to antipornography organizations. President Richard Nixon put him on the federal Commission on Obscenity and Pornography. In 1970, Keating traveled 200,000 miles giving speeches against pornography. He cannot explain his passion in this matter, his quick tongue hesitates when he is questioned about it, and he mumbles something about his Catholic education, his moral training.

But then he cannot explain his interest in women either. He will walk around his company and peer down the blouses of the secretaries he has hired. The head of his insurance subsidiary, Chip Wischer, walks around unhooking brassiere straps. At least twelve women on Keating's staff have had breast enlargement surgery—a local plastic surgeon has offered ACC employees a special discount. Keating has never commanded such alterations in his employees, not at all. But they know, they see him walking up to a secretary at her desk and staring at her breasts. They hear him say, "Good grief, talk about hidden assets!" They can feel his desire. They know he watches them. A woman will suddenly get, say, a $5,000 bonus, and then a few weeks later come in on a Monday with huge new breasts. Once an ACC woman went to the plastic surgeon and found the entire waiting room filled with other ACC women. Keating will walk a visitor past the scattered desks of sec-

retaries, and he will watch for a sign of appreciation. If he does
not see it, he will know what kind of man he is dealing with and
tell people the visitor was a "queer."

It is not easy to nail down this part of Charlie Keating. He likes
bawdy humor, is one of the boys, but no one can be quite sure.
Once the employees at one of the branches of Lincoln in California
pulled a prank on a woman whose husband was away in the navy
for a year. They popped a pornographic film into the VCR in the
company lunchroom, the images glowed from the screen for about
thirty seconds, and suddenly the woman looked up from her sand-
wich, saw the lusty bodies copulating, and fled the lunchroom in
horror. When Keating heard of the incident, his reaction was simple: fire everyone at the branch. When his attorneys calmed him
down and explained he couldn't do that, he said, well, then, fire
whoever put the cassette in the machine. No one doubted his anger was real and deeply felt. And the person who had brought the
tape to work, a woman, was fired.

On the other hand, he likes to stare at women, to be surrounded
by beautiful women. When a reporter questioned him once about
this fact, he sighed and said, look, I work seven days a week,
maybe fifteen hours a day, and if you were me just what kind of
people would you surround yourself with? He also seems to enjoy
watching the bodies of young women as they run. He will take a
dozen of his secretaries to an ice cream shop at a nearby mall that
features expensive dress shops. As the secretaries lick their cones,
Charlie will suddenly hand each of them $500 or $1,000 or
$2,000 and tell them they have ten minutes to go buy a dress, or
fifteen minutes, and if they cannot do it that swiftly, he will take
the money back. As they race out of the ice cream shop on their
high heels, Charlie Keating watches their bouncing bodies. He will
feel very good at that moment, and he will laugh.

Darrel Dochow, the director in the Office of Regulatory Affairs,
has been to enough meetings and worked long enough for the government to know one must get that memo into the file, make sure
a point is in the record—just in case things turn out differently in
the future. As the meeting on May 5 rolls along like a polite Ro-
tarian luncheon, he speaks up with that telling phrase known to
all bureaucrats: "For the record, let me draw the board's
attention . . ." He speaks carefully, almost deferentially, saying

that he merely wants to aid the board, make them aware of a few points their own auditors in San Francisco have made again and again. To begin with, well, the auditors think Lincoln is short of cash, or, as they put it, "Lincoln's capital is insufficient." Also, the profits have gone down sharply. Then there is the matter of what Keating and his staff are reporting as Lincoln's income: "misleading." Losses are also understated; in fact, "the financial statement should not be relied upon." Also, there is another small matter Dochow thinks the board should consider: "Future prospects are for increased risk losses and probable failure." The San Francisco auditors, he continues, think Lincoln's staff lies all the time or, as it is stated in the lingua franca of the federal government: "They point to lack of credibility in the 407 findings."

Shortly after Dochow speaks, the chairman of the board, Danny Wall, suggests a five-minute recess.

Charlie Keating also enjoys parties. He does not care what they cost. In 1986, he threw an office Christmas party. He spent $27,143 for the entertainment—Peter Duchin's orchestra was flown in from New York. The banquet hall and the bar bills ran to $65,319, wreaths for the tables cost $3,452. Special lights were necessary, and that ran to $4,021, and naturally, there must be Christmas trees, another $2,449. And of course, Silly String, the aerosol spaghetti that partygoers could shoot out of cans at each other—figure $1,948 for Silly String. Why not? American Continental was hot in 1986, *Forbes* wrote about it, everyone noticed it, noticed this company based in Phoenix, Arizona, that suddenly had billions in play, this corporation run by a man called Charles H. Keating, Jr. There were so many parties, why, from 1983 to 1989, ACC officially dropped at least $460,000 on them.

And of course, the best parties were in private homes. Robert Kielty, Charlie's senior executive, gave some of them. Charlie would come and break things. He loves breaking furniture and fine crystal. He also does this in restaurants. Keating would grab a tablecloth and try to jerk it off without smashing the plates and crystal. He would always fail at this stunt, but this did not seem to disturb him. Nor did Charlie's love of destroying things bother Kielty. After each party at his home, he would simply send him the bill for the damages.

When Keating's daughter Elaine got engaged to Keith Dickson

in 1983, Judy Wischer, the number two executive at ACC, hosted the party for the couple. Wischer sensed that Charlie wanted this party to be elegant, so she told her guests to dress formally. Her husband, Chip, sensed that Charlie wanted the party to be informal, so he told the guests to dress casually. It was never easy to know what Charlie wanted. Chip greeted everyone wearing a blazer, tie, and Bermuda shorts. Soon the men who had worn jackets turned them inside out, and when Donald Loback, one of Keating's executives, arrived wearing a new Gucci tie, Charlie ripped it off him and tossed it into a pot of simmering beans. There was so much to drink that soon red wine stains were fingering across the Wischers' fine white carpet. Charlie sat there drinking from a bottle of Dom Perignon.

Then it started getting a little crazy. People were throwing each other into the swimming pool. Charlie liked seeing people get wet. He would sometimes offer a good-looking woman a hundred bucks to jump into a pool with her clothes on. But this time everybody was so drunk that Chip worried about somebody drowning. He rolled out his pool cover but was too late; the night was so warm and pleasant, the wine so good, no one wished to stop. People began jumping on the cover, which quivered like a trampoline, women in spikes laughed as they bounced and drilled holes through the fabric. Charlie got angry. He liked to see people get wet, enjoyed watching women climb out with their clothes soaked and clinging, so he picked up a beer can from an ice chest and hit Chip Wischer in the head with it. Wischer understood finally, and he removed his pool cover.

Charlie wanted more of that good feeling he had when he watched people jump into the water. He gathered up the china and threw that into the pool, followed by the crystal, the silverware. He ripped the clock off the wall and threw that also. And the telephone. Still he needed more of this wonderful sensation. He stalked around the backyard, wandered into the garden, and . . . the liquor hit him. He fell over and sprawled out under the desert sky while the hired disc jockey kept playing records, while people continued leaping into the pool and inside the house other guests staggered around barefoot in a sea of shattered glass and blood ran across the white carpet. Dickson, the man about to marry into the Keating family, caught Charlie's spirit. He kneed Chip Wischer in the back. Perhaps Dickson was still feeling the rush

he'd started in his ride over in a limo when he'd drunk champagne and done a few lines of cocaine. Soon he and Wischer had
a fine fight on with Chip pushing him down on a sofa and diligently pounding him into mush. But nothing could stop the party.
That is what Charlie Keating wanted, that is how he lived, that is
what he spent money for: to make sure no one could stop his
party, his life.

The next morning the house was in ruins, but Judy Wischer
never sent Charlie a bill. Why should she? Keating had one of his
own daughters on the ACC payroll at $30,000 a year to baby-sit
Judy Wischer's children. Later the next day, when Chip decided to
clean the beans and broken crockery from the bottom of the pool,
he got his finger caught in the drain at the deep end and almost
drowned.

The 1985 company Christmas party was held at a resort in
Phoenix. It was a place where Charlie was likely to feel at ease—
the owner, Texas rich, once strode into the lobby and saw a man
standing there in a blue blazer with brass buttons and wearing a
red tie. Something about this manner of dress offended the owner,
so he walked up and fired the guy on the spot. Except the man
was a guest, not an employee.

ACC had been gearing up for weeks. Annual bonuses—ranging
from one week's to one month's pay—were given out early with the
explicit instruction that female employees were to go out and buy
new formal outfits for the party. Kim Campbell had worked at
ACC as a customer service representative in the insurance subsidiary only since February 1985, but she dutifully went out and
bought a fancy dress. When she arrived at the ballroom she was
stunned to find out that this corporation in Phoenix, Arizona, had
the Four Tops for the entertainment. Soon everyone was busy getting drunk, food started to fly, and people were staggering around
spilling drinks on the fine carpet. Senator John McCain and his
wife made an appearance, Father Bruce Ritter attended, and so
did some officials from local government. But the center of the
party, like all such occasions, was the Keating family clustered at
a couple of tables up front. They formed a considerable tribe:
Charlie, his wife, and then five daughters and a son, all with their
spouses. Charlie began flipping out matchbooks with bonuses
scribbled in them, like he often did, and of course tossing food,
but this did not seem to be enough. So Keating and company put

Christmas wreaths on their heads and then they mounted the tables. They leapt from one to another across the big room, smashing glasses, toppling bottles, and whooping it up. The bill from the hotel ran high. Later Kim glimpsed the order from ACC central to the subsidiary where she worked: Insurance West was to ante up $50,000 to cover its end of the party.

Board Member Larry White is still having trouble going along with the bulk of the people at the May 5 meeting. He is a different kind of personality, a university scholar who is comfortable in a world of theory. He does not like arguments and confrontation. He has told the San Francisco office of FHLBB that when it comes to Keating and Lincoln, "I'll probably end up voting with you. But I'm not going to make this a *cause célèbre* and go out of my way to kill it." He does not want to alienate Chairman Wall, he prefers to keep a low profile and fight his battles on the bigger issues that he senses loom ahead. The proposal on the table is fairly simple; it is to draft a Memorandum of Understanding, an MOU. This memo will allow Lincoln to get a new audit out of Washington, D.C., that will essentially trash all the earlier audits by the regulators in San Francisco, will forgive Lincoln and its staff for any actions taken before the MOU, for all those deals like the Hotel Pontchartrain, and will, eventually, allow Lincoln to move out from under the scrutiny of the San Francisco office and into another district.

"And I'm very troubled," Mr. White explains, "by what I will characterize as the current position that many of the people around this table have described the board as having been put in, which is we've got a high-risk institution and to get out of this situation, we have to follow the words of Charles Keating; that it's a two-word admonition: Trust Me. . . . I realize that's a broad characterization of what's been said around the table, but I don't think it's an unfair characterization. 'Trust me in this very high-risk situation.' And that bothers me a great deal. . . . [I]s he really ready to reform?"

There are clues. Nine days before this May 5 meeting an advertisement appeared in the *Los Angeles Times* touting an investment opportunity. Lincoln Savings and Loan was offering what are politely called high-yield bonds or, more commonly, junk bonds. Actually, it was not Lincoln but its parent ACC that was peddling millions of dollars of the stuff through the Lincoln branch offices. The ad was headlined "AVOID GETTING STUNG EN ROUTE TO THE HONEY." The bonds, backed by nothing except hope, as is true of junk bonds in general, were described as "backed by the resources and stability of a savings and loan that's made Southern California home since 1926." The bonds were selling very well, mainly to very, very old people.

But the board does not touch on these bonds. After White's remarks the board drifts back to considering its various options: seizing Lincoln, letting Keating run it and go on his way, or possibly doing the MOU, a new lease on life for everyone. There is another factor: Danny Wall has to catch a plane, he must leave for personal business, and the board will either have to wrap up this matter of Charlie Keating or continue the discussion at a later meeting. And they realize they have been having meetings about Charlie Keating for months and months.

Besides, as Wall points out, "It seems to me that Mr. Keating, in my own knowledge, has been a very active, and a very entrepreneurial businessman for at least the last thirteen years that I've known him. . . ."

A vote is taken. The measure for drafting an MOU passes two to one, Mr. White dissenting. Keating has won as long as he can get the MOU through the thickets of government bureaucrats in essentially the same form as the draft copy the board has just voted on. And that is what has him waiting on May 20. That day is supposed to be the occasion of the signing of the final agreement: the word made legal document. Almost a hunting license for a man who likes to stalk a deal.

In the quiet governmental world of regulators, this MOU will be christened in honor of Ms. Rosemary Stewart, the head of enforcement who insists that the case against Charlie Keating does not legally justify seizing his savings and loan and booting him out. Everyone will call the MOU "Rosemary's Baby."

The federal regulators from the San Francisco office have been searching his files for months. They want to shut him down. They say his company is a fraud, a giant Ponzi scheme. The term comes from one Charles Ponzi, who started up Securities Exchange Company in Boston in 1919. He offered people a 50 percent return on their money in forty-five days. For a while everyone got rich and

Ponzi lived in the best hotels and ate at the best restaurants. He simply paid old investors off with the money he got from new investors. But in 1920, the local newspaper figured all this out, and Ponzi's bubble burst. He did three years in prison, moved to Brazil, and died a pauper. But his innovative idea lived on after him.

What the regulators have pounced upon are tiny details in Charlie Keating's eyes. Why shouldn't he throw Christmas parties? What's wrong with corporate jets? And what do they know about business deals, these little men who sit all day at gray metal government desks? Keating is enraged when he thinks about government, about rules, about all these federal flunkies trying to tell him what to do. He says, "Government is basically inoperable, I think. To survive under that circumstance—it would be like in my company if everybody could do their own thing. We'd be gone in a week. Same old syndrome that is rampant everywhere: when you have the type of structure that the federal government has, you won't tell an underling, you won't contradict him sufficiently to do the right thing even though you know it's right. You're hidebound by regulations, rules, protocol. There's nobody at the top. It's so ironic that in the Reagan administration, which was going to get rid of all regulations, it's worse than it ever was. The spending, the deficit."

Meanwhile, he has to try to keep his company and, by extension, the U.S. economy, going. Dammit, don't they realize this? On May 4, the day before the bank board meets to decide his fate, Keating has shipped another $260,000 from CLC to the Hotel Pontchartrain. He can't survive with endless meetings, with niggling rules. Deals don't wait, nothing that matters in life will wait. It is not a safe place.

He does not believe in credentials, degrees, restrictions. He knows his nation is losing, he can see it in all the economic indices, and he will not abide by limits, he will not operate with his hands tied. He can launch things, he can make people do things. Back in early 1983, he took a look at a prospective son-in-law, Keith Dickson, and saw potential. The guy was a national swimming champ, and besides, he had made a few bucks doing public relations for a swimsuit company. So one day he called Dickson into his office and said, "How would you like to be a stockbroker?" Dickson was taken aback and replied, "I don't really know what one is." God, won't they ever learn? Keating flared back, "I didn't ask you that. I asked you if you wanted to be one." That's it, can't they ever see it? Reach for it, take a chance, make it work. Dickson turned out to be okay as a stockbroker. He hired a bunch of ex–college athletes, figuring they would have self-discipline, and Charlie loved the idea. Keating suggested Dickson also recruit some Hoover vacuum cleaner salesmen too, since they would not be afraid of cold calling. And it worked; the boiler room pushed the product, and soon Keating had the company chef coming in at 5:30 A.M. to cook breakfast for the boys as they scanned their *Wall Street Journal*s before the market bell rang.

He is alone. He is at risk. He is decisive. He does things. He makes things move. And he knows the true facts. Billions are flowing through his hands, the clock is always running, the market is open in Singapore, something is happening in Zurich, the Wall Street operators have this deal for him in New York, the Kuwaitis have endless billions of oil dollars that they must put somewhere and he rolls dice with these very same sheiks, and the money shifts and enters accounts, crosses oceans, mutates into bonds, shares, acres, deals. "A large part of our business," he patiently explains, "is trading, and we trade globally. You asked if we had to operate twenty-four hours a day . . . that's exactly what we do and where we're headed. We want to be involved in the globe. We want to be where we think tomorrow is economically, and that is across all borders."

The pace is killing, just killing. On May 9 the Kuwaitis arrive in Phoenix, and besides that he has to meet with a representative of the Saudi-European Bank (the French-based institution of which he is a part owner). Two days later, Peter Fishbein, his high-powered lawyer from Kaye Scholer in New York (and also the attorney of Carl Lindner), descends so that they can work out strategy for dealing with the regulators. Prudential Bache sends a squad out to examine the financial possibilities of his operation. And after them comes Bankers Trust Company. On the eighteenth, Charlie pops over to the West Coast to see about dealing with Imperial Savings and the Imperial Corporation and to check out joint ventures and stock purchase ideas with Leisure Technology. The next day it's Security Pacific Bank and then back to Phoenix. It just never stops. He has to keep this place afloat.

The young women, those good-looking blond women, are running in his outer office, and he pays for that. A herd of gardeners is toiling outside his window, and he pays for that. Mother Teresa needs a million dollars, and he pays for that. The homeless clogging America's streets? He gives them a hundred thousand a year. People work for him, and he works for no one. He is self-made, practically an invention. He has remained married to the same woman for forty years, he has raised six children, he has created thousands of jobs, he is a friend of the rich and powerful, he is a good Catholic. He is beyond their rules because he senses something in American life that others do not and at ACC he is attempting to prove what he senses. He is making his intuition into a reality, a physical thing that can be touched, seen, bought, and sold. He understands that people can do almost anything they wish if they have money. And that they can have the money if they have the nerve to take it. He will never surrender this insight, never. He will not let them take the money away. Fuck 'em.

It is nearly noon in Washington, D.C., when Jim Grogan, an ACC counsel, is ushered into a conference room at the Federal Home Loan Bank Board. Keating's representative is a former aide to Senator John Glenn—Charlie always likes to hire the best. Besides, he is a good Catholic boy from Cincinnati, just like Charlie, and when he was a boy he used to pop into Keating's house because one of his friends, Bob Wurzelbacher, was dating Beth Keating and eventually married her. With him is Peter Fishbein of Kaye Scholer. To have such a legal weapon along is not unusual for an ACC employee—Keating keeps seventy-seven law firms on retainer. The atmosphere in the room is very formal. Dochow is there to sign for the bank board and is surrounded by six staffers. Kevin O'Connell, one of the onlookers, has a special feeling for this moment. He came to work for the FHLBB in June 1984, just a few months after Keating bought Lincoln. For four years he has dealt with problem thrifts, starting with some wild-man operations down in Texas where under deregulation billions have vanished and strange owners had proposed notions like opening branches on the moon. In April 1987, he was brought to the Washington office and handed a special assignment, Lincoln Savings and Loan. He has a unique background in the matter—O'Connell's father is the head of the industry's U.S. League of Savings Institutions and is a personal adversary of Charlie Keating. And so, just as Dochow picks up the pen to sign the MOU, O'Connell explodes and beseeches him not to sign the document, not to go through with the agreement. O'Connell rolls on and on, but Dochow does not waver, he signs for the bank board, and Grogan signs for Lincoln and ACC.

Done deal. Keating is the rainmaker in the corporation, and today he has truly made rain. It is around 9 A.M. in Phoenix when the telephone call comes from Washington and Keating yells across his corporate headquarters, "Get the champagne colder!" He has won. Secretaries are dancing on their desk tops. Cans of beer fly through the air, and there is an endless supply of Dom Perignon. Soon Charlie is wearing only a T-shirt with a hand-drawn skull and crossbones on it. He has a thin, drunken smile on his face, the look of a man who has just bet all his chips on sixteen black at Monte Carlo and broken the bank. Robert Kielty pours a bottle of champagne onto a woman's breasts, then sees a secretary taking photos on a desk top and jumps up beside her. Suddenly Charlie is there and binds their bodies together with duct tape. Two computers are airborne and crash through the glass windows of the building—one smashes into a truck parked below.* ACC will foot that bill gladly. Later, when Judy Wischer goes home to be den mother to her daughter's Brownie troop, she is so drunk that she walks into her house and vomits into the sink. The next day people will have gray memories, blacked-out memories. They will not be sure exactly what happened to them—only when the Polaroid shots appear in a scrapbook will they begin to recall their relief and sense of jubilation on May 20. Charlie Keating has won, he has made the federal government back down. Charlie Keating is the man who always wins.

But the government regulators will be back, and Charlie Keating knows this because he knows what is really going on. He carries it all in his mind. Paper can be dangerous, it can be used as a weapon by enemies. The mind of Charlie Keating is a safe place, and wherever he is, that is the location of a financial empire called American Continental Corporation. Still, the party is a pleasure, a respite from his toil. And he has bought time. As one of his close

---

*Part of this description is based on a scrapbook of Polaroid images taken at the party. Keating showed the scrapbook to Bowden in June 1988 with the request that no mention of it be published at that time. He said he was afraid of angering the federal regulators. He turned the pages almost tenderly as he displayed the photos and paused and smiled with satisfaction when he came upon the image of himself in the T-shirt with the skull and crossbones.

aides explains, "For Charlie it was always you cut a deal so that you can live to fight another day." Now he has that next day in his grip. In the coming year, yet another billion dollars will flow through his hands. The night of the twentieth, after the hours of partying and whooping it up at the headquarters on Camelback Road, he will host a dinner for Citizens for Decency Through Law, his pet antipornography organization. The next day he will entertain the official Irish delegation visiting Phoenix. And also, his jet and chopper will fly Mother Teresa around the Southwest and he will spend the whole day with this living saint. It just never stops. Three days later, on June 1, eleven days after the Memorandum of Understanding is signed at the bank board conference table in Washington, Charlie Keating's empire will ship $240,000 through a subsidiary and various banks to the Hotel Pontchartrain. Two weeks later, on June 13, another $245,000 will be dispatched. On June 29, yet another $365,000. In his world, one cannot hesitate, one cannot falter. His God judges, his God can be harsh. That is why he swims that mile a day. He must keep in shape, he must be ready for this fight. He will not tolerate losing. Ever. The financial seas teem with sharks, the clock is a whip at his back. Time is very important for Charlie. He hates waiting.

PART TWO

PANCHO & LEFTY

Living on the road my friend
Was gonna keep you free and clean
Now you wear your skin like iron
And your breath's as hard as kerosone
You weren't your mama's only boy
But her favorite one it seems
She began to cry when you said good-bye
Sank into your dreams.

—Townes Van Zandt, "Pancho and Lefty"

He was the national champion in the breaststroke in 1946, but now it's 1973 and Charlie Keating is fifty years old as he does lap after lap in the pool in Cincinnati, Ohio. He is collecting on a kind of challenge: he will swim a hundred laps in the twenty-five-meter pool, well over a mile, in order to raise $10,000 in pledges for the private swimming club he sponsors. The audience watches as the middle-aged man ticks off ten laps, then twenty, thirty, forty, fifty laps, and still his pace never falters.

A friend watching from the sidelines shouts, "I'll give you $10,000 if you finish." And Keating does his hundred laps. The friend is not yet satisfied. He shouts again, "I'll give $10,000 more if you swim five more laps, and I'll give $20,000 on top of that if you do those five on butterfly strokes."

And Charlie Keating does.

A SQUIRREL
IN THE
YARD

He does not understand this interest in the past. For Charlie Keating, the past barely exists. How can it possibly compete with the richness of the present moment and the possibilities of the future? He is sixty-five years old, it is midmorning on a May day in Phoenix, Arizona, outside the heat is inching up on one hundred degrees, and now someone is asking him about his childhood back in Cincinnati. He gives a puzzled look, not angry or secretive, simply puzzled.

"You really want to know about that stuff?" he asks.

Okay, he decides, he'll give it a shot. He's got a few spare moments—he's just hedged that currency play in London and handled a phone call in his effort to flip that Midwestern drugstore chain. One of his secretaries scurries in with a small note on a yellow scrap of paper, and Keating pauses, stares at it intensely in total silence for twenty seconds, then crumples it and puts it into his pocket. He looks up and smiles, and she hurries away.

He looks down at the small bronze squirrel he keeps on the coffee table in his office, almost the only personal touch in the large suite.

"I had a father," he begins, "who was a total cripple. He used to sit in the front yard in a chair. We'd lift him and put him in that chair. He had a pet squirrel that came up all the time. I've got that bronze there of the squirrel—I'm not nostalgic or anything, I'm just surrounded by things that I like.

"My father was one of those few that got lucky. It was back in the days when they first introduced a disability insurance policy.

76

He got two hundred dollars a month as a result of that for all of his life. In those days, two hundred dollars a month was fine. It wasn't bad back in the thirties and forties. He had come out of the streets of Kentucky, and he had done well—he didn't have any real money, but he maybe had ten or twenty thousand bucks in the bank. It wasn't uncomfortable. . . . No log cabins, we lived modestly but had ample means."

And then Charlie Keating runs out of words. After all, that was then, and this is now.

He was born the son of a one-legged man on December 4, 1923, in Cincinnati, Ohio. His father, a manager in a local dairy, came from Kentucky, just across the river, and had lost his limb in a hunting accident. Another son, William, soon followed, and then when Charles Keating, Jr., was seven his father went down with Parkinson's disease, a degenerative disorder that slowly robs a person of everything but a beating heart. Two hundred dollars a month in disability insurance kept the small family going through the Depression, and the sons held many part-time jobs.

Six feet four, the senior Keating was soon trapped in a wheelchair, a helpless man who drooled. His wife, Adelle, would turn him over in bed so that his sores could heal. When strangers would stare at him, her husband would scream, "Don't look at me that way!" Or his boys would carry him outside and he would sit in his chair in the front yard all day, watching a world he could not join and feeding a squirrel that would scurry down from a tree to take tidbits from his hand. Then he lost the power of speech and spent the remaining decades of his life in silence until finally death came in 1964. The decades of nursing him gave his wife an indestructible heart, and as late as 1990, she lived in a Cincinnati nursing home.

One summer, Charlie discovered swimming at a Catholic camp and the sport became his passion—a solitary war against an implacable adversary, time, and one in which his large feet and hands gave him an edge. He became the natural leader of his boyhood friends, and what he sought was not, in their memories, simply power but a kind of love. It was important to him that people like him. He came of age in a city that since the nineteenth century had missed many of the changes that had whipped across American life. The great influx of immigrants was long past in Cincinnati, and its dominant blend of Germans, Irish, and Southern whites had been in place since around the time of the Civil War, when it was a pork-packing center, called by many Pigopolis. The initial great fortunes were made by gouging during the Civil War as loyal Cincinnatians cranked out goods for the Union cause at inflated prices. It was a city of tree-lined streets and simple houses tucked between the hills facing the Ohio River, a conservative city with many of the restrictive mores of a small town. Mark Twain allegedly once said, "I'd like to be in Cincinnati when the world ends, because it will happen ten years later there."

This Midwestern sense of a world floored on moral certainty was reinforced for Keating by his Catholic education, particularly under the Jesuit fathers at the city's downtown parochial high school, St. Francis Xavier, a Cincinnati institution founded in 1831. Keating was a good student. The fathers ran a tight ship, segregating their charges from the heathen world of other faiths. The entrance to school dances was policed by priests who whispered into the ears of strange boys questions about rites or prayers that only a sound Catholic lad could answer. The students were warned to watch themselves for any sign of sexual stirrings. If they felt their bodies coming to life at a dance, they were advised to sit down until the moment passed. The school motto was "Men for Others." St. Francis Xavier rejoiced in sending men into the world "who are stabilizing forces in a crumbling civilization because they are Men of Character."

Keating entered the University of Cincinnati in the fall of 1941. He flunked out. On December 4, he turned eighteen, on December 7 the Japanese bombed Pearl Harbor. He enlisted in the navy ("All my life I've wanted to be in the navy, I can say that, I always wanted to be in the navy.") and spent four years as a fighter pilot ("shooting down a lot of pilots, all you had to do was stand in line"). He never saw combat or was shipped overseas ("got my wings, and they formed a new squadron, a night-fighter, low-level-intercept air base, and they transferred me to that and it took another year of training, they transferred me out of harm's way"), and when the war ended he was twenty-one years old.

In December 1988, when his empire is in its death throes, he speaks off the cuff to a meeting of Lincoln employees in a session closed to the press—"for the first time in my entire business career

I have not been able to speak with my people without fear of a leak"—and at that meeting in some stuffy room in southern California, he rolls on for more than an hour. He has brought with him a Catholic bishop from the back country of Indonesia, as if to exorcise the demons who pursue him. In four months he will be in bankruptcy, his bank seized. In nine months he will be indicted. He starts talking about the federal regulators, the savings and loan problems, the prospects for investments, the future of the company, but somehow he is drawn back to a memory, to the joy of being a navy pilot.

"I can remember a couple of major decisions in my life," he begins simply. "One was, I flew for the United States Navy. I was a carrier-based night-fighter pilot. I loved every minute of it. I served a number of years and probably didn't have one incident that wasn't delightful and challenging. I was about twenty-one, I think. The time came for me to make a career choice. Did I want to continue in that exciting life or get out? I had no reason to get out. I was unmarried. I couldn't even find any girls to go out with me. . . . What finally convinced me to get out was that I remembered it wasn't all so glamorous. There were times when the grease that came out of the engines and those old fumes would seep through and soak you with oil and sweat from the un-air-conditioned cockpit.

"But the main thing that convinced me was that when I got to be thirty-five years old I wouldn't be flying anymore. What I was in love with wasn't the military service particularly. It was flying. So I left, and it was a good decision and then we made other decisions."

And then Charlie drifts off into a denunciation of everything that has happened to him lately. He can't contain his spleen about the federal government—"That means war. It's a war that we will probably lose. But it's a war that I fully intend to fight." He can't shut up, he's rolling now, and he launches into an elaborate defense of his investments, explaining complicated deals, the fine points of accounting, the beauty of the vision he brought to Lincoln. For half an hour, forty-five minutes, who can count? he talks and talks, his words plain, colloquial, and blunt. And then he turns back to his war, as he often has. He talks about the flying, the freedom of the skies. And of the sensation, the intensity he found and loved, of punching a hole into the heavens with a Grumman

Hellcat. Charlie Keating cannot help himself, life is so good for him when he transports himself back to 1945.

His audience is surely puzzled. For months and months these employees have been under siege by federal and state bank examiners and have heard rumors of collapse. They think about payments, bills, job security. And now suddenly, without warning, Charlie Keating has stormed into their California office with a strange foreign bishop from some island where there is nothing but the hoe and the bullock, and he is talking about a war that ended forty-three years ago. The subject just seems to come up out of some secret but tender part of himself.

"I'm not rich anymore," he suddenly blurts out. "They've managed to get me down to where it's very close for me and I probably don't have the same financial base that you do at this point. I'm very much at risk. . . . I can't walk away from the bondholders, I can't walk away from the people that have put deposits in here. I have a tremendous obligation. So, you know, you fight for it. In order to fight for it you have to have that capability to be willing to say that you can leave it. I remember when I was, I hate to keep going back to the war, but I was proud of it. Actually, you know it is true . . . once you fly for the navy . . . I hate the government so much today . . . I keep forgetting . . .

"But when you flew for the navy in my years," he resumes, "it probably sounds strange to you, but we were not allowed to be married or engaged. You could not fly for the U.S. Naval Air Corps in World War II if you had a wife, if you were married or engaged. If they found out you were married after you got in, they threw you out. They needed pilots very badly. That's how I got in. But the reason was, that they didn't want you to be worried about dying. If you were going to go up there, they wanted you to be gung ho. They wanted you to face the fray, and that wasn't something they wanted you to worry about . . . when you had to figure out who to hit and how to do it and so forth and so on. . . . The equipment was very expensive, was the reason. It wasn't because they were worried about losing a pilot, it was because the equipment was very expensive.

"As a matter of fact, one time I landed a plane with its wheels up. I had a date with the only broad—pardon me, Father—the only girl down at what's now NASA Station, it used to be Banana Creek. . . . I was flying night fighters out of there and we'd go up and fly all night and there was one good-looking blonde in town and she dated most of the aviators and I was flying and I'll never forget it.

"I don't know if you've ever heard of Harry James, he used to play the trumpet. I had Harry James on the radio, the rest of the flight was out over the ocean somewhere, and I was hanging around the tower all night because when they called you in those days they teach you to fly silent and they [signal] and flash it out like that and when you saw the [signal] you knew the flight was called in. No radio contact, but I had the radio on, you had to leave the radio on for emergency.

"So I had the radio on, I don't know why I'm telling you all this.

"So Harry James is playing 'Cherry' and I'm having a ball and I'm wanting to get down and all the boys figured I was entitled to fly in first because you get tied up in traffic and I could get down to Banana Creek and have a date. So it was about two in the morning and I'm going in for a landing and in the navy they teach you to land tail first so your hook catches the carrier wire. So I'm flying into the landing and ol' Harry's playing and the tower is screaming 'Your wheels aren't down! Your wheels aren't down!' I forgot all about it, I was . . . so I hit, and the minute I hit I knew I was in deep trouble because the plane just sank. And instead of doing the smart thing and letting it sink, I poured on the coal and almost made it. I almost got out, just the tip of the prop caught."

Harry James has come out of Albany, Georgia, but he is way past such places now. He has a regular radio show. Helen Forrest, Connie Haines, and Frank Sinatra all have sung for his band. He is married to Betty Grable, the woman with the most famous legs in the world, the woman in a swimming suit who is smiling from posters on the walls of every American barracks on earth.

"Some flames came running back, fire started in the engine. I was full of gas because I hadn't spent it out there, so I jumped out—and we all wore parachutes in those days—I jump out, I hop on the wing of this careening airplane and blow off of it and I'm sitting down on the runway and the plane goes down and blows up down the runway. And all the poor guys are out in their [firefighting] suits looking for the pilot in the cockpit and everything . . .

"So they court-martialed me the next day and all of the officers were friends of mine and they decided I was the dumbest idiot that ever lived and what reminded me was the cost of the equipment."

Reminded? Reminded of what? It is 1988, the world runs on money, it is getting late, and this man, this old guy is saying the money, the money for the plane was the key thing.

"He told me that if I spent the rest of my life in the U.S. Navy and they never paid me a nickel, I'd never pay for that airplane. That airplane was a brand-new night fighter. It was a fleet plane. It cost $50,000. Now just imagine compared to today. But anyway. The point is, that you didn't care and to a certain extent you have to not care a whole lot about the enemy. That's why we don't care at this point, yes. . . .

"I never made the date.

". . . If I could tell you more, I'd tell you."*

He can't stay with his war. The night air of Florida, the date waiting at Banana Creek, his Hellcat bursting into flame, the fire against the tropical night. He looks out at the room, the sea of young faces, young ambitious faces, faces that are being paid very well. . . . The bishop is at his side, Charlie Keating must go on. He tells of the real estate recession . . . the investments in Playtex . . . he must reach his audience, make them like him.

"If the bishop weren't here," he smiles and says, "I'd tell about the Irishman that said his wife hated him so much she didn't even open her eyes when they made love because she didn't want to see him having any fun."

The war is always with him, but it never seems more than an anecdote about a night flight, Harry James on the radio, a kid flying through the blackness. We are in a war, they will probably win, but we must fight. We are being trained to die. We can't have permanent women, not a fiancée, not a wife. There is an edge, and that is where we live. And we accept this fact because we know the other places. Because the other places will rob us of our edge.

And we all know this is true. Here, feed that squirrel coming down the trunk of that tree. There is a man trapped in a chair, he is drooling, who can make out exactly what that man is saying? Charlie Keating is talking to a roomful of employees in southern California. They are very young, most of them were born after his war was over.

---

*A stenographic record of Charlie Keating talking to staff at Lincoln Savings and Loan, December 1988. Interviews with Keating over the years are studded with brief, allusive references to his days as a navy pilot.

Carol Kassick, his faithful secretary, his Boswell—"And also I have with me my secretary, my aide, Carol Kassick. Carol."—she is blending into the audience, faithfully recording every word.

The man who obsesses Charlie Keating also begins his life without promise. Carl Henry Lindner, Jr., is born in 1919. He comes of age in Norwood, a small working-class section of Cincinnati. Norwood is an enclave of Kentuckians, hillbillies in the eyes of the city's powers. Carl Lindner does not go to St. Xavier High School, he does not finish high school for that matter. By age eleven he is working in a small ice cream store owned by his father—three scoops for a nickel. He also looks after his younger brothers, Robert and Richard. The business fails in 1931. He goes to work full time in the family dairy at age fourteen to help his family survive the Depression. And he drops out of school. He works twelve- to fourteen-hour days and keeps this pace six days a week. For the rest of his life, he will maintain this schedule. Because of the economic grind of the thirties, his two brothers drop out of high school also and join him at the dairy. Only their sister, Dorothy, ever graduates. In 1940, he is twenty years old and he has an idea. He gets hold of a twenty-foot-by-fifty-foot store, stocks it with milk, and undercuts the market by a nickel or so. The local milkmen who specialize in home delivery do not like this new idea, and the very first day the store opens for business they beat up Carl's father. His brothers want to use their fists to respond to the attack. Carl has a different idea. He sues the dairymen, wins $1,000 in a settlement, and puts the money into the business. Then he adds ice cream to the depots (the Lindner boys make it themselves), then he adds stores, then he buys a truck (with $1,200 borrowed from a bank). When the war comes, his two brothers go into the service and Carl remains at home as the sole support of the family and runs the dairy and discount outlet.

He is a Baptist, he does not drink, he does not smoke. He contributes to his church. No one takes note of his actions. There is no reason to pay attention. When the war ends, Carl Lindner is twenty-six years old and no one in Cincinnati, Ohio, beyond his own kinfolk knows who he is. He has never had a childhood. Years later, whenever he cannot reach one of his executives because the person is off playing golf or tennis, he will grow testy. He has no tolerance for games since he was never allowed time to play as a child. Charlie Keating is four years younger and better educated, but he faces exactly the same future of unimportance.

Their city prides itself on conservative values but enjoys certain vices. By the late 1940s, there's hardly a saloon or grocery store in the county that is not booking bets or hosting a crap table. And across the river in Newport, Kentucky, are full-blown casinos. Cincinnati has room for players if they uphold its middle-class values and do not draw attention to themselves.*

The tall young man stands on the block staring down at his lane in the Yale University pool. He has been out of the navy for less than a year, and he has been busy cutting deals. First he tries Ohio State, where they offer him a scholarship if he will join their swimming team. He accepts but then backs out when the University of Cincinnati sweetens its offer. Back in 1941, Charlie Keating flunked out of college his freshman semester. Now, four years later, years spent flying navy planes and working out at military swimming pools, Charlie Keating is scheduled to take six months of liberal arts courses and then enter law school. And swim. He has come to New Haven to compete in the two-hundred-yard-breaststroke. He has thirty-six-inch arms, big feet and hands. And willpower. When the race ends his time is 2:26:2 and he finishes a yard ahead of his closest competitor. He is the disarming victor, telling reporters that he is really out of shape, that he needs to train more. Besides, he says, he comes "close to drowning when I try to swim on my back."

He wins a gold medal as the National Collegiate champion.

That year he also takes the gold in the Pan Am games.

He is the practical joker. When his friend Ted Toma marries, Charlie stuffs mothballs under the front seat of the honeymoon car. He meets Mary Elaine Fette, an athletic Catholic girl from an established Cincinnati family. One night they double-date with the

*Al Schottelkotte worked for decades at the *Cincinnati Enquirer* and recalls Cincinnati night life before the rise of Las Vegas in the late forties: "Illegal gambling was everywhere then, crap tables and handbooks in every saloon and grocery in Hamilton County, glittering legal casinos across the river in Kentucky. I won my first car at a crap table. Nightclubs, big stars, big bands—some of the best musicians in America lived around here. . . . Miami, Philadelphia, even Chicago could hardly match our nightlife in those days. Las Vegas was a burg compared to Newport, Kentucky." (Johnson, "City of the Year: Cincinnati," *Sports Illustrated,* December 31, 1990.)

Tomas and all go to a striptease joint. The starring attraction is
Rose da Rose. He sits at his table pounding a cane on the floor
and shouting "Come on. Take it off! Take it off!" Charlie's face is
red, he is enjoying himself. But he will not let Mary Elaine lift her
eyes and see the naked woman who dances before them. He and
Mary Elaine wed in 1949 and soon the children start to arrive.

He graduates from law school in 1948. His friend Ted Toma
goes to work for the FBI, and Charlie Keating picks up whatever
legal work he can ("They would pay me a buck, did a lot of insurance work, trial work, tried cases, police court work, street level.
I liked it, I liked trying cases, for a while."). Then he joins a law
firm ("just stumbled into corporate work, friend of my father's did
a lot of business—you really want to know this stuff? . . . We tried
a lot of cases, guy I knew, my dad knew, ran some businesses
and I started representing him and found a home, corporate law
business.").

For a while, he sells life insurance. Then he runs a fruit stand
and he learns to read people, learns to tell if people are going to
come across with the money or cheat him. He gets up at 3 A.M.
each morning to go down to the wholesale market and haggle for
fruit. He loses money financing the stand, but he remembers every
lesson. On Sundays, Keating and Toma pick up some extra money
working as Roto-Rooter men. Once they unclog a drain at a large
public housing project and hundreds of used condoms come flowing out. Charlie Keating is appalled at this evidence of sin and
willful violation of God's injunction to be fruitful and multiply.
One Sunday morning they work on an apartment building full of
poor people. The landlord is a rich speculator. The job goes very
quickly, and Ted Toma suggests charging their routine fee of
twenty bucks. "Hell, no," Charlie Keating snaps. "Charge that guy
sixty bucks. You see how much money he's making off these
people."

Maurice Niehaus is a partner in the law firm where Keating
works. "Charlie," Niehaus remembers forty years later, "was an
opportunist if there ever was one. He was the kind of guy who
would walk in where angels fear to tread."

Keating is not offended by this opinion. Facing federal and state
charges in 1990, he responds, "I can see where he could say that,
that I was opportunistic, aggressive. You've got to remember, I wasn't
a young kid out of law school. I was a navy officer, flew fighter pla-

nes, I'd had authority and commissions. I didn't look at it quite like I was there to work for others. . . . I got my own business."

During the Korean War, Niehaus took a leave of absence to work for the Office of Price Stabilization. Keating, he remembers, suddenly began representing people in various industries who had price problems. Niehaus was questioned by the FBI because Keating was using a letterhead with Niehaus's name on it. "It was a little ethical thing," Niehaus thinks now, decades later. ". . . It's name dropping. I could never say he was dishonest."*

In 1952, he decides to strike out on his own and founds a law firm with his brother, William, and a classmate from law school, Keating, Meuthing, & Keating. He always remembers his first big case representing a woman who owned an ice cream business. She paid him ten thousand dollars in cash in a paper bag. Charlie Keating raced home, went to his bedroom, and threw all of that money up in the air and watched it float down and carpet the room.

In 1953, Julius and Ethel Rosenberg are electrocuted in New York State for giving atomic secrets to the Soviet Union. In 1956, if not earlier, the Cincinnati office of the FBI opens a file on Charles H. Keating, Jr. He is the focus of an Atomic Energy Act–Fraud Against the Government and Espionage-X investigation. Keating has represented a private company, Research Laboratories of Colorado, Inc., a small outfit of former scientists from the Los Alamos laboratory who maintained offices in Colorado Springs and Newtown, Ohio. He seeks Q clearances—a category in the growing federal security system—for employees so that they could have access to Atomic Energy Commission information. That is when the FBI pounces, suspecting fraud in the application.

Keating—a hungry young lawyer, a young father—does not know that he is suspected of some form of treason by his government. He sees himself as a patriot and a regular churchgoer. One day in 1956 while the FBI builds its case against him for betraying his country, Charlie Keating sits among fir and beech trees seventeen miles from downtown Cincinnati and prays with other Catholic men to God for guidance. He is spending a weekend at the Milford Retreat.

*Charlie Keating's memory is more blunt: "I don't know what the hell he's talking about. . . . He's nuts."

Reverend Nicholas Gelin, S.J., a charismatic church leader, does not like smutty things, and as the group of Catholic men listens at the retreat in the fall of 1956, the priest denounces "the filth flooding our newsstands" and assigns Charlie Keating to do something about it personally. Keating, as it happens, is the president of Men of Milford, a fellowship based in the retreat center. Soon Keating is meeting with a close circle of twenty friends to discuss this issue. Cincinnati is a town open to campaigns against naked ladies and bad thoughts, a place with a history of making war against the bare breast. When Nicholas Longworth commissioned a naked statue of Eve in 1830, local pressure made him cover the figure with a calico dress.

His first blow against pornography comes when he participates in a raid against a small candy store near a school where an elderly woman also sells what he describes as "rubber pricks and dildos." Keating uses expert witnesses—an innovation—in the trial to prove that the obscene materials are harmful. The old woman is fined $100.

He discovers the joys of performance and begins talking to auditoriums full of parents. On the way to his first big talk, he pulls off the highway, goes into a cigar store, and buys about $50 worth of dirty magazines and books. Soon he is before a crowd shouting about the danger of pornography ("ranting and raving," as he will recall years later) and holding up the material he's just bought as proof that this menace is in the neighborhood. He tells them that pornography is a half-billion-dollar-a-year industry and he suspects that the Communists are behind it. The applause is deafening and Keating is hooked, a fact he will admit again and again over the years.

By January 1958, Keating is in Washington, D.C., with two of his daughters, seven-year-old Kathleen and six-year-old Mary, so that they can see him sworn in to practice before the Supreme Court. That done, he goes to the Hill and testifies before the House Judiciary Committee on the topic of mailing obscene matter. He sees a conspiracy "capable of poisoning any mind at any age and of perverting our entire younger generation." Every single case of juvenile delinquency is tied to pornography, and behind the pornography are Reds—"part of the Communist conspiracy," he explains, "was to print and deposit for mailing and delivery obscene, lewd, lascivious, and filthy books, etc. . . . The enemies of our country recognize the effects of pornography upon our country and our youth." One congressman wonders if his antiporn group has taken on the current best-seller, *Peyton Place.* "No, sir," Keating responds, "although with respect to *Peyton Place,* it would be my personal desire to do so."

On November 1, 1958, he incorporates his organization as Citizens for Decent Literature—his pitch is that people should read classics, not smut. That same day Keating and his CDL supporters put on workshops to train police, prosecutors, and clergy from fifteen states. Soon CDL has 300 chapters nationwide (eventually there will be 100,000 members), and it becomes the biggest antipornography organization in the country. Charlie Keating becomes its biggest single contributor.

The Lindner brothers keep adding little stores, and then they move up and try their hand at supermarkets. Buying stores gives the brothers a good eye for real estate, and then they start building strip shopping centers that include their stores. Carl Lindner learns to borrow lots of money. His little milk depots are debt driven.

He is a hands-on manager, a person obsessed with the smallest detail. He is suspicious of organization. Cincinnati is dominated by Procter & Gamble, a company of routine, order, and ritual. All P&G men wear suits, and they all wear their fountain pens in their suit pockets, not their shirt pockets. Cincinnati is the kind of a town where a man worth $15 or $20 million will drive a modest sedan. It is a city that hates flash, a place where the big money was made long ago and has been seasoned and now resides in the hands of a hereditary elite. Once Lindner comments on the Procter & Gamble headquarters over on Sycamore Street: "If someone went over to Sycamore Street and shot fifty guys at the top, the only thing that would happen would be that the fifty guys down below would be smiling more."

Lindner runs things differently. His critics say he runs everything as if it were "an ice cream store." That's okay with Lindner; ice cream has been good to him. He supports his Baptist church and votes for conservative candidates. He drinks ginger ale. In 1955, at the age of thirty-six, he is elected to be on the board of Central Trust Co., the city's second biggest bank. He goes to the board meetings, and he is surprised by what he hears and how he is treated. People listen to him. "Me," he says, "with my three years of night school.* I had to pinch myself to realize such men were treating me as an equal." And the profits that banks make for simply moving paper around catch his eye.

He takes stock of the situation. He speaks very slowly, his voice high pitched, his words coming out with difficulty. A lot of people who hear him talk decide he is stupid. He works closely with his brothers, Bob and Richard, and his sister, Dorothy. He has this idea: if a person can only control money, he can control everything. Money is in banks. The rest is simple. In 1959, he pays $1.3 million for three little savings and loans with assets of about $12 million. To swing the deal the Lindners borrow $800,000.

He is not testifying in Congress about pornography, but he is moving up in a city that does not take him seriously.

Keating becomes a national figure, a warrior in the fight against filth. He is a successful lawyer, he is on his way to moderate wealth. And he is becoming an expert at ferreting out and destroying the moral rot in his society. But there is a ghost in the machinery of his life that he does not know exists. His FBI file is still active. The original investigation in 1956 and 1957 did not lead to the filing of any charges. But in 1963, the Cincinnati FBI office advises Director Hoover, "because of derogatory information available on Keating, their [the FBI's Cincinnati office] relationship with [Keating] has been very circumspect and will remain that way. Cincinnati further suggests that Keating not be dignified in any manner by apparent FBI backing." "Prosecution," a memo from William L. Sullivan, the head of FBI counterespionage division, to Director J. Edgar Hoover on May 14, 1964, notes, "was declined at the Department level but the Cincinnati office advised that this was a close decision and serious consideration had been given to prosecuting Keating."**

Like Charlie Keating, the FBI is relentless in protecting the nation from filth and foreign ideas. As the young lawyer moves to or-

---

*Over the years, Lindner attended some night classes in an effort to get a high school diploma.

**Material gathered under the Freedom of Information Act from Keating's FBI file; also, Stephen Pizzo, "Keating's Troubles with the Federal Government Began Back in the '50s," *National Thrift News,* November 18, 1991.

ganize people against pornography, the Bureau tracks him. He writes J. Edgar Hoover on September 16, 1960, asking him to speak before a meeting of Citizens for Decent Literature, and alarm bells go off inside the agency. A memo is dispatched on September 27, 1960, to the director warning:

> The forthcoming *February 1961* meeting does not appear to be sponsored by the CITIZENS FOR DECENT LITERATURE but appears to be KEATING's own personal idea. There is no apparent group sponsoring the meeting. The letter from the Archbishop ALTER *was obviously requested by KEATING,* who has the Archbishop's ear, and the Archbishop believes that KEATING is doing a good job in combating pornographic literature. KEATING is a relatively prominent Catholic layman. Note that the Archbishop is unable to name any specific organization sponsoring the meeting to which the Director is invited.

BACKGROUND OF KEATING

CHARLES H. KEATING, JR., et al. (RESEARCH LABORATORIES OF COLORADO, INC., aka), ATOMIC ENERGY ACT; FRAUD AGAINST THE GOVERNMENT; ESPIONAGE-X, is an investigation reflected in Bufile 117-2070, in which Assistant Attorney General felt the facts do not constitute a suitable basis for prosecution.

Observe Bulet to Cincinnati, 2/21/57, captioned, "CHARLES H. KEATING, JR., CINCINNATI, OHIO, INTERSTATE TRANSPORTATION OF OBSCENE MATTER," relating to a call KEATING made to the Bureau concerning the work of his Committee in combating pornographic literature, and the forthcoming trial on this topic in Cincinnati.

KEATING appeared as representative for the CITIZENS FOR DECENT LITERATURE, INC., before a House of Representatives Sub-Committee in Washington, 5/28/60, concerning problems in combating smut publications.

Relations between KEATING and the FBI in Cincinnati are circumspect by virtue of the foregoing information relating to KEATING.

Keating has become ensnared in a world that he fervently prays actually exists, a kind of police state guarding the nation, a place where there is an effort to read thoughts, to judge morals, to put the nation's cops into the nation's bedrooms. Where Keating does not trust any American to behave properly if he beholds a photo of a naked woman, the Bureau does not trust any American, period. The report on Keating goes on for another page:

SAC'S OPINION OF WHAT IS BEHIND KEATING'S INVITATION

1) It would give KEATING great publicity.

2) The presence of the Director before a group of 10,000 students in Cincinnati would *be a feather in* KEATING'*s cap* and would lend an aura of FBI endorsement or association to KEATING personally and his Committee generally.

KEATING left word with our office receptionist that Judge BENJAMIN S. SCHWARTZ, Common Pleas Court (Juvenile Division), Hamilton County, Cincinnati, Ohio, was requested to write a letter and did so, but sent it directly to Mr. HOOVER. That letter is undoubtedly at the Bureau by now.

RECOMMENDATION

This entire program is in the earliest *formative state;* there has been no publicity whatsoever; *it is my guess that it will go through only if* KEATING *can lure the Director or, in his absence, some other big name to Cincinnati to "promote" it.*

It is therefore recommended that the Director decline, and that a copy of the declination be made available to us for our files.

Presidents come and go, movie stars streak across the nation's consciousness and then flame out. But the file, the sacred file, never dies, never ceases to grow. It is the only certain piece of immortality an American citizen is likely to achieve. On August 28, 1963, Keating writes Hoover again about getting copies of a child molester poster. Hoover's lifetime secretary, Helen Gandy, writes Keating on behalf of Hoover, and by this simple exchange of letters, Keating's file is opened again and new additions are made.

Somewhere in the file, looming out of view, is a wad of documents detailing the two-year investigation for espionage. Somewhere in the file hides that bundle of "derogatory information." It is the fourteenth day of May 1964, and J. Edgar Hoover replies to a letter from DeWitt Wallace, cofounder and co-owner with his wife of the *Reader's Digest.* He thanks him for sending a copy of the May issue. Naturally, Wallace's letter is filed, everybody's letters are filed. And a copy is bumped down the line to Sullivan, now in charge of Foreign Intelligence and Espionage. Charlie Keating appears in that particular issue of the magazine as part of a piece denouncing pornography. A Bureau note is also slapped onto Wallace's letter so that there can be no misunderstanding the darker realities hidden behind its innocent statements.

Keating feels he has arrived. His organization is national, he is a prominent figure, his words are published in the *Reader's Digest.* But he does not really understand how the system works. He is the outsider. It is all in his file, that thing he does not even know persists. The root cause of his problem is that application for Q clearances for those scientists who had an invention, a "titanium suboxide rectifier," a device that never worked. In 1955, a year before the FBI investigation, the device was written off in a federal tax return for $45,000. The company itself lost its incorporation in Colorado and Ohio in 1960 because it failed to pay its state taxes. It lives on as a ghost in the files, babbling away forever to itself in the wonderful newspeak the director has devised.

And as for the director of the Federal Bureau of Investigation, J. Edgar Hoover, the man Keating admires and wishes to have address his antipornography organization, well, Hoover has a special room in the basement of the FBI headquarters in Washington where he retires from time to time with his colleague and lifetime companion, Clyde Tolson. There they sit and watch a screen as an FBI projectionist runs pornographic movies. The supply is all but limitless. Hoover has his dedicated agents constantly seizing such smut so the American people can be protected from such enemies within.

He's trying to remember, but it's not easy. It was all so long ago. Lindner? Yes, he remembers Carl H. Lindner. Even now, as he talks in the spring of 1988, now that he has access to a $5 billion corporation of his own, he still can't quite get Lindner out of his system. It all happened way back when he was about thirty-five years old. "I practiced law until the 1970s," he begins. "We were corporate lawyers and real successful. Ninety-nine percent of my time was involved with corporate matters. Actually, I wasn't so much a lawyer as I was involved with the companies. Lindner became an obsession. He started off as a client about '58. I became more and more involved, and by '59 or '60 he was seventy-five percent, and shortly thereafter became ninety-nine and nine-tenths percent of my business. I was with him for twenty-five years. He and I worked very closely together. A number of times he referred to me as a cofounder of the company, American Financial Corporation. I was there from the beginning. From Lindner you learn decency and honesty. He had a brilliant analytical mind that was very concentrated on financial matters. He always had the bottom line straight. There's a lot of guys that are pretty bright in depth of financial matters, but they can't make it all come down to what the real world's about."

Like Charlie Keating, Mike Manning's father was a navy Hellcat pilot in World War II who never saw any action. He is now a traveling salesman and is gone a lot of the time. The family gets by, but there is never really any extra money. Mike was born in Missouri but has spent his short life in Lincoln, Nebraska. He lives in what he will describe years later as a middle-class neighborhood, the kind of spot where everyone tries to own a home and raise a family but where such goals require a real effort. Lincoln is a conservative, Republican, Protestant town on the plains. Michael Manning is Catholic (head of his church's youth group), and now in the summer and fall of 1960, when he is eleven, he feels stirrings he cannot really name. He has seen John Fitzgerald Kennedy on television, and he is attracted to something he sees and hears in the grainy black-and-white images on the screen.

He gets a 2×6 and paints VOTE KENNEDY on the board and then nails two posters of JFK at the top. Every day after school he stands for hours on a street corner in Lincoln, Nebraska, waving his message as the cars roll past taking people home from work. The drivers and passengers in the conservative town lean out the window, and they yell and they jeer and they make catcalls and they spit at him. And still the eleven-year-old boy is out there day after day after day, hour after hour, waving his sign.

Lindner is out to buy another supermarket in 1958, and Charlie Keating represents the person he is buying out. Soon, Keating, Meuthing, & Keating's business is simply one client, Carl H. Lindner, Jr. Within a year, Lindner takes over his three little savings and loan associations. And then the stamp of a new hand at play in Cincinnati is made plain. Interest rates for deposits are raised, and Lindner chases new loan business all over town. A strange kind of holding company, one called American Financial Corporation, rises in 1960 from the bare bones of ice cream stores, milk depots, strip shopping centers, grocery stores, and banks. Charlie Keating is the coinventor with Lindner of this new beast. Within two years, earnings are way up, and Lindner and his family take the company public. They are instantly paper million-aires. A year later, in 1962, AFC buys a little bank in Athens, Ohio. Lindner has this dream for AFC: he will make it a "financial department store." He starts creating subsidiaries underneath AFC, eventually has fifty-some wheeling and dealing with each other. Of course, below the subsidiaries are yet more entities, sub-sidiaries of subsidiaries. And he creates financial instruments con-stantly, new warrants, common stock, preferred stock, debentures, a whirligig of debts interlaced through the maze of subsidiaries. One SEC official in Washington thinks that Lindner, this stranger from Cincinnati who had to leave school after the eighth grade, is creating more issues of paper than any other corporation in the United States. When finally a Wall Street analyst takes a look at AFC's records, he concludes that he has "never come across a company that has so much strange paper on its books." Lindner bags United Liberty Life Insurance in 1963, then invents some-thing called American Computer Leasing, changes his mind, and renames it American Financial Leasing & Services. All these moves give the Lindners and Keating access to cash or credit.

On October 15, 1959, Charlie Keating travels to Chicago to give a speech. "If, God willing," he intones, "and your child escapes di-rect contact with the pernicious influence in the minds of this junk . . . he still will be exposed to the evil influences in the minds and breasts of his companions." The filth industry, he now calculates, is a $2-billion-per-year operation. "It's almost beyond belief," he says. In 1962, CDL has mutated to another name, Citizens for De-cent Literature and Motion Pictures, and Charlie Keating is named the head of the group. The organization is distributing its own movie, a color flick entitled *Pages of Death,* which recounts the rape-slaying of a young girl by a guy addicted to obscene literature.

Around midnight on August 31, 1965, Charlie Keating is prowl-ing around Washington, D.C., first at the corner of Fourteenth Street and Kenyon Northwest, then Eighteenth and Columbia, then he walks over toward the White House and stops at Fifteenth and F. He is hitting corner newsstands, buying dirty books. He picks up *His Brother's Love,* a volume on homosexual passion. He selects *Sensational Step Daughter,* a celebration of incest. He buys *Fiseek Art Quarterly,* thumbs the pages, and notes the images of erections. And then there is *Jaybird Safari,* with images of male genitals and female genitals in contact. The next day Keating testifies before a House subcommittee investigating pornography. He brings the dirty books and pictures with him. "I want to emphasize," he says, "that this filth is available practically anywhere in Washington, or New York, or Los Angeles . . . for that matter, practically anywhere in the United States." And this is a serious matter because "these magazines are the catalytic agents to warp and twist the minds of youth and destroy their souls and wreck their lives."

Then Keating seems to go too far. He picks up one title, *Love's Lash,* about the joys of sadism, and he tries to read it out loud to the congressmen, everything from page 126 to page 132. The chair will have none of this. "I suggest," says Committee Chairman John H. Dent, Jr., "you mark the passages and spare the committee." Keating is reasonable. He replies, "I will spare you." Keating also appears before another House committee, one exploring the possibility of creating a presidential committee to figure out ways to fight pornography.

He is busy speaking at the schools in Cincinnati, particularly the parochial schools. He will show up and endorse chasity, denounce pornography, explain how the Communists are really behind this effort to rot the American character. He will give homely examples of the risk of rampant sexuality. One day he tells an auditorium of high school girls about a young mother who was struck down by a car as she pushed her baby in a stroller across the street. Why? She was wearing Bermuda shorts and her exposed legs distracted the male driver. He asks all the girls in the school to sign a pledge never to wear Bermuda shorts.

He seems to be everywhere now. He is in Salt Lake City talking to the students at Highland High School. "The masters of evil," he warns, "are here." And to prove it he reads excerpts from some books he's just bought in the City of the Saints, titles like *Lesbian Lust, The Gay Boys,* and *Sex Rampage.*

Of course, Charlie Keating must be careful. He is like a doctor fighting an epidemic: the disease could strike him down also. That is the risk of so much exposure. CDL itself carefully screens applicants for membership. They must be at least twenty-five years old, have a family and church affiliations—in short, as a CDL public relations director explains, "people who can handle such [explicit] material over an extended period of time without being adversely affected."

That fall Xavier University awards Keating the St. Francis Xavier Medal for his war against filth. First there is a Communion service. The award is given annually to men who "demonstrate in today's world the qualities of heart and mind that distinguished St. Francis Xavier."

Charlie Keating is forty-one years old and rising.

It is not easy for Mike Manning to impress his father, who motivates his son in an almost negative fashion. Partly, it is that Midwestern quality where bragging is suspect, where everything is understated. Michael Manning attends a parochial high school. He is determined to win a major letter, and he goes out for golf. At the end of his first year he wins a varsity letter in golf, one of only two beginning students in his school to win such an award. He is immensely proud of himself when he brings his prize home.

His father asks, "What did you get that for?"

"Varsity golf."

"Well," he says, "that's not as big as a letter for football, is it?"

And the next year Michael Manning goes out for the football team and wins another varsity letter.

Every year for fifteen straight years the earnings of AFC go up and up. Finally Lindner and Keating are ready for a really big play. Provident Savings and Loan has $200 million in assets and is one of the treasures of the Cincinnati establishment. It is their bank. Barney Kroger, who founded the Kroger grocery chain, started up Provident. For months Charlie Keating travels and looks up odd shareholders in order to gain shares or the votes of shares. This band of outsiders, the tall, pornography-crazed Catholic from St. Xavier and the family of dairy farmers, pours $20 million into the move. They are making the first hostile takeover of a U.S. bank since the end of World War II. It is 1966.

Around midnight, they get a call from the Federal Reserve Board informing them that they now have themselves a bank. They promptly hold a board meeting at two in the morning. Then they catch a little sleep. Around two that afternoon, they stroll down to take a look at their new property. All the employees are going home. Lindner and Keating discover that in the gentlemanly world of this bank, the doors shut at two, Monday through Friday. They promptly extend closing hours to 5 P.M. and stay open on Saturdays. And they chase down every possible scrap of loan business in town. They install a former mailman as the new head of the bank.

Lindner does not talk to the press. He has scrutinized the careers of various financial heroes, and he thinks that what has taken many of them down is that they get too big for their britches. They stand out. What is he like? people wonder. No one will talk publicly for the record, but guarded comments surface. "Carl is a very positive person," a former colleague offers. "Carl's glass has always been half full, not half empty. He wants total commitment. He is a believer that almost anything can be done if you do it the right way. . . . I think [Lindner's skill is] very intuitive, kind of a combination of street smarts, great instincts, and—in some way that's strange to the average guy—he's oblivious to the risk."

The Cincinnati business community is appalled at what they see happening before their eyes. Lindner and Keating do not care about tradition. They have met these people, they have sat on the same boards. And they know they can take them out. They will not wear pens in the pocket of their suits, they will not drive modest sedans. Lindner picks up a Stutz Bearcat, complete with car phone. He wears tan linen suits, which become his trademark. Then come the planes, eventually a Gulfstream II, also with a phone. Soon there is a fleet of three corporate jets. Charlie Keating gets a Cadillac convertible. And a car phone. He will be remembered decades later for driving around Cincinnati, even in winter, with the top down, his head sticking up over the windshield, talking on his car phone, one of the very first in the entire city.

Lindner never slackens his pace in creating new paper, swallowing more companies, flipping more deals. He hires a blond and very attractive assistant, Sandy Heiman. And she will eventually make $300,000 a year. Lindner believes in paying his people very well. Then he hires her father, a mailman, who takes down around $250,000 a year. When his children's baby-sitter grows up, he hires him at $150,000 a year. Every year he throws a big Christmas party for all of his employees and flies in major talent to entertain them. He gives them all shares of stock as presents. At the top, the company is run very thinly, the executives have unclear responsibilities, and there are not many of them. This is a new kind of business, and it operates in a new way.

AFC's headquarters in downtown Cincinnati has no name on the building. Lindner hires an armed security force and puts the men in domed cars just like regular cops. His home is constantly guarded, and when he makes his twenty-minute trip to work each day, accompanied by a bodyguard, he always varies the route. When he dines out with his wife, his police force makes security checks of the restaurants. When one of his sons graduates from high school, Lindner has armed guards posted at the celebration lest any kid smuggle in a bottle of booze. He does not like booze at all. AFC's private box at Riverfront Stadium serves only ice cream.

In 1969, the *Cincinnati Enquirer* runs a series on the city's "movers and shakers." Lindner is portrayed by the paper as an upstart, a man left out of the community's power structure, kept at arm's length by the city's loftier social circles. Lindner does not like this series. He buys the *Cincinnati Enquirer.* Soon after the buy, he asks the editor, Betsy Bliss, if the writer of that series is still on the payroll. But the reporter has moved on. He swiftly makes some changes in the *Enquirer:* more business coverage and more listing of over-the-counter stocks, the kind of off-brand securities that provide the financial blood for AFC. The corporation's press releases also find a warmer welcome in the pages of the *Enquirer.* Between them, the Lindner brothers and Charlie Keating have created families of swimmers, horse riders, and wrestlers. Soon coverage of these activities is expanded in the sports pages. Everyone on the paper gets free checking privileges at the Provident Bank and, of course, is invited to the famous Christmas parties.

Charlie Keating becomes the sponsor of an amateur swimming team in Cincinnati, the Marlins. He is determined to train Olympic champions. One morning at 5:30 A.M. his friend Ted Toma sees Charlie Keating before a training session in the school parking lot directing traffic with a whistle. In 1969, he and his brother Bill donate $600,000 for the construction at St. Xavier of an eight-lane, fifty-meter indoor pool. They toss in a $50,000 scoreboard that is accurate to one-thousandth of a second. The brothers name the pool after their father, Charles H. Keating.

Politics also calls. Charlie Keating in his porn wars has learned his way around Capitol Hill and around many statehouses and court-houses and city halls. When his brother decides to run for judge, he directs the campaign, he raises the money. His brother wins and becomes one of the most popular politicians in Cincinnati.

It is all going well. AFC is a new kind of corporation run by a new kind of people. People not afraid of risk, people not timid about debt. People who come from a different background than Cincinnati is used to seeing in the boardroom. Charlie Keating has his St. Francis Xavier Medal. Charlie Keating has a crap table in his house. He always carries a roll of hundred-dollar bills so that he can tip people.

When Mike Manning graduates, he tries for football scholarships but is handicapped by his size, which is that of a normal male. Finally, he wins an athletic ride at Kansas State Teachers College in Emporia, Kansas, a small institution with about eight thousand students. His father gives him five bucks toward his education. There is no money to spare. He never cracks a book but manages a B average. He works three jobs. He is elected student body president.

It is the spring of 1970, the time of the Cambodian invasion, of the endless war in Southeast Asia. Manning has long hair, does not wear a necktie. He looks at the radical groups talking revolution and he does not believe his nation will have a revolution and he does not think such talk will cause change. He believes in working within the system. One night there is a near riot on campus, and since he is the student body president, he is called out by the school's brass to try and defuse it. He stands there in the darkness before the angry throng; a Molotov cocktail is tossed but fizzles out. He tells them he will take their grievances against the war and the draft and the government to the administration of Kansas State Teachers College. And they buy it and slowly melt away into the night.

In August 1970, he marries and he sees some vague specter of a normal life. He promises this to himself and to his new wife. That November he is at the convention of the National Association of Student Governments (NASG). He promises his wife that he will accept no nomination for national office. He comes home elected executive vice president, and by December they are living in an apartment in Washington, D.C. Manning has a mission: to get young voters registered under the new law lowering the voting age to eighteen. One evening Manning is in the NASG offices, when Allard Lowenstein wanders in. Lowenstein is older, a former college wrestler, who had been a key force behind the civil rights movement's Freedom Summer project in Mississippi in 1964. He is also the man who launched a Dump Johnson movement in 1967, and now LBJ is out of office and waiting to die on his ranch down in Texas. Lowenstein is a committed liberal, a close friend of the Kennedy family, a man who believes in the capacity of the system to reform itself and achieve social change. He never tires, sometimes giving ten or fifteen speeches a day. And he is one of the best public speakers in the United States, a man who sets audiences on fire. Now he has just launched a new crusade, Dump Nixon.

Manning is instantly taken with Lowenstein's passion, his skills, and his absolute faith that an individual can make a difference. He notices that Lowenstein treats everyone well, that he is not pompous. One night Lowenstein wanders into the office and pulls a book out of his pocket, Philip Roth's scathing new comic novel (*Our Gang*) on Nixon, and begins reading it out loud. He reads the whole damn thing and has everyone spellbound. And suddenly Manning is meeting people. One evening he is having a drink with Lowenstein when young congressman Don Riegle of Michigan sits down, and they go over his involvement in the Dump Nixon movement. Manning is constantly on the road holding campus events on how to register young voters and how to get them out to boot the president out of office, and he bumps against people like Senator Birch Bayh of Indiana, Congressman Pete McCloskey of California, congresswomen Shirley Chisholm and Bella Abzug of New York, and Senator Ted Kennedy.

Manning gets Lowenstein to appear before students at Manhattan, Kansas. This is the first time he ever hears him speak in public. Jack Kemp is also on the program. The meeting is technically about registering young voters, but the campus Young Republicans have sensed its real goal, dumping Nixon, and they have packed the auditorium with supporters. When Lowenstein is introduced, a small handful in the crowd applaud. And then he unleashes his power and explains why Richard Nixon must be dumped, and when he concludes he receives a standing ovation. That evening he and Manning go to dinner. It is not so much that

Manning becomes a disciple of Lowenstein as that Lowenstein shows him what can be done, what really is possible. And Lowenstein does this day in and day out. (When he is murdered in 1980, fifty veterans of his crusades sit in various state legislatures.)

She's just been hired and she wants to do it right, but she can sense it is not going to be easy fixing the public face and public image of Charlie Keating. God knows she's connected in Phoenix, lived there all her life, and when she goes downtown she knows everybody right up to and including the mayor. The problem is Charlie. It's the summer of 1988, he's just busted the chops of those federal regulators again, and he's feeling like he should patch up his image in the community. So he agrees to do a little television, let the press get near him and breathe on him and fire off their dumb questions. God, he hates it, he knows they can never be fair. But he'll do it.

They go down to the television studio for the interview, and she acts as his guide through this media jungle. At first everything seems to go fine, Charlie is in his hi-I'm-just-your-neighbor kind of thing and he comes across as some geek of an old uncle with a few crotchety opinions but what the hell, not a bad guy all in all. And then just when she starts to relax and think this is a snap, she can hear Keating's voice rising, his face goes tight and hard, and he's spouting over the airwaves how that filth freak Larry Flynt had his daughter raped. She starts slashing her hand across her throat in a desperate effort to get Keating to shut up, but he doesn't even break stride. During a break in the taping he comes over and asks, "Why can't I say that? Flynt did it." And she knows, she really knows, this is never going to be easy.

SUCH AN
ADVOCACY OF
MORAL ANARCHY!

By the late sixties and early seventies, American Financial Corporation is growing at more than 20 percent a year—the average compounded growth rate in earnings for the years 1960 to 1972 hits 28 percent per annum. Many are puzzled by the numbers. The company seems to lack a factory door where an observer can see the product coming off the line and being stacked up on a loading dock. It is a new thing, something there is barely a word for in the language of finance, a company that is not so much economically driven as accounting driven. The proof of this pudding is in the books. Be that as it may, the money comes tumbling in for Carl Lindner and Charlie Keating. And they both begin to feel its power—Lindner with his seizure of banks and, of course, his move on the local elite's house organ, the *Cincinnati Enquirer.* Keating moves into the political arena.

Through his brother's campaigns for local office he has gotten connected to the local pols. He has also been appointed by President Richard M. Nixon to the eighteen-member Commission on Obscenity and Pornography. But it has not been as easy as Charlie Keating might think. The White House, when considering his name, had asked the FBI for a SPIN (Special Presidential Inquiry), and the old espionage charges from the investigation in the fifties came bobbing up from the files. On May 5, 1969, an FBI memo to White House Chief of Staff John D. Ehrlichman points out that the espionage charge was dropped because of "insufficient evidence." Ehrlichman lets the appointment go through. But the White House is aware of Lindner and Keating, and particularly in

Keating's case they wonder what he is after.* CDL, Keating's antiporn powerhouse, by now has four U.S. senators and seventy House members on its honorary committee (one of them, Donald E. Lukens, will be convicted in 1989 of having sex with a sixteen-year-old girl; another, Speaker of the House Jim Wright, will end his career in Congress in general scandal, a part of it due to the savings and loan disaster of the 1980s).

Keating wastes no time seizing the spotlight. In September 1969, he acts as a private attorney and argues in court that the Russ Meyer film *Vixen* is obscene. The movie is confiscated by police the first day it opens in Cincinnati. Meyer had started out making industrial films in California after World War II but by the early sixties had hit his stride when he focused on his true interest, gigantic breasts. As he explained years later, "Preoccupation with tits. Still have it. Love 'em. Go out of my way to be with somebody that's new, that's built like a brick shithouse."** For *Vixen* (released in 1968), he cast as the star one Erica Gavin, a woman he found stripping at The Losers in Los Angeles. By Meyer's standards, she did not have the usual assets ("didn't have the best body or the biggest tits"), but she did project sex appeal. "I have a sixteen-millimeter print," he explained years later in a effort to clarify his film's artistic force, "and [his wife, Edy Williams, would] just come out fucking like hell that night. The whole thing turned her on so."

Meyer held a different worldview from Charlie Keating, and *Vixen* was his means of spreading his message. Decades later, he summed up their collision: "Yeah, there was this guy Charles Keating. . . . [F]ormer head honcho of the Citizens for Decent Literature. The elite of porn busters. Grandmothers in tennis shoes. And what a success he enjoyed. He got to *Vixen,* his primo target . . . stopping it cold in the sovereign state of Ohio. I spent a quarter of a million dollars. Tried to put me in jail. . . . Keating volunteered something like this: 'Russ Meyer has done more to

*Jim Bishop, former bureau chief for *Newsweek* in Washington, recalls this White House concern based on his talks with John Ehrlichman and Alexander Butterfield.

**Sergei Hasenecz and Charles Schneider, "A Clean Breast: Titillating Talk with Russ Meyer," in *Cad: A Handbook for Heels,* Feral House, Inc., Los Angeles, California, 1992, p. 40.

undermine the morals in these United States than anyone else.'
And my retort would be: 'I was glad to do it.' "

When a local Cincinnati judge tackles the movie *Vixen* in a
decision, Keating touts the twenty-two-page decision to the newspapers, television, *Time, Life,* and *Newsweek.* No one shows up except local reporters. And so Charlie Keating writes a letter to Vice
President Spiro Agnew complaining of neglect. "In this case," he
protests, "in spite of the fact that the news release went out on a
CDL letterhead—which is impressive enough to say the least—that
it came from a member of the Presidential Commission, and that
a decent judge, properly outraged, really 'laid down the law,' the
amount of coverage wasn't worth mentioning."

He seeks to do better with the presidential commission. He
brings his normal style to this assignment. First, attack: he decides
that other members of the commission, appointees of former president Lyndon Johnson, are too easy on pornography, so he boy-
cotts the public hearings. Second, intimidate: he refers to himself
as the "Nixon appointee" and tells them that the majority report
will create great political opposition. He should know; for a year
he has apparently sought to have Nixon dismiss the head of the
commission, William B. Lockhart, the dean of the University of
Minnesota Law School. Third, claim a conspiracy: he believes
most of the other members are in cahoots. He says "all but a few
of them have a stake in the business"—meaning they hail from the
book and film business and are therefore pornographers. And finally, operate behind the scenes: the White House assigns presidential speechwriter Patrick Buchanan to take a strong hand in
writing the dissent. The commission report argues that pornography is basically harmless, that obscenity laws should be junked,
and that what the nation needs is more sex education. The report
also demolishes the notion that the pornography industry is a
multi-billion-dollar affair (the commission figures its gross in
1969 was less than $200 million) or that the industry is a sinister
monolith ("several distinct markets and submarkets . . . extremely
chaotic"). And it finds no convincing link between pornography
and behavior. Keating brings a suit to stop publication of the document (seven hundred pages long and with a trail of "technical
reports" following in its wake) unless dissents by him and several
other upset members of the commission are appended. He wins

and writes a rebuttal that, together with the dissents of some colleagues, eventually takes up almost a third of the published report.

"Such an advocacy of moral anarchy!" he notes in his dissent. ". . . For those who believe in God, in His absolute supremacy as the Creator and Lawgiver of life, in the dignity and destiny which He has conferred upon the human person—for those who believe in these 'things,' no argument against pornography should be necessary." He rambles on about the difference between sex and love, the poisoning of novelist Marcel Proust by erotica, and the lethal link between pornography and marital infidelity, divorce, abortion, and suicide. Keating hauls out the metaphors and images he has used on platforms for years—"our nation is imperiled by a poison which is all-pervasive"—and his language resounds with the thunder of a classic Jeremiad. "Never in the history of modern civilization," he warns, "have we seen more obvious evidence of a decline in public morality than we see today. . . . [O]ne factor has to be the deluge of pornography." Filth, he explains, stirs up the sexual appetite, "one of the most volatile appetites of human nature. Once the appetite is aroused, it will seek satisfaction."

Regardless of his standing on the commission, Keating is hardly in a true minority. The report is given to Congress at the end of September 1970, and two weeks later the Senate rejects it by a vote of sixty to five. Nixon denounces it several days later in terms that sound almost like Charlie Keating: "Moreover, if an attitude of permissiveness were to be adopted regarding pornography, this would contribute to an atmosphere condoning anarchy in every other field—and would increase the threat to our social order as well as to our moral principles."

Keating is busy on other fronts. His law firm now has elegant offices, he has established a fine home, and he is the mastermind behind his brother's successful 1970 campaign for the House of Representatives. He raises the money, he plots the tactics. He is also in Washington a great deal of the time lobbying for laws against smut. And he represents a corporation, AFC, that is becoming a bankroller of politicians. When Nixon runs for reelection in 1972, officials of the corporation donate $259,969 to his campaign, an amount so generous that even the Committee to Re-elect the President (CREEP) cannot figure out how to swallow it all. A month after the election, Maurice Stans, the finance head of CREEP, returns thirty-six checks totaling $107,000 and includes a note explaining why. "It now appears," Stans says, "that we have adequate funds on hand to pay all of the costs of the campaign and also provide a reasonable reserve to take care of other contingencies. If I may make a suggestion, I would like to urge that you hold some of this money in reserve for 1974 when I am sure that the person sitting in my place at that time will be looking for a major effort to elect Republican senators and congressmen."

The thirty-six checks show a curious pattern for such a spontaneous outpouring of political support. Although they are issued by various executives in Cincinnati, Ohio, they go to Nixon reelection committees in twenty-nine states and the District of Columbia. Also, all of them, save one, are made out for exactly $3,000. As for the remaining $149,969, kicked in by AFC folks in 1972, it, too, has a peculiar touch. On April 7, 1972, a new campaign law came into effect that required the listing of contributors. Four days before this new legal requirement, AFC donated 4,511 shares of AFC stock to CREEP in the name of one of Lindner's many subsidiaries, United Dairy Farmers Investment Company. The stock was sold by CREEP and the cash pocketed. As for the $107,000 chunk shipped after the new law, Keating later bluntly explains its purpose to the Watergate committee investigating the election: "Shortly before the election, Robert and Carl Lindner (unsolicited) offered Maurice Stans, in a phone call initiated by Carl Lindner, to contribute additional funds if needed. The contribution was ideologically inspired. . . ."

The two outsiders from Cincinnati, one a teetotaling Baptist without a high school diploma, the other a fiercely competitive Irish Catholic, are making their way in a larger world. Lindner is on his way to being the largest single contributor to Jewish causes, among other feats. Keating, besides traveling 200,000 miles in one year waging the good fight against pornography, has put his brother into Congress, made connections with the Nixon White House, and finally risen from being a private attorney to getting his hands on some real money.

In July 1972, he leaves his law practice and joins Carl Lindner in the company they have created, AFC, as executive vice president. AFC is now worth about $1 billion. He is now a power in Cincinnati. He and Lindner control the key bank, Provident, they control the key newspaper, the *Enquirer.* They gush money to the Republican Party. Charlie Keating is busy picking up the knickknacks that signify arrival into the establishment of old, honored money. He is the president of the Cincinnati Marlins, a nationally recognized swimming club that he runs as his own private laboratory for creating Olympians. He is celebrated at a banquet by the Cincinnati chapter of the National Conference of Christians and Jews. He heads the fund drive to raise $2 million for the Little Sisters of the Poor, who tend to the aged in two Cincinnati facilities. His brother, Bill, and Carl Lindner serve on the committee.

He is intoxicated with his new standing. He has his secretary, Marty Lang, keep an annual tabulation of two things: how many miles he has flown and how many nights a year he spends in hotels. He loves telling people both statistics. Jimmy Schneider, his old friend from parochial school, is constantly coming to his office for clean clothes or a handout. Charlie Keating also does a certain number of pro bono legal cases for criminals in the local courts. Various lowlifes are always dropping by his office, either because he is going to defend them against assorted felonies, armed robbery and the like, or because they have just done their time and need some help to get back on their feet. Keating gives them help, loans them money for the first rent payment, ferrets out jobs. There is an endless stream of the needy in his life now, women without men who need a few bucks to avoid eviction or to keep the heat turned on in the heart of the winter, ex-convicts making their way back into the world. One guy always shows up with a weapon, either a gun or a huge knife strapped to his leg. He will say something like "It's getting close to Christmas, Charlie, and I don't have any money to buy presents for my family." And Charlie Keating will give him a handout. His life is a whirl of different connections from the White House to the slums. From the church to the swim team. From the courthouse to the boardroom. And when he decides his longtime secretary, Marty Lang, has done a helluva job, why, he gives her a new Porsche. And if this raises eyebrows in straitlaced Cincinnati, well, to hell with Cincinnati. Charlie Keating has moved on to a greater world.

So has Carl Lindner. He takes to having little sayings printed on small cards and handing them out to people as words of wisdom from the chairman of AFC, sayings like "The harder I work, the luckier I get"; "Life is hard by the yard, but a cinch by the inch"; "I never worked a day in my life"; "Only in America! Gee, am I lucky!" And perhaps his favorite card of all reads "The old rich sometimes look down on the nouveau riche . . . but it is better to be nouveau riche than not rich at all."

He still does not talk to the press but at least now he controls the key part of the local press. And he enjoys this power. On election night 1972, Lindner flies off to Washington for the celebration. He plans on being photographed with a victorious President Nixon at the party in the Shoreham Hotel and has even blocked off a section of the front page of the *Cincinnati Enquirer* for this special picture. But as the evening staggers on Nixon fails to arrive, and finally Lindner has himself snapped posing with Vice President Agnew. The photo runs as planned. Of course, due to the delay, all the readers get their newspaper late the next morning.

After thirteen months in Washington, D.C., it is time for Michael Manning to go home to Kansas. He has a plan: he will enroll in graduate school, get a master's degree, and settle down to a normal life. It is December 1971. He has one last bit of unfinished business. Lowenstein has made him promise to scout Kansas for some candidate who will run on an antiwar/Dump Nixon platform, someone who will capitalize on all the newly minted eighteen-year-old voters. For months Manning cruises the state seeking a hungry young Democrat on some campus. But he can't seem to find such a person, so Lowenstein says, why don't you run? Manning's wife is against the idea. On May 1, 1972, he announces his candidacy for secretary of state. He is twenty-one years old, and his opponent, a woman, comes from a powerful political family. She and her husband between them have held the secretary of state office for twenty-two years. Manning campaigns every single day until the election in November. His wife runs his home office, and Lowenstein comes out to give speeches. In his campaign literature ("Taking politics to the people"), Manning looks like a tousle-haired young Kennedy who has come out of the wheatfields of Kansas. His short political bio can credit him with little beyond having graduated from Kansas State Teachers College in Emporia ("Mike likes to read and to think") and marrying a Kansas girl. He pushes a simple notion, that "Kansas does a better job collecting taxes than registering voters." His brochure ends with a shot of the Winnebago he lives in for months and a Robert

Frost quote: "I have promises to keep,/And miles to go before I sleep." He hits every county in the state and receives 46 percent of the vote.

During the campaign he comes to the attention of Kansas Governor Bob Docking, a Democrat with close ties to the Kennedys. After Manning's defeat, Docking invites him to join his staff. He is now twenty-two years old, and for the next twenty-four months, Manning is in charge of all patronage in Kansas.

When Chip Wischer is four years old, he comes down with ulcers. He comes from a home without a lot of warmth and spends his summers and spare time working on farms. He attends St. Thomas More, a small Catholic college in the Cincinnati area, and there he meets Judy, who is majoring in accounting. They marry in 1970 and move into Cincinnati. Chip has saved about $15,000 from all those summer jobs. They both hail from northern Kentucky, and, like many people in the area, they do not want to leave. So Chip scrutinizes the job opportunities in Cincinnati, seeking a local company that will not put him through a career ladder that demands he move around the country. He gets a job selling insurance for a subsidiary of AFC. Judy works as a public accountant and after two years hates her job. One night looking over the want ads she sights a job opening at a law firm, Charlie Keating's firm. Chip recommends applying; he once dated the daughter of Keating's partner. Charlie hires her on the spot.

One week later, Charlie moves up to an executive vice presidency job at AFC, so Chip and Judy suddenly wind up working for the same people. The marriage has grown cool after two years, and their lives are mainly work. In the evenings, Chip goes out drinking with the boys. Soon Judy succumbs to the Keating regimen and is working until eight or nine at night. Chip realizes he's lost his wife to the Keatings. But the money is so good, he does not complain.

Judy Wischer almost instantly learns that her new boss has some habits she must somehow understand. He is almost always in debt; in fact, he seems to crave debt. And yet he cannot quite face this fact. He might be on the phone to American Express, and his face will show surprise at their claim that his bill is overdue. He will turn to Judy and shout so his voice can be heard clearly by the American Express representative on the phone, "What? You mean *you* didn't mail out that check I ordered you to send last week? What is going on here? Check on it right now." And she will know there was never a request for a check to be cut, that she is being used. Soon she is doing this effortlessly, telling little lies as if it were the most natural thing in the world. But they will not seem like lies, they will seem like—like the way Charlie Keating sees the world, and he is a very persuasive man, a visionary.

Keating will explain to her one of his great insights: why debt is powerful and good. He will teach her that if you sell, say, stock or form a partnership with a person, then it is true you have access to capital but you also have other people on board who have rights and who can tell you what to do, who can demand a vote on decisions, insist on dividends, criticize policies. This he wishes to avoid at all costs. That is why giving people an equity position is not desirable. So he prefers debt, simple, naked debt. Because a lender is helpless, a lender has bet a fortune on the borrower's abilities but can do little to interfere. Debt, as Charlie Keating explains it, becomes a thing of beauty: money without constraints. And Charlie Keating, she soon learns, hates constraints.

Judy Wischer will in some ways become as close to Charlie Keating as any human being, but after twenty years she will be able to remember him being in her home only once. She will have a sense of never really being a part of his family—she is invited to the wedding of only one of his children. And every day when she goes into work for him she will have a single fear: that she will be fired. She will never overcome this fear no matter how high she rises or how much money she makes. She will always believe that it can end in the next second.

Chip also learns to take some precautions. Charlie is said to get the subscription lists of *Playboy* and *Penthouse* to see who is buying them. Chip cancels his subscriptions and starts buying the magazines off the rack. And Chip must learn to live with Charlie's arrogance. Once, Keating punches him hard on the arm—a gesture he often makes—and Wischer chips his front tooth. Once at a party Chip brings a friend over to meet Keating. His friend sticks out his hand, and Charlie just looks down at it and says, "Well, any friend of Chip's is a friend of Chip's," turns his back, and walks away.

AFC itself takes some getting used to. Keating and Lindner have their offices close together on the executive floor, and around them swirls a nervous constellation of other executives. Employees are always on call—Lindner has phones installed in the rest rooms so that no one can escape him when he wants something. No one feels secure because no one has a clear job. Employees spend a lot of energy trying to discover secrets about one another, damaging bits of gossip that may pay off in some power struggle. A lot of this climate is created by Lindner and Keating. Both have the habit of secretly assigning people to the same task and then watching them compete and flounder as they try to perform the job. For a while Charlie Keating functions in part as Carl Lindner's hatchet man, the person who fires and fires often. As new corporations are seized and absorbed, Charlie Keating becomes the visitor who leaves a shower of pink slips in his wake. One day he and Carl decide to fire another executive, and Keating goes into the man's office to deliver the news. The executive listens and then opens a desk drawer and pulls out a pistol. At first Charlie thinks the man is going to shoot him. But instead, the executive puts the gun to his own temple and announces he is going to blow his brains out. Keating talks the man down, and he keeps his job. After that, Keating develops a method he will adhere to for the rest of his career: he has letters prepared announcing firings, and then, when he and his family take a vacation, the letters are delivered. To avoid lawsuits, large severances are paid.

There is the corporate fleet parked in a private hangar, and the floors of the hangar are snow white and spotless. The colors of the company are black and gold. The secretaries at AFC headquarters are beautiful, and the men dress immaculately. Keating is addicted to French cuffs and cuff links (a passion he shares with Carl Lindner), and the shirts, of course, must be monogrammed on the pocket. Charlie Keating keeps a limousine in New York for use on his three or four visits there a year. He travels a great deal, down to his condo in Florida or off to the East Coast. In Cincinnati, he leaves work whenever he feels like it—takes in a Reds game to relax. When the plans for building Riverfront Stadium are announced, he goes to the club's management and buys the eight seats behind home plate for cash. He knows that when the television cameras pan home, Charlie Keating's face is going to be on the screen. He tips big. He tells his staff, "These poor slobs, they make no money, and you're lucky to have the kind of job you have.

These people are the backbone of America, hardworking people."
And he insists on paying attention to secretaries and the like at
the office. He brags that his most important meetings are about
the secretaries—do they have any problems, are they being paid
right?

When a newsdealer near AFC headquarters carries *Playboy,*
Charlie Keating tries to stop him. When *Oh! Calcutta!* is scheduled to open at the Civic Center in 1971, city officials track
Keating down in Texas to ask how he feels about it. He tells them
not to let it open. The county prosecutor has the show closed (the
decision is overturned on appeal).

Carl Lindner has a habit of eating lunch each day at a fine restaurant just across the river in Kentucky, the Mike Fink. He always has his own table complete with a phone. One day he comes
in and the place is packed with conventioneers. The maître d'
apologizes that he has no table for Mr. Lindner. An hour later, a
truck pulls up to the restaurant and men unload a table and
chairs, carry them into the Mike Fink, and plop them down. Then
the telephone rings, and it is Carl Lindner on the line. "Don't ever
tell me," he says, "that there is not a table for Carl Lindner at the
Mike Fink."

These little quirks are easy to overlook because Carl Lindner is
making people rich. If the maître d' at the Mike Fink had bought
$1,350 worth of AFC stock at its first offering in 1961, it would
have been worth $25,116 by 1971.

The financial department store continues to buy up companies
other people have built. Lindner proceeds cautiously. He starts by
buying small blocks of stock in a company, and then, using this
toehold, he analyzes its management and reports. He seldom
sleeps more than three or four hours a night, a trait he shares with
Keating, Donald Trump, Ivan Boesky, and Michael Milken. Increasingly, not sleeping is becoming a prerequisite for anyone
claiming bragging rights in American business. He takes home a
full briefcase each night and reads prospectuses and annual reports. He is a fiend for numbers. Milken at this same moment is
beginning his ascent in Drexel Burnham Lambert's junk bond department and catching a bus in from New Jersey each morning
before dawn. According to his legend, he spends the trip reading

prospectuses by the light of a miner's hat.* When Lindner finds a company with numbers he likes, he buys more and more stock. And then, as often happens, a company will falter, and Lindner, as a large shareholder, will force in his own management team from his staff at AFC. It is a patient, insidious process, and usually it works.

In 1971, Lindner and Keating set out to swallow a property and casualty insurance company. Two years before they made a run at Ohio Casualty and the Chubb Corporation and failed. Lawsuits resulted. Now they buy two smaller operations, Agricultural Insurance and Selective Insurance. This merely whets their appetite. A conglomerate, National General, is weakened by management fights, and they buy a big chunk of its stock. For two years, AFC maneuvers, a minnow seeking to swallow a whale. They issue an array of securities—debentures, preferred stocks, warrants, notes—to raise cash. They borrow $319 million from First Bank of Boston for precisely two days. And in April 1974, AFC swallows up National General. Having taken over the target, it instantly dips into the new acquisition's coffers and repays the bank its $319 million. Inside National General is Great American Casualty, a subsidiary that in itself is almost as large as AFC.

Years later Lindner's brother Robert explains this appetite for leverage, for debt. "Carl and the rest of us," he points out, "have always resorted to leverage because it was the only way that underdogs and have-nots like us could get ahead."

Keating and Lindner have achieved a kind of financial magic. And it is noticed. The Christmas parties get larger and larger. Now 5,500 employees attend. There is a banquet, free shares of stock, bonuses. For entertainment they get people such as Sammy Davis, Jr. Lindner is so taken with Davis's show that he gives him, besides his fee, five shares of stock and a $35,000 black Stutz Bearcat.

The fine life has a price. Between 1971 and 1974 AFC's debt has grown from $194 million to $692 million while its stockholders' equity has moved from $103 million to only $192 million. The

---

*Milken denies the bit about wearing a lamp, pointing out with some logic that buses have lights (Jesse Kornbluth, *Highly Confident: The Crime and Punishment of Michael Milken,* William Morrow, New York, 1992, p. 46). In any event, during these early years at Drexel he was given a miner's helmet with a light as a gift.

company is buried in debt—its interest payments rise from $11 million in 1971 to $63 million in 1974. For AFC to meet its payments, it must upstream money from its subsidiaries in the form of dividends and advances. But many of its subsidiaries are in regulated industries, like banking or savings and loans or insurance companies.

But Lindner and Keating are ripe with inventions. They may look peculiar to Wall Street, but they are full of self-confidence. They visit Drexel Burnham Lambert in New York, and while taking a tour are told they should meet this new hire who has an office in the basement. There they find a young guy, just out of college, named Mike Milken. He is about the only Jew in the WASP firm, and so he has been shunted to the cellar. Milken believes in a new source of money for corporations, a thing called subordinated debentures, junk bonds in short. Lindner and Keating have been issuing unsecured paper for over a decade. They feel they have met a kindred soul and a genius, one who like them truly sees what is now possible in this country.

First, Charlie Keating goes out to inspect the new subsidiary, Great American Casualty, and he leaves a trail of pink slips behind him on desk tops. Then the headquarters is moved from New York to Ohio, where the laws for insurance companies are more lenient. This single act immediately raises the possible dividends that can be upstreamed to AFC from $15 million to $40 million. They also peddle other parts of National General—Bantam Books, Grosset & Dunlap, First Insurance Company of Hawaii. They sell the *Cincinnati Enquirer* (booking an $11 million profit), although in many ways Lindner retains control by keeping his title as publisher and having Charlie's brother, Bill, installed as the paper's president.

Then Charlie Keating has a brainstorm. Because of AFC's enormous debt and the bite the interest payments have made into profits, Wall Street is not anxious to issue new paper for the company. Keating decides to put out $50 million worth of junk bonds and offer the securities to small stockbrokers in units as small as $1,000 that pay 11¾ percent annual interest—a lot higher than any banks are offering. He advertises the bonds not in Chicago or New York City or the major capital markets, but in small-town newspapers across Ohio and Kentucky and remote cities like Buffalo, New York, where he senses there are lots of small savers greedy for big interest. And he figures such small-time buyers would just stick the certificates away as nest eggs—in other words, he could get long-term money out of them. There are no reserves to back up this issue, reserves that would have been required if he had syndicated the offering. And Charlie Keating's plan works.

In the sixties and seventies, some of the initial experimental laboratory work for what would later be called the eighties was done in Cincinnati by two guys nobody ever expected would amount to much. Since its inception in 1960, AFC has plotted the way to a new world characterized by debt, and it has done this by acquiring companies and then dismembering them to pay the bills, by creating new and bizarre financial instruments, by setting up a maze of subsidiaries sufficient to baffle all but the most zealous regulators, by operating outside the established business community, by running lean in management and rich in credit, by buying things with other people's money and then paying people by borrowing yet more money. And what did they create? Basically, a business that sucked up money through premiums or deposits and then survived or died depending on how well Carl Lindner and Charlie invested that money. A speculative kind of thing. A crapshoot.

The money just flows and flows. The most important force in U.S. business life is within reach: power. Keating has built his swim club, the Cincinnati Marlins, into a national power, and all of his kids swim for it. In 1976, his son is on the U.S. Olympic team, and the whole family travels to Montreal to watch him compete. The family has some condos down in Florida, and when they want to escape the Cincinnati weather, they just fly down for a few days. One time while vacationing Charlie calls up his aide Judy Wischer and asks her to bring him some business papers. She and Chip fly down to enjoy a free vacation. It is as simple as that.

Keating loves the beach, the sun. He is a swimming machine with his big hands and feet. "Totally effortless," Wischer discovers, "swimming up the swells, down the swells, same stroke, never wavering or anything, just the same speed. . . ." Everything is possible if you just do it, if you do not give in. Keating buys a piece of Cat Cay, an exclusive island in the Bahamas. It is a dot of land rising out of the blue sea with a handful of rich estates and, at one end, a partitioned-off enclave of poor Bahamian blacks who serve as help.

He thinks of his times in the sun when his good times are coming to a close in December 1988. The federal government is closing in, bankruptcy is near, the lawyers are gnawing at his bones, and he pauses in his diatribe against the regulators before a surprised group of Lincoln Savings and Loan employees in Los Angeles and begins to speak of a hideaway. "I go to an island in the Caribbean," he says without preamble. "It's called Cat Cay. And there's a lot of Bahamian natives there. And they live in hovels. One time I built them a basketball court and I gave them a little money to clean up some of their houses, paint their houses. There's thirty-three houses on the island and about one hundred members, and they're mostly rich people—the Americans, the whites. The natives got restless one time, and they had a big party and they had too much, whatever they drink in the Bahamas, and they started a Keating for Premier campaign. And they painted all these signs and they are walking all around the island beating their bongo drums and so forth and so on and the next day I was called before the board of directors of the island. And they wanted me to cut all that stuff out. I said all I did was try to keep the rats out by patching the holes and giving them a little paint and bought them a few refrigerators and basketball courts. It just never stopped. And it got to the point where I became an outcast on that island."

He is on a kind of ground here that his audience does not anticipate. Charlie Keating, troublemaker instead of corporate mogul. He seems to sense this himself.

"I don't want to paint myself," he continues, "as being some kind of a revolutionary. I'm not at all. But that's very typical and very simple in terms of what happened. I just basically left the white society of the island and lived in my own home. I have a perfectly good time with my family and my friends, but the natives haven't gotten anywhere in the fifteen years or so since that occurred. It all occurred because of jealousy. Not wanting other people to stir things up and to change the commonplace, and that's exactly what's happened here. So it's all your fault. You shouldn't run the branches that way, and I'm taking the consequences. So don't blame me that I have to sell Lincoln. Look in the mirror. I've talked too long, and I haven't probably said much."

He will build a special place on Cat Cay. He buys a beautiful slice of beach. Cat Cay is very small and all the construction materials must be brought in. Keating acquires a World War II landing barge and begins to haul over tons of equipment. As the costs escalate, Judy Wischer is concerned, but he will not be stopped.

There is a kind of Gypsy trader who comes around in a small boat peddling pots and pans, eggs, a little produce, and Keating makes him the captain of his barge. He hauls drywall, cement, glass. The Americans on the island are rich, but as the project continues they grow alarmed at the outlay of money. The two-story ocean side of the house is a glass wall. The building is on a small spit carved into a hill on the land side with a white crescent beach in front. The interior is light and airy. There are many bedrooms; Charlie Keating likes to be surrounded by his children and grandchildren. Judy Wischer makes him a pillow that says "Keating's Folly," and when the house is ready he places it prominently on a couch in the living room.

At Cat Cay, he makes his own rules. He likes the local black people, helps them out with odds and ends, pays random medical bills. He causes a scandal when he goes to their little ghetto on the island and drinks beer from the same bottle they do. He does not care. He makes that offer of one hundred dollars to any mother who names her baby Charlie. In the eyes of his white guests, Keating is looked up to like a god by the natives.

He loves speed, and so he buys fast boats, cigarette boats. He is stopped repeatedly by the Coast Guard as he runs between his island and Florida. They board his boat toting machine guns. He is moving so fast, they are convinced he must be a drug smuggler.

He finds the best builder, Don Aronow, and commissions a special cigarette boat with two 454-horsepower Chevrolet engines. He makes the passage from Miami to the island at night, bucking twelve-foot waves. He is after the feel of the sea. Keating can put six people into the boat and plane out on the water at sixty, sixty-five miles an hour. He decides to enter races.

He is streaking toward the finish line and cannot gain on his opponents. His whole family is in the boat with him, and Charlie is standing decked out in shorts, a ball cap, and boat shoes. He decides to lighten the load, and they begin throwing overboard life jackets, water skis, diving tanks, anything not tied down. The other racers are two to a boat and wearing protective helmets. Keating roars along with his family. He cannot sit down, the pounding of the waves is too severe. He loves the speed. He talks about forming a partnership to design and build faster and faster boats.

Everything is coming together for Charlie Keating. Washington, D.C., has become his new backyard. He goes to Europe when he wishes. He slips down to the Bahamas when he wants the sea and sun. One day in Scotland, he bumps into John Connally, the former Texas governor, and his wife. Connally is a protégé of both Lyndon Johnson and Sid Richardson, a legendary wheeler-dealer from Texas who, like his partner, Clint Murchison, Sr., never felt good if he went to bed at night with money in the bank instead of money in play. He is wealthy, powerful, and respected. Keating is all but star-struck, and he and Connally become friends. One day Connally stops by his office in Cincinnati, and the group photograph with the game-legged, boozy Jimmy Schneider comes into being.

Mike Manning works for Bob Docking until 1974, when the governor decides he is going to retire from office. For a guy in his early twenties it is a heady experience to hand out all the political plums in the state of Kansas; it is a total-immersion course in American politics. When Docking decides to end his distinguished career, he takes Manning aside and says, "You will be governor, senator, whatever you want to be in Kansas. You've got tickets, I'll turn over my organization to you." And Manning knows this is not simply idle talk. Docking has been an enormously popular governor, his father had been governor before him. His organization is real, Manning has just spent two years tending to its lubrication. And Bob Docking is connected—he is a good friend of the Kennedy family. But Docking has more to his message than simply offering Manning the keys to his kingdom. He also says, "You need to be something more than just a professional politician. You need to be something—I'm an insurance man, I'm a banker. You need to be something else, all you are right now is a politician. Why don't you go to law school?"

Manning says, "Fine, I'll talk to my wife." His wife encourages this new plan, and Manning enrolls at Washburn University's School of Law in Topeka, even though he could have gotten into schools elsewhere. In part he picks the school so he'll have an in-state pedigree when he resumes his political career. But also he chooses Washburn because he has no money, and Docking is going to allow him to work while attending classes. He tells Manning that he can't miss work, he has to work forty-plus hours a week, but he will let him fit his hours around his classes. So Manning puts in forty to fifty hours a week during his first year in law school, working for the governor until his term expires.

To his surprise, he does incredibly well. For the first time in his life, he is an A student. He is cracking the books, too. He falls in love with the law—is editor in chief of the law review, sixth or seventh in his class. Sometime in his second year, he realizes he never wants to return to politics. He just wants to be a lawyer. He has this sense of mission, that with the law he can make a difference. Manning goes through his Ralph Nader period of considering a public interest law practice but discovers to his amazement that he is addicted to the complexities of commercial litigation. The Dump Nixon veteran is set on fire by an antitrust class. He is also heavily influenced by two professors who stress that lawyers charge a hell of a lot of money and it is the duty of every attorney to sacrifice whatever it takes to ensure that the client gets the best result possible while being billed for the fewest hours possible.

He holds down two jobs, and by the time he graduates Manning and his wife are subsisting off vegetables from their garden. In the final semester they are saved when their basset hound has a litter. They sell the pups for $75 apiece, and this windfall gets him through his last exams.

His appetite for commercial law and antitrust action means Manning will have to find a firm in a major metropolitan area. He decides he will interview in New York, Chicago, Phoenix, and Kansas City and picks a firm in the last city because the partners stress that law is not a business but a profession. And that anyone who joins them will make a nice living but never be rich. He is easily seduced and in 1977 joins Morrison & Hecker and becomes one of their thirty-five or forty lawyers.

Charlie Keating is given to pronouncements like "Homosexuals should be prosecuted and put in jail." A reporter comes to his office to quiz him on his obsession about pornography and he whips some color photographs out of his desk of women having sex with pigs and says, "Is this what you meant when you said you wanted to discuss pornography? These are the latest imports from Denmark." He lives surrounded by filthy pictures—for his work he must have a collection as evidence.

In 1977, Keating's hatred of pornography seems to grow fiercer. He speaks to a Cincinnati "Rally for Decency" on Friday, May 13, and attacks the clergy for their weakness in the fight against filth, insisting they have "permitted the roaring lion to destroy the lamb." The rally is supposed to be a celebration. In February, a Cincinnati jury convicted Larry Flynt, the publisher of *Hustler,* of pandering obscenity and engaging in organized crime. Flynt is a native of neighboring Kentucky (from a county so poor that jury duty was said to be *the* economy) and as a boy wanted to be either a gynecologist or an evangelist. Now he resides in southern Ohio. Flynt has brought a new perspective to the increasingly popular skin magazines: open vulval shots, the "pink." His movie reviewer considers only pornographic movies. His readers send in snapshots of their wives and girlfriends to sustain another monthly feature, "Beaver Hunt." Flynt works with gusto, with an almost messianic desire to tear down the standards of proper behavior. He has risen up from his poor roots, his spotty education, his ventures as a nightclub operator, and now he deliberately assaults whatever pillars of the community he can locate. And he is fighting his war not in back alleys, not through mail drops for salacious photos, not in after-hours joints and brothels parading as massage parlors, but at the neighborhood newsstand.

Flynt is far more ambitious than Keating's earlier demon, Russ Meyer, with his limited fixation on enormous breasts. Flynt, in the realm of selling photographs of naked women, takes no prisoners, stops at no line. He says he wants to learn if the First Amendment really means what it says. He now lives in a mansion; his wife, Althea, procures him about fifteen women a week. She is a self-professed bisexual, and in 1975 she poses nude for *Hustler.* She is not the kind of woman Charlie Keating is likely to hire. When she was eight years old, her father came home and killed her mother, her mother's best friend, her grandfather, and then himself. When she was seventeen and a runaway from an orphanage, Flynt hired her to be a go-go dancer in his nightclub. She also is the copublisher of *Hustler* and at $800,000 the highest-paid woman in the country. And *Hustler* is hauling in tens of millions of dollars a year, a bottom line that can make even a Charlie Keating take notice. When Althea and Flynt decide to marry in 1976, they celebrate the decision by going to the best brothel in New York and having sex with an array of beautiful women. His magazine hails from and is read by the blue-collar world, that special part of the nation that Charlie Keating believes he knows as bone of his bone and flesh of his flesh.

But the rally that is supposed to thank the local jury for nailing Larry Flynt becomes a lament in Keating's hands. "I've been very, very wrong," he confesses. "That's right, I've been wrong." He quotes from St. Paul, he quotes from Alexis de Tocqueville, and he charges that the churches of the country have let people "exchange God's truth for lies. This is what the churches are here to stop." It is all so clear to him tonight, he is tired of nitpicking arguments about what is pornography and what is not: "There is no difference between Brigitte Bardot taking off her clothes in movies and children doing it. It's all pornography; it's just a matter of degree."

The problem is spreading; now even hotels are showing dirty movies to anyone "shoving money into a slot in their television sets. What if my son or daughter [stays in a hotel]? He can do whatever he pleases in the room, but he is tempted because he can see pornography, intercourse, and all sorts of perversion. . . ."

Ah, he senses he may have gone too far, his voice trails off, he laughs and says, "Now, I want to make it clear that I have nothing against intercourse. I've got six kids," and then his wife, Mary Elaine, stands up for a round of applause. He goes on saying, "I love you for coming. I know some people thought it would just be Keating and a bunch of little old ladies in tennis shoes. Stick with it. We've got a lot to tell you."

In March 1977, Larry Flynt spoke at Sigma Alpha Epsilon fraternity house at the University of Cincinnati. Charlie Keating will later believe that Flynt referred to a local girl by name and said he would pay money to embarrass her. On April 12, 1977, a coed parks her car on the University of Cincinnati campus at high noon and gets out to go to class. She is struck from behind on the back and ordered to go into Burnet Woods. The man she confronts stands about five feet ten inches tall, he has light brown hair and a tattoo of a star on his right forearm. He rapes her. She is a daughter of Charlie Keating.

When Keating gives his impassioned speech that night in May at the Rally for Decency, he describes this abduction and rape. Without naming names he makes it painfully clear that he's referring to his own child. He shares with his audience, there to celebrate the conviction of Larry Flynt, the fact that the girl "is physically and emotionally all right today. Her mother and the girl—before the consequences were known—ruled out murder if a child were to be born. I cannot tell you how proud I am of my wife and daughter for their faith and courage." And then he mentions the talk at Sigma Alpha Epsilon house and the offer by a "well-known pornographer."

Keating has been fighting Larry Flynt hammer and tongs—what other response is conceivable for Charlie Keating when he is confronted by a man who is said to keep in the foyer of his home a life-size statue of himself fornicating with a chicken to commemorate his first sexual experience? He and his organization, CDL, have been instrumental in Flynt's recent conviction. After his daughter's rape, a new hardness surfaces in Charlie Keating. He contacts the FBI, he digs into his Rolodex of people in power, seeking information. And then on March 6, 1978, Larry Flynt is on trial before the Superior Court of Gwinnett County, Georgia, on obscenity charges. When the court breaks for lunch, he ambles down to the V & J Cafeteria, where he orders two tumblers of grapefruit juice. Flynt is undergoing a new dietary regime, one recommended by his friend comedian Dick Gregory. He is a complete vegetarian. He has been through a lot of changes recently. Ruth Stapleton, sister of President Jimmy Carter, converted Flynt to Christianity during a plane ride on his labia pink jet. During that flight, Flynt suddenly felt a tingling sensation and saw St. Paul and Christ. "I promised to give up my life for Him," Flynt explains later. "I promised to see myself castrated, to look down and see myself with no sex organs. . . . I spoke in tongues." He becomes a complete celibate and commissions a series of photographs based on great nude scenes from the Bible.

His meager lunch consumed, he heads back up the street with his lawyer, Gene Reeves. His bodyguards have been dismissed for the day—none of the good ol' boys in Gwinnett County seem to be riled up about his magazine, *Hustler*. As Reeves and Flynt pass a transient hotel on the other side of the street, two shots ring out from a doorway and both men go down, hit by bullets from a .44. Flynt shouts, "Help me! Help me! Somebody help me!" His spinal cord is severed, and for the rest of his life Larry Flynt will be dead from the waist down. He will never again feel the sexual pleasure of a woman. He survives in part because he has adopted Gregory's regimen of morning enemas and his intestines are empty. Ruth

Stapleton comes to his bedside and tells the press, "I believe in miracles. I just thank God he's alive." But when Flynt learns he will never walk again, he has a different response: "I stopped being spiritual."

There are many guesses about who did the shooting, which is viewed as a very smooth and professional job. Some suspect Flynt's Mafia competitors in the dirty magazine business. Others see the hand of an intelligence agency because Flynt is obsessed with discovering who really shot John Fitzgerald Kennedy. There are those who think it could be the work of the Ku Klux Klan, whose members might be offended by Flynt's current mixture of Christ and vaginas. No one will ever be arrested for the shooting that noonday in Georgia. Flynt will offer tens of thousands of dollars as a reward, but his money will not bring him an answer.

Charlie Keating has talked of Flynt often during his war against his publications and ideas. But when Flynt is shot, he says nothing at the office. Years later, according to Keating's colleagues, his son will say that he thinks his father had the shooting done. Some of the people who worked around him don't think he could ever have killed Larry Flynt. That would have been a mortal sin for a devout Catholic. But of course, Larry Flynt does not die. The rumors surround Charlie Keating like a dark cloud. But he says nothing. He presses on.*

*In June 1988, Bowden asked Charles Keating about his daughter's rape and about Larry Flynt being gunned down. They were alone in the boardroom at ACC, into which Keating had led Bowden after he had brought up the subject. The room was huge, the walls wood paneled, the table polished and immense. Keating led Bowden to a corner. He acknowledged his daughter's rape and said that after that event Larry Flynt was shot and now he'll spend the rest of his life in a wheelchair. His voice was very calm and even and he stared with determination into Bowden's eyes as he recounted this string of events. This was just moments after he had held secretaries on his lap for a series of gag photographs—the warrior against pornography wall-eyed and ogling the bimbos—and showed Bowden the crucifix given him by Mother Teresa, the one said to contain a piece of the True Cross. He was as intense when he displayed the piece of the True Cross as he was when he spoke of Flynt being gunned down. The Flynt case has never been solved. One executive who worked with him for years says, "I can see it, I can see it as a father, for one thing. I can see it from the standpoint of Charlie, knowing that [his daughter] had been raped, knowing that they really suspected that it was a rape for hire. . . . Charlie liked to brag about things no matter whether he did them or he wanted to lay claim to doing them. I can't even remember him saying anything about Flynt, about the Flynt shooting. It seems to me he was uncharacteristically quiet."

*   *   *

Citizens for Decent Literature has now become Citizens for Decency Through Law, runs on a budget of over a million dollars a year, and tackles motion pictures as well as the printed word. In Cincinnati it has won almost a total victory: the city has no adult bookstores, no X-rated videos or cable, no massage parlors, and no strip joints, and it is next to impossible to buy a copy of *Hustler* magazine. Keating's new role as executive vice president at AFC takes up so much of his time that in 1971 he contracts out CDL's fund raising to Richard A. Viguerie Co. of Washington, D.C. Viguerie is the guru of right-wing fund raising by mail. And he doesn't come cheap. Soon most of what CDL raises goes to pay Viguerie to raise yet more money. Five states—Florida, Pennsylvania, Arkansas, North Carolina, and New York—ban CDL from seeking money. And there is another problem: CDL invests more than $230,000 of its take in AFC stocks and bonds. The *Cincinnati Post* (the afternoon paper not controlled by Lindner and Keating) breaks the story on August 30, 1974. A day later, Keating responds through the pages of the *Enquirer.* He admits he's been busy and not tending the shop. The mailing abuses will be corrected ("The new laws are good"), and as for investing the money in the company he helps run, AFC, why that is the very point in Keating's eyes. He argues that the logical place for the funds is in a corporation in which he believes, and AFC certainly fills that bill.

But there are problems at AFC. Because of Lindner and Keating's constant acquisitions the debt is vast. Because of servicing the debt, and because of a slump in the housing market and the economy in general, dividends and earnings decline in the mid-seventies. Profits shrink from $25 million in 1974 to $9 million in 1975, and dividends collapse from $1.43 to $.22. And because of these conditions and others, the lawsuits are finally served on the company, focusing on its endless growth and adventurous investment.

On June 1, 1976, some shareholders file suit in U.S. District Court in Cincinnati against American Financial Corporation, and later that day AFC denies the charges. The suits are brought by one Richard G. Donohoo and by Piedmont Paper Products, Inc., an investment company that has put some money into American Continental Homes, one of AFC's many subsidiaries. They think some funny deals have gone down in AFC that have diluted or diminished their interests. They want to know about $700,000 paid by AFC directors to Charles H. Keating, Jr., on September 25, 1975, for warrants to buy 200,000 shares of AFC stock. They point out that the warrants (which would have expired on June 1, 1979) went for $22 a throw. Tuesday, the day the suit was filed, AFC common stock traded over the counter at $7.12. This seems like an unusually sweet deal to the claimants, one which so far as they can tell benefits none other than Charlie Keating, the executive vice president of AFC. And there are other matters: a couple of shareholders, the suit charges, managed a deal similar to Keating's where they got a loan for $6.274 million at 9.5 percent about New Year's Eve 1974. In exchange for the loan the couple forked over 62,128 shares of AFC common stock and $355,000 of convertible debentures and warrants for purchase of 902,779 shares of AFC common stock. The claimants figure that the value of the loan was way over the value of the stuff put up against it. But there is more: the claimants argue that Charlie Keating in 1975 got a $600,000 fee for his part in the sale of the *Cincinnati Enquirer* (for $55 million) and that he didn't really earn it. Carl Lindner disputes this charge, saying that Keating's fee simply was a case of "rewarding achievement." A few weeks before the suit, an AFC proxy statement had noted that there was an SEC investigation of the company but that AFC did not think it would come to much. (By October 1976, there will be a flurry of shareholders' suits seeking about $10 million they figured the management of the company ripped off.)

The house of corporate cards constructed by Lindner and Keating came under federal inspection, and in August 1976, the SEC filed suit. It had some questions about stock dealing. The suit noted that on March 21, 1975, AFC bought 42,000 shares of Warner and accomplished this purchase by having two brokers on the floor of the New York Stock Exchange making the buys. At the same moment, a third broker representing AFC sold 690,000 shares of Warner. The SEC suspects that Lindner and his colleagues were trying to drive up the price of Warner so that their big sell order would go for more money. And indeed, at those moments when the three brokers were executing AFC's orders, Warner bumped up from $13 a share to well over $14. Facing this suit, Lindner capitulates, accepts a consent decree (in which the company admits to no wrong and agrees not to do whatever it was doing again) and sets up a $1.1 million reserve in case Warner sues for stock manipulation. And naturally, Warner sues.

But there are still more problems. A bunch of suits question the way Lindner and Keating have shared profits with the employees of AFC, especially the executives at the top. Lindner has always believed in encouraging his people to buy lots of AFC stock, a habit some view as propping up the stock to keep its value high. In order to achieve this goal, AFC has made big, generous loans to insiders to buy stock in AFC and its subsidiaries and from time to time bought back warrants (rights to buy AFC stock at a certain price) from insiders. The gist of the suits is that AFC is being run not for the benefit of the shareholders but for the benefit of the executives who work for AFC.

Heading the list in this issue of insider trading is Charlie Keating. By August 1976, AFC and its subsidiaries have loaned Keating $6,328,000, and all of these loans are unsecured. And this does not include some other details such as buying warrants from Keating in 1975 for $700,000. Or paying him a $600,000 bonus (in addition to his base salary of $193,000 a year) for helping to sell the *Cincinnati Enquirer*. The bonus is all the more generous since the man who bought the *Enquirer,* Karl Eller, claims never to have dealt with Keating at all when doing the deal, a negotiation that took six solid months.

The SEC returns to the fray with a laundry list of charges that in effect review the years of work Carl Lindner and Charlie Keating poured into their invention, American Financial Corporation, the financial department store.* Besides objecting to specific deals,

*When they sold the Athens National Bank, they had their captive Provident Bank buy up $3 million worth of loans made to friends of AFC.

When they took over National General, they paid a $500,000 bonus to the vice president of that company.

When they made a profit of $440,000 in 1972 selling an aircraft leased by an AFC subsidiary to Lindair, Inc., it was really an inside job since Lindner and his brother owned Lindair.

When Provident Bank, in January 1975, guaranteed a $400,000 loan to Charlie Keating from the Royal Bank of Canada, this was not simply a business decision but preferential treatment for an insider.

When AFC's captive Provident Bank repurchased a loan from the Union Commerce Bank of Cleveland, a loan secured by AFC stock, this was not simply normal business either, since the quid pro quo was that Keating would get a loan of $600,000 and another AFC director would bag one for $400,000.

the SEC raises general questions. Since 1971, the government argues, Keating and his law firm have not been totally forthright when peddling AFC securities. Rather, they have used "devices, schemes and articles to defraud" and made "untrue statements of material facts," all this in order to perpetrate "fraud and deceit upon purchasers and sellers of securities of AFC. . . ." Besides these claims, the SEC is convinced that Lindner and Keating have used Provident Bank for sweetheart loans to insiders, loans that totaled $5 to $10 million between 1972 and 1975 and shot up to $14 million in 1976. They provide an example. In 1972, Donald L. Klekamp, vice president of an AFC subsidiary, wanted to borrow $600,000 to buy some AFC stock. Lindner and Keating loaned him $1.7 million instead. When Klekamp's finances hit the skids in May 1974, he complained about the extra amount packaged into the original loan. So in December 1975, AFC let him transfer stock back to itself and forgave the rest of the debt. But AFC fibbed when it reported the deal because it claimed that $1.1 million of the loan had been repaid and only $247,000 written off. In short, the government believed AFC was cooking its books to make them look good.

Suddenly, Carl Lindner, now fifty-seven, is described this way by a fellow Cincinnati businessman: "He's a character. A nut. He must have a tremendous brain; you have to think that, considering everything he's accomplished. I know he's got one of the most tremendous egos I've ever seen. If you think as a psychiatrist might, it's clear he wants to be loved. He's clamoring for love. In business, when I've dealt with him, he's been fair and honest and professional. But if you were to ask me whether I trust him one hundred percent, I'd have to say I really don't. . . ." Charlie Keating, now fifty-two, does not fare as well. *Fortune* magazine looks into Keating's reputation in Cincinnati and reports, "Indeed, it seems almost impossible to find anyone who actually likes Charlie Keating."

More than a decade later, Keating still cannot get past what happened to him in Cincinnati, cannot get it out of his mind. Like that night he landed his navy Hellcat with the wheels up, the days with AFC and Lindner have become one of his touchstones. The audience listening to him speak off the cuff at Lincoln Savings and Loan in December 1988 cannot know what he is referring to. They live in Los Angeles, they are branch managers and other staff members from the twenty-nine offices of the bank, and suddenly this man in his mid-sixties is making vague allusions to a place they have never been and a time that is part of their childhoods, not their lives.

"I was a lawyer," Charlie Keating announces, "believe it or not, for twenty-five years. And as a matter of fact had a lot of success as a lawyer. With a small firm of thirteen people and I'm not here to tell you all about me or my life or anything else but I thought some of this might be germane to the issue later on. . . . We did well, we had a small firm of thirteen people, and we were ranked on an income basis with the top fifteen law firms in the United States and there wasn't one other one that had less than one hundred lawyers. . . . The time came to get out of that business. The opportunity came, and I took it. I went with a company called American Financial Corporation which had meant to be a public company in which I played an important role. And we succeeded beyond our wildest dreams. We got to the point where we were attacked by the Securities and Exchange Commission, and the people that owned more stock than I did decided to take it private. At which point the company had no more interest for me because it was a family company and it wasn't something I wanted to do. The reason I was in a position not to vote and carry more weight was I had made a mistake. When I was at first with the company and they decided to go public, I did a lot of work for them and was instrumental and successful strategizing what they did and they asked me how much I wanted to be paid for my services. I said that I didn't want to be paid for my services, that I wanted a piece of stock that was fairly important and that put me in an ownership position that would be of consequence. I was dealing with a guy smarter than I was, I had a wife and six kids at the time, and he said, well, my family, we really have never had outside influence in the company, why don't I give you a fee. He named a number that was staggering to me, and he bought me for thirty ounces of silver. I took the cash and he took the stock. . . . That was the first time in my life where my action, my decision what to do with the future was conditioned to some extent outside of my own volition. There were influences that exerted, that pushed me to a decision that I didn't want to make particularly and I probably wouldn't have for my best interest had I been totally independent of any outside influence. Today, we find ourselves in the same position. . . ."

*　　　*　　　*

On August 5, 1976, Charles H. Keating, Jr., resigns from AFC. Years later he will say, "I hated to leave and left a lot on the table when I did." AFC is inching up toward being a $2 billion operation, and Charlie Keating has no doubt in his mind that he is the cofounder and cocreator of this strange holding company.

Stories grow up around his leave-taking. One is simply that Carl Lindner and his family decide that Charlie Keating is too wild, too uncontrollable for their operation, and the suits by the SEC prove this. Another is that Charlie Keating decides he does not want to work for AFC, that he sees no future for himself in a family-run outfit when the company begins buying up its own stock so that it can go private. Inside the walls of AFC two other tales circulate. They both involve a board meeting. In one story, Charlie Keating pushes Carl Lindner to step down and make him the CEO of the company. Carl responds that if anybody is going to be the boss besides himself, it will be his brother Bob. Charlie flares back, "Bob is an asshole." The second legend within AFC has darker colors. In this one, Carl and Charlie get into an argument—no one remembers quite what the argument is about. There are so many choices, the massive debt load, the shareholders' suits, the SEC breathing fire down their necks, the fact that one little subsidiary, American Continental Homes, is losing a ton of money through a slump in the housing market. Charlie, who is much taller than Lindner, leans down into his face, starts shouting, and suddenly the two men come to blows. And Carl Lindner, Jr., starts crying.

When Charlie Keating resigns from the corporation he helped create, AFC agrees to pay him a consulting fee of $150,000 a year for four years. And generous loans are offered so that he can spin off a subsidiary, American Continental, a home-building business that is losing millions per month. Charlie Keating is fifty-three years old when he makes this shift, and he is starting over.

Larry Flynt has disappeared as a person but not as an idea. He is in constant pain from his injuries, he has a big drug habit, but he has not lost his spirit. In 1977 *Hustler* offers television anchorwoman Barbara Walters a million dollars to pose in the magazine buck naked with her legs spread. Then Flynt takes on an icon of middle America, Grant Wood's painting of an Iowa farm couple, *American Gothic,* and runs it in *Hustler.* Only this time the dour, harsh-looking farmwife with the severe hairstyle is topless. As it happens, the woman actually exists—she is Grant Wood's sister, and she sues *Hustler* for $10 million. But this does not slow Larry Flynt down. He is used to lawsuits, and he will not be kept down by the courts.

The ending is so quiet, it is almost a whisper. After years of headlines in the Cincinnati papers about Charlie Keating the swimming champ, Charlie Keating the rising young attorney, Charlie Keating the crusader against pornography, Charlie Keating the executive at AFC, on October 26, 1978, a tiny three-inch item appears in the Cincinnati *Post,* with the simple heading "Keating Goes West."

"Charles H. Keating, Cincinnati attorney," the story explains, "anti-pornography crusader, and businessman, is moving his family from Finneytown to Phoenix, Ariz.

"Keating is the chairman, chief executive officer and largest shareholder in American Continental Corp., residential home-builder in Phoenix and Flagstaff, Ariz., Salt Lake City, Cheyenne, Wyo., Denver and Ft. Collins, Colo. and Chicago.

"American Continental is a spinoff of American Financial Corp., Cincinnati-based insurance and banking conglomerate. . . .

"He also is known nationally as a champion swimmer."

Cincinnati says good-bye with a grand total of one hundred and twelve words.

The night of his going-away party, Jimmy Schneider, his boyhood friend and adult ward, gets drunk, falls down a stairway, hits his head, and dies. He will keep Jimmy's obituary on his office wall until he is put out of business for good. He is finished in this place.

But he is not finished. *Fortune,* that bible of big business, has announced that no one in Cincinnati likes Charlie Keating, and Charlie Keating will never forget that charge, that indictment of his half-century of life in his hometown. He will have big yellow buttons made that read "I Like Charlie Keating." And when people ask him about that slur on his name, he will say, "There are a lot of people that would say nasty things, I'm sure, about me, but it ain't true that nobody ever liked Charlie Keating."

And of course, there will be those two other big yellow buttons, perhaps the most important ones. They will say simply, "I am Charlie Keating."

PART THREE

STANDING ON THE EDGE OF LOVE

Late last night I was dreaming,
I was dreaming of your charms.
I was standing on the edge of love, darling,
With you in my arms. . . .

I'll promise that I'll stop all my gambling . . .

—B. B. King,
"Standing on the Edge of Love"

Charlie Keating is on a tear. He's got this home-building business to run, he's making a future for his family in a new town, in a new state. He is being reborn, after a fashion. He's got subdivisions popping up all over the region. And he is making good money at this rebirth.

One of his salesmen calls him up and says, "I've got a guy out here you might like to meet, a Vietnam veteran." The salesman figures he'll score a few points with the boss. After all, the company colors are red, white, and blue. So Charlie drops what he is doing and drives out there. And there is this guy waiting with his three kids, and when he tells his sad story it seems life hasn't been so good for him since he shipped back from 'Nam. Keating tells him to pick out any house he wants in any of his developments around Phoenix.

"You've done more for our country and me and my kids," he says, "than anyone can imagine. Pick out a home. It's yours."

WELCOME
HOME

He wants it back, all of it. There is no welcoming committee, there is no announcement in the newspapers. Charlie Keating is an unknown in these parts. And best of all, there is no history. Phoenix is not about history.

"Ended up out here," Keating explained casually in May 1988, "with resuscitation of a loser. I took over a company that was sort of down on its uppers, Continental Homes. So I was going to liquidate Continental Homes, it was sort of a nonevent, it wasn't in too good a shape. That led me out here, I love Phoenix, and so the whole family came. In the process of dissolving it in '76–'77, we decided it might still be viable and continued as a home builder."

When he cut loose from AFC, Keating had some money—estimates vary, some say as high as $15 or $20 million if all the stock is counted, but certainly a couple of million. When those who worked around Keating at this time are asked the status of his personal wealth, their estimates vary by not millions but tens of millions. There is a reason for this: money has become not simply the amount one possesses after paying off debts and expenses, but rather the amount one can command, the amount one can get one's hands on. Money has become a figure, a number that one can conjure up, and if others believe that figure, then that money really exists and the force of that figure becomes a measure of personal power.*

---

*Bowden remembers asking Keating in May 1988 how it felt to get out of bed with a couple of billion dollars in his britches, and Keating looked at him with both

Keating's door prize after his banishment from Lindner's AFC is a financial vagary. American Continental Homes (ACH) is a subsidiary of AFC and operates in Cincinnati, Chicago, Phoenix, Flagstaff, Denver, and Salt Lake City. ACH is losing a fortune. On April 1, 1976, for example, ACH reports losing $6.5 million in 1975, up from a 1974 loss of $168,000. And it is worse than that: ACH owes its parent, AFC, $25 million, and AFC has guaranteed $37 million more in bank loans to ACH. This is truly the black hole in Lindner's accounting-driven operation. Keating himself is not in great financial shape—when he resigns from AFC in August 1976, he owes Lindner's Provident Bank $6,328,000 in unsecured loans. But what is ACH worth? That is a matter difficult to figure out when one confronts the kind of books Carl Lindner, Jr., likes to keep. For example, on August 31, 1976, AFC distributes all of its ACH stock to AFC's shareholders with Lindner, at 1.4 million shares, owning the biggest chunk. That same day a subsidiary of ACH, American Continental Mortgage, is sold to a Phoenix thrift, but the subsidiary's loans—$2.5 million to Keating and another $2 million to various AFC insiders—are severed and moved over to yet another subsidiary, American Wholesale, Inc., which once manufactured panels for prefab housing units. Keating winds up with Lindner's 1.4 million shares, but just how this happens is not clear. Few things are ever clear in Lindner's empire—for example, buried in the SEC charges is not simply the allegation that Lindner, Keating, and others indulged in $14 million worth of insider loans but that Charlie Keating at one point loaned himself $500,000 and then wrote off the loan as a corporate loss.

For the first time in his life, Keating separates from his family and is gone for three months, surveying the damage. The largest wound is in Flagstaff, a small Arizona community of about 50,000 squatting along the tracks of the Santa Fe and the tired asphalt of old Route 66 and sheared off on one side by the dull four lanes of

amusement and pity and said calmly, "It doesn't really work that way." And then he went on to explain how investments go up and down, bond folios flourish and then sink under water, and this goes on day and night and there is no simple fixed point where one can calculate one's wealth with certainty. It is in flux, and of course, ultimately and always, it is a game. For examples of the difficulty modern bankers have in assessing a notion as simple as how much money a borrower actually possesses, see Tom Bower, *Maxwell: The Outsider,* Viking, New York, 1992, and Wayne Barrett, *Trump: The Deals and the Downfall,* HarperCollins, New York, 1992.

Interstate 40. Flagstaff is in some ways a peculiarly Arizonan achievement: a remarkably ugly town erected in one of the most beautiful locations on earth.

Charlie Keating is a man in his early fifties, a man broken in reputation, a man with his career snapped neatly in half like a stick broken over the knee. And he is ready and eager for whatever comes next. He is the kind of person Arizona has always found a place for, a man on the make in a state with no hallowed institutions, no traditional or esteemed groupings of wealth, and no reverence for the past or much else.

Continental Homes's attempt to develop a country club in Flagstaff bleeds cash. Keating discovers one key asset, a salesman who goes by the name of Jim "Saltlick" Taylor. Taylor has won his nickname by dumping ten-pound blocks of salt near the model homes and reaping sales as the salt brings in dozens of deer and the deer bring in buyers. He hails from some money in Dallas and is said to like good-looking blondes and Cadillac convertibles. He always keeps his glove compartment well stocked with pistols. Keating, a salesman of the first water, instantly recognizes one of his own breed. Soon he and Taylor are posing for snapshots like Mexican revolutionaries with pistols, carbines, and bandoliers.

At first, Continental Homes keeps its main office back in Cincinnati, and Keating brings Judy Wischer to this new venture. She is making about $80,000 a year, and Chip is pulling down $35,000 at Lindner's AFC. They have a farm in Kentucky, a nice house in Cincinnati, and no debt. They are about thirty years old. Then Keating begins to shut down profitless operations in Chicago and Cincinnati and by 1978 is determined to move everything to Phoenix. Judy decides to quit working for Keating; she does not wish to leave her parents and sisters. Keating counters with more and more money. Finally, Chip goes to Carl Lindner III, a close friend, and says he and Judy are thinking of moving to Arizona for a year or two and can AFC give him some work there? Lindner's son warns him about Keating, about his recklessness, and says he will go to his father and get him to make Judy an offer she can't refuse. But Keating, a man intensely competitive when it comes to Carl Lindner, counters again and wins with a promise of over a hundred thousand a year. AFC pays Chip $50,000 to run the Phoenix office of one of its insurance subsidiaries.

What they join is one of the more debt-ridden companies in the

United States. As of January 1, 1978, Continental Homes has assets of $510,000 and debts of $110,051,000, an equity-to-debt ratio of 1 to 216. Keating has a plan to resolve this situation: dump bad developments; refinance debt; diversify the company by expanding from simply building houses to also financing mortgages, peddling mortgage-backed bonds, and selling insurance. In short, reinvent AFC, only now using the initials ACH (later changed to American Continental Corporation, ACC). The colors of the company are red, white, and blue like the American flag. The motto is: Welcome Home. He sets out consciously to show Carl Lindner he can do it on his own and do it better. And to begin this project, he uses Carl Lindner's money.

In 1979, the SEC settlement is made with Charlie Keating taking most of the fall for the charges against American Financial Corporation. (Almost all SEC defendants settle rather than fight—neither businesses nor the agency is interested in actually going to court. The agency lacks the staff to prosecute very many violators, the businesses find it more cost effective to cop nolo pleas and continue with their practices.) For years, Keating will tell people he took the rap for Lindner. He will deny any knowledge of insider loans and say things like "They [SEC] were trying to get Lindner and took me along." The head of the SEC, Stanley Sporkin, will become a special object of his scorn, a man he claims has "a vendetta against all American business." He will never admit to any guilt—"I'm not guilty, they made the case up. Those loans were made on competitive terms, the same or higher interest rates. There was never a loss to the bank or AFC." The decision itself devastates Keating. The SEC had taken many depositions from people who knew Keating in Cincinnati, and he is shaken when he discovers what his fellow businessmen think of him. Like Lindner himself, Charlie Keating has a deep need to be loved. Judy Wischer tells her husband of the SEC settlement, "I've saved a box of files, and if Charlie ever tries to fire me these files could emerge." Keating, people around him at the time say, repeatedly goes to Lindner for more capital as he struggles to bail out Continental Homes. And he repeatedly gets it.

What ensues becomes the legend of the economic and personal rebirth. Between January 1, 1978, and the end of 1983, Keating's company builds 18,816 homes, by 1982 hitting a pace of eight a day. In Phoenix and Denver it becomes the largest builder of single-family homes. The books go from red to black, and Charlie Keating is back.

He has certain notions about his home-building business. One is that his strength is in selling. The second is that things are easier to sell if they are beautifully landscaped. He meets a Cuban refugee down in Florida, Manuel Diaz, who runs a nursery, and soon Keating is dedicated to having Diaz produce all of his trees and shrubs and shipping them from Florida. It costs more, of course, but Charlie Keating is not into nickels and dimes. Over time, Diaz becomes a fixture at the company, a man Keating brings out often to tell of his flight from Castro's Cuba, his rise to success in the United States, his loyalty and patriotism toward his new nation. And finally, there is Keating's belief in what he calls the water element. In the Sonoran Desert water is so scarce that the federal government is bankrolling a huge canal to salvage Arizona's cities with a $5 billion public works project called the Central Arizona Project. Even so, Charlie Keating insists on studding his projects with lakes filled with drinking water. He fights the city over this issue, he fights in the legislature. He contributes heavily to politicians. He may be in Arizona, but in many ways he is building an outpost of Cincinnati.

This is evident in his dress code for employees. Phoenix is a volcano in the summer with the temperature riding steadily above one hundred degrees for months. But Keating's people must all wear dark suits and ties. They could not stand out more from the local business community if they were parading about in Chairman Mao suits. But then, they have little to do with the local community at any level. Keating demands complete dedication to the company and does not want his people getting distracted by other matters. He takes care of any charitable contributions, he dictates any political contributions.

As ACC expands into places like Colorado Springs, Cheyenne, Wyoming, and Seattle, the family is brought into the business. C3, who fails to finish college and then works as a busboy, is made an executive. There is a tension between the father and the son. During an executive meeting C3 will fall asleep with his mouth agape. His father, Charlie Keating, Jr., will say nothing but slowly begin pitching paper clips across the table into his son's open mouth. When he finally tires of this sport, Keating will announce, "Somebody wake up that lousy lout of a son of mine." His son is the heir apparent to an empire that does not yet exist, but he is a reluctant heir. C3 is not quick at business and prefers to fire off model rockets and work with animals on the family ranch outside of Phoenix. His father constantly belittles him. At dinner in a fine restaurant Keating is asked about a questionable investment and points toward his son and says, "This jerk got me into that." And when the bill comes for the prime rib, the bottles of champagne, the rich desserts, Charlie Keating walks away and leaves his son fumbling with the payment.

The family that in Keating's view of the world is inviolate seems to be often violated within the family. There is little holding or comforting, a slap to the face is not unusual, even when the children are full grown. Everything is justified by the idea of the family and based upon the sacred value of the family, but within this creed there is little or no space for tenderness.

Politics beckons again. When his friend John Connally decides to run for president, Charlie Keating initially becomes his Western finance chairman. Connally has the traits Keating admires: he is tall, he is rich, and he is addicted to power. He shares Keating's penchant for offhanded renditions of his own past: "I really wanted to practice law," he once said in summing up his life, "but I was frustrated for so many years of my life. I didn't ask to be secretary of the navy. That came because of Sam Rayburn. I didn't ask to be secretary of the Treasury. That was President Nixon's idea." He also didn't resist being Lyndon Johnson's protégé, and he didn't resist being boy Friday to Sid Richardson, one of the richest men in the world in the forties and fifties and a crony of J. Edgar Hoover. When Richardson died, Connally became an executor of his estate, and that act was the source of his fortune. Basically, Connally would have spent his life being a player in the right wing of the Texas Democratic Party if he hadn't been shot with John F. Kennedy on November 22, 1963. The bullets transformed him into Mr. Texas. He didn't ask to be tried for bribery; that happened because when he was secretary of the Treasury in 1972 he was accused of taking $10,000 from milk producers who sought to get the price support on their product raised. Edward Bennett Williams got him off.

Connally collects the work of Elmyr de Hory, a forger who peddled $150 million worth of bogus old masters in his lifetime. After Hory's apparent suicide, Mr. Texas and a friend bought a hundred of the fakes. Years later, he defended his acquisitions by saying, "I like the quality of the paintings. This fellow, even though he was a faker, was a really superb artist." For Charlie Keating, John Connally represents legitimacy. Connally hobnobs with the rich and powerful, sits on boards of banks and corporations like Ford. And he knows the oil-rich Arabs, men like Ghaith Pharaon of Saudi Arabia, who once explained his love of the United States by saying, "In America, a $400 million bank can be acquired for $20 million. Where else can you do that?" In 1975, Connally smooths the way for Pharaon to buy a bank in Detroit by calling on his old friend Henry Ford II, who calms the local Jewish community. And then he helps Pharaon buy a piece of a bank in Houston in which Connally is a shareholder. Connally also has ties to the Kuwaitis.

On November 2, 1979, Connally is in Phoenix giving speeches and Charlie Keating hosts a fund-raising dinner for him at his home and raises $100,000. When the quest for the nomination falters (it is destined to spend $12 million and harvest one delegate), Keating is put in charge of the entire campaign, goes east, and fires staff wholesale. One friend he makes is an attorney and player in the Atlanta real estate market named Lee Henkel. Back in 1971, Henkel, a law graduate of Duke University, had been appointed general counsel for the Internal Revenue Service, and in that job he brushed up against two secretaries of the Treasury, George Shultz and Connally. Eventually, he returned to Georgia to be a tax lawyer and to dabble in real estate development. Keating gives Henkel some ACC legal work, and their business involvement slowly blossoms.

There is in Charlie Keating a hatred of control. And also, a deep hatred of things out of control. Or perhaps not a hatred but a deep fear. Normally it is masked, hidden from view like an underground river. But it sometimes surfaces in the one area of life where he absolutely cannot control himself. Pornography.

It is, for example, October 15, 1979, and Charles H. Keating, Jr., LL.D., is testifying before the Senate Judiciary Committee on obscenity laws. He tells them the truth: "I am a Doctor of Law . . . the father of six children. . . . Though I do not relish the assignment, it has become my avocation to speak out about hard truths many people in government seem to have forgotten." Don't the senators realize that pornographers are raking in $4 billion a year?

And don't they understand what these people are selling? "Hetero-sexual porn . . . ," he intones, "homosexual porn . . . kiddie porn . . . bondage porn . . . sexual devices porn. . . ." And he will ex-plain. American women can walk into stores in this country and buy two-headed dildos so that they can lie with another woman and each have a head to insert. There are pillows made especially for fornication. There are massage parlors. There are . . .

What can he say? "There are hundreds of magazines and mov-ies," he announces, "showing scenes of unspeakable vileness right within five miles of the Senate Office Building, scenes so perverted no senator would want anyone, much less his own family, to look at them even once."

Women are having intercourse with dogs and horses. Gangs are raping young girls—"chain her to a post and then simultaneously have sex with her in groups of two or three or even more." These films show "close-ups of male and female sex organs in massively turgid arousal."

Women lying side by side, on sheets, their skin sweating, and then they take in hand a two-headed dildo, and the insertion be-gins. The films are everywhere. Your little daughter baby-sits, and she finds such a film. Your young son goes to a friend's party, the room goes dark, the screen lights up. "Then on dates!!"

There have to be constraints.

Two-headed dildos.

Never clean anyone out in a business deal, Charlie Keating tells his young staff. Always leave the other person something. Also, pay attention to your secretaries. Tip people very well. You should be grateful. They are working hard, damn hard. You could be them.

Insertion.

By 1981, ACC is ready for new offices and Keating bags a build-ing on Camelback Road that some other developers cannot carry financially. Keating is so alarmed by the littered condition of the offices as the crews race to finish them that he insists his staff show up at 7 A.M. each Saturday and again Sunday afternoon. Charlie gives orders like a general, and his secretary blows a whis-tle whenever Charlie issues a new command. For years Chip Wischer will remember the sight of his wife, Judy, down on her knees in a bathroom scrubbing tiles with a toothbrush. The cleanup drills go on for six weeks.

For the first time in his life, Charlie Keating answers to no one. He has no law partners to bully or placate, he has no Carl Lindner to argue with. He is the company. He hires every employee, and they tend to look the same: all are tall, white, blue-eyed, and the women are blond, thin, good-looking, and buxom. His job interviews spook his staff. He will ask someone if he or she is Mexican or black. He will ask a female applicant if she intends to get knocked up after she is hired. His staff will tell him that he cannot ask questions like that. But he can and does. His employees function as followers. He supervises their dress and appearance and tends to their social life. Because he deems that Phoenix has limited entertainment possibilities, he hosts barbecues and films at his home for the staff. Everyone who brushes up against Keating's home-building company has a feeling that it is not simply a company, it is a kind of private world in which all power flows from Charlie Keating.

He fires easily and often. His hatred of personnel departments and rules is manifest. But he never confronts the person who is to be fired. First, he isolates the person, talks behind his or her back, tells everyone he bumps into that the person is worthless. Slowly, the victim sinks into a state of paranoia. No raises come, no bonuses. Other workers will start avoiding the person. It becomes, in the words of one of his executives, "almost like Keating's version of Amish shunning." Once this state is achieved, more and more problems are blamed on the selected victim. Ideally, the target will resign as this slow torture continues. If not, Keating and his family will take a vacation, and as soon as their plane clears the runway, pink slips will begin to flutter down on desks back at headquarters. He constantly pits one staff member against another, one day praising a person to the sky and then without warning cutting the same person off at the knees. Charlie Keating believes that people work better if they are not secure—especially management, for his rage seldom falls upon lower-level employees.

The people around him scramble to keep up with his sudden shifts in position. One day he will make a decision and say it is black. The next day he will call the decision gray. Soon he will insist on white. Suddenly, he will go back to black. Keeping up with this swirl of alternations becomes a full-time job for his executives—the phone can ring at any hour of the day or night, and does. No one is ever off duty. No one can ever be secure. There is an incident from the early eighties that captures all of Charlie Keating's needs and fears. He is convinced that one of his aides in the home-building business is getting kickbacks from subcontractors. Then he discovers that the man has his résumé out and at any moment may jump to a new job before Charlie Keating can prove he's been ripping off the company and have the sweet pleasure of firing him. How to stop the guy from bolting? He does the one thing he knows will ensure that the man will stick around for a while: he hosts a banquet, invites the guy, and announces he is making him a corporate vice president. In a few weeks, Charlie Keating is ready with his evidence and at that moment fires the man. No one gets to walk out on Charlie Keating. But the man sues, and Keating cannot stomach going into the court and having his actions examined by strangers. To avoid this fate, he agrees to pay the man such a big severance payment that the guy is able to live a life of leisure for several years. But he still got to fire him.

He sees someone who is overweight and offers a bonus if he or she will lose weight. An employee is a smoker, a habit Keating abhors, so he promises the guy $100,000 if he'll kick for one year. The man does, collects his hundred grand, and then lights up again. If someone working for him has a financial problem, Keating steps in and makes the problem go away with a bonus. If children are distracting a worker from work, Keating assigns a baby-sitter. "I pay you enough," he'll say to an employee. "Don't be screwing around cleaning your own pool or cutting your own grass." But of course, in the company based on the family and home life, no one really gets to see his or her family or have much home life. This is a common fact of life in American business, perhaps in American life itself. In the eighties, the nation will have a president who preaches family values as a veritable mantra and yet has little to do with his own children and does not even see a new grandchild until the toddler is almost two years old. Keating easily handles this contradiction by constantly ordering family gestures. When his top executives are out of town, they are commanded to buy gifts for their wives. Keating will say, "Go to a nice shop and buy her a really nice something." He is a master at sending out conflicting signals. A grandchild will wander into a key meeting, and everything will stop while Charlie Keating deals with the child as if nothing else in the world could possibly be as important. His daughter Beth is in labor and his son-in-law Robert Wurzelbacher skips a meeting to be with her in the delivery room. "He's not having a baby," Keating snaps. "What the hell's he doing down there?" Someone in the meeting is momentarily stunned and then thinks that Charlie Keating does not fully understand the reasons the father is at the birth, does not remember that his daughter has a history of problem pregnancies, that the baby might be lost. But this assumption is wrong. "Hey," he responds, "kids are born every day, some of them live and some of them die. That's just part of life. Wurz should know where his priorities are."

Chip and Judy Wischer have been married a decade when he finally wears down her resistance to having children. The birth is not easy, the child's chance of surviving seems slim. So Wischer looks to the church. He prays, he makes vows, he swears he will alter his conduct and return to his faith if this child lives. He remains at the hospital throughout the week with his wife. Finally, Keating calls and he tells them that what will be will be and what they both need to do is get back to work, get back to their desks at ACC. And they do. The child lives.

Like Carl Lindner, Keating despises the normal hierarchies of the corporate world and switches titles around so whimsically they become meaningless. Like Lindner, he makes the onetime baby-sitter of his children, Robert Kielty, a high-paid executive. Like Lindner, he stuffs the company with family members. Like Lindner, his key assistant, Judy Wischer, is a tall, attractive blonde. Like Lindner, he has ambitions that far exceed something as plain as throwing up houses. He has not forgotten his former life at AFC, where he played with $2 billion.

Little flickers of the rush he felt at AFC surface from time to time. Stan Demory is his barber in Phoenix, and he opens his shop at 7 A.M. whenever Keating needs a haircut. When, because of the hurly-burly of Keating's life, he misses a few appointments, Demory jokingly tells him, "What you ought to do is put a little chair down in your office and I'd drop by in the morning on my way in here to give you a trim."

"Would you do that?" Keating asks.

"I'd be delighted," Demory replies.

"Done."

"Pardon me?"

"Done," Keating repeats. "I'll find you a nice spot."

Keating targets a ten-by-ten storage room at his office and installs a marble floor, oak cabinets, a fancy sink, artificial plants, a stereo system, a barber's chair, and a giant air conditioner. Stan Demory is impressed. And he is busy. Keating has him cutting everyone's hair so that his executives will have no excuse for not being at work. One day, Demory tells Keating that all he really needs now is a window so that he can grow some plants. The next day he finds a hole has been knocked out in the wall and the window is being installed.

Keating buys the former estate of a local car dealer—a frieze of the Chevrolet emblem circles the rooms. The house squats on twenty-six landscaped and walled acres. It has the feel of a church with the front door leading to a hallway about thirty feet wide and sixty feet long lit by overhead windows. Keating cannot abide the sound of air-conditioning, so a contractor is called in and spends a fortune moving the heating and cooling systems. The $2.5 million mansion is where Charlie Keating dines on fried chicken or corned beef and cabbage and the meals are prepared by his wife and daughters. There is no cook. There is no butler. There is a growing swarm of grandchildren as his daughters marry and Keating houses them in homes nearby or directly on the grounds.

He decides to add a wine cellar and the plans keep changing and his vision of the cellar keeps growing and when it is finished it costs over a hundred thousand dollars. The chamber runs sixty feet deep, is a brick-lined vault with water carefully piped so that it artfully drips down the walls. In the front is a tasting room with a table and chairs. An exit is cut in the cellar, the land is carved, and a patio is created where guests can also drink. Keating uses his cellar for parties. But he never builds a great collection of wines; he seems to have little interest in being judged a connoisseur.

He has more interest in spending money than he has in what money buys. He is always in debt—one of his aides thinks that if Keating had one dollar he would use it as leverage to borrow ten more. He is always competing—he constantly keeps track of Lindner's fleet of planes and tries to upstage him with a finer corporate jet. He knows that money is a way of keeping score in business, and so he diligently tries to increase his own net worth and that of his company. But there is something deeper in Keating's feelings about money. Contempt. He will spend a fortune on clothes and yet never appear strikingly dressed. He will spend $2 million on a house, and yet no one ever seems able to clearly remember much about it. Once Chip Wischer sends a man up to videotape the rooms of the house for insurance purposes in case there is a loss by fire or theft. The camera accidentally topples and shatters a giant Boehm porcelain bird, a gift from Lindner. Wischer is terrified about telling Keating of the mishap. But Charlie Keating explains that the kids had busted the bird up once before and he had just glued it back together. It is important to have things, to be able to buy things, but the things themselves are not important. For Keating money is something to toss away in impulsive gifts to charity, in unexpected bonuses to employees, in outsize tips to waiters. Keating's feelings toward money are perhaps most clearly expressed in his appetite for smashing things, smashing windows, wineglasses, plates, furniture. Money has a power over people, and Charlie Keating knows this, and the way he exorcises this power of money, the way he proves to himself it cannot control him is by destroying things, by squandering money, by living buried with debt and still sailing boldly into the future. His staff can never figure out quite what to give him as a present since he spends so freely and buys whatever he wants whenever he wants it. So they start giving him silver ingots. When they come up to the house for a meeting, they discover the ingots scattered about the house. Charlie Keating is using them as doorstops.

When he finally turns the country club development in Flagstaff around, thanks to salesmanship, hard work, and salt blocks, he brings out his old friend Ted Toma, now retired from the FBI, to be the beverage manager. Toma is appalled when Keating orders a champagne cocktail and lets the rest of the hundred-dollar bottle go flat and unconsumed. He thinks his old friend has changed, suffered some kind of corruption. But then Ted Toma was not in the room when Charlie Keating came home with that first big fee, $10,000 cash in a grocery bag, threw it into the air, and watched it float down to cover the bed and floor.

Debt seems to make Charlie Keating free. The 1983 ACC annual report contains a small announcement on Keating's zeal for debt buried in footnote M, Related Party Transactions. The long note details his recent history of constantly borrowing money from his own company. On December 31, 1982, Keating owed ACC $2,500,000, the sum the result of various loans dating back to 1974 when AFC still owned the home builder. He paid off this sum in full on September 20, 1983. But the note goes on to explain that on November 1, 1983, he borrowed another $2,000,000. Also, the chairman and other officers sell the company hundreds of thousands of shares a year, shares that hardly ever publicly trade and that Keating and his family all but totally control.

To track Charlie Keating is to witness a pattern of constant cash injections, constant purges of money by big spending and yet a strange lack of avarice. He builds up no big bank accounts, he does not seem to sock much away. He is always worth millions on paper, but the millions are in stock in his company and its subsidiaries and the value of this stock is always in question and his companies are always at risk. Like his friend Carl Lindner, he seems drawn to risk. Money is the unexamined value of American society because the society takes its value and importance for granted. In many ways Charlie Keating does not. He is almost a student of the absurdity of money, and perhaps that is why his efforts to mock it—those bottles of champagne left to go flat, the destruction of glasses and tables at parties, the periodic need to pitch tens of thousands of dollars into the air and watch it flutter to the ground—offend almost everyone who witnesses them.

Mike Manning is in Jakarta, he is in Singapore, he is in Oslo, he is in Seoul, he is in Bangkok. He is all over Europe and Asia. Three years out of law school, he has worked on the firm's biggest and most complex commercial litigation. He has done securities fraud cases, patent cases, bank fraud cases. He has defended clients against conspiracy charges. His best friends at the firm make jokes about him. They say he has a separate engine inside of him that others lack and that this engine lacks any kind of governor. Manning does not simply work, he does not seem to know how to stop. On airplanes, he works from takeoff to landing. When he is on the road, he frequently has dinner delivered to his room so that he can continue working until midnight. When he is in Kansas City, he willingly takes work home most nights. He is convinced that hard work can overcome almost any obstacle. He forces himself to think like his opponent and does not feel right about a case until he can predict the moves of his opposition before he makes them. When he is beaten, he studies his defeat and copies things from his adversaries. Once in a patent case, the other lawyer always referred to Manning's client's invention as Brand X, and pretty soon the judge was calling it Brand X, too. Manning was furious, he realized the negative ring the term had. So after that case, he always created a lexicon and used it in every motion, every paper, every statement because he was never going to let an opponent invent the language of one of his cases again.

He is a father now, his first daughter was born in 1979, the same day John Connally announced his candidacy for president. He works long hours, to be sure, but his life has a regular contour. He can schedule weekend golf games. He can attend functions with his wife. He can schedule hours with his daughter. By accident he drifts into international commercial law, and for over three years, from 1981 through 1983, he is often abroad negotiating contracts. He becomes one of the few people in Kansas City who realizes the enormous future lurking in that new term the Pacific Rim. In Asia, he learns a key lesson: patience. Europeans he finds much like Americans—tight schedules, in a hurry, quick to make a deal. But in the Orient, he falls into a different world.

What really stuns him is the infinite patience of Orientals in negotiations and how very good they are at it. Things seem to move slowly, and yet behind this screen of ease and politeness loom the toughest bargainers he has ever faced. He learns that his aggressive nature is not useful when doing a deal in Asia. After three years of this kind of education, Michael Manning is surprised that the Americans who negotiated with the Koreans at the 38th parallel to end the war did not have to give up, say, California.

In the eyes of many who work for him in Phoenix, Charlie Keating seems bored. When Ronald Reagan is elected president in 1980, Keating makes a run at being appointed ambassador to the Bahamas. But his chances end when his settlement with the SEC surfaces (in, to his rage, the *Cincinnati Enquirer*), and this leaves Keating bitter.

On a trip to Salt Lake City Keating attends an outdoor banquet and learns that the dinner has been prepared by a group of South Sea islanders. Tongans. About one hundred and twenty-five of them have been converted, at least partially, by Mormon missionaries in Tonga and have come en masse to Utah under the sway of their leader. The Tongans are a big people and heavy. Their leader maintains his power over the group in part by lifting weights each morning before they begin work. He can bench press three to four hundred pounds. They are gardeners and landscapers, which Keating needs for his developments. Keating hires the whole group, and soon they move as a unit to Phoenix. Now his kingdom has its appropriate vassals.

He moves his antipornography group west with his family. His daughters start popping up on the board, and Keating fights video stores in the Phoenix area that rent blue movies. He reenacts the antifilth rallies he once held in Ohio, and Arizona senator Dennis DeConcini speaks at one in 1979. He also cultivates the young war hero and congressman John McCain. His nemesis, Larry Flynt, has also moved west and settled in Los Angeles, where he pays $2 million for the mansion of Sonny Bono, then spends $3 million remodeling it. Among other new features are 500-pound steel front doors, armed guards, and patrols of attack dogs.

By 1980, high inflation (about 14 percent in 1979) and tight money are killing the real estate business. Housing starts ride at 1.7 million units in 1979 but sink to 940,000 in 1980. Builders begin going bankrupt in a wholesale fashion. Developers mail Federal Reserve chief Paul Volcker hundreds of stamped two-by-fours, and Charlie Keating is inflamed by the Fed's tight money policy. In 1978 Salomon Brothers in New York begins packaging mortgages together and selling shares in the mortgage pool as bonds. The new instrument takes off with inflation, and the mortgage pool zooms from $500 million in 1976 to $1.7 billion by January 1980. (Mortgage bonds will grow to $150 billion by 1986.) Taking a lesson from Salomon, Keating begins issuing a variation on mortgage-backed bonds and in essence provides his own financing for the homes he builds and sells. He closes out his weak operations and loses tens of millions of dollars in Denver when poor soil under one development causes furnaces to bolt through walls and chimneys to separate from houses. Keating makes good on the homes he has sold there and fixes up all the damage. Then he discovers he is being robbed blind by employees in Denver, where his son-in-law Bob Hubbard is in charge of the operation. Hubbard has a habit of coming into his office, then going for a jog and then plotting his lunch. Eventually, ACC drops perhaps $75 million to patch up this wound. Keating does what comes naturally—he humiliates his son-in-law and then promotes him. As for the lost money, he follows his instinct: make it up somewhere else. Like any serious crapshooter, Charlie Keating can accept the inevitability of losses from time to time.

He has only one real strategy: offense. In 1983, he and his associates pump $80,000 into the Phoenix city council races and the election for mayor. This infusion dwarfs all the other contributions, and when the local newspapers question him on tossing so much money into the campaigns, he expresses amazement at the very question and says he is puzzled that other people don't make investments of the same size in the local democracy. What Charlie Keating wants is water for his developments, which he is convinced will work only if built around lakes. In water-short Arizona, this is a red flag to many local citizens (and to other developers), and Keating is constantly fighting to stave off city council votes that might outlaw his ponds. Charlie Keating is not one to take a chance when he can protect himself by making a friend. In the state's attorney general race he gives $50,000 to one candidate, even though the man is running unopposed and raises total contributions from all sources (including Charlie Keating) of $53,000.*

Still, he is losing interest in the business, and it is obvious.

He starts talking about something called merchant banking and hands out to his staff a book on the subject. It is obvious to him that home building is deadly ground and finance is not. He begins taking trips to Europe and cold-calling merchant bankers and financiers like Sir James Goldsmith.

A merchant banker can make direct investments in projects as opposed to merely making loans. And a merchant banker can assume a profit-sharing position. In London, such firms have fine offices with old oil paintings and expensive antique furniture. The

*In 1988, Keating, in an interview with Bowden, said his oversize contribution in the state's attorney race was an honest mistake because he did not realize just how cheaply one could buy Arizona politicians. He explained that back in Ohio you had to kick in fifty grand for a county sheriff. Perhaps the best testament to the political world Keating found in Phoenix comes from a statement by then legislator Bobby Raymond in Stedino and Matera's *What's In It for Me?*, p. 144:

"Understand where I'm comin' from. I don't give a fuck about issues. There's not an issue in this world I give a shit about. I do deals. That's what I do. I mean I do deals. I mean, there's two or three issues that got me here . . . Other than that, I don't give a fuck if school keeps tomorrow."

"If what?" [responds Stedino]

"If school keeps tomorrow. I don't care. I mean, I like the deals of the legislature."

atmosphere is reserved and conservative. But what merchant bankers really do is plunge, they gamble, they take big risks, and they can make big winnings. They are the heart of casino capitalism. In fact, the book Keating loves to hand out has a chapter on the daily business meetings of merchant banking firms and it is entitled "11 A.M. in the Casino." Keating is drawn to the idea, tells people he wants to be one. So far as his staff can tell, ACC is running fine now and making money. But as Chip Wischer senses, for Keating this is hardly enough. "Problem is, it is boring now," Wischer explains. "No thrills."

Larry Flynt cannot seem to stop being sued. He calls *Penthouse* publisher Bob Guccione a homosexual, he calls novelist Jackie Collins a hooker, and naturally they file. In the early eighties he mails a free issue of *Hustler* every month to 535 members of Congress plus the nine judges of the Supreme Court. Justice Sandra Day O'Connor tosses the magazine into the trash along with the rest of her junk mail. But this does not still her anger. So she sits down and writes to *Hustler*'s headquarters in Los Angeles asking to be removed from the mailing list. She gets a personal letter back from Flynt in which he displays his extensive knowledge of abusive and obscene language.

Keith Dickson's brother Bruce works for Charlie Keating in Phoenix. His father lives there also and is self-employed. And he thinks of this one day in November 1982 as he goes about his job in Florida as the public relations director for a swimsuit company. A graduate of the University of Florida and a former member of a world championship swimming team, he realizes he is bored and wonders if maybe he shouldn't go out west and try someplace new. He talks about his restlessness with a friend, and two weeks later they are driving west pulling a U-Haul trailer. He stays with his brother and scouts Phoenix for a job. His brother suggests he try selling insurance for a subsidiary of ACC, the one run by Chip Wischer, who has left Lindner for Keating by that time. Dickson gets the job.

One month later he meets Elaine Keating at the company Christmas party, and they hit it off and begin dating. As the romance blossoms, his brother Bruce gets worried. He warns Keith that the Keatings are a different kind of family than theirs. Bruce likes working for ACC and loves the pay, but he is leery of the Keatings' style and of the power that family members have over anyone in the company. He senses a need for domination in Keating that makes him cautious. But Keith is twenty-two years old, having a good time, and dating the daughter of a multimillionaire. He plunges ahead.

Once Keating realizes that his daughter is enamored of Dickson, he gives him a new job with a big salary, he includes him on trips, he drops hints about what a great future he might have. Elaine and Keith decide to marry in 1983, and she tells him he must ask her father formally for her hand. So he and Keating dine at a French restaurant in Scottsdale and seal the occasion with a bottle of Dom Perignon. Keating gives them a new Mercedes 380 SL as a present. He flies with Dickson to New York to help him select an engagement ring. Dickson is determined to buy his future wife's ring with his own money and spends $4,000. Only much later does he learn that Keating had prearranged with the jeweler to lie about the price. The ring actually costs $20,000 with Keating making up the difference on the side. When they marry in April 1983, Keating spends $150,000 redecorating the church—he tells Keith he was going to do it anyway—and invites Representative John McCain and senators Dennis DeConcini and John Glenn. At the reception at Keating's house there are two bands. There are some small problems. When Keith picks a friend of his to be best man, Keating says he does not like the person and demands that Dickson select someone else. Only after a great deal of skirmishing does he relent.

There are other warning signs, but Dickson ignores them. For example, his friends are ill at ease because Keating has had private investigators search out details of Dickson's life. He assembles a file on his prospective son-in-law and discovers that Dickson was not only a swimming champ in college, but also a hell-raiser and a leader in wild fraternity blowouts. Keating grills him relentlessly on these matters until he is satisfied. After all, Dickson is an athlete, and Keating has a predilection for athletes. His daughter Mary is married to Gary Hall, an Olympic swimmer and Mark Spitz's former roommate.

Keith Dickson is twenty-three years old and no longer shopping at K mart but on Rodeo Drive. He honeymoons in Hawaii, and Keating picks up the tab. And he is being led to believe he will go very far. "My dad really likes you," Elaine tells her new husband. "He thinks you have a good business brain. And if you play your cards right, you might really move up." There are conditions, of course. Dickson plans to buy a house, but Keating puts his foot down. Family members buy the houses Keating picks out, and they live near him. He dictates that Dickson take over the home of another son-in-law, Wurzelbacher.

One thing that keeps Dickson in line is that he believes in Charlie Keating's destiny. He studies him and sees how he breaks all the rules and yet somehow keeps winning and winning. He knows that Keating has this plan: he will buy a deregulated savings and loan, he will use the bank's money to build up the company, he will create a dynasty through his son, son-in-laws, and possibly grandchildren, and he will retire in 1990 and become a kind of monarch in residence. "Charlie Keating," he recalls years later, "was the type of guy who could take a helicopter ride over Phoenix and say, 'There's millions of dollars down there.' The guy just saw opportunity everywhere." Dickson wants to be part of this future. Keating teaches him lessons, such as he should always pay people too much. That way when you fire them they don't sue. And if they are good, they won't leave.

Dickson is instantly drafted into the regimen of Charlie Keating's world and adjusts to a new life of travel, lots of money, parties with the rich. He senses the company is, for lack of a better word, a cult. Everyone kind of looks the same—white, clean, well dressed, fair-haired—and the employees have no other real life beyond the company. By the time he gets to work at 5:30 in the morning, there are already three or four pages of agenda notes on his desk from Keating. They spell out his day—who he will meet, what car he will drive, whether he will attend a political function that night (two or three a week, usually), when and where he must show up for a family dinner, and so forth. Each day every member of the Keating family gets an agenda, fashioned and dictated by Charlie Keating. One day Dickson comes home from work and finds his entire house refurnished—furniture, rugs, china, lamps, everything—and neither he nor his wife has made any of the selections or known such a thing was in the offing. Sometimes his wife complains about her life, about being rich but really a puppet. But in the next moment, she is running off to see her father. Dickson decides the family members are under a spell.

But for all of Keating's efforts at control, for all of his intelligence gathering, there is one thing about Keith Dickson he has failed to discover or curb: two or three times a week, Keith does cocaine. He feels it is natural, that it goes with driving a Mercedes, with having lots of money, with drinking champagne, with being a powerful person. And he knows he is not the only person in the company snorting powder.

On July 20, 1983, Elaine and Keith hold a housewarming party and celebrate Dickson's birthday. While the party is in full swing, Keith calls a friend in San Francisco and his friend hears all the noise in the background and says that it sounds like Dickson has been doing some "marching powder." Dickson confesses that his friend is right and says he picked some up that afternoon. Elaine is listening in on this conversation, and she explodes with anger. Their guests flee. C3 comes over and is very upset, and Keith's brother stops by and tries to calm the situation. At two or three in the morning, Elaine does the inevitable; she calls her father who is vacationing in Ireland. "You son of a bitch," Keating tells Dickson over the phone. "I've given you everything. You've blown it all." He summons them both.

Because of flight schedules, the couple has a stopover in Washington, D.C., and as soon as they've checked into the Watergate Hotel, Dickson calls the priest in Phoenix who married them. In the past, Charlie Keating has sent the priest on a trip around the world, redecorated his church to the tune of $150,000, and given a great deal of money. Keith Dickson tells the priest that he is in trouble and needs counseling. He finds no solace in the priest.

Dickson refuses to give up. He walks the streets, knocking on church doors regardless of denomination, and finally he finds a priest. The father at first protests that he is in the middle of dinner, but eventually he gives in. Dickson tells him his story for three solid hours, and the priest is stunned. He says to Dickson, "Let me tell you something, son. The biggest mistake you can make in your life is to get on that plane and go to Ireland. I don't care who the man is, you and your wife are the family. Why don't you sit down and work this out amongst yourselves?" Dickson returns to the hotel and relates this conversation to Elaine, and she agrees they should try to work it out themselves. Then C3 calls, and she explains their new plan to him. He asks her to put Keith on the phone and then explains to him, "If you don't get on that plane, I will fly to Washington and break every bone in your body."

When they arrive in Ireland, Keith has been up for forty-eight hours straight. As they ride out to the castle where Keating is staying, Dickson finds the countryside beautiful. Charlie is standing outside, his body shaking, his lips quivering. He asks, "Why did you do it? Why did you do it?" Dickson can only say, "I don't know. I just don't know. I'm sorry. We're going to have to work this out." But Dickson is wrong. "The only thing I can give you," Keating explains, "is a plane ticket home to your mama." And then he pulls out seven one-hundred-dollar bills, hands them over, and says good-bye. Keith Dickson leaves his wife weeping in her mother's arms.

He flies to his parents' home in North Carolina and promptly has a nervous breakdown. Then a sheaf of documents arrives seeking an annulment. Dickson fills them out and tells the Vatican his side of the story. Keating has a sixty-page deposition assembled as evidence for the annulment, a document Dickson views as a pack of lies. Dickson has decided that he wants no money, no property, that he will take nothing from the marriage. But when he reads over the deposition vilifying him, he balks at signing the annulment papers. The terms are stiff. He discovers Elaine is pregnant, and the documents Keating has prepared insist that Dickson's name cannot and will not be on the birth certificate.

Dickson has another brother, Rob, who works for Senator John Tower, and at 1 A.M. Rob gets a call from an ACC executive, who gets right to the point: "If your brother does not sign that document, Bruce will lose all of his stock options, you will lose your job with John Tower, and your father will never work again." So the three brothers have a conference call, and Keith says he does not want to sign the document because it is a lie. But as they talk they come to believe the threats, and as their belief in the threats grows, Keith falters. And he signs.

He never visits Phoenix again and becomes a dark legend within ACC, a symbol of Charlie Keating's ability to break anyone. He speaks with Elaine Keating only once after he leaves her in Ireland. Months later, she calls late at night and she sounds as if she has been drinking. She wants to get back together, and Keith is tempted since he still loves Elaine. He says he will do it if she will move to North Carolina. He never hears from her again.

In November 1983 Keating's aide Robert Kielty is in Washington on business and is picked up by the driver for Representative McCain, a Brad Boland. Kielty notices that Boland is tall, as is Elaine. He tells McCain that Elaine needs a date for the company Christmas party and asks if Boland is available. A few months later, McCain is touring Vietnam with Walter Cronkite and his phone rings in the middle of the night. It is Boland, announcing his resignation from the staff. He tells McCain he is going to marry Elaine Keating. Not long afterward, McCain's wife, Cindy, sees Boland driving around Phoenix in a Mercedes and wearing a ruby-studded tuxedo.

Keating is a compulsive reader, a man always rooting through books and magazines looking for clues. He may not finish a book, he may simply devour chapters until he gets the drift, but he is eager to educate himself. As the U.S. economy in the late seventies and early eighties begins to move from equity to debt, from stable money to inflation, from production to finance, he is well aware of this change. His staff is constantly being inundated by him with newspaper stories, magazine pieces, books. He hires them young so that they will obey and fires information at them wholesale so that they will learn. And what Charlie Keating knows is that it is time to get out of home building.

"We looked at the home-building business," he sums up in 1988, "as a financial business—which, if we have any capabilities, it's probably there in finances. We decided we had to figure out how to finance the buyer and so forth and so on. We became the largest home builder in Phoenix and the largest home builder in Colorado. As a result of that we became one of the top ten home builders in the country in short order and stayed there until we got out of the business. We were building three to five thousand houses a year. We weren't smart enough to stay out of Houston, we were lucky enough. We just didn't go there. We were dumb enough to go into Utah and Seattle. We just didn't get big enough quick enough. The market soured and taught us a lesson before we could get trapped. A lot of business is luck, not skill. We just happened to have gotten lucky in Denver. We weren't smart enough to get out of Denver, we were in Denver when it got dead. But by that time we were in other businesses. We were able to carry it. We got killed in Denver, we closed down in Denver."

Of course, there is a vision. "Here in Phoenix," he continues, "we never got hurt, we always relied on Phoenix, and when we got out in Phoenix in '85 we simply sold the management of the company, but it was a thriving business then and it is today. We had always thought, even from the day we started in '76–'77, we had had a program that roughly in '85 we would get out because we felt that the demographics didn't underscore a strong housing market for the rest of the century. We had that right. We had always projected it, but we didn't act properly on it. But the caution, that was constantly with us, served us in good stead. It kept us from some excessive things that killed other builders. It wasn't intuition or instinct, we just always felt it was there, we felt that the demographics would phase out, which indeed they have. Some guys brighter than us have seen the viability of adult-only leisure communities. Those are real good. Basically, we didn't see the boom continuing."

It is luck, of course, that must always be emphasized. It is almost as if Keating fears God will strike him down like some modern Job if he claims too much credit, if he does not stress the mistakes, the bumbling, the importance of fate. But there are other matters Keating does not bring up. Perhaps they do not matter to him, and in any event it will be years before anyone really notices what is buried in the annual financial reports that tally his success as a home builder. Continental Homes may build thousands of homes, but what drives the profits are accounting techniques. Keating follows an accounting procedure that books interest payments—money paid out on loans—as an asset, not a debit. This practice is called capitalizing interest. For example, in 1980, his company pays $25 million in interest on its debts but books $15 million of this as income. In 1981, ACC pays out $32 million in interest but books $18 million of this as income. The effect can be magical. In 1981 ACC lost $2.6 million building and selling houses but, after working over the books, reported net income of $3.7 million. By 1983, he is reporting net earnings of $19,119,000, yet through the magic of numbers is carrying $120,000,000 in losses forward to shield himself from taxes. All of this is perfectly acceptable under GAAP, generally accepted accounting principles. But then, if one shops around, there is very little that is not satisfactory in the wonderland that is GAAP.

One thing Keating notices in his reading is a bill signing in the

Rose Garden of the White House by Ronald Reagan on October 15, 1982. The legislation item has the dull, safe name of the Garn–St. Germain Depository Institutions Act. "All in all, I think we hit the jackpot," Reagan notes as he inscribes his name. In fact, the president considers the bill "the most important legislation for financial institutions in the last fifty years."*

The jackpot that enthralls the president is quite simple: the federal government will guarantee deposits in savings and loans while at the same time allowing the thrifts' managers a wide latitude as to where they invest these deposits. While in the past several years savings and loans were restricted to home loans and killed by the spread between what they paid for money and what they could charge for money, now they are free to taste the strong waters of direct investment, of junk bonds, of pretty much anything that catches their fancy. This is called deregulation, and it is the essence of Ronald Reagan's faith: that U.S. businessmen, left to their own devices, will create great wealth. Like many of his insights, this is one based on his lack of experience. He has never been a businessman, but he did spend years as a spokesman for General Electric, and so he thinks he has been a businessman.

When Keating was ten years old, there was a political battle over the issue of thrifts. The Great Depression had busted many of the savings and loans (then uninsured) and cost Americans $200 million. Franklin Delano Roosevelt ran in 1932 railing against the idea of insuring thrifts, noting, "We do not wish to make the United States government liable for the mistakes and errors of individual banks, and put a premium on unsound banking in the future." But once in office, he succumbed to the notion and created federal insurance for thrifts to the tune of $5,000 per depositor. He was building on a bill signed by Herbert Hoover in 1932 that created the Federal Home Loan Bank Board, a safety net of twelve regional banks that was supposed to function for thrifts the way

---

*On August 22, 1990, when U.S. District Judge Stanley Sporkin hands down the decision that finally and forever strips Charlie Keating and ACC of Lincoln, he will dryly comment in a footnote, "It must be remembered that the purpose of deregulation is to foster the ability of private organizations to compete and not to provide a license to steal." (Sporkin decision, p. 47, note 30.) Sporkin also, while at the SEC, headed the prosecution in 1979 that argued that Charlie Keating was guilty of numerous security violations and that fined him $1.4 million and barred him from the securities markets for three months.

the Federal Reserve functioned for other banks. This system more or less worked until the 1970s, when it became apparent that no one could buy money at 15 percent or 20 percent and survive if legally restricted to selling money at 5.5 percent. By 1980, 85 percent of the thrifts were losing money. Congress inched its way toward deregulation. In 1980, it removed the cap on what thrifts could pay for deposits. Depositors came back to the savings and loans when they offered 17 percent interest. But the thrifts were still caught in the home mortgage business and buried alive under old loans at a low rate of fixed interest.

The solution was the bill Reagan signed in 1982, which gave the thrifts freedom to do pretty much whatever they wanted with the money. Almost instantly, a new industry came into being, the brokering of jumbo accounts, $100,000 units. By 1984, there were $34 billion in brokered deposits in federally insured thrifts. All this was accomplished by one of the most cost-effective lobbying actions in the history of the republic. The U.S. Savings and Loan League represented the nation's thrifts, and it invested heavily in a representative from Rhode Island, Fernand St. Germain, the chairman of the House Banking Committee. St. Germain had two joys in life, food and women. So day in and day out the U.S. League picked up the tab for him and his companions at the best restaurants in Washington. This bill ran to about $20,000 a year.

Shortly after the Garn–St. Germain bill was made law, the California legislature sweetened the deal by passing the Nolan bill. Where the federal government still retained some limits on the percentage of deposits that could go into speculative investments, the Nolan bill removed any restrictions and made it possible to plunge 100 percent of a thrift's assets into anything. One motive for this act of bravado by California legislators was their fear that the new loose federal charters would prompt a wholesale flight by the state's chartered thrifts. And if that happened, how could a state politician collect contributions from them? Something akin to a gold rush takes place. John Connally's friends from the Middle East begin shopping around to buy U.S. thrifts. Michael Milken and his colleagues at Drexel hold meetings to plot how thrifts can fit into their speculative plans. And Charlie Keating, the man who wishes to be a merchant banker, now sees his chance to be one with federally guaranteed dollars.

*　　　*　　　*

Years later, the players in this production will be characterized as crooks, bad apples, financial deviants. They will be considered villains who plunged massively into debt, took big risks, failed to follow prudent business practices. They will be individuals who invested in junk bonds and real estate, who played currency markets, tackled global markets. The public will see them in this light and be appalled at the risks they ran, the eagerness they displayed in assuming debt. This same public will itself embrace a debt—government and private—that by 1984 stood at $7.1 trillion. Many businessmen also will scorn these high flyers, somehow forgetting that in 1984 alone, U.S. business took on $140 billion in new debt solely to finance corporate mergers and takeovers. In other words, a massive new debt was swallowed that on balance hardly added one job or built one new factory. And finally, government will denounce these players, investigate them, hold hearings about them, while it streaks toward new levels of debt, eventually floating in an annual sea of red ink of $400 billion.

All will over time share a contempt for a strange speech given by President Jimmy Carter in the summer of 1979, a talk to the American people that was filed under the category of "malaise," a word that never appeared in the statement itself. And almost everyone will forget what Carter said:

> In a nation that was proud of hard work, strong families, close-knit communities and our faith in God, too many of us now tend to worship self-indulgence and consumption. Human identity is no longer defined by what one does, but what one owns. But we have discovered that owning things and consuming things does not satisfy our longing for meaning. We have learned that piling up material goods cannot fill the emptiness of lives which have no confidence or purpose.

In the early eighties, Charlie Keating is anxious to be a player again. Carl Lindner has finally succeeded in taking his company private, buying up outstanding shares at bargain prices in the depressed stock market. And now Lindner no longer has to answer to obnoxious shareholders or listen to the nagging authorities at the SEC. He and Keating often talk on the phone before dawn. Lindner has deepened his relationship with Michael Milken, become almost a father figure to him. With a short phone call, Milken can count on Lindner to sign on for, say, $300 million. Milken has crisscrossed the country preaching his faith in junk bonds, showing with charts how they outperform more traditional and secure bonds. He has converted so many investors that his junk bond operation has functionally become the key business of Drexel. In 1978, when he learns that his father has cancer, he moves his operation to southern California, where he was raised. He buys the guesthouse on Clark Gable's old estate in Encino, ten blocks from his mother's home. He opens an office in Century City, fills it with fifteen employees, and spreads them out along his famous X-shaped trading desk. They start work at 4 A.M. in order to be in sync with the New York markets, and they work until 8 P.M. Many of them have little or no experience. Milken prefers that. He wants people who have fire in their bellies, who want to be rich. And who will do what he tells them. No one leaves for lunch or dinner. No one is allowed to be distracted—Milken hires people to take care of their dry cleaning, to drop their mail off at the post office, to fix appliances in their houses, to tend to their pets. And he pays them very well—Jim Dahl is hired, for example, in 1981 for a salary of $20,000 a month, plus commissions. Even this pay soon seems paltry. By 1982, Dahl is making $1 million. But of course this is small change for Milken. He takes home $45 million that year. The pressure is very great, of course. Once a salesman starts screaming hysterically because his phone has gone dead during trading hours. The staff discovers the salesman has nervously chewed through the phone cord. Yet Milken's world remains a kind of national secret. He gives no interviews, he allows no photographs of himself to circulate—he buys every copy the wire services have. In Drexel's annual report he is not pictured, and he insists that any listing of his bond department be alphabetical, not by rank. But Milken is not a secret to Charlie Keating, nor to a legion of many other outsiders who know just what they would do if they could just get their hands on some capital, on some money.

In January 1983, Keating is in Los Angeles to tour various home builders, then moves on to Snowmass for an ACC directors' meeting. February finds him in Aspen, then a brief stopover in Cincinnati, and finally on to New York, where he stays at the

Helmsley Palace and dines at Le Cirque. He visits bankers—
Manufacturers Hanover, Chase Manhattan—to sell them on ACC's
success and seek yet more credit. He meets with representatives of
something called the Saudi-European Bank, and then he flies
down to Florida and on to Cat Cay. Finally, on March 18, he lands
in Los Angeles, and at 11 A.M. he meets with Tom Spiegel of Columbia Savings and Loan, a leader in the newly deregulated thrift
world and a gluttonous consumer of junk bonds. Later he meets
with Michael Milken. Keating is setting up a junk bond issue on
ACC of $125 million. Some of the money will go to pay down old
debt. But about half is for a shopping spree. Charlie Keating is in
the market for a California savings and loan.

It is summer, and for the first time in years Larry Flynt feels
somewhat comfortable in his twenty-room Bel-Air mansion. For
years he has lived in pain. "Imagine," he says, "standing up to
your thighs in boiling water. From the moment I was shot, that's
what it was like for me, unbearable pain with no letup." To blot
out this sensation, he turned to Dilaudid, a morphinelike pain
killer. His wife turned to coke. And now an operation has ended
Flynt's pain, and he and his wife have kicked their drug habits.
Larry Flynt is anxious to return to the world. His cash flow is
$30 million a year from the magazine. He has put out an offer that
he will pay $1 million to any top television or movie actress who
will spread her legs for *Hustler*. And he has a more innovative project. He is going to produce a porn movie. He has located a medically certified eighteen-year-old virgin. She will be deflowered on
camera. "She was holding out for the right man," Flynt explains,
"but the right price won out."

He tells people, "I've done more than anybody in modern history to protect the First Amendment—I've given up my manhood."
When a court slaps a gag rule on him because of his outbursts,
he shows up in his wheelchair wearing a diaper made out of the
American flag.

He will not be put down. He hates the Rev. Jerry Falwell, a television evangelist and kingpin in a configuration of the religious
right that goes by the name of the Moral Majority. So Larry Flynt
publishes a parody advertisement for Campari that consists of an
interview with Jerry Falwell.

*   *   *

JERRY FALWELL TALKS ABOUT THE FIRST TIME

Falwell: My first time was in an outhouse outside Lynchburg, Virginia.

Interviewer: Wasn't it a little cramped?

Falwell: Not after I kicked the goat out.

Interviewer: I see, you must tell me about it.

Falwell: I never really expected to make it with Mom, but then after she showed all the other guys in town such a good time, I figured, "What the hell?"

Interviewer: But your Mom? Isn't that a little odd?

Falwell: I don't think so. Looks don't mean that much in a woman.

Interviewer: Go on.

Falwell: Well, we were drunk off our God-fearing asses on Campari . . . and Mom looked better than a Baptist whore with a $100 donation.

Interviewer: Campari in the crapper with Mom . . . how interesting. Well, how was it?

Falwell: The Campari was great, but Mom passed out. . . .

Interviewer: Did you ever try it again?

Falwell: Sure . . . lots of times. But not in the outhouse. Between Mom and the shit, the flies were too much to bear.

Interviewer: We meant the Campari.

Falwell: Oh, yeah. I always get sloshed before I go out to the pulpit. You don't think I could lay down all that bullshit sober, do you?

When Charlie Keating comes to Los Angeles to meet with Michael Milken he must drive very near to where Larry Flynt lives and plots his exploration of the First Amendment. But it is unlikely he enjoys the parody of Falwell in *Hustler.* Keating knows Falwell and donates money to his fight against smut and declining morals. If there is one thing that truly seems to unnerve Charlie Keating, it is disorder. That is why desks must be spotless, employees perfectly groomed, and why he can look out his office window and see a huge Tongan gardener bending over to pick up a single leaf on the lawn. And yet, like Larry Flynt, he cannot seem to act without creating disorder, without shattering other people's calm. So naturally he hates Larry Flynt. And just as naturally, as he speeds past Flynt's mansion in Los Angeles while the porn king contemplates a virgin being deflowered on camera, Charlie Keating has his own dreams of how to shake things up.

Donald Crocker is not really interested in the call from the banking lawyer, but the attorney tells him that he has a client who would like to buy Lincoln Savings and Loan, the bank Crocker heads, for $16 a share. Crocker is in no hurry to sell, but since he is going to a convention in Scottsdale anyway he agrees to talk to the proposed buyer, Charlie Keating. He waits until his last day in Arizona to make the call. Keating is upset. "I was waiting for your call," he says. "I thought you were going to call earlier in the week. I could have taken you to dinner." Keating dispatches a driver to pick Crocker up and bring him over to ACC headquarters.

Keating gets right to the point: "I want to buy your company."

"We're not for sale," Crocker responds, "but if we ever sold to anybody I'd have to make sure that the Federal Home Loan Bank Board would approve him as a buyer. I read an article in 1979 in *The Wall Street Journal* about your having a problem with the SEC. I want to make sure I don't enter negotiations with someone when it turns out he isn't a qualified buyer."

Keating goes immediately into his sell. For half an hour, he explains how he never really did anything wrong, how the SEC was hypersensitive, how he'd pled rather than fight the charges in order to protect himself and his family and to avoid legal costs. And then he makes one more point: he'll raise his offer to $21 a share in cash. Crocker may have been holding out for the right man, but he recognizes the right price. Lincoln at the moment has an actual net worth of $34 million, and here is Charlie Keating offering to pay $51 million. In September 1983, they close the deal at the Burbank Airport. At this moment Keating hauls out a copy of *Forbes,* which lists Carl Lindner as one of the nation's richest men, pegged at a personal worth of $250 million, stabs at the name with his finger, and tells the mystified Crocker, "Soon you'll see me in here." The transaction has taken one week.

Technical hurdles in the regulatory agencies will take up a few more months. The federal government wishes to know Keating's plans for the thrift, and he tells them he will finance home loans and keep the institution's regular management.* He presents himself as a successful businessman, and certainly ACC's books look very fine that fall of 1983. The company's stock has split 400 to 1, and yet somehow even with this massive new issue, the per share value has gone from a low bid of $3.75 in the third quarter to $10.50 in the fourth quarter. Where these numbers come from is never quite clear since Keating and his family control almost all of the stock and little is ever publicly traded. Also, the onerous debt-to-equity ratio of 216 to 1 in 1978 has shrunk to a 1.5 to 1 ratio, this despite the new $125 million junk bond sale peddled by Michael Milken. But no one questions the company's numbers, certainly not Keating's auditor, the Big Eight accounting firm of Arthur Andersen & Co. American Continental Corporation is a successful home-building business—just look at the books—and now for $51 million it has bought a savings and loan with a billion dollars worth of assets. And Charlie Keating is about to embark on his dream of being a merchant banker. He can feel the rush of doing deals, he can feel the power. In December 1983, he announces that his company will give $100,000 a year for ten years to the St. Vincent de Paul Society in order to help out the homeless. He is already giving large amounts to Mother Teresa and Father Ritter of Covenant House. Robert Kielty, former baby-sitter to his children and now Keating's key in-house attorney, explains that this giving has no significant tax advantages since ACC is already rich with tax loss carryforwards. It is prompted by other motives. Besides, ACC has plenty of money—projected after-tax profits for 1983 are expected to be around $18 million, the company announces. A merchant banker, a prince of finance.

At the time Charlie Keating buys Lincoln Savings and Loan, Larry Flynt is, among other things, running for president as a Republican and seeking to place X-rated ads on television touting his

---

*For example, in its Change of Control Application, October 13, 1983, ACC stated, "While it is anticipated that the current officers of the Holding Company [ACC] and the Institution [Lincoln] will remain upon consummation of the proposed transaction, the Applicant [ACC] intends to augment this management team. . . . In accordance with the provisions of the Community Reinvestment Act of 1977 ("CRA"), no changes are expected in the performance by the Institution [Lincoln] after the proposed acquisition in helping to meet the credit needs of its entire service area, including low- and moderate-income neighborhoods."

candidacy. But he is also busy in the nation's courts. In 1983, he wheels into the chamber of the U.S. Supreme Court with a King James Bible in his lap—the very chamber where Charlie Keating's two daughters watched in the late fifties as their father was admitted to practice before the high bench. Flynt has asked to represent himself (the root of this case is a cartoon in *Hustler* that implies that *Penthouse* publisher Bob Guccione has given his female vice president a venereal disease), but the court insists he have counsel. Flynt is not about to be denied. Nor does he seem to be awed by the judges, a group Justice Oliver Wendell Holmes, Jr., once described as "nine scorpions in a bottle."

He surveys the nine justices in their black robes and says, "You goddamn fuckin' assholes, all nine of you," and then turning to Justice Sandra Day O'Connor, he adds, "and you token cunt, you. Yeah, you, you bitch. All of you are denyin' me my constitutional right to counsel of my choice, namely myself, an' when I get to 1600 Pennsylvania Avenue, I'm sendin' the FBI over to lock every one of you motherfuckers up. I'm gonna charge you with obstructin' justice."

Chief Justice Warren Burger shouts, "Remove that man! . . . Take him into custody!"

As Flynt is wheeled from the room he roars, "Fuck this court!"

A day later Flynt explains his feelings to a reporter. "You shoulda seen Sandra Day O'Connor's face," he notes. "I didn't wanna be sexist, you know. I started to jus' call 'em eight assholes and one cunt, but I thought that would be a sexist remark. . . ."

Later, many will see Keating's ambitions and his successes as a fraud, an illusion perpetrated on an innocent and basically sound society. This belief will eventually become a rock-hard certainty in the press and in the minds of millions of American citizens. But Charlie Keating is probably more in step with the mores and standards of his country than at any other time of his long and busy life.* As a religious man, he is witnessing the rise of the

---

*In 1982, for example, General Electric, Boeing, General Dynamics, and fifty-seven other large U.S. corporations did not pay a penny in taxes to the federal government. This fact was used by Secretary of the Treasury Donald Regan to educate President Ronald Reagan in late 1983 on the need for tax reform. (See Donald T. Regan, *For the Record: From Wall Street to Washington,* Harcourt Brace Jovanovich, New York, 1988, pp. 194–195.) When so informed, President Reagan said, "I just didn't realize that things had gotten that far out of line."

religious right. He is also witnessing the assault by both fundamentalist preachers and feminists on pornography. He is living at a time where there is a growing revolt against the idea of women having the right to an abortion. Nor are his lavish tastes out of step with the times. The public is fascinated with the conspicuous consumption of the rich and the wily tactics used to stay rich. The vice president will maintain an unoccupied hotel room in Texas in order to avoid paying state income tax. At the time Charlie Keating buys Lincoln Savings and Loan, Steve Ross will be running Warner Communications and will find it essential that the corporation maintain a $6 million hideaway in Acapulco, Mexico. Ross will routinely turn in business expenses for odd necessities such as $24,000 for sneakers. He will keep a briefcase stuffed with cash in his office. He will take the company jet to Vegas and generally play high-stakes blackjack—a particular pastime at which he says he makes $60,000 to $90,000 a visit. He will not report these feats to the IRS, since, as he finally concludes, his losses balance out his winnings. He will become a regular feature in society pages. When allegations of fraud arise from time to time, he will select the Fifth Amendment as his best response. All his friends will say that what he craves is to be loved and what he really gives is charm. And by the end of the decade, he will essentially pay himself about $78 million for three hundred and sixty-five days' work and no one will try to file criminal charges against him for this act of self-evaluation.*

The very rules for making clean money, for having a decent living, are in flux at this moment in the early eighties. In the first few months of 1984, as Charlie Keating dreams his dream of being a merchant banker, Michael Milken and Carl Lindner help T. Boone Pickens of Texas make a run on the Gulf Oil Company. This is in a business sense no easy game since Gulf has 497 subsidiaries, so many that there is no swift and sure way even to analyze the company. They are beaten by an offer from Chevron of $80 a share, a $13.3 billion offer. Milken financed the move against Gulf by es-

---

*There is almost nothing to be said about how Americans confront the challenge of great wealth that has not already been said brilliantly by Thorstein Veblen in his turn-of-the-century classic, *A Theory of the Leisure Class.* Naturally, Veblen is little read by economists or anyone else. Periodically his works surface in odd volumes like William Grieder's *Secrets of the Temple* and then sink again beneath the waves of conspicuous consumption.

sentially penning notes and making phone calls: he got people to promise to contribute money if they ever had to someday, the famous "highly confident" letter with which Drexel will terrify the boardrooms of America. Their profits from this feint against Chevron total $760 million. Ivan Boesky, operating independently, clears $70 million on this play. As for Milken himself, in 1984, as Keating makes his move toward the big money in the big casino, Milken will take home $123.8 million in pay. Others notice these feats. That spring Milken raises $500 million for Pickens's further raids and also helps Saul Steinberg make a move on the Walt Disney Company. These are not freak events: in one week that spring it is said Milken raises through junk bonds $1.3 billion for Metromedia, $1.2 billion for Occidental Petroleum, $325 million for Saul Steinberg, and $100 million for Kohlberg Kravis Roberts & Company, the leveraged buyout specialists. These actions will not clean up the air or the water, feed the poor or save the dwindling forests. These actions will not necessarily create jobs. These actions will not build factories. These actions will not fend off the competition of the Japanese. These actions will not make the economy stronger or the national debt less. Nor will these actions offend the administration in Washington, one gearing to run for reelection on the slogan of a new morning in America. But these actions will catch the attention of Charlie Keating because he is a man alert to the world in which God has placed him.

Keating does not formally assume possession of Lincoln until February 22, 1984. Five days later, the local business journal in Phoenix asks him, "If there was one statement you could make to the public about Charles Keating, Jr., what would it be?"

And Charlie Keating answers, "I don't really know. I don't really know."

Charlie Keating is eager. He has the savings and loan, he has billions he can invest and increase. He can get into rooms where he was not welcomed before. And so he is excited, he is in a hurry, and he is very difficult to be around. When he decides to add some coverage to his life insurance, Chip Wischer strikes back. Keating has had a prostate condition for years and problems with hemorrhoids. So as part of the medical examination Wischer, head of all company insurance policies, orders up the use of a proctoscope. Keating comes back to the office grumbling, "How can they do these goddamn things to you? Goddamn, I can't even sit down!"

The test was totally unnecessary, but Wischer had ordered it anyway. Because it was necessary for him.

SOMEDAY
THE WALL STREET JOURNAL
IS GOING TO WRITE
ABOUT US

The year 1984 will remain a blur to Charlie Keating's employees. He hits the ground running. When he visits his new possession, Lincoln Savings and Loan, he discovers musty branch offices decorated with various works of stained glass, a hobby of Donald Crocker's. In the back room, women work over their tallies with crank adding machines, and two-hour lunches are the norm. For recreation the staff puts together huge jigsaw puzzles, and when these are completed they are hung on the walls. They have a Ping-Pong table at work and hold in-house tournaments. Charlie Keating has promised the federal regulators that he will keep Lincoln's management intact. He spends his first month of ownership largely in Los Angeles and discovers one Lincoln executive has been selling Amway to other employees during most of his work hours. Swiftly, the management figures are pink slipped. Keating hates personnel departments, so he fires everyone in Lincoln's personnel department. His lawyers try to stop him, but he insists. Severance pay is very generous, and no one sues. The branches have no automatic teller machines. Boom, they are installed. Keating hosts a contest to name them, and his own entry wins: "Teller Yes." He explains that for years he has been constantly answering questions about whether his daughters can do something by saying "Tell her yes." No one questions his choice.

He needs more room, much more room. The headquarters he inherits are not adequate to his ambitions, so new space is rented and decorated with fine furniture and paintings. He hires young, quick-witted talent. Ray Fidel, a man dedicated to competing in marathons and to motivating people, is brought in to run the branches. Keating sees the branches as vacuums for sucking up money, and Fidel is his cheerleader. At first Fidel is abashed at his new position. He sees himself as an entrepreneur, and because of this self-image, he quite naturally hates bankers. "I can't believe I'm getting involved with banking," he laments. "My father would disown me." He adjusts, perhaps by devising his own personnel policy. Anyone who wants a job must race him in pushing office chairs down the hallway with the winner getting hired. For the day-to-day operations, Robin Symes, a kind of human computer, is in charge. He is electric with the possibilities and announces in one staff meeting, "Someday they are going to be writing about us in *The Wall Street Journal.*"

They are part of a new master race being constructed by Keating. They tend to look alike; young, clean-cut overachievers. Their jobs are shuffled regularly, their titles meaningless. They are picked by Keating because he senses they possess the right genetic stock and are at his whim parachuted into one of the dozens of subsidiaries. A joke among management is that one day they will get onto one of the corporate jets and discover that Keating's favorite chef has been made the pilot.

Keating's dream of being a merchant banker has now fused with his staff's dream of making history. And making money, a lot of money. What will become known as the savings and loan crisis begins with a group of people who think they are better than other people and who know they will do things no one before them has imagined. "It was an atmosphere," one ACC executive recalls, "of real positive excitement that we were at the dawn of a whole new age in banking for the United States, and Charlie really felt that the California law [the Nolan bill] was a precursor to what was going to be happening internationally. He thought the Japanese had started it all by having aggressive investment powers, and that the Japanese banks were growing aggressively. He saw that as a threat to the United States' full system of financial institutions. . . . What this legislature had done in California was create in effect a merchant bank and charter. . . . A merchant bank lends money but also gets equity participation. . . . We would sit in the conference room up in the second floor, and he'd have the key people who were going to be involved with Lincoln. . . . What he would talk to people about, you know, get your mind set on how this was going to be tremendous investment opportunities, and one of the things I will never forget is that he used to talk a lot about underwriting and the proper way to determine who to lend money to. . . . I mean, there was a general feeling that, hey, this company is gonna make history."

What this new invention does is harvest assets. The money is guaranteed by the federal government. The regulations are at the moment all but extinct. "At the end of every quarter," a Keating aide remembers, "he'd sit down with his top executives and say, 'Let's look over our crop. What's right to harvest? Where are the gains?' It was an accounting-driven company. But he wouldn't apologize for that. He'd say, 'You're right, we buy and sell assets and the accountants are an integral part of that.' What's fascinating to me when I watched him up close, he'd push, he'd scream, he'd yell, he'd berate, he'd be aggressive, but in the end, he'd do whatever the accountants told him. He might get pissed off and then get new accountants, but . . ."

He is driven, he is gracious, he is savage, he is kind. He walks through his offices, and he knows every secretary by name. He goes into the men's room, and standing by him at the next urinal is Joe Calluchi, the husband of one of his three executive secretaries. He asks him what the federal funds rate is that day, and Joe Calluchi does not know but says he will go and check. Keating goes into a meeting and rants and raves about how nobody is taking their job seriously enough, about how he just asked for the federal funds rate and a staff member did not know. He tells them to fire that man. Fire him right now. Keep everyone off balance.

This is the big casino. For $51 million dollars, raised by selling a stock issue, he has bought a bank with a billion dollars' worth of assets, and now he is putting them into play. He will not fail this time. This will not be a repeat of Cincinnati. He is very careful: he makes every decision concerning Lincoln, he is a micromanager. But he holds no position at the bank. He will not be charged by federal regulators again; he is determined to avoid the punishment once dished out to him by Stanley Sporkin at the SEC.

His staff lives on a kind of red alert. Robert Kielty, who heads his legal department, keeps a bag packed in his office, carries his passport on him at all times, as do Keating's three personal secretaries. They are making history, and history can be made without any warning. But even careful attention to Keating's rapid-fire mind, to his mood swings, to his impulsive nature, to his unwritten guidelines for personnel, even this close attention is no guarantee of security. Sometimes an employee blessed with a huge bonus will ask Keating to delay it until January 1 for tax purposes. And then the explosion occurs. Charlie Keating will say, "This is the greatest country in the world, and you ought to pay for it and don't come to me with this bullshit about avoiding your taxes. You pay your damn taxes, 'cause this is a wonderful country, and it's because of this country that you're getting this bonus, and some of it deservedly should go to the government."

This might confuse some of them. They know that this same man had spent a fortune on lawyers and accounting firms in late 1983 after buying Lincoln to seek a way to fold ACC into the bank. And that he had given up on this quest only when no one could figure out a way to fuse the two without ACC losing over $100 million worth of theoretical tax losses that it was carrying forward.

Judy Wischer has her own way of living with her daily fear of being fired by Charlie Keating. She becomes a kind of dragon lady to many in the company, a woman who fires easily and seems to delight in this act. She is a cool professional, a woman who has an extraordinary ability to carry in her head the minutiae of Charlie Keating's endless and complicated deals, a woman who can attend to the thousands of small decisions that follow in the wake of her boss's impulsive moves. She develops a policy for those who rise in ACC, who aspire to the top rungs of the corporate ladder. One of their first acts must be to fire someone. She knows after all these years what it takes to survive. A person must be blooded.

While Keating has whipped ACC into shape as a home builder and then gone on to capture a savings and loan (just as he and Lindner did in the sixties), Lindner also has been busy. In 1983, he becomes the chairman of Penn Central, a conglomerate slowly returning from the near death of bankruptcy. Lindner's AFC now is pegged as a $4 billion company, and for a man of his appetites, Penn Central has certain charms. Its credit line runs to hundreds of millions (should borrowing be an appealing idea), and it carries forward a tax loss credit of $1.7 billion, a sum that rather dwarfs Keating's credit of a hundred million or so. Lindner is also toying with positions in American Can and other ventures. And as

Keating is making his play to buy Lincoln, Lindner has been plunging into high-paying ventures with Milken, things like his $300 million position in T. Boone Pickens's move on Gulf Oil.

He has also sharpened his skills in supporting politicians. The new reforms that limit donations to $2,000 and that have led to the creation of legions of political action committees (PACs) have not even given Carl Lindner, Jr., pause. He has put together something observers call the Lindner Circle, a band of business associates and relatives that overnight can shower legal donations on appropriate candidates. Also, in the area of what are called soft money donations, funds channeled to the national committees of the political parties for their general use, the Lindner Circle in 1982 coughed up $135,000.

Nor has he neglected the home front. By the end of the decade his support of Ohio politicians will reach into the millions of dollars. These contributions to the representatives of democracy do not go unnoticed. For example, in 1985, a year after Keating manages to buy a California savings and loan, Lindner is in a fight with Chemical Bank of New York for Home State Savings of Ohio. The depositors do not want his participation and picket his home. Lindner sends out for four gallons of cold punch (from one of his own dairy depots) to quench their thirst. "I try to be nice to people," he once explains, "because as my friend Billy Graham says, you meet the same people on the way down as you meet on the way up."

He manages to win the prize of Home State Savings thanks to a provision of Ohio state law giving Ohio businesses the chance to top any out-of-state bid for a bank. This provision is the work of State Senator Stanley J. Aronoff, who in 1984 received a $6,000 contribution from Carl Lindner. After buying Home State Lindner sells off most of its branches, thus instantly recovering most of his cost. He changes the name of the bank and by the end of the decade will have used its assets to buy a 17 percent stake in Columbia Savings and Loan of Beverly Hills, an institution that will base much of its investment policies on buying junk bonds from Michael Milken (that is, until Columbia fails in 1990 at a cost to taxpayers of about $1 billion).

In January 1984, Mike Manning is dispatched to look into Indian Springs State Bank in Kansas City. The bank has gone bust, and the FDIC has hired Morrison & Hecker to clean up the accounts. Manning is assigned to handle the matter because four years before he helped a partner in the firm with a similar bank failure in Kansas.

Indian Springs does not look to be a big case—one federal regulator refers to it as "a flyshit on the wall bank in the basement of a shopping center." Manning works with a team of Morrison & Hecker lawyers. He sifts the files, separating the loans and contracts that will be settled in state court from those that will go to federal court. He takes the federal cases himself because they are bigger and the judges are better. He notices a bunch of bad loans from the little Kansas City bank to people in California and Hawaii, and he sets these thirty-four files in a third stack.

By February he notices that he has not yet gotten to this third stack of files, so one day, he decides to stay late and go through the bad loans in Hawaii and California. He takes the files down to the conference room, spreads them out on the big table, and makes two pots of coffee. On one side of the manila folders are the loan applications listing the collateral and on other side the actual loans. He begins making notes. Christ, it seems some of these people borrowing a hundred thousand dollars or two hundred thousand dollars are listing the exact same pieces of property for collateral and the bank does not seem to notice this fact. Similar names keep popping up in the paperwork, names of strange, fishy-sounding guys who purport to be hotshot developers in Hawaii. It is past midnight now, he is chain-smoking and drinking cup after cup of coffee. He checks bank deposits and discovers that suddenly the tiny Indian Springs bank in a Kansas City shopping center will get massive brokered deposits from all over the country and instantly make huge unsecured loans to these odd people in Hawaii and California. He senses that these people are lying, lying right there on their applications. What makes thirty-four people lie? And where is all this money coming from? Why is it flowing into this nothing bank? And who is behind it?

Manning begins to make a drawing on a piece of paper, a set of concentric rings. In the outer ring, he lists the names of the borrowers who do not seem to be legitimate. In the next ring, he lists the names of corporate people who seem magically to appear on the loan documents. And in the exact center is a giant hole, a person or force Manning feels in his gut is directing this movement of money. Here Manning draws a small circle and writes "Mr. X."

At four in the morning, he knocks off for the night. He has gone through two packs of cigarettes. When he gets home, he showers and goes to bed, but he cannot sleep. He gets up, throws on his army parka, and drives back to his office. He is not the least bit tired. He knows he is onto something. Millions of dollars are passing before his eyes. In his gut he believes that he is looking at a conspiracy, at a giant fraud, and it is so brilliantly devised that it is fully documented because whoever dreamed up this fraud believed that no one would ever detect it. Still, he wonders: is he really seeing this? Can this small bank be of interest to anyone but some two-bit con? He begins rifling the seized bank's files for any correspondence, anything containing the names he culled from the documents the night before.

Manning realizes he is looking at the handiwork of some kind of genius even though he does not know his or her name and cannot quite fathom how the scheme works. But he feels several things as he feeds on the files hour after hour. One he will never admit to others for years—that to catch this genius it will take someone as obsessed and focused and determined as the guy himself, someone as crazed about things as, say, Mike Manning. He does not care if Mr. X is smarter than he is. He will work harder, he will be aggressive, he will not give up. And second, Manning feels a kind of stirring, like the sense of mission he had in his days with Allard Lowenstein. Whoever Mr. X is, he has just bankrupted a bank, essentially bilked millions from the public treasury because the deposits are federally insured. And he is getting away with it, and . . . that is wrong. Finally, what Manning feels is the exhilaration of litigation, of being in court after three years of cutting contracts. Because for him there is no substitute for litigation—it is a legally and publicly approved playground fight.

When his associates come in to work that morning, Manning makes only vague allusions to what he has found. He is concerned that his discoveries may be the product of a caffeine delusion. He knows if he says conspiracy and organized bank fraud out loud, they will look at him with disbelief. And he knows he cannot yet prove what he senses. Also, he knows if he starts talking about conspiracy and bank fraud there is a good chance that word may somehow trickle back to the mysterious Mr. X and his case will

vanish in a shredder in some distant office he does not even know
the name of. So Mike Manning is very careful about what he says.
He knows this case will take time. He is right; he will not be home
in any real sense for more than four years.

They will never unravel it all. Not the federal regulators. Not the
federal prosecutors. Not the lawyers representing all the civil suits.
Not the more than fifty accountants humming along inside American Continental Corporation. Not Charles H. Keating, Jr. For almost twelve solid months, Lincoln Savings and Loan will operate
at a new velocity, one that auditing techniques can barely approx-
imate. It will be two years before even guidelines for making loans
can be banged together by the corporation. There is no time for
such things. Vacuum money through the branches, plant assets,
and then, when the crop is ripe, harvest.

Go. There are not enough days now, not enough nights. Lincoln
has assets, and these can grow simply by someone's picking up a
phone and buying some of those jumbo deposits. In 1983, when
Keating buys Lincoln, it has assets (meaning deposits) of about
$1.2 billion. By the end of 1984, this sum has risen to $2.5 billion.
In 1983, about $250 million worth of the assets are judged by fed-
eral regulators to be in risky ventures. By 1984, this number is almost $400 million, and a year later it is $1.6 billion. And for every
deposit acquired by the savings and loan a place must be discovered to plant the money, a place where when harvesttime comes the
money has grown and is larger than the deposit plus the interest.
Or Lincoln goes broke. But with lots of money and lots of nerve and
some luck, the possibilities of wealth are all but endless.

If there is one deal that mesmerizes the Charlie Keatings of the
world in the early eighties, it is a piece of work done by former
secretary of the Treasury William E. Simon. In 1982, Simon and
some associates bought Gibson Greeting Cards from RCA in a
leveraged deal. The cost was $80 million, a sum obtained by bor-
rowing the money against Gibson's assets and then, once ownership was assumed, paying the debt with Gibson's assets. A year
later, in May 1983, just when Charlie Keating was scouting for a
California savings and loan to purchase, Simon and his partners
made a public stock offering of Gibson—a deal in which Simon's
end came to $80 million and still left him with stock worth $50
million. A hustler's dream. No one thinks that in a few short

months Gibson has suddenly altered the world of greeting cards or
has invented some new and highly profitable form of condolence
notes. Not at all. This is the beauty of the deal, of the tens of millions gushing out in sudden profit. No better mousetrap has been
developed, no new plants have been built, there has been no
breathtaking new marketing plan. The whole string of events has
pivoted on financial instruments, on small scraps of paper traded
here and there. A dealmaker's deal.

The BAC 1-11 leaves Phoenix for Los Angeles on February 24,
two days after ACC assumes possession of Lincoln. Keating
spends six or seven hours in the city, then takes off again, returns
to Phoenix, and continues on to Austin. The next day he is in Cincinnati and then on Sunday arrives in Miami, where his party is
joined by Mr. and Mrs. Lee Henkel of Atlanta, friends from
Keating's days in the Connally presidential campaign. There is a
dinner dance at the country club at Indian Creek, and then everyone goes to Cat Cay for almost a week.

Lee Henkel is the chairman of Continental Southern, and Continental Southern in time will have housed underneath it a fistful
of entities such as Hickory Partnership, Wishbone Associates,
Ocean Club Partners, Ocean Dunes, and the like, and they have
investments in various slabs of land in the south—a 112-unit con-
dominium in Myrtle Beach, a 147-unit hotel, a proposed 84-unit
condo tower. The nature of these ventures is not always immediately clear—for example, the 112-unit condo in Myrtle Beach is actually an old Howard Johnson's that Henkel and his partners have
bought. Nor are the appraisals always higher than the loans. The
loans from Lincoln begin in 1984 and by 1986 reach $90.6 mil-
lion. Or so it seems. Some of the paperwork is hard to find. For
example, there is said to be a $300,000 personal loan to Henkel,
but no one can find any documents. At one point Chip Wischer
discovers that a hurricane is bearing down on the various coastal
projects and not one of them appears to be insured. When he
points this out to Keating and his lieutenants, they do not seem
very concerned and are a bit miffed at his alarm. They act as
if Wischer did not grasp the nature of deals, the essence of
business.

On March 5 Charlie Keating returns to Phoenix, and the next
day he jets to Los Angeles. He has dinner with thirteen others at

the Dinner Regency Club and bunks at L'Ermitage in Beverly Hills. By the eighth he is home hosting a dinner for John Connally and Ben Barnes. They've come to cut a deal. Barnes, once the youngest legislator in Texas and later the state's lieutenant governor, is Connally's partner in an air charter service, a catering company, and, more importantly, real estate developments—by 1986, they will have $300 million in dirt. Eventually Connally will explain that Barnes "talked to me about one or two projects, and that quickly expanded into more. It's kind of like Topsy. The whole thing just grew until it became rather huge." Barnes has shown up at the dinner with what Keating's aides will remember as a "hot woman," but for Charlie such matters are minor details when a deal is at hand. Before the pair arrives, he cautions his staff about Connally, one of the few men on earth he considers a real peer.

Recently, Connally has sold Keating's son some cattle—Connally raises Santa Gertrudis stock, part of his Texas ranching image like the multimillion-dollar livestock auction and Western art show he hosts each year. The cattle are not what C3 expected, and he is skinned in the deal. So Charlie Keating tells his staff that as a person Connally is a ten but in a deal he is only a four, because, well, he's a Texan and you've got to watch those guys. On the other hand, Keating sizes up the possibilities of plowing money into ventures with Connally and Barnes and figures that with their political connections, if anyone is going to make money in Texas, it will be they.

The deal on the table that night in Phoenix is called the Uplands, a parcel of 3,280 acres of land outside Austin with a creek winding through it. Connally and Barnes will spend most of the week in ACC's offices going over the venture. In April, the millions will begin to flow from Lincoln into their hands. And by the fall of 1984, the deal will start to unravel—Keating will discover that Barnes is not very good at managing a development—and ACC and Lincoln will deepen its involvement in the project, send staff out to Austin to take it over, and rewrite the terms of the deal so that Connally and Barnes are forgiven payments they are unable to make. But the deal itself will not be questioned—there isn't time for that.

On March 19, Keating returns to Los Angeles, meets with Ben Barnes among others, and stays until March 26. Then it's back to Phoenix and then almost instantly back to Los Angeles. There is so much to do. Carl Lindner is not slowing down, either. He is running with a crowd Keating hopes to join, a world of corporate raiders like Saul Steinberg, Victor Posner, and Meshulam Riklis. Perhaps this seems odd company for a teetotaling Baptist and 33rd-degree Mason. After all, Posner's mistress is the daughter of his former mistress, who still works for him. But this is business. By riding positions in Steinberg and Riklis's moves in the early eighties, Lindner makes $170 million. Whenever Riklis's young wife, actress/singer Pia Zadora, appears in Cincinnati for a concert, Lindner buys any unsold tickets, and there are a lot to buy. He borrows (through the sale of junk bonds) hundreds of millions at a time from Drexel. And each spring when Drexel hosts its high-yield bond conference, a fiesta generally known as the Predator's Ball, Carl Lindner, Jr., is there.

On April 4, 1984, Charles H. Keating, Jr., joins this elite crowd and for three days attends the conference, a kind of boys' night out for the planet's corporate raiders. Milken gives his usual rousing speech (he was a cheerleader in high school), the surprise entertainer appears (this year it is Frank Sinatra), and the famous gathering of the elite of the elite takes place in Bungalow 8 at the Beverly Hills, a hotel owned as it happens by Ivan Boesky. What is special about the small gathering in Bungalow 8 is very simple and reveals how little ever really changes in American business. Capitalism at its best is always seeking to avoid the waste entailed in real competition and constantly shifting to inside information or cartels or sweetheart deals. Bungalow 8 is in many ways a fine example of this essence of capitalism. Old men who run corporations gather in a room and drink with young women, many of them whores.* Then they all go to dinner, but their wives do not accompany them.

They all share a sense of risk, a sense of being on the inside, a sense of knowing how the economy really works and taking advantage of this knowledge. Keating, upon assuming possession of Lincoln, immediately begins pouring hundreds of millions into junk

---

*According to Connie Bruck in *The Predator's Ball: The Junk Bond Raiders and the Man Who Staked Them* (Simon & Schuster, New York, 1988), the practice of packing the party with prostitutes had gone on at Drexel for years—see p. 15. Milken himself never attended the parties in Bungalow 8 and denies any knowledge of prostitutes being procured for clients. (See also Kornbluth, *Highly Confident.*)

bonds. There is little analysis; usually the amount of study required takes place during a brief phone call. Keating will be sitting in his office during those early morning hours while the rest of the world sleeps and the phone will ring and it will be Milken's salesman Jim Dahl peddling a new issue of paper. Keating will listen, turn it over in his mind. And buy. All the prospectuses, all the due diligence and analysis will come later. The world moves too swiftly for such practices now. That is why in Charlie Keating's mind all the traditional savings and loans are going broke. They are mired in the past, in that maudlin world captured by Jimmy Stewart in *It's a Wonderful Life.* In 1984, Lincoln increases its liabilities by almost 200 percent by buying junk bonds, buying dirt for development, loaning money to other corporations so that they can play the stock market, buying jumbo accounts from brokers, pouring hundreds of millions into its own service corporations (the subsidiaries have $7 million in Lincoln money on March 31, 1984, and $1,391,790,000 by June 30, 1986), playing options. This is all done deliberately; this is all part of the dream called merchant banking.

Lincoln was formed in 1925 and came under federal regulation in 1938. For decades it took in deposits in southern California and then loaned the money out to people who wanted to buy houses. It had an unusually high number of home loans to minorities when compared to the rest of the thrift industry. When interest rates soared in the late seventies and the law held Lincoln to a limit on what it could charge for loans, it began to lose money, like most thrifts. Not big money—basically, the old management massaged the books by selling a branch here and there to keep the thrift in the black or close to it. When Keating bought the bank, the regulators were told that the old management would be kept in place and things would go on pretty much as they had before. But that is not what happened. What happened is that Charlie Keating—and hundreds of other new owners just like him—got out of home loans (which lost money) and plunged into new markets, looking for the big killing. Under the new federal and California state deregulation, this is legal. In fact, it is what deregulation is all about. Traditionally savings and loan officials were renowned for 3-6-3—that is, borrowing money at 3 percent, lending it out for home mortgages at 6 percent, and always being on the golf course by three in the afternoon. But there is no time for games now.

Three days after the Drexel conference, Keating is in Austin again to meet with Ben Barnes, then on to Phoenix, Cincinnati, and finally New York, where he keeps a series of appointments with bankers, among them a man named Richard Fenn, a vice chairman of an Arab financial group based in France called the Saudi-European Bank. After that come Ireland, London, Paris, Monte Carlo, St. Tropez, Biarritz. And the shrines at Lourdes and Fatima. On the fourth, fifth, and sixth of May, and again on the seventh and eighth, Charlie Keating is on his knees praying to the Blessed Mother for mercy and divine intercession.

His son, C3, has headaches, and they get worse and worse. There is so much to do—buy junk bonds, buy land, fix up the branches of Lincoln, create new subsidiaries, fly to distant cities and cut deals. The only son, the heir apparent in a patriarchal family with five daughters, does not excel at school or business. But when Charlie Keating reinvents himself in Arizona, C3 is made a highly paid executive in ACC. A woman begins working at ACC, and her name is Krista. She rolls into work the first day in a beat-up old car belching smoke. Her hair is blond and she is athletic, on the track team in college. She has blue eyes. And C3 marries her and children begin to arrive, one a son called C4.

His father continues to berate him, to call him dummy in front of others, to toss paper clips at his gaping mouth when he falls asleep in meetings. C3 retreats into the things he loves—model rockets, outdoor work at that ranch his family buys, and land. He loves land. One day he stumbles on a huge parcel about twenty miles west of Phoenix in a high desert valley tucked away in the Estrella Mountains. The land has a bizarre history. For decades the Navajos and Hopis have warred over a joint use area in northern Arizona, and the federal government, in order to end the dispute, decides to relocate the Navajos. So they go to a local rancher and seek his land, and he tells them he'll trade it for a parcel held by the Bureau of Land Management near Phoenix in the foothills of the Estrella Mountains. The deal goes through, and then he immediately goes to ACC since they are known to be in a buying frenzy, and best of all they pay top dollar.

C3 goes out, walks the land, and comes back and tells his father he has found the deal of the decade, thousands of perfect acres ready for development. They are on the wrong side of town, official projections do not suggest the tract will be necessary for development for decades, but this kind of reasoning is for the timid, the losers. Charlie Keating buys the land, and the deed comes back listing as owners Spain, Mexico, the government of the United States, and now Charlie Keating. Keating has an idea that he thinks could make enormous amounts of money. He will not do a subdivision, he will not do a little retirement community, he will not add one more tract to the sprawl of Phoenix. He will build a city, a city of 200,000 people. He will bring in industry. He will create an international airport. He will bring into being a total world, one that will ignore Phoenix. It will look west. It will advertise itself as Los Angeles's newest addition, a mere six hours or so down the freeway, a place where housing is cheaper, where labor is cheaper, where factories can be built away from all the costs of southern California. Yet this new city will be an overnight drive away from LA's markets and in a state where union busting is a favorite form of exercise. Charlie Keating in the mid-eighties anticipates what will become a fact by the early nineties—the flight of human beings and jobs from Los Angeles to Nevada, Utah, and Arizona. He senses that he is not stuck in the middle of the desert but located in a new, cheap zone of the booming Pacific Rim. And since he will own the raw land and since with his deregulated savings and loan he has access to almost limitless amounts of capital, the whole idea is doable. Done deal.

Such ideas are in the air at the time. At the same time, Billy Bob Burns, a local kid in his twenties turned real estate promoter, is launching a similar scheme west of Phoenix. He, too, is weary of small-time deals like subdivisions—he started out in high school peddling vegetables—and he too never sleeps. He travels with a tape recorder and endlessly dictates memos to his staff. He has a forty-acre estate outside of London, likes double-breasted silk suits, and lives in a 14,000-square-foot Phoenix mansion equipped with eleven fireplaces, a pink marble tub, and a wife, a Miss America runner-up. In 1984, when Keating embraces his dream called Estrella, Billy Bob Burns embraces his dream called Sun Valley, a vacant tract of 48,000 desert acres. He then floats a $82 million bond and uses the money to build a four-lane highway connecting the land with major thoroughfares. He figures he will plant 300,000 Americans in Sun Valley.

It is a time when individuals, with a little help from endless sources of credit, can dream their debt-driven dreams. The early covenants for Estrella demand that no abortions can be performed in the community, that no pornography can exist within the city limits, that the pictures people put on their walls must meet certain moral guidelines. When the press gets ahold of these requirements, feeds on them like a blood-crazed wolf and the public outcry floods ACC's switchboard, Keating swiftly retreats and does what comes naturally. He blames his son, denies any knowledge of such covenants, lays it all at the door of the dummy.

But the headaches get worse. A tumor is found in C3's brain. He is flown repeatedly to Houston for treatment by the best physicians, and Charlie Keating, not trusting mere medical science, goes to his knees and prays. He flies in his BAC 1-11 to the most famous shrines in Christendom. His knows where the ultimate power resides, where the final bastion is against a world of sin, of pornography, of avarice, of infidels. His plane always has a crucifix on the wall. His religion is not a light garment, his belief is not easily understood or dismissed. He will never talk about his faith much with others. He will read a book, say, about miracles or sanctity and then give copies to his staff. But there will be no lectures, no sermons. The visits to the shrines do not surprise his staff. They know Charlie Keating is not the kind of man to take the word of others. He must go and experience the thing himself.

By May 15, 1984, Charlie Keating is back in Phoenix, and two days later guests arrive, Toufic Aboukhater and his sons Bassam and Kamal. They live in various spots on the globe, including Monte Carlo, and they are friends of John Connally, who just closed his deal with Keating a month before. When one of Toufic's sons marries, John Connally and Keating attend the wedding in London. They are the kind of friends it can be very good to have. What Toufic and sons do is know people, and the people they know are oil-rich sheiks, particularly Kuwaitis. For two days Keating entertains them in Arizona, and they talk. The Kuwaitis have more money than they know what to do with, and since they live in a rather dangerous part of the world, they are always looking for a haven for their treasure. Charlie Keating sees the Kuwaitis as the ultimate safety net for his plans at Estrella* and for a new dream that is just emerging.

Like Lindner, like Milken, like others in the world of finance, Charlie Keating leaves a trail of deals and various forms of paper. But no monument. And like many men who taste power, he eventually wants to produce something that is physical, that he can show people who do not know a bond from a bidet. He wants to build hotels. There are financial reasons—under the current tax laws governing limited partnerships such investments can be very lucrative shelters. In the current buying frenzy, they can be sold at a great profit. If a hotel is kept occupied, it becomes a cash cow as guests fling money into the till on a daily basis. And cash flow is like blood for anyone who loves to do deals. But the reason of the heart is that Charlie Keating wants a monument.

Charlie Keating is going to build the finest hotel on the surface of the earth. Not a Hilton, but a place to rival and exceed the grand hotels of Europe. He is going to build it in Phoenix, Arizona. In order to do this he needs deep pockets that are not anxious about immediate returns on capital. He has, under deregulation, part of the necessary equation in Lincoln Savings and Loan. And now, as Toufic Aboukhater and his sons dine at his table, he has within reach the other piece of the equation, Middle Eastern oil money. He will need it all because before the Phoenician opens its doors on October 1, 1988, over $300 million will have vanished into its six hundred rooms.

He has already made explorations into this world of Islamic money. For years, Charlie Keating will patiently explain to people that his house happens to be in Phoenix, Arizona, but he is not of Phoenix, Arizona. He belongs to a much larger and increasingly borderless world. He will constantly try to explain to people that the ACC headquarters on Camelback Road, the red, white, and blue branches of Lincoln Savings and Loan, are merely faces of a

*Some former ACC executives argue that many of Keating's larger schemes—Estrella and the $300 million-plus Phoenician Hotel, for example—were based on the huge resources of the Kuwaitis and on the fact that they were driven not by a need for high immediate returns but by a craving for long-term security and profit. Keating repeatedly argued with critics that his investments were not risky, and given his apparent assumption that he had Kuwaiti backing, his point has merit. After all, how many family firms—like the Kuwaiti emir and his kin—can get a war fought, essentially by proxy, when harm comes their way?

much larger and more complicated thing. For example, almost a year earlier, in August 1983, when Keating is walking around with tens of millions of dollars in cash from the sale of Michael Milken's junk bonds, he sits down in Phoenix with Richard Fenn and Jamal Radwan of the Saudi-European Bank. Radwan is a Syrian-born U.S. citizen who has headed the bank since its inception in 1979. Radwan had met Keating earlier in 1983, when he helped finance an ACC bank loan with Saudi money. They talk about what might be mutual deals—they are both looking for a California savings and loan to buy, with Radwan and Fenn pursuing Southern California Savings and Loan (a pursuit that fails).

By 1984, Radwan decides to increase the amount of capital in his bank by issuing stock, and he puts out a private memorandum saying the offering will total 600,000 shares. Through ACC and Lincoln Keating buys 180,000 of the shares for $18 million. Under the law, Radwan cannot make the offering in the United States without dealing with the SEC, and since he does not wish to do that, Keating forms a subsidiary in Curaçao, Netherlands Antilles. He keeps the actual stock certificates in his vault in Phoenix. Shortly after the purchase, Keating discovers he has been misled—that Radwan has peddled 1.2 million shares, not 600,000. In essence, he has watered the stock. But Keating does not join other shareholders in protesting this apparent fraud. When his high-powered New York law firm, Kaye Scholer, sends him a memorandum outlining the scam in 1984, he writes a one-sentence response to his aide: "Do *not* spend any more money on this." He realizes that he now has access to Saudi money. He puts one of his aides on the bank's board, where John Connally also serves. And through Radwan he meets other interesting players like German financial consultant George Herrdum—who claims to have clients such as General Motors and who entices him into an offshore Caribbean investment speculation that swallows about $17 million.

Keating is not simply making deals, he is entering a new world, and it is not a simple one. In some ways it has the feel of the intelligence community, this world of mainly men who are not afraid of debt, not afraid of borrowing. It is a world in which it is very easy to lose one's way. There is no longer a Henry Ford whom one can point to and say, ah, he makes automobiles. There is no John D. Rockefeller locking up oil lands. There is instead Sir James Goldsmith. In the ACC balance sheet tracking its dealings with the Saudi-European Bank over the years a $2 million payment is listed as an introduction fee for a deal with Sir James. Behind that simple notation lies another realm, one Charlie Keating is alert enough to discover and join.

Keating first ran into Goldsmith when he was cold-calling Europe's merchant bankers in the early 1980s as he struggled to teach himself the manners and moves of global finance. Goldsmith was born in 1933 to a French mother and English father and lives with dual passports and a divided identity. He leaves Eton at age seventeen, takes a job in a hotel kitchen, then enters the British Army at eighteen as a private. When he gets out two years later he is a lieutenant and runs off with Isabel Patino, a Bolivian tin heiress who dies a year later in childbirth. He buys the rights to a French rheumatism cream for $200 and three years later has parlayed this into a half-million dollars. He marries twice, fathers six children, has mistresses, and acquires homes in London, Paris, New York City, and Spain, plus a vast estate in Mexico. He is very conservative, yet he holds the traditional European order in contempt for being hopelessly decadent. His brother, Edward, is one of England's leading ecologists, and Sir James shares this passion, along with a dislike of nuclear energy and a strong support of AIDS research. His is not a simple picture. When he tries to take over Continental Group in 1984, his opponents drag him to court before the Virginia state insurance commissioner. They rest their case on a simple tale of Sir James's recent vacation in Sardinia: he put his wife and children into one seaside villa and his mistress and their children on a nearby peninsula, commuting between his two broods and lovers by speedboat. The commissioner hears out the attorneys and says, "Anybody who can pull that off can't be that bad."

What Sir James is about in the early 1980s is seizing corporations that he considers ill run and running them better. He is particularly interested in trees, in forests. He feels that their value will rise as his fellow human beings destroy the planet, so he forms a plan to take over major timber companies, split off their vast tracts of forest, and hold them. He puts together funds for these ventures, things that wind up as acronyms like General Oriental Investments Limited (GOIL) and General Oriental Securities Limited Partnership (GOSLP). These entities exist in places like the Cayman Islands but operate in a much wider arena. From a move against St. Regis, a paper and timber company, Sir James makes $50 million; from his play against Continental, he makes $35 million. And now as 1984 ripens he moves against Crown Zellerbach Corporation. Charlie Keating, who prides himself on betting on winners, on riding other people's insights, begins to buy in. He activates some of the subsidiaries riding under the umbrella of American Continental Corporation, names like AMCOR Funding Corporation, Crescent Lending Corporation, LINFIN Corporation, American Founders Life, and Phoenician Financial Corporation. And these entities pour money into GOIL and GOSLP, a sum that in a few short years will reach $134,245,594. What this money does is back the notions of Sir James. They are not investments in houses or factories or normal bonds. They are a bankroll for the casino. Sir James almost always wins, and GOIL and GOSLP make money for Lincoln and ACC and Charlie Keating. These deals offend the traditional notion of what a savings and loan does with its deposits, but giving offense is not an alarming idea for either Sir James Goldsmith or Charlie Keating.

On Tuesday, May 22, Keating and his staff are back in Los Angeles for more meetings about Lincoln, particularly the federal and state regulations that still limit savings and loans. And then the next day, May 23, he travels by limo to Michael Milken's warren at 9560 Wilshire Boulevard. Everyone is still high from the Predator's Ball a few weeks before. And later that evening he has dinner with Jamal Radwan.

Early June is devoured by a flurry of meetings with Connally, Ben Barnes, and Toufic Aboukhater, plus visits to Milken's operation. Within two years Keating will have hundreds of millions in junk bonds and will have traded $1.4 billion. The march to this position is steady: in February 1984, the holdings are $5,000, by March they stand at $4,284,000, come June this has grown to $48,403,000, and by December it rises to $209,155,000. Two years later, when federal regulators finally intrude into Keating's financial workshop, they will be given a short course in the virtues of junk: junk bonds are less fuss than home mortgages and pay better. The Lincoln staff of four handling the junk is very young, and none has ever worked for an investment banking firm before. They range from the mid-twenties to early thirties—Amy Hunt, for example, is twenty-five and previously worked five years for the accounting firm of Arthur Anderson, and before that was the assistant to the sports information director at her college. They make no written evaluations of bonds, and often they hear of bonds only after they have been bought.

None of this alarms Charlie Keating. He hates experts; they seem trained to tell people what they can't do. He does not need evaluations; he is on the phone with Jim Dahl and Mike Milken and Sir James Goldsmith and Carl Lindner, Jr. Keating isn't interested in the blandishments with which issuers stuff their prospectuses. He wants inside dope, and he has it. There is no time. Go.

Mike Manning fences with the defense lawyers throughout the spring of 1984. He wants to consolidate the thirty-four bad loan cases and gets the judge to agree by arguing that it will be more efficient for the court and save money for the clients on both sides. And he wants to depose the borrowers without alerting their attorneys to the fact that he suspects a massive bank fraud conspiracy. Normally, bad debts are quickly settled—a two- or three-page filing, a bang of a gavel in a courtroom and a judgment is rendered. Unsecured loans made to borrowers five thousand miles away such as those Manning is looking at—$100,000 to $200,000—are all but blown off since the chances of recovery are usually slight and the cost of chasing borrowers is usually high. Finally, the court permits him to depose the people in Hawaii.

He arrives in Honolulu on June 26, and his first target is the borrower who told the most obvious lies on her financial statements. To his mind, she is the weakest person. She is thirty-two—"I don't look just at the evidence to find out who is most culpable. At this stage I want to know who is most vulnerable. How much money is she making? Is she heavily in debt? Is she married? Lots of little things. It's the art side of litigation rather than the science." She lives with a guy who has also gotten funny loans with phony collateral. Manning senses from the documents that her boyfriend talked her into signing them. So she has a psychological out, a door Manning can open for her ("I want her to let her boyfriend know when she goes home and gets in bed with him that night that this country bumpkin from Kansas City may have stumbled onto something and how is he, her boyfriend, going to get her out of the deal?")

She comes to her deposition thinking Manning is trying to collect on a debt for a tiny bank in Kansas City. He has her loan form before him, and he looks up innocently from the list of collateral—"Is this your property? How long have you owned that? Can you provide documentation? Do you know so-and-so?" She breaks down in tears halfway through the procedure. She spends the night with her boyfriend, and the next day Manning takes his deposition.

He is the hunter. He calls in one man because he seems stupid—"Did you really want to do this?"—picks another because he hangs with the press and pretends to be a reporter—"I thought he might still have retained some of that belief in truth and social justice that journalists are supposed to start out with." By the third deposition, the defense lawyers smell something—"Can I see you in the hall for a minute? What are you doing? Are you about to allege that my client committed fraud?"—and a wide-eyed Manning tells them, "Look, I got questions, there appear to be irregularities on this loan application that I've gotta know. Did somebody tell you this was just gonna be a collection case depostion? I didn't."

He is in the office in downtown Honolulu at six-thirty, he takes a deposition until two or two-thirty and then another one from two until six or seven, and then he goes back to his hotel and eats dinner in his room and spends his evening from say, nine, until twelve getting ready for the next day's depositions. He works Saturdays and Sundays. He has come with a woman court reporter who has visions of spending time on Waikiki beach. ("I bring a court reporter from Kansas City because they are cheaper than the ones in Honolulu and I say I need a hardy one. They send a tough one out. She finally leaves frustrated and exhausted, and she says, 'You know, when I took this assignment I thought I'd have some time off to go to the beach. I'm in Hawaii, for God's sake. You're taking depositions from seven in the morning and going until seven-thirty or eight at night.' ")

Finally, after days of grinding away, a name has floated up, Mario Renda, Mr. X. Manning has saved the last deposition for one Stan Tobias, a borrower. He nibbles at the outer ring of his drawing, at the weak, at those most likely to flip—"These cases are never made unless you get early flips and you get the documents, and the documents alone will never make these cases. Juries won't listen to documents, won't understand them. You've got to have somebody who will breathe life into those documents."

He senses weakness in Tobias because the man is in trouble with the real estate commission and because other people in their depositions kept fingering Tobias as their excuse for lying on the forms. In Manning's drawing, Tobias sits in the ring closest to Mr. X. Originally, Manning had Tobias listed much earlier in the rounds of depositions, but he crossed him out and scheduled him for the last day—"I decided I can get to this guy. And he's also the smartest." Tobias takes the Fifth Amendment fifty-two times. Manning, listening to his rote replies, is now convinced that his suspicions about Tobias are correct. But he does not understand the scale of the operation, how many banks might be penetrated, and what this Mr. X, Mario Renda, is truly about.

Manning takes depositions every day until July 10. ("I got on the plane and passed out—I don't ever remember being that exhausted before—but boy oh boy, was I enriched with information. In my mind I had the scheme. I still didn't quite understand Mr. X's role. *But I had the scheme.* I knew a name, Renda, Mario Renda.")

Manning arrives home in Kansas City late on the night of July 10 and starts depositions in southern California on the seventeenth with another set of phony borrowers (doctors, engineers, people in the defense industry). He is almost in a panic to get to these people before Renda can put out a uniform party line for them to follow. "Every lawyer during depositions," Manning explains, "has throwaway questions in either their notes or brain tapes, and mine was 'Did anyone ever make tapes of these meetings? Of these loan pitches?' " And he is told yes.

By June 20, Charlie Keating has had enough of work. The jet stops in Gander for refueling, then continues on to France. Three days later it is in Cairo, and then he wanders Africa with his family until July 10, seeing the sights. He is rounding out his résumé as a man of the world. After a few days in Phoenix, he is back in Beverly Hills at Drexel and touring Lincoln Savings and Loan. Toward the end of July and into the middle of August, he drops business to attend the Olympic Games in Los Angeles. The people flow in and out like a parade—Ben Barnes, John McCain, Lee Henkel, the folks at Drexel, herds of accountants, the players at the Saudi-

European Bank. His life of only a year ago seems like a thin, pale thing compared to this. In late October he is back in Europe—London, Germany, Paris ("Pick up CHK," his logs note, "with two limos at airport"). When they land in London, only two Rolls-Royces will do. And then Cat Cay, yet again. And besides this fine life, he is making financial history and everyone around him feels he or she is a part of this creation. By taking a traditional, stodgy savings and loan and plunking its capital into new places, they are creating a new world. That fall he begins his venture in the huge Pontchartrain hotel in Detroit. He is making the ground explode in southern California, in Colorado, in Florida, in Georgia, in Texas, in South Carolina. He is part of Milken's circle, a community that will soon begin issuing junk for hostile takeovers of corporations.

On December 17, 1984, he meets with Alan Greenspan, with Danny Wall, with Senator Alan Cranston, Senator John Glenn, Senator Mack Mattingly, Senator Paul Laxalt. That evening he dines with Senator Dennis DeConcini and his wife. He loves roaming the Hill. He has been wandering it since the 1950s, when he was often the uninvited speaker at a hearing on pornography. According to an aide, Charlie Keating has an odd view of congressmen: he believes in them. He actually thinks democracy works. His brother was a congressman for two terms, and Charlie Keating thinks that all in all the federal representatives are on the level. He goes around preaching the virtues of deregulation, decrying the danger of the Japanese though he has no real specific requests. He is a born-again announcing the new economic gospel. And he is somebody. Not Carl Lindner's appendage. Not a list of charges in an SEC suit. Not a nobody from Arizona. He is Charlie Keating, a merchant banker who flies on his own jets and dines at the finest restaurants.

He can now stand in a casino in London with his friend Toufic Aboukhater and shoot craps and lose twenty-five thousand dollars, fifty thousand, hell, a hundred grand, and the casino will take his marker. He is in a larger, more intriguing world now. Why, his friend Sir James Goldsmith *owns* casinos in London.

He is living at a speed that eclipses even his days at AFC in Cincinnati with Carl Lindner. He has more than money now, much more. He has power. He will not be constrained by quibbling clerks who do not understand, who have never been there, who have never tasted risk—never, not once—who have never tasted defeat, and who will never, ever know victory.

Larry Flynt's wife, Althea, is faithful in her own way. She does not sleep with other men. There may be sexual adventures, but not with men. She says she is a one-man woman. She is clean of drugs now; Flynt is free from pain. But he is disturbed by her decision. He cannot imagine a life without sex—except as he lives now, dead from the waist down because of a bullet to the spine. He lives a life oddly incongruous with his image. As he rolls in his wheelchair down a hallway in his mansion in Los Angeles, a reporter is startled when a half-naked nymphet in a negligée pops out of a bedroom and embraces Flynt. But it is only his fourteen-year-old daughter.

His magazines continue to pour in cash. Since he has gotten rid of the needless overhead—the labia pink, full-bodied personal jet is gone—he has no need of accounting tricks to doctor his books. Instead, he has become a kind of loose cannon in American culture, a man of great wealth and great cash flow who has very little need of money since he is stuck in a wheelchair. But he has a lot of time to think. And he has ideas.

In December 1984, he is on trial again for libel. A psychiatrist testifies and offers this portrait of what goes on inside the mind of Larry Flynt: "At times, [Flynt] sees himself as a great human being fighting for noble causes and failing to achieve greatness only because of the malice of others. At other times he sees himself as a 'hustler' or 'prankster' who is not really serious about anything. . . . The most basic psychological characteristic of Mr. Flynt is that he thrives on attention and being in the limelight. The world of plots and counterplots he has created with himself as the central figure is a world in which he cannot be ignored."

When he returns from Hawaii, Manning meets with Ed Leon, a Kansas City FBI agent. To Manning's relief, Leon buys into the notion that he has stumbled onto a conspiracy. Manning tells him he has people on record admitting to wholesale bank fraud. When the deposition transcripts come in, Leon reads them and says, "I see you've got these people, but why is this a big case?" And Manning tells him, "It's a big case because there is something big behind it. These people did it for a purpose, they are part of a larger conspiracy. I feel it, I believe it down to my marrow. I know I'm right." Leon believes Manning, and together they go to the U.S. Attorney for Kansas City in August 1984. They lay out what they have and what they suspect—a set of borrowers who admit to lying on their loan applications, who are fronting for someone else, and who immediately turn the proceeds of their loans over to a third party and take a cash payment for committing this fraud. The USA says she cannot prosecute such a case, she lacks the resources, it will take too long to turn the case, if she doesn't turn the case quickly she won't have convictions for her stats, and besides she has drug cases that are easier. Manning is not surprised, but he does not think her position is reasonable. What really bothers him is that she does not read the depositions in which the people admit fraud that they have committed, that they are fronting for other people. Also, he is the man who insists that the system works and that people should work within the system. Now the criminal justice system has spoken to him. At the same time, he is trying to sell the FDIC on a bigger picture, and they are beginning to buy it. The FHLBB's Steven Hershkowitz has already scrutinized Renda and found that he was okay in 1983 or early 1984. If the federal prosecutor refuses to mount a criminal case, Manning decides he will pursue a civil suit on his own. In July 1984, he pulls in the FDIC lawyer who is the federal liaison for his firm. The man takes some of the California depositions and, as he listens to the tales of borrower after borrower, soon understands that a giant fraud is staring him in the face. People back at Manning's firm wonder about where he is headed. He has remained very circumspect about announcing the discovery of a broad-based bank fraud conspiracy. The facts and theories necessary to prosecute this conspiracy case are not yet sufficiently framed to withstand lawyerly scrutiny—even by his own colleagues.

He does not believe in plans. They are constraints, they are crutches. Charlie Keating sees the world as very fluid, and in order to survive he believes he must stay flexible, open to opportunity. When he buys Lincoln in September 1983, the federal regulators ask for a business plan, and of course he gives them one about running a traditional savings and loan dedicated to home mortgages and serving the residents of southern California. But he does not take this plan—this sketch of the future—seriously.

He has bought a totally unregulated thrift because such a financial institution gives him almost total freedom to act. So in 1983 and repeatedly in 1984 he supplies the regulators with updated business plans, but in fact he goes his own way. It's almost as if the state and federal regulators were a swarm of obnoxious gnats swirling around the giant financial frame of Lincoln. He does not pay much attention to them because his charter grants him so much power. Finally he tells the regulators that he cannot give them a five-year plan, or a five-month plan, or even a five-week plan. But he might be able to give them a five-day plan. That's the point, though they can't seem to get it: finance capitalism thrives in shark-infested waters, and long-term plans can get you killed. You have to remain loose, open, ready. Keating represents a culture that is alien to the civil servants who watch over his savings and loan. They are trained to do it by the book, to follow procedures, to document carefully and analyze and then prudently act. Keating is trained to beg or borrow money, then belly up to the crap table and roll the dice. Behind the prestige and trappings of the fabled world of merchant banking, that is the reality. Reach quick decisions, face down risk, make a killing. It is the world of the phone call versus the world of the long form.

Nor does he take admonitions from his staff with much grace. His investments—hotels, raw land, new cities, takeover funds, junk bonds, currency markets—all these things swallow up enormous amounts of money. But unlike conventional home mortgages, they do not necessarily produce regular and predictable returns. The Phoenician Hotel will require $300 million before the first customer pays to stay there. Estrella will demand $100 million to $150 million (roads, lakes, sewers, utilities, and so forth) before the first developer will buy an acre and begin building. Junk bonds can shift in value, go underwater for a while, and then they must be held until the market bounces back. It is that way all across the portfolio of Keating's new investments in the first golden year, 1984, when he has his own bank. Soon the spread between income from investments and costs is about $10 million a month. Charlie Keating's hunches about where to invest may be brilliant, but it will take time for them to pay off. So at one staff meeting, one of his executives points out this shortfall and presents a long-term plan to salvage the situation. And Charlie Keating explodes in a rage, denounces the plan, denounces the ideas of plans. And then he goes out and does Gulf Broadcasting.

Gulf is a media company that owns television stations, and Keating loves the numbers. Television stations in the early eighties have great cash flow. So he begins to buy a position in Gulf, he is going to stage his own hostile takeover just like his friend Sir James Goldsmith does. And he is in a perfect position to do it because he has almost an unlimited source of money in Lincoln's deposits. Naturally, the stock goes up and down as he keeps buying and the regulators grow nervous. Charlie Keating is taking a broken-down thrift mired in home mortgages and putting the money into something that might pay off enormously, a corporate takeover. And this is legal under deregulation. What the regulators see is an operator from Phoenix, Arizona, making a massive plunge into the stock market and using federally insured dollars to make his play. They see a reckless gambler. Keating looks into the mirror and sees a man wise to Wall Street who can and will make a tremendous return on his investment.

On October 5, 1984, a subsidiary of ACC buys 8,314,846 shares of Gulf Broadcasting (12 percent of all outstanding common stock) from Carl Lindner's AFC and pays about $12.37 per share, or $102,896,210. That same day the stock is actually trading at $9.25 per share. In short, ACC has paid about 30 percent over market. By November, Keating boosts his ownership position to 24.9 percent. Lincoln officially says it is buying up Gulf stock as an investment, but internal memos circulate about taking it over. One memo, pegging a possible 75 percent position, is clipped to an article entitled "Regard Drexel Burnham Lambert, Inc., 'Junk Financing' Option." There are certain steps necessary in this theater of paper money. Keating hosts a meeting aboard his jet with E. Grant Fitts, the chairman of Gulf. Fitts naturally wonders what Keating has in mind, and he tells him that he hasn't quite decided yet. But he might be interested in buying up Fitts's stock. On December 7, one of Keating's lawyers sends information on Gulf and ACC to Michael Milken, and by the end of the month ACC has hired Drexel to help them in their fight. Gulf turns to Goldman Sachs in New York. The company is in play.

Four days later, the two heads of their corporations meet again and kick around ideas like Lincoln maybe having some seats on the board, or Gulf liquidating itself, or perhaps Lincoln buying

some more of the stock. It is a dance of numbers. Fitts wonders
if perhaps he could become a consultant for Lincoln. A memo is
drafted that month that entertains the notion of Lincoln swallowing Gulf and Fitts getting a five-year consulting fee at $500,000
per year, a box seat at Texas stadium, and a television station for
about $4,200,000. But in early February 1985, Gulf announces it
is being bought by Taft Broadcasting for $775 million—ACC says
the price is too low and that it will fight the move at the shareholders' meeting on April Fool's Day. Lincoln starts filing lawsuits—
"Keating never saw a lawsuit he didn't like," explains one of his
attorneys. But on April 1, ACC and Gulf sign an agreement with
Gulf giving ACC $10,925,000 for its legal expenses, and the sale
of Taft goes through. In six months Charlie Keating has cleared
$50 million on the deal. He has won big in the casino.

But the regulators are worried. Lincoln had bought the stock over
the market price, and if the deal had not gone through, if Gulf had
not been forced into play, they think Charlie Keating would have
lost his shirt. Lincoln's huge buys in the junk bond market also
bother them. And all those direct investments in real estate
schemes: they just can't seem to fathom this kind of an operation.
So on February 5, 1985, ACC president Judy Wischer fires off a
letter to the regulators describing the government's attitude and its
desire for more regulations as an "ill-advised imposition of a regulatory straitjacket on Lincoln." The authorities just don't seem to
get it, so she spells it out for them: "[W]e remain nonplussed that
the Association [Lincoln] should be called upon to explain why
these investments are 'safe and sound,' while 'traditional' California
thrifts exercise unfettered authority to loan (1) without recourse,
(2) to developer-borrowers of dubious net worth and expertise and
(3) on the security of projects which management has convincingly
demonstrated it could more safely and profitably complete itself."
Keating himself allows that he is considering getting out of junk
bonds. As for Gulf, Wischer wants the regulators to know that this
deal is "a good example of our internal operations."

It just seems to get worse. When he was angling to buy Lincoln,
Keating had presented himself to the regulators as a successful
home builder. In the spring of 1985, he sells off that part of his
operation. It is kind of dull after the excitement of doing a Gulf
deal, after bankrolling the takeover ideas of Sir James Goldsmith.
After plotting out an entire city. A deregulated thrift provides a

man with a headier experience. A perfect example sits a few miles from his office at Western Savings and Loan, a local thrift that has been under the control of the same Mormon family for generations. With the new availability of hot money from brokered accounts, Western Savings flowers. It loans local developer Conley Wolfswinkel around $100 million, bankrolls some Tucson operators with $219 million for a Colorado land deal, and builds itself a new headquarters for $32 million. One of the owners has himself hoisted up in a cherry picker before construction starts to assure himself that his new office will have a suitable view. And this staid old family firm is suddenly in a hurry, so busy, in fact, that it forks over $4.1 million to one party three weeks before the loan application even comes before the bank's committee.

What creates this new, frisky spirit is the dream of sudden and great wealth. For example, in 1981, Mobil bought a ranch in Colorado for $22.6 million, or about $880 an acre. Four years later it sold it for $80 million, or about $4,000 an acre. Western Savings looks at this 355 percent increase in value in forty-eight months and wants a piece of the action—which is how it winds up bankrolling some players to the tune of $219 million when they buy a piece of that very same ranch. Charlie Keating can feel this action going on all around him. He can hear it when he talks on the phone to Carl Lindner or Mike Milken or Sir James. He can see it when he drives around Phoenix or when he flies in his jet to Texas or Georgia or Michigan. There is a boom going on, and he has the money to ride this boom. And he is tired of flying out to Los Angeles. He asks and is given permission by California to move most of Lincoln's back-room operations to Phoenix.

For years he will try to explain this to people, to the regulators, to reporters, to politicians. When his business practices are questioned, a part of him always thinks that his critics just don't understand, that if they come out and see his operation, if they listen to him explain it, they will agree with him. He is not a fool; he knows he has enemies, and he pays out large sums of money for attorneys, lobbyists, politicians, intelligence reports from private investigators. But there is still a part of him that cannot really believe that people dislike him or that people do not approve of what he senses he is inventing at Lincoln and ACC. He often wars with his own staff—his own staff!—because even they cannot seem to grasp his vision.

Mark Sauter is a bright young lawyer from Cincinnati brought on board at ACC early in 1984 and assigned to dealing with the regulators. Sauter has close-cropped hair and wears glasses, walks around hunched over, and never smiles. He is an encyclopedia of bank regulations and functions as a reference guide to what the government says Lincoln can and can't do. He is the opposite of a deal maker, of a rainmaker. And soon he is constantly butting heads with Keating over his deals. He has hardly been there a month when he is questioning the deal with Ben Barnes and John Connally to develop land in Texas. Then in April he whips out some documents about Lincoln's professed plans to continue issuing mortgages to homeowners, but he does not push them with Keating because he senses Keating hates the idea. A week later he is back in Keating's office talking about the regulation that limits a loan to any one borrower to no more than 1 percent of a thrift's assets. Charlie hates this limit and wonders if they can just bust up loans into segments and avoid the rule. Finally Keating meets in the Regency Club in Los Angeles with the California commissioner in charge of savings and loans, Larry Taggart, and gets a waiver from the limit. But the conflict does not stop. In late November 1984 Charlie is upset by some of the attitudes of his people. His staff, he complains, is resisting deals that, dammit, he wants to do. Second, all the lawyers he is paying for are not helping find ways to do these deals. Look, he tells the doubters in his own house, Charlie Keating's lending philosophy will eventually develop and become apparent to everyone, and then they will all understand. He is setting out to make history. He will show them. And in the first twelve months at the helm of the thrift he instantly does what he had planned to do all along: he gets out of mortgages and plunges into the more exciting markets.

It is January 1985, and Conley Wolfswinkel visits Charlie Keating in his office. He is in some ways not Keating's type. He is fat. He loves pornography. But he is a deal maker. For months, Wolfswinkel has cultivated Keating's son, C3. He is a well-known figure in the Phoenix area, and when his day is done, he likes to have a drink at his favorite bar, the Downside Risk. He is a farm boy from the east valley and while in high school began bagging money by growing alfalfa on vacant lots and selling the hay. For years as a teenager, he and his older brother, Clifford, were partners, but they split up in 1980 and have not spoken to each other since. Wolfswinkel is a millionaire by age thirty, and in 1980 he builds his dream home. The twelve-room house faces a pond with fountains and swans, and out back are the bathhouse, pool, tennis courts, and stables. The master bedroom stretches for 1,200 square feet and holds a Jacuzzi and a shower big enough for five people. He hosts charity benefits on a regular basis at the mansion, and two or three thousand people will show up. Wolfswinkel likes to say things like "The greatest advantage in the world, in my opinion, is being raised poor." But this day in 1985, he is busy not becoming poor again. He has a deal that will go up in flames unless he can get some financing in a few days. Though he and Keating have bumped into each other socially, they do not really know each other. They talk for twenty minutes, and Conley Wolfswinkel walks out with $70,828,035. The deal involves a parcel of more than seven thousand acres near Tucson, a plot called Rancho Vistoso. Ten days after the loan is made Lincoln's board of directors will meet and approve it. An appraisal on the land will drift in months later, in May. The loan application will not be filled out until ten days after the board approves the loan. The collateral pledged never seems to arrive. There simply isn't time. Keating prides himself on betting on individuals, not in following dull guidelines. In the next eighteen months or so he will hand over to Wolfswinkel about $130 million. Wolfswinkel is a dealer, or, as he puts it, "I'm a dirt peddler." To Charlie Keating he is a player, and that is what Charlie Keating seeks. When later Keating discovers that his damn staff is balking again about his zest for deals and is seeking to shut down his business with Wolfswinkel, he has a meeting with the dissenters on July 15, 1986, and hears their petty worries. Then, on July 20, Bruce Dickson, the brother of Keating's ex-son-in-law, weighs in with a memo that also questions the deals. That rips it for Charlie Keating. Two days later he makes several more loans to Wolfswinkel—that'll show 'em! Wolfswinkel, for his part, does not choke either. He builds, among other things, a sixteen-story office tower in Mesa, Arizona, the structure outlined with neon. In front he places a sculpture of his parents sitting on a park bench, the way they first met. The plaque reads: "without whose love and guidance this building never would have been possible." The $52.5 million he borrowed from Western Savings and Loan also helped.

Keating is in Florida. Send a Cadillac, he instructs, send a

Cadillac to the Miami airport, pick up Jamal Radwan, and bring him back to the mansion on Indian Creek. They talk for more than three hours about the Saudi-European Bank, about the possibility of Keating maybe picking up some of the stock for $8 million, about the Saudi-European Bank perhaps plunking down some of its money for U.S. investments. They consider the various investments of Sir James Goldsmith and toss around hotel management possibilities for Keating's people, both domestically and overseas.

There is also the matter of the Saudi-European Bank loan to Clint Murchison, Jr., of Texas. The previous fall *Forbes* had listed his net worth at around $250 million, and he owned a 100 percent share in 140 corporations and slices of another 110. On February 22, 1985, he files for Chapter 11, and that June, when the accountants finally tally up debts and assets, they discover that he personally owes $396,693,827.89. This figure later swells to $560 million. As for his assets, they run only to $70,767,295.88. The world is not always a safe place.

A week later Charlie Keating is in Beverly Hills for Drexel's annual Predator's Ball. This year he is truly a player; in a week he will bring Gulf to its knees and greenmail will gush forth into his hands. Carl Lindner is there, as are Ivan Boesky, T. Boone Pickens, and Sir James Goldsmith. On Thursday night, the annual cocktail party for the big players is held in Bungalow 8 at the Beverly Hills Hotel, and when one of the high rollers gets excited by all the beautiful women and locks into a conversation with one for hours—"I've got to hand it to these guys, I've never seen so many beautiful wives!"—another player looking on says, "Tell Irwin he doesn't have to work so hard. She's already paid for." Of course she is, because if you're going to make it in business you can't leave anything to chance. Guys who've spent their days and nights looking at dull columns of numbers have a lot of making up to do. One of the partygoers explains it this way: "All the big takeover guys were in that place together and we've all got tremendous egos, we're all trying to prove ourselves all the time, to show we can get the girl we didn't get in high school, we're basically a bunch of exhibitionists—things just got out of hand."* At the Friday night banquet another Drexel specialty, the in-house comic ad, opens the program, and this year it is a takeoff on the E. F. Hutton

*Connie Bruck, *The Predator's Ball,* pp. 14-16.

ad ("When E. F. Hutton talks . . .") backed by theme music from
Ghostbusters. Except in this ad a great-looking woman walks past
and a guy asks, "Did you see the tits on that broad?" Then artificial fog rolls across the stage and Diana Ross walks out singing
"Ain't No Mountain High Enough." Her medley runs forty minutes. She pauses ever so briefly and says, "I can't believe how
much money is in this room, how much power is here." The audience erupts in applause for itself. At the end of her act she
comes off the stage still singing, walking amid the tables, and then
settles onto Carl Lindner's lap and sings to him.

Everything Keating has ever wanted is within reach now. His
employees all call him Charlie, and he is the center of their world.
His fleet of planes stands ready to travel anywhere. He has moved
his antipornography organization to within his corporate headquarters, and some days he will go to its offices and watch dirty
movies and help create elaborate précis of this filth. He holds an
annual $1,000-per-plate charity ball to finance Citizens for De-
cency Through Law—the party in the fall of 1985 raises more than
$1 million. Charlie Keating the zealot is also Charlie Keating the
man of the world. At the CDL benefit in 1985, Conley
Wolfswinkel walks up to Keating, gives him a check for $50,000
or $100,000, and says, "Charlie, I love you and I love what you're
doing. But I got to be honest with you: I love this stuff, I watch it
all the time." And Charlie Keating takes the check and just
smiles.*

Charlie Keating is hot now. He can support his church with millions in loans to Father Ritter's work with homeless children, millions to Mother Teresa to sustain her saintly tasks, a hundred
grand a year to the fathers in Phoenix to help ease the suffering of
the homeless. A bundle of money to Father Brian to help train

---

*One ACC executive who is also Catholic tries to explain this aspect of Charlie
Keating and himself this way: "I think this a phenomenon that anyone who has religious belief has to deal with on a daily basis. I mean, I can tell you personally as a
Catholic that I personally struggle with—if you really believe in Mass, and if you really believe that God is present, what the fuck am I doing sitting here with you? I
should be in church. I mean, I should be kneeling down in church and trying to save
my soul. I mean, if you really believe it. So I think that's just something that anybody
struggles with. I mean, whatever your religious beliefs are, if you really believe them,
shouldn't you be off helping the poor or doing something to make sure you don't end
up going to Hell? I don't know if Charlie really believed it, but I know . . ."

those promising young students in Harlem. And why not a swimming club like the one he sponsored in Cincinnati? Yes, he will build the pool, hire a national-level coach, and write the thing off, so to speak, by making it a health facility of the Phoenician, which is rising up several miles away. He looks out of his office, and my God, there is a line of nuns waiting to see him and get his contribution. He looks out of his office, and there are all these beautiful young people working for him. *Forbes* has just announced that ACC is number one in the nation in percentage of asset growth for 1984 and ranks 338th in terms of assets. His company claims to have experienced a 60 percent compounded growth rate since 1977. One thousand people now work for him, and his payroll runs to $50 million a year. By May, his company claims assets of $3.3 billion and sells off Continental Homes, Keating's original Phoenix grubstake. American Continental explains it is getting out of building houses so that it can focus on financial services.

This is not like the bad time in Cincinnati with that snotty article appearing in *Fortune* that said nobody liked Charlie Keating. No, no, this is a new hand, and in April 1985, Charlie Keating feels he holds nothing but aces.

$\mathbb{M}$ark *Sauter, one of ACC's attorneys, is in Los Angeles to cut a deal with the federal prosecutors. It is October 1989, Lincoln has been seized by the government, ACC is in Chapter 11, and the menace of lawsuits is everywhere. Sauter wants a few things about ACC understood. No one, he insists, can grasp what has happened unless they understand the company's almost unique culture. So the federal lawyers sit back and listen and scribble down what Mark Sauter is teaching them. When he finishes speaking, his audience of attorneys has made a record of his comments that is sixty pages long.*

"At the commencement of the proffer, Sauter advised us that when we looked at and analyzed the case we should understand the corporate culture of the ACC corporate family. He advised us that the ACC corporate family was, in fact, the sole proprietorship of Charles Keating and that the entire corporate group was run by a very close knit inner circle. He divided the inner circle into two groups. The first was the family group. . . . The nonfamily group [had three real members]. . . . Each of the nonfamily group members attained their significant corporate status by virtue of demonstration of unfaltering loyalty to Mr. Keating. According to Sauter, to Mr. Keating loyalty was the highest virtue.

"Judy [Wischer] had been with CHK since 1972 in his days at American Financial Corporation. According to Sauter, CHK told him that Judy had 'stood by me' through the SEC matter. . . . According to Sauter, she was a person who perpetually demonstrated extreme loyalty. . . .

"Bob Kielty had a long history with CHK as well. According to Sauter, he did chores around the CHK home as a boy. . . . He is also a person who has demonstrated perpetual and long-term loyalty to CHK. . . .

"Sauter describes the various boards of the corporations within the ACC corporate family as 'fictitious.' Positions on those various boards were used by CHK to make various people feel like they *were being rewarded. A paralegal in Sauter's office kept a list of officers and directors. It was frequently marked in red by CHK and changed monthly. This indicated who was in favor with CHK and who was out. . . .*

"Whenever Sauter got into a safety and soundness discussion with Keating, he would become impatient and say there was nothing unsafe or unsound about the operation."

Sauter gives the puzzled federal lawyers a glimpse into the world of Charlie Keating. But what his story means to them is very difficult to say because they are not of Charlie Keating's corporate world.

Perhaps they should consider the importance of games. Charlie Keating always does. He is a player, always. He wants the best, dammit, the best. His employees must understand excellence. He puts a basketball hoop up behind the headquarters of American Continental Corporation on Camelback Road, and he gets his people out there to practice, practice. But still it does not seem quite enough. Although he tends to recruit athletes to his company, although he surely has enough raw talent among his staff, he can sense their play is not quite right. Phoenix has an NBA team, the Suns. Keating hires their coach to come over and run a basketball clinic one weekend. And then the employees get very serious. The game gets very rough.

THE
COLOR OF
WHITE

Edwin Gray is not cut out for Washington, D.C. He is the son of a Modesto, California, salesman who had come from Texas as a boy when his family had followed the crops as migrant workers. His father never forgot his suffering and remained a Baptist fundamentalist and populist all of his life. Ed Gray stutters as a boy, yet graduates as valedictorian (and champion debater) of his high school and plans on a career in radio. He winds up doing public relations for Pacific Telephone and Telegraph in Sacramento. When Ronald Reagan runs for governor of California in 1966, he asks the phone company for volunteers and they ship over Ed Gray and pay his salary. (He changes his registration from Democrat to Republican.) When Reagan is elected, Ed Gray has the kind of position in the campaign where he is assigned to find the oldest possible Bible in California for the swearing-in ceremony. For the next six years, he is on leave from the phone company and works for Reagan. Reagan retires after two terms, and Gray gets a job as senior vice president for public affairs with a thrift in San Diego.

Then Reagan makes his move for the presidency in 1980, and Gray helps out again. When Reagan wins, Gray becomes an official in the White House office of policy development. He is a man without influential friendships in a city that runs on clout. Ed Gray is not a man who impresses a lot of people: he is a balding, white-shoes kind of guy. Reporters once locked him in the campaign plane's bathroom by putting masking tape over the door. He was called "Mr. Ed" after the talking horse on a television comedy. He is not happy in his new job—the hours are long, his wife, Monique, is left alone as he toils in the White House, the people around him are brutal. Finally he says he has had enough, and in August 1982, there is a party for him in the Roosevelt Room of the White House, Reagan and Vice President George Bush attend, and then Ed Gray heads home to California with a handwritten note from the president thanking him for almost two decades of service. When he crosses the bridge over the Potomac, he pulls off onto the side of the road, gets out, and cuts loose with a shout of jubilation.

In California, he takes a job doing public relations for the recently deregulated savings and loan industry. Ed Gray preaches the virtue of deregulation, he works hand in glove with the industry lobbying group in D.C., the U.S. League of Savings Institutions. The league is powerful, and for years there has been an informal understanding that it gets to pick (or at least veto) the president's choice for chairman of the Federal Home Loan Bank Board. The league officials look around for a new candidate and notice Ed Gray working the convention. Who could be better than a friendly PR guy from California who won't rock any boats and who is putting out copy every day celebrating the new era coming with deregulation? So in May 1983, just as Charlie Keating is scouting California for a thrift to buy, Ed Gray goes back to the capital, promising his wife he will stay only two years. He believes he has assumed a rocking-chair kind of job.

Five weeks into the job, Ed Gray smells trouble. He is in Dallas, Texas, to address a regional meeting of savings and loan owners, and one of them invites him to dinner. Gray notices with surprise that the man is wearing an expensive Rolex watch and a big diamond ring. They ride to the restaurant in a blue Rolls-Royce. When Gray asks about the fine things, the man explains, "Our institution is very profitable."

Two months later, in August, Ed Gray sits in a meeting organized by the Federal Savings and Loan Insurance Corporation (FSLIC), the outfit that insures all those deposits. These regulators run a few facts by him. The thrifts, they point out, are increasingly not running on the deposits of local people but feeding off big brokered jumbo accounts ("hot money" in the parlance of the trade)—$100,000 units. And these federally insured monies are, under deregulation, pouring into risky loans and investments. On the books, the industry is now bankrupt: the bad deals exceed the size of the insurance fund, and there is little that can be done. The deals are happening so fast and money is flowing so swiftly, the agency lacks the personnel even to track it.

Ed Gray begins to live like a monk. His $70,000-a-year salary is not enough to take care of his family, what with his wife still living in their house in California and his two daughters in college. So he rents a one-bedroom apartment. The living room has a peeling imitation leather couch and a small table with a bare-bulb lamp and his IBM Selectric typewriter on which he writes all his speeches about the U.S. savings and loan industry. The walls are lined with bank board documents, and for entertainment at night Ed Gray listens to his shortwave radio. He dines at McDonald's. For a while he pops into the National Presbyterian Center to listen to the choir, but one day the minister rails about the sorry state of the church's finances and Gray flees, never to return. He does not want to hear about money problems. He has to take out a $10,000 loan from his widowed mother and get cash advances from his credit cards just to meet his current expenses.

He works all the time, and on days when he must appear before a congressional committee, Ed Gray comes to the office at 3 A.M. so he can cram. One day, just before he is to go up on the Hill, his people cannot find him. Finally his chief of staff, Shannon Fairbanks, looks in his private bathroom, and there is Ed Gray curled up on the floor, sound asleep.

He begins to believe that the problem in the industry is the hot money from the jumbo accounts and the lack of any constraint on how this hot money is invested. He begins to circulate new guidelines, which if implemented will amount to reregulation. He wants to restrict the percentage of jumbos that thrifts can buy, he wants to cut back on direct investment. He does not make friends with these ideas. His own staff thinks he is wrong. The president has put Donald Regan in command over at Treasury, and the former head of Merrill Lynch, whose brokers are making a killing on their commissions from peddling jumbos ($770 million in federally insured jumbos in 1985 alone), is not keen on Ed Gray's new restrictions. Regan and his staff argue that brokers help the nation by speeding capital to those regions that need it.

Gray is not convinced, but then he knows he is not a man from Wall Street. He's the son of a migrant worker who never got past the seventh grade. And he has not spent his life in fights; quite the opposite, he is a public relations man. Still, on March 14, 1984, he gets out of bed around 4 A.M. to type out his remarks for an up-coming appearance before a congressional committee looking into his plans for new regulations. Then he goes down to his office at the bank board building, where some of his people from Texas want to show him a twenty-minute videotape. The tape is not very fancy; it was shot by an appraiser hired to check out some of the projects a thrift is backing around Dallas, a thrift run, as it happens, by the same man who drove Gray to dinner in a blue Rolls-Royce the previous June.

A road map appears on the screen; then a hand holding a pen stabs at the path of I-30 from Dallas to Lake Ray Hubbard. Acres float past the eye, acres of half-built condos and completed condos; piles of unused construction material rot in the sun, sacked and burned units come into focus. The tape rolls on and on, showing mile after mile of half-finished or finished and unoccupied developments. There is nothing else—no stores, no schools, no sales force, no residents. Even the top developments are 60 to 80 percent empty. Gray watches and then turns his head because, as he later explains, "It was so shameful." He calls Paul Volcker of the Federal Reserve and asks him to come over and view the tape. He begins to carry it around the Hill with him. And he starts telling Congress, "The list of horror stories resulting from the misuse of brokered funds by desperate financial institutions is growing as the weeks and months go on." It is about this time in 1984 that Ed Gray, the former public relations man, tells his aide, Shannon Fairbanks, "Everything from here on out is for history." On May 16, 1984, the bank board, led by Ed Gray, proposes new guidelines for savings and loans that would slash direct investment to no more than 10 percent of a thrift's net worth.

As Gray speaks, Charlie Keating is in the process of cutting deals with Connally and Barnes, forming an alliance with oil sheiks in the Middle East, dreaming of creating an entirely new city, plotting his entrance into the world of grand hotels. He is working his staff eighty to a hundred hours a week to fulfill his vi-sion of what this country can do when it has access to capital.

By September 1984 Charlie Keating appears as a blip on the screen of a federal regulator in Washington, D.C. William Black of the FHLBB notices hostile letters coming in from Charlie Keating's lawyers, men like Arthur Liman and Peter Fishbein, and he knows who they are and what their participation means. They are heavy hitters (Fishbein has represented Carl Lindner since the early seventies and was Keating's lawyer before the SEC in the 1979 settlement), and if this is the company Charlie Keating keeps, why then he must be somebody or at least somebody who knows how the game is played. And these attorneys are true hired guns. Fishbein, for example, is Harvard Law, a former Supreme Court clerk, and a dabbler in politics. He has worked for the Peace Corps and participated in the campaigns of Robert Kennedy, Arthur Goldberg, and Mario Cuomo. But he is flexible. In 1982, he helps rich New York State school districts beat back an effort to equalize support for all public schools. The year before, when preservationists sought to save New York's Biltmore Hotel, Fishbein got it demolished. As one of his former associates explains, "Peter is not the world's friendliest guy."

Bill Black knows intimately the dance between legislation and regulation, between administrators and politicians, among power and money and law. He is a small man with a scraggly beard, a mop of red hair, and a carelessness in dress—he spends his spare time in old Levi's and torn sweatshirts. He is the son of a beer and wine advertising salesman for the *Detroit News.* In high school and college he is a debater, and by the eighth grade Clarence Darrow is his hero and the law is his future.

He is in private practice and doing quite well when Ed Gray asks him to join him at the bank board. His partners argue against the move; they tell him Gray is a little person, a fool. But Black is attracted, he still in some sense wants to be a Clarence Darrow, to serve. He tells people that by working for government, at least he is trying to make the world a better place. In private practice he often sees lawyers using their skills in ways he finds socially detrimental. He says that as a government lawyer he can look at himself in the mirror. He is a Democrat, but this identity is not sufficient. He wishes to represent something larger than a party. Some people find him a zealot; all find him committed. And in the fall of 1984 he begins to take note of Charlie Keating and Lincoln Savings and Loan. He is close to Gray; they work in the same building, speak to each other each day. And Bill Black, like Charlie Keating, is implacable and not afraid of a fight. He defines his duty as a public servant simply: to keep federally insured financial institutions from taking risks. In his mind he is a guard, and what he guards is the public treasury and the public trust.

In the fall of 1984, it becomes apparent that Gray is really seeking to reduce the amount of money thrifts can invest directly—meaning the bucks they can put into deals not as loans but as actual players in real estate schemes and the like. And Charlie Keating, who has just paid $51 million for a thrift that is legally allowed to do all those things, begins to fight—fight with lawyers, fight with lobbyists, fight with people on the Hill. He is in the midst of the Gulf Broadcast deal, which will eventually make him $50 million, he is launched into the Pontchartrain Hotel, into Estrella, into the Phoenician, into a new universe, and now the federal government wants to welsh on the deal and shut down the party. He will not abide this.

He knows this sensation so very well. In 1975, he was the key partner, in his eyes the cofounder, of American Financial Corporation in Cincinnati, a $2 billion operation. And then the SEC charges came down and he was out. Out because of niggling rules, out of a company that he not only had helped create, but one that would go on to have $12 billion in assets. This must not happen again. He will see to that. His aides tell him to back off, to deal with the regulators, to cut back on investments in questioned areas. He says no, he says fuck 'em. He refuses to hold any office at Lincoln Savings and Loan, he will not let them do to him what they did in 1979 when he had to plead no contest to a laundry list of charges lodged by the SEC. He has learned one lesson: fuck 'em.

Luck is always a factor. In September 1984, Manning discovers the Seven Dwarfs. They are six of Mario Renda's brokers plus a secretary who launched their own company and were then sued by Renda. One of them had gone to Washington to dig up dirt on his former boss in hopes of helping their case. And had looked up the same FDIC attorney Manning had brought into the California depositions and offered to trade information. And then, with Renda almost within reach, they settled and the deal was off. Manning had been drooling at this break—he applies the term "Seven Dwarfs" to their group—and when they back off, he decides to play hardball. He tells them he is going to depose them for the thirty-four cases he is preparing, and of course in such depositions other counsel must be present and Renda will soon know what they say. Manning knows that the dwarfs are terrified of Renda; people come to visit him who carry guns, and Renda has told them that he is connected—mobbed up. They opt for Manning's offer of an administrative subpoena, which means they and their lawyers can meet with him alone and they'll talk on the record but Renda will not know.

They begin meeting in Babylon, New York, in the late afternoon of October 3. Manning senses that one of the dwarfs wants to help but is scared to death. "He said, I can't, I can't give you documents. You don't understand about this guy, you don't understand how dangerous he is, he'll stop at nothing." By this time Manning knows that Renda has penetrated over a hundred banks and some are starting to fail. "The rest of the people [dwarfs], the shells were too hard. I'd knock on each one of the shells and tap for spots that are soft and hollow and it just wasn't there. But with this one guy, I could tell the way he looked at me. And I'd say to him, I think this can be stopped, I made him believe this was more than another assignment for me. That this was going to get done. I was going to win this." The man keeps telling Manning he can't provide documents, it's too dangerous. "They talk about getting hit, they were very clear about it. A couple say, 'If it were just me . . . but it's my family.' " Nor can Manning make light of their fears. On his third deposition, Manning learns that someone has called Renda and said, "The Seven Dwarfs are talking to the FDIC." He is shaken—is the phone in his New York hotel room tapped?

After dark on Saturday, Manning finishes with his questions. He walks out to the parking lot, one of the dwarfs follows him out to say good-bye. Manning opens the trunk, throws his overnight bag in. Then he opens the car door for the court reporter, and as he puts his briefcase in the car behind the driver's side, Manning sees the dwarf put something into the trunk and shut it. He drives out of the lot, and a few blocks away he pulls over and looks into the trunk and sees that he has some documents. On the flight back home he fans through them, and he knows. Now he has Renda. He learns a new lexicon from the documents: the deals are called special deals, or black magic deals. Manning calls the FBI and the U.S. Attorney's office. On October 19, Renda's office is hit by federal agents along with a law office in Honolulu.

He now understands in detail how the scheme operates. Renda runs a brokered deposit business and offers clients a high rate of return in federally insured jumbo deposits. He deals with large pension funds, union funds, credit unions, and the like and places their money in hundreds of banks around the country. He becomes one of the country's two or three largest hot money brokers. These banks are generally quite small, and more than a hundred of them are targeted by Renda for loan requests from his emissaries. In many cases, the people who apply for these loans are told they will never have to pay them back. All they must do is turn over the money to Renda's organization, and they are paid for this service. The blocks of borrowed money, a hundred thousand here, two hundred thousand there, wend their way back to Renda as profit. His own brokered deposit clients cannot lose, for their money is in federally insured deposits. Occasionally the money managers he is dealing with are too busy to keep track of everything, and often he does not even pay them the high interest he has promised. The borrowers default on their loans, and the banks write them off. And Mario Renda's fingerprints are nowhere to be found—in fact, there is no clear linkage between the deposits his company has brokered into these small banks and the sudden eruptions of strange, unsecured loans. The only minor flaw, that greed on his part can and does make many of the small banks fail, is truly very minor. Who is ever going to look through the mountain of paper a dead bank leaves in its wake and piece it all together? There is no rational reason to anticipate the existence of a lawyer in Kansas City named Michael Manning. Nor does Renda seem to be aware of Manning's existence even after his business is raided by federal agents.

Late that fall Manning finds a phone message on his desk. A man in New York needs a lawyer for some litigation he is caught up in in Kansas City. Would Manning be interested? The man's name is Mario Renda. Manning relishes the irony but does not return the call.

Kim Campbell comes to work at American Continental Corporation in February 1985. She moved to Phoenix the previous December and quickly learns that ACC pays very well. She hears other things, of course. Her husband, who is a real estate appraiser, is leery of the company, sensing something not quite right in ACC, something unusually risky. He tells her they are crooks. But this sense that ACC is different, that it is a unique corporate culture, is precisely what Charlie Keating wants people to realize: he is building an original corporation, and for it he wants a different kind of person. That is why he is still trying to interview every job applicant himself. He wants his stamp on everything.

She goes to work in the insurance end of the company, and Chip Wischer, Judy's husband, is her boss. Kim was born in eastern New Mexico in 1964, her parents divorced, her mother remarried several times, and she has learned to survive on her own. When she was fourteen, back in 1978 when the Wischers were contemplating their big move to Phoenix and their new, large paychecks, Kim appeared in court demanding her custody be shifted from her mother to her father. The judge looked down at her and asked, "Don't you remember me?", then cleared the courtroom and explained that he had known her mother. By sixteen she is absolutely on her own, but she finishes high school. Her marriage is not working, but she is the kind of person who is used to things not working. She is petite, her hair is blond, her eyes are blue, and there is a sense of life about her that makes her five-foot height seem irrelevant. She is almost indestructible. She cannot be threatened by firing, by power, by money. She knows she can survive anything—because she already has.

Wischer's operation, Insurance West, has moved out of the ACC headquarters on Camelback to a new building in Scottsdale, a complex it shares with Keating's antipornography organization, Citizens for Decency Through Law. When Kim is first interviewed, six people grill her for two hours. They do not so much ask her things as tell her things and watch how she reacts. They preach that ACC is wonderful, that Charlie Keating is wonderful, that Chip Wischer is wonderful—things Kim perceives as "this kind of crap." The next day they call her back for more interviews, and she is hired. At first the pay is not spectacular. But then things begin to occur that are not typical of American business.

The Gucci bonus, for example. A woman will be working there a week, two weeks, maybe three weeks, and suddenly her supervisor will say, "Come with me" and take her down to Gucci and tell her to pick out a handbag. Or simply hand over $500 or $1,000 and say, "Go buy some nice clothes." A tailor comes into the office to measure the men and make up suits. The suits must be of a certain cut, shirts cannot be short sleeved, and the pockets must always be monogrammed. A shoeshine man—Heels on Wheels—roams the company. Patronizing him is not an option; the man comes up to someone with suspect shoes, says, "Let me take care of that," and then the employee must pay five dollars. Nothing is left to chance.

Of course, some things are never stated in the invisible rule book, but Kim is very quick to notice things. The fixation with large breasts strikes her ("if you're the only flat-chested girl in the whole legal department, it is kind of obvious you had better get some tits"). Weight also matters. Supervisors walk over to a woman and say, "You go on a diet and lose the weight, or you're out of here." Fingernails must be perfectly manicured. "I want professionals here," Keating will snap. "I don't want you to look like you worked on a farm all day." In many ways Kim has immunity. She is the blonde with the well-formed body. She is trim. She has the blue eyes. Still, some things kind of surprise her. One day she goes around ACC and asks the young women who work there, the attractive women often called Charlie's Angels, just how much they would want to pose for *Playboy* or *Hustler.* And they uniformly answer, well, a thousand, maybe two thousand dollars.

But what Kim Campbell notices most is the color of white. It is everywhere. The carpeting is white, the walls are white, the desks are white. She thinks she is working in a hospital. Desk tops must be spotless, utterly clear of any material. No one can have candy in the desks. This cleanliness is a preoccupation of the staff. Charlie Keating often comes to the building to visit CDL in order to examine and critique new pornographic material. But the people never really know if that is his mission or if he will sweep into their offices. So when he is sighted, someone will shout, "Charlie's coming! Charlie's coming!" and there will be a scramble as everyone polishes his desk top. Even casual day is never really casual at ACC. Women must look professional. Kim is told never to wear anything risqué, yet when she runs errands over to headquarters on Camelback Road, she notices that on casual day the women are dressed in a manner she can only perceive as raunchy. None of them is wearing flats, either. Charlie Keating loves high heels and nylons. He loves legs, she believes.

Keating's daughters often swing through the work areas, and they are the enforcers, Kim discovers. Everyone fears them. One of Charlie Keating's habits is to call someone up and ask about his daughters. One day he is out at Lincoln and calls up an employee and says, "Now, tell me about my daughter, isn't she screwing up? Getting in your hair, right?" And if you understand, you say there is no problem, we really love working with her. But this day at Lincoln, the person says, "So glad to hear you say that. She's driving me crazy." The person is instantly fired. Chip Wischer knows of at least two people who are fired and live for five years off their severance pay. One day when Kim is out of the office on an errand, two of Keating's daughters sweep into Insurance West and instantly notice a black file case on wheels. Kim has the key to this chest; it is where the entire staff hides their forbidden candies and snacks. The daughters ask, "What is this black box?" It is an affront to the whiteness of the entire office. The staff says, "It's Kim's, it's Kim's." And the daughters then ask, just who is this Kim? They decide to fire her. But a Keating son-in-law works at Insurance West, and he too hides all his candy in the black box. He intervenes and saves her job. But it is a close call.

She notices that this professional company is not always that professional. She goes to C3's office and is stopped by his secretary, who tells her that C3 is very busy. When she looks through the doorway, she sees him wadding up paper and playing basketball with a wastebasket.

About 80 percent of Insurance West's business is outside the company with outfits needing commercial coverage. Almost all of the video stores in Phoenix, as it happens, buy their policies from this subsidiary of ACC. Keating insists that these stores—every single one of them—be inspected to see if they rent pornographic movies. And if they do, their policies must be canceled. So Kim spends a lot of time popping into mom-and-pop video stores and inspecting their stock.

She is not sure she likes Charlie Keating. He will call and insist she go get some man out of the bathroom so he can speak to him. Yet he will not return a call for weeks. Once she is instructed to find an employee who has gone to the bathroom, and she opens the door and shouts, "Goddamnit, Charlie's on the phone and I'm tired of coming in the crapper to get you, get your ass out here now." And then she thinks that what she has just done is stupid, that she has become yet another pawn of Charlie Keating. She decides she will never do things like that again.

She is attracted to Chip. She likes his sense of humor. He's always making jokes, and Kim appreciates laughter. And so they get closer. This is noticed, but no one knows quite what to do about it. Chip is Judy Wischer's husband, and she is the president of ACC and one of Keating's closest aides. Kim seems not to care about the rules and acts as if she were immune to threats. Or rewards. Kim senses her peculiar standing the first time she meets Charlie Keating. He walks right up to her, looks her over carefully, and says, "You're Kim Campbell, aren't you?" She is a customer representative, about the lowliest job at Insurance West, making $22,000 a year. But Charlie Keating knows who she is.

He is six foot five, she is five foot even, and he will tower over her, deliberately crowd her, she thinks. Charlie Keating notices her but does not fire her. He rules through fear, he likes to keep people off balance, to keep people unsure of what is safe and what is not. And what can keep them more off balance than not firing Kim Campbell?

By the fall of 1984, it is apparent to Charlie Keating that Ed Gray is trying to cut back the direct investment rule from the level guaranteed to Lincoln under its California charter, 100 percent, to a new federal level of 10 percent. And this act will tinker with net worth, meaning it will increase the amount of money a thrift will have to keep in reserve and out of play. On October 19, 1984, Charlie Keating examines a newsletter called "The Bank Board Watch," which states "linkage of direct investment net worth regulations now seems unlikely." He does not believe the report and scribbles across the newsletter a note to the head of his legal department, Robert Kielty: "Kielty, it ain't over. Gray must be fired. CHK." He will tell everyone in Washington what he thinks of Gray—from Treasury Secretary Don Regan to Vice President George Bush. In another note he sends Kielty that fall about the proposed regulations, he is adamant: "Kielty, this absolutely must be stopped. By far the most negative impact on us we have ever faced." He didn't buy Lincoln to have the employees or the branches or even the assets for that matter. He bought the charter, the scrap of paper that instantly fulfilled his dream of being a merchant banker. So he hires the best lawyers, and they look at the situation and tell him he has a case. Charlie Keating believes in lawyers—in the next five years Lincoln will hire dozens of firms, including twenty of the nation's largest, and drop $4 million to $9 million a year on them. The lawyers suggest he get some economists to study his operation and those of other deregulated thrifts and give an opinion on their merits. They suggest Alan Greenspan. Keating thinks this is a fantastic idea. Greenspan dutifully prepares a report endorsing deregulated thrifts—for a fee of more than $32,000. The threat of lawsuits is hurled at the regulators. A favorite tactic is to send the regulators drafts of complaints with the warning that the next time they won't be just drafts. It is the instinctive way Charlie Keating always deals with government opponents—drag them out of their bureaucracies, get them into court where there are rules, a level playing field.

Also, there is lobbying, and he begins hiring people to work Congress, a squad that will eventually reach fifteen. Len Beckwit, who has worked in Senator John Glenn's office, comes on board. Eventually, they hire Bill White, once Glenn's administrative assistant and still his personal attorney. They pick up Dave Evans, once a member of the House Banking Committee. Also, former congressman Don Clancy. Keating himself begins going to Washington more often, visiting congressmen, giving his case for deregulated thrifts. Of course, he denounces Ed Gray; how can this former flack administer a trillion-dollar thrift industry? The deals keep going forward—all the Gulfs, Pontchartrains, Estrellas, Conley Wolfswinkels, and John Connallys. He flies people out to Phoenix, shows them around. Charlie Keating always thinks that if his critics can only see his operation, they will convert.

And he loses. On January 31, 1985, Gray gets the bank board to roll back the limit on direct investments, and the rollback is retroactive to December 10, 1984. Suddenly Lincoln is hundreds of millions of dollars over the line, it is out of compliance with the regulation. Even worse, some of its deals, like the Pontchartrain, occur before the new ruling but after the retroactive date. They are at best invalid, at worst illegal, and there is a scramble at Lincoln to straighten out the records so that they accord with the new mandates.

There are many problems to face. In September 1984, the bank regulators have just finished examining Lincoln's books, and when they exit, Keating terminates the entire accounting staff, including one of his sons-in-law. Though he does not even hold a position at Lincoln, Keating becomes the chief loan officer, and until July 1985 does deals without consulting anyone or doing any underwriting. He lives the life of a merchant banker. When Gray successfully makes his first move to reinstate regulations, Charlie Keating is naked. A new mind-set begins to appear at Lincoln and among the staff of ACC. If a loan lacks documentation, underwriting, appraisals, and the like, then this means the file must be corrected, brought up to the standards of the regulators. If a direct investment is suddenly in excess of the new direct investment limit, this means a way must be found to characterize it as a loan, not a direct investment. If a deal involving executives at ACC and Lincoln is suddenly viewed as illicit insider trading or self-dealing, this means it must be restructured through subsidiaries so that it cannot be seen this way. Things must be corrected. Laws are not broken, they are rethought and reinterpreted. That is why so many accountants are necessary. That is why so many lawyers are necessary. Step by step, reregulation is seen as an obstacle, not a wall. Avoiding the intent of regulations is seen as not breaking laws but evading them. It is a gradual process, but it is relentless. When a Lincoln employee plucks a file months after a deal and inserts the paperwork that was actually required before the deal could even be done, he is bringing the file up to date. Not falsifying, not backdating, not file stuffing. Over time, as these practices grow and finally become the norm, a bizarre circumstance will arise: a situation where the federal government and the staff of ACC agree largely on the facts and disagree violently on what the facts mean.

On January 28, 1985, Michael Manning gets a call from Stan Tobias in Hawaii. When Tobias was deposed in July, he took the Fifth Amendment fifty-two times. Now he is Manning's key witness, able to link actions in New York City, Honolulu, Kansas City, and California as all part of a centrally planned scheme, a conspiracy. On the phone Tobias is very secretive and nervous. On the thirty-first, they meet in Orange County, California, and Tobias hands over boxes of documents. For three days, Manning grills him—thirteen hours the first day, fourteen hours the second, fourteen and a half hours the third. Tobias is upset by this schedule, which disrupts his exercise regime. At one point, Tobias does his workout on the conference room floor. As he pumps out push-ups, Manning continues to fire questions at him and he gasps out answers.

In April 1985 in the U.S. District Court in Kansas City, Mario Renda and his colleagues are sued for $65 million by the FDIC. In a little over a year, Manning has proven that his suspicions have merit. Now he must win in court. He figures that will take him two solid years but Renda is no simple subject to take apart. Before his indictment he was managing $5 billion. Michael Manning is embarking on postgraduate work in the most advanced techniques of U.S. bank fraud.

Mark Sauter is Keating's expert on federal bank regulations, and between June 1985 and March 1986 he is involved in forty separate meetings or telephone conferences about how to get the documentation in the loan files up to snuff. When Sauter says that the lack of appraisals in the files means the deals are not in compliance, he is told that a letter of value will do and a full appraisal can come later. This happens repeatedly on different aspects of deals—any problems are seen as technical, something to be worked out between the accountants and the lawyers, a clerical matter. The important thing is that the deals must go forward and that Charlie Keating not be stopped.

This state of mind can occur in part because Charlie Keating is a salesman and he sells enthusiasm and ideas and belief. He does this almost effortlessly. First he petitions the regulators to be exempted from their new rules, and his request is denied. Then in February 1985, he appears as a witness before a congressional committee that is looking into whether the thrifts should be reregulated, and whether Chairman Gray's new rules, either proposed or implemented, are good rules. And Charlie Keating comes across once again as a missionary for his faith in wide-open thrifts. Even if some are out of control, he allows, it is too late to back off. You cannot simply turn off the faucet. This he knows. He has already put hundreds of millions of dollars into play based on the earlier understanding.

Keating's testimony is disarming and has an off-the-cuff quality. When the chairman welcomes him as Charles Keating, he instantly sets the record straight—"My name is Charlie Keating."

"To reregulate today," he allows, "in a world of financial institutions being deregulated and with institutions that are not now regulated competing on a level playing field, is suicidal. It is burning down the house to roast the pig."

He has ideas. He thinks the premium charged for federal insurance should be raised—"that is part of life." He thinks that the need for thrifts to provide home loans has ended; after all there is a huge market of Ginnie Maes and Freddie Macs out there right now providing people with money to buy homes. And more important, he has real problems with this whole notion of his federal government insuring deposits for guys like himself.

"I think that the FSLIC," he announces, "and the FDIC could phase out of the insurance business. The government just plain is not good at it. I think one of the ways to do that would be to immediately begin to reduce the amount insured, which is now $100,000, which, in my opinion, is excessive."

As for the rest, he continues, let the market decide. If a thrift can raise capital, then leave it alone when it seeks to make a profit. And what is wrong with direct investment? he asks. Why should he let some developer make all the profit through a loan when he can make a killing himself through an equity investment? The whole talk going on now is crazy, he thinks. Take subordinated debentures, junk bonds.

"[W]e filed in May for a subordinated debenture," he blurts out. "We have not heard yet. I do not care whether they tell me yes or no. I do not happen to think subordinated debenture is viable capital; I think it is a sham. So I do not really care, but everybody else was doing it, so we filed; but that was May of 1984; we have not heard yet."

And that brings him to what really burns him up: this attitude that things can wait. "Speed to invest," he explains, "—I've heard someone today say that you—thirty days is plenty of time. I have been in business over forty-five years and—I'm sixty-one years old; since I've been in business—I have never known when thirty days was available on a very good investment, including real estate. Maybe I operate in a different business investment. . . . The FHLBB staff is not competent, in my opinion, to make business judgments on the processing of these investment applications. If they were, they would be out in the business world."

And when the hearings fail to achieve what he wants, he takes to the Hill to fight for a bill to roll back reregulation and he gets over two hundred congressmen to endorse it. Keating has had his aides and lobbyists toiling together with the staff of Representative Frank Annunzio in pushing for H. Cong. Res. 34, a bill tossed into the hopper on January 21, 1985, which seeks to stop reregulation of direct investments. Nor does he ignore the Senate side, where his troops are working over the members of the Senate Banking Committee. One aide, in citing his good deeds for this period, lists the senators he has done the most with: Thurmond, Mattingly, Cranston, Glenn, Armstrong, Laxalt, Hecht, DeConcini, Dole, Hawkins, Proxmire, and Wilson. Like most American businessmen, Charlie Keating has cultivated politicians for years. Like Carl Lindner with his formidable circle bundling cash to various PACs, like Michael Milken at Drexel with his own bundling operation, he knows that congressmen always need money. In 1986, Senator Alan Cranston will spend $13 million getting reelected, and he will defeat an opponent who spends $15 million. In a nation where there are many regulatory agencies and where the biggest business of all is government itself, Charlie Keating knows he needs relationships with politicians. Keating has given money to Senator Cranston, Senator Glenn, Senator DeConcini, and Congressman McCain. He asks them to speak with Gray about this new regulation on direct investments, so they all write to Gray and urge him to delay enforcing the new rule until there can be a congressional debate on the matter—a classic stalling tactic. DeConcini and Glenn also write to members of the Senate Banking Committee, and DeConcini drafts and circulates a bill that seeks to delay the rule for a year.

Glenn is a hero to Keating because of his space shot. In July 1984, the employees of ACC contribute $10,000 to Glenn, in December they are moved to give another $8,200. On July 10, 1985, Charlie Keating meets with Glenn and his wife, Annie, in his Washington office. Keating has known him slightly since his days in Cincinnati, and after this visit, they become closer. Soon Keating and Glenn, both former fighter pilots, are swapping flying stories. Then, without warning, Keating shifts gears and begins telling Glenn how much he admires his career as an astronaut, how he has been a personal hero for years—including his work as a public servant. Charlie Keating is drifting off into one of his monologues. He says he understands the sacrifice involved in giving up business and wealth for a career in politics. He truly knows, he says, because he is a businessman, a capitalist, and he is wealthy, that in fact, 1984 was a great year for ACC and 1985 looks to be even better. Is there anything his company can do to help? The key distinction Keating is touching on is between soft money and hard, between corporate donations to political committees and federally restricted donations by individuals to individuals. Glenn answers that he'll have to check with Bill White, his former assistant, about the laws and so forth. Then Keating suddenly blurts out that he will raise $100,000 corporately in 1985 and another $100,000 in 1986 for the senator's captive organization, the National Council on Public Policy. Besides, he wants to help Glenn with the campaign debt he incurred in his failed run for the presidency. Charlie Keating feels that it is humiliating for a hero like John Glenn to have to panhandle to pay his old debts. He has access to mailing lists, he knows heavy contributors, he will do anything to help. Mrs. Glenn is so moved by Charlie Keating's unexpected offer that she hugs him and says that it is a terrible burden for her husband to raise money, that he is not suited to such a task and does poorly at it. Annie Glenn has always struggled with a severe stutter, and articulating her feelings is not an easy task for her. Her eyes tear up.

This is the way U.S. citizens and U.S. politicians speak of money and power. It is almost like listening in on Victorian gentlemen as they struggle to find a way to express their desire to take women to bed and what kind and shape of women they like to bed. And just as fornication continued apace and babies were conceived in Victorian England beneath the constraints placed on discussing sexuality and parts of the human anatomy, so too in modern U.S. politics torrents of dollars flow beneath the polite language of hard money and soft money and PACs and general-purpose policy committees. The facts are out in plain view, the take is duly noted by both givers and recipients. The enormous cost of running for public office is lamented, piously denounced, and then ignored. The fact is that the high cost of public office benefits people who hold public office—they can raise the money, they can stay in power. And they do. As the costs increase, reelection becomes almost automatic. Charlie Keating understands this world. He did not invent it. But he understands it. He will always tell some simple facts to people who question his giving. He will say that politicians come to him, he will say that they always have their hands out, he will say that neither he nor anyone like him in business can survive without giving such money. And then he will shrug, as though puzzled that anyone would be surprised by this fact.

With Keating, there are many moments of bonding, like his session with John Glenn in July 1985. He first meets John McCain at a Navy League dinner in 1981, where the survivor of five and a half years as a prisoner of war in Hanoi is the speaker. After the speech, Keating comes up to McCain, says he, too, was once a navy fighter pilot and that he deeply admires McCain's record and considers him to be a hero. McCain, the son of an admiral who was also the son of an admiral, got shot down on a mission over Hanoi at a time when his father commanded the entire U.S. naval fleet. He broke both arms and one knee, took a bayonet through the foot when a mob of Vietnamese tried to beat him to death, and was not treated kindly in captivity since his father, the admiral, was directing the bombing of Vietnam. After years of therapy he still has a dissolving shoulder joint and can barely raise one arm. Keating wants to know McCain better and takes him over to his table to meet his wife and family. All McCain knows is that Charlie Keating is an extremely successful home builder in Phoenix. But soon he learns that he is a heavy contributor to charities and political campaigns. When he runs for the House in 1982, he calls up Keating, who arranges a fund-raiser for him. They become closer, and in 1984, '85, and '86, McCain and his family vacation in Cat Cay with Keating. The place strikes him as a day camp with Keating's six children and grandchildren boating and swimming. McCain loves the water. Because of his injuries, swimming is one of the few forms of exercise he can do.

He sees Charlie Keating once every few months. They are friends in the way that busy men who are seeking power and who never have time for people consider each other friends. There are things about Charlie Keating that seem odd to McCain. His obsession with obliterating pornography does not seem to jibe with his penchant for wild, drunken parties. Also, he finds a habit of Keating's embarrassing: they will be at some function together, and Keating, without warning, will drift into one of his seemingly spontaneous monologues. He will tell people that John McCain is a true hero, a torture victim of the North Vietnamese. "Do you know what they did to John McCain? . . . John McCain never cracked when they . . ." and so forth, while McCain stands uncomfortably at his side. Eventually, McCain will receive $110,000, DeConcini will receive more than $40,000, Glenn more than $200,000, and Cranston almost $1,000,000.

In the summer of 1984, an ACC executive is at the Democratic National Convention in San Francisco when he sights Cranston. He introduces himself and says, "I represent American Continental, an Arizona company that owns a major California savings and loan. We're constituents of yours. Sometimes issues come before you that have interest to us, and I wanted to say hello."

Cranston whips out a three-by-five card and a pen and asks, "What's your name again? You work for a savings and loan? I do a lot for S and Ls. I've been very supportive of S and Ls. You should help me. I need your help."

The executive brings up ACC's troubles with Ed Gray, and Cranston says, "Ed Gray—I've already had run-ins with him. I agree with you. He's a problem."

A few days later Cranston's full-time fund-raiser, Joy Jacobson, calls the executive and says, "I understand that you met Senator Cranston and expressed that you might be able to help him."

Charlie Keating calls on Cranston on his next trip to Washington. He gives his set speech about how the Japanese are eating our lunch, how the regulators are destroying the financial industry. The senator says he believes in what Lincoln is doing, believes in the lack of constraints embodied in the Nolan act. Keating asks for nothing in particular, Cranston sticks with a vague hope that Keating will be willing to help him. It is all so informal and polite. Later an aide asks if ACC could possibly raise $10,000, and Keating responds with $25,000.

Bill Black, sitting over at the bank board, takes notice. He realizes that Charlie Keating is not just some hick from Arizona. That he is a sophisticated player in politics. In short, a menace. Soon Chairman Gray receives a report each morning on Lincoln. Charlie Keating becomes not just another wild-man thrift owner, he grows to be the symbol of what is wrong with the savings and loan industry.

But life goes on. In June, Keating is in Europe visiting friends, doing business, enjoying the fine hotels. On Monday, June 17, he comes to rest in Germany and a curious note enters his log:

1. Add to Lincoln Reserves
2. WJK 100
3. Mickey 900 m
4. Fishbein 750 m
5. RCF and RSS 100
6. Mother Teresa and Fr. Ritter
7. ACC dividend and stock repurchase
8. Bishop $100 + $250
9. $150,000 Xavier High School

And so forth. The note recognizes the world of regulations with the different estimates of how much of a reserve Lincoln must make to meet the federal regulators' net worth requirement. But for Charlie Keating this world blends easily with donations to his old high school and his support of Mother Teresa and Father Ritter. It is all of a piece for Charlie Keating, it all goes together with the white offices, the fight against pornography, the hatred of dirty desks, the scorn for rules. He is not alone in this curious mixture of a lust for money and a penchant for charity, in presenting his role in life as that of some kind of social reformer. Sir James Goldsmith—in between bouts of corporate takeover—injects money into the ecology movement and supports efforts to increase AIDS research. Michael Milken, when he interviews Dennis Levine (later convicted of insider trading) in early 1985 for a job at Drexel, promises him fifteen minutes and then rambles on for three hours, a strange monologue in which he sees himself as a kind of social scientist and savior who will raise so much capital through junk bonds that he will feed the hungry, shelter the homeless, dress the naked, and put the Third World on its feet.

By the summer of 1985, Dennis DeConcini has joined Charlie Keating's campaign to get rid of Ed Gray. He makes calls, he writes letters. And during the month of July he receives $20,000 in contributions from ACC employees.

In 1985, because of Mario Renda's dangerous connection, the FBI visits Manning and says, look, you need to be careful. Next time you go back to Long Island you shouldn't rent a car in your own name, you shouldn't have a hotel room in your own name, you should make reservations on a number of flights going into different airports. Manning follows their advice. And tells his wife.

They both visit their daughter's school and give the principal and her teachers instructions—no one is to pick her up at school except her mother or father. His wife is upset by the need for these precautions. This is not the way life in Kansas City is supposed to be. He promises her that after Renda their life will be normal, that he will stick to a conventional law practice.

Then an old college friend of Manning's who's now in public relations in Kansas City writes to him that a prospective client had come in offering the firm a large contract to mount an offensive against a local lawyer named Michael Manning. He also wants Manning followed and photographed. Money is no object. About the same time, the FBI in New York and Kansas City says that discrediting you is the focus of Renda's defense. They're saying you're too aggressive, you're getting people to lie, you're extorting money. Next Manning hears from Tobias that the word is that narcotics are going to be planted in his hotel room and he will be arrested. One day Manning goes to lunch and a mob-connected figure in Kansas City, who is also a former officer of the bank under investigation, enters the empty restaurant. He sits at a table right across from Manning and stares at him throughout lunch. Even as he eats he never looks down at his plate, he never breaks his stare.

One Friday afternoon in July 1985, a limousine pulls up to a nondescript Washington office building and out climbs White House chief of staff Donald Regan and two Secret Service men. Regan is making his first and last visit to columnist Jack Anderson, whose muckraking work appears in about six hundred dailies. Regan parks his two Secret Service officers in a secretary's office and enters Anderson's inner sanctum, where he sips a Cutty Sark while the Mormon Anderson sticks to Diet Coke. Regan has come with a message: the administration has a made a mistake. They have appointed this guy Ed Gray as the head of the bank board and he is a dud, in fact a disaster who may ruin the entire industry. After Regan leaves, Anderson calls in one of his staff people, Michael Binstein, tells him what he has heard, and asks him to look into it—Washington parlance for doing a hit. In a town that runs on leaks, the Jack Anderson column has just been given a silver bullet.

So Binstein sets up an appointment, but when he shows up to interview Gray at his chairman-of-the-bank-board office, Gray sits on one side of the table surrounded by lawyers and staff and Binstein on the other and nothing is forthcoming. Binstein is irked by Gray's apparent fear and inability to talk frankly. But something holds him back from writing the column he has been assigned, from pulling the trigger on the man referred to derisively as Mr. Ed. Like some reporters, Binstein is a victim of his own heroes. When he was in college, I. F. Stone once plunked himself down next to him in the Senate cafeteria, and he never forgot the conversation. Then, when he went to work for Anderson years later, he was honed in the strange mores of what some call investigative journalism—in plain speech, muckraking. Anderson has simple, brutal rules: if he ever discovers that one of his staff is at an official news conference, he'll fire the fool. He is not paying people to listen to the propaganda of political hacks. Binstein has learned to go away from the pack and research things on his own. For some time he has been hanging around one of the most boring and unreported agencies in all of Washington, the Federal Home Loan Bank Board. And so he hesitates when Gray refuses to talk straight with him and keeps putting off the column, even though Anderson repeatedly tells him Gray is a zero and he should get on with it.

And then Don Regan grows impatient—his voyage out to the grubby offices of Jack Anderson has apparently been a waste of time. So he instructs a key White House political operative, Ed Rollins, to deliver a simple message to Gray. Rollins requests a meeting at his White House office with the chairman of the bank board, and Gray comes over at 10 A.M. on Monday, September 30.

Rollins begins by explaining that he has a message to deliver on behalf of Don Regan. "You know why you're here," he continues. "Today's my last day. I'm acting as a messenger, and only in that capacity. We're old friends. Regan was going to haul you over to the White House himself, but I told him, you don't do this to Ed Gray. He's worked for the president for a long time. He's an old friend, a personal friend."

When the niceties are out of the way, Rollins fires the bullet: "Regan wants you to leave in several months. They want to have their own chairman."

Gray asks, "Who is 'they'?" and is told, "You know." And then he protests, asks what he has done wrong, and is told only that they feel there is turmoil in the savings and loan industry.

"Does the president know about this?" Gray asks.

"No, not very much."

"Does the president know *anything* about this?"

"No, I'm sure he doesn't."

"Well, who's in charge?"

"Regan. He runs about eighty percent of the place now."

But there is a note of kindness. Gray is offered the confidential post office box number of the president so he can send him a note no one else will see. But, Rollins warns, it will do no good. "The last person," he says, "who talks to Ronald Reagan is likely to prevail. That's Regan."

Ed Gray is crushed—he has served Ronald Reagan twenty years for this?—and mentally begins to pack his bags. The following evening he is at a Washington reception and a line of supplicants crowds around him seeking an audience. Binstein wanders in looking for not much more than a free meal and a drink, notices Gray, and ambles over. He waits his turn and then takes a chance: "Why don't you talk to me like a man instead of hiding behind an entourage, for God's sake?" And Gray begins to talk, and then they sit down and continue talking, and when the reception is over three hours later and the janitors are stacking chairs and vacuuming, they are still talking.

Ed Gray begins to slowly emerge from behind Mr. Ed the talking horse. He spent a bad night after Rollins delivered his political death notice, and he reached a decision that is not in keeping with his career as a public relations man. He has thought about Don Regan and concluded, "There's no way that this asshole is going to do this to me."

Things have been happening that have triggered his suspicions and brought back memories. The high-flying thrift operators he witnessed in Texas in 1983 still bother him, but that moment that occurred in December 1984 brought Charlie Keating to Ed Gray's attention in a way he could not overlook. When Ed Gray worked in the Reagan White House as a deputy to the president, he would be dispatched to the airport from time to time to pick up Alan Greenspan, the chairman of the Economic Policy Advisory Board. In late 1984, he noticed that Alan Greenspan, now an independent consultant, was writing a brief to defend Charlie Keating and the way he ran Lincoln Savings and Loan. And Ed Gray had but one simple, immediate thought: "I quickly came to the conclusion that Alan Greenspan was doing this for the money." The bank board staff soon engaged in a guessing game over Greenspan's fee with estimates running as high as a million dollars. Gray was sickened by what he saw even though he knew this was the way of Reagan's Washington—"If you paid enough, you got a well-known person to be your spear-carrier. It was all over Washington in 1984." From that moment on, Ed Gray kept track of Charlie Keating.

He faced down Keating's lobbying on the Hill, he testified at the Barnard hearings, he fought the bills in the House and Senate to stall reregulation. And now, in late September 1985, he refused to obey Don Regan ("this asshole") or President Ronald Reagan. Also, he has been going through a lot in his private life. His father died after a lingering illness on Thanksgiving Day 1984. His family is angry that he is staying in Washington, where his wages cannot even pay their bills and wants to know why he does not return to California. His aged mother has to loan him money. He shops at the Price Club, a warehouse discounter where he can buy cases of soup cheap. Something comes alive in Ed Gray that breaks the mores of the normal Washington power game. He does not simply want power or to save his career. He elects to self-destruct. He decides to be just what his nameplate says, head of the Federal Home Loan Bank Board.

By October 1985, one of his colleagues on the three-member bank board is openly lobbying for his job. Ed Gray goes to the national meeting of thrifts in Dallas and is greeted by full-page ads denouncing him, paid for by Texas thrifts. He gives a speech announcing he will not resign, he will serve out his term. And then something happens that to Ed Gray seems like a dream, and he decides to set a trap.

That fall of 1985, Charlie Keating has yet another idea on how to solve his growing problems with the regulators. He is talking on the phone one day and complaining to a friend that Ed Gray is screwing up the industry, bringing ruin to it, and his friend says he should not worry because he has heard Gray is looking for a job and will soon be leaving. Keating says, really? Do you think Gray would come to work for me? In part, this is because Charlie Keating thinks he can convert anyone—"Charlie," one ACC executive says, "really believed that if Ed Gray followed him around for a month he'd have a whole other view of direct investments. Charlie felt he could buy anything." An offer is delivered to Gray through intermediaries, a vague promise to pay "a lot of money."

Gray is stunned and decides to get the offer on record. He sends his chief assistant, Shannon Fairbanks, to the meeting to pursue the job offer and to trap Charlie Keating in an attempt to buy off a regulator. Fairbanks is a small, refined woman married to a wealthy Washington lawyer, and in many ways she and Gray hail from different worlds, but she is totally loyal to him. During his early efforts to reregulate in 1984, she is his only supporter at the bank board. When she comes down with cancer in the spring of 1985, her sense of duty demands that she resign, but Gray will not let her. He prefers to leave the job vacant until she can return.

At 8:30 in the morning of November 22, 1985, she sits down with Keating and two of his staff in the main dining room of the Four Seasons Hotel. By this time, Keating has gotten cold feet and tried to call off the meeting—only to be stopped by the anger of friends who had used their influence to set it up. He speaks vaguely to Fairbanks of "using Mr. Gray's contacts and skill to further the corporate interests and activities of Lincoln Savings. . . . Three seems to be some problem in getting our message heard." Keating feels he needs someone like Gray to "get our corporate initiatives past the existing regulatory roadblocks."

The offer is rejected, and Keating is angry. He does not like to be made to look a fool. But he is not beaten. He can take yet other steps toward his goal.

Carl Lindner prides himself on not leaving things to chance. Although others tend to see his stock plays as the fearless acts of a buccaneer, he buys small positions and then slowly builds them up as he masters the numbers of a company and studies and meets their managers. In politics, he is much the same—not a man to leave things to chance.

His Lindner Circle—the pattern of swift and massive giving that he and Keating perfected in the seventies—continues to grow in muscle. During the 1980s he and his family and colleagues will give more than $1.5 million to candidates for federal office. For example, Senator Bob Dole of Kansas, the Republican minority leader, gets $34,000 in 1986 for his Senate race, and when he reaches for the presidency in 1987, the Lindner Circle kicks in $47,000. When the mayor of Cleveland, George Voinovich, makes his move in 1988 against Senator Howard Metzenbaum, the Lindner Circle gives $50,000. Metzenbaum chairs the Senate Judiciary Subcommittee on Antitrust, Monopolies and Business Rights and is basically the Senate cop on matters of high finance. He has not looked kindly on the innovative tactics of corporate raiders. The Lindner Circle gives Metzenbaum $5,000. The money is delivered in a swift, impressive fashion, lest someone fail to notice it. The $47,000 for Dole dribbled in from about sixty people, but it all arrived on December 3, 1987. Senator Dole's staff says that there is nothing in the record to suggest that their senator has ever done anything for Carl Lindner. Presumably, that is also true of Representative Bob McEwen, who received $38,000 on June 30, 1987, and later inserted in the *Congressional Record* "A Salute to Carl Lindner," which in part said, "Wherever this caring citizen goes, he brings a concerned interest in his fellow man, and in those pursuits which enrich our earthly existence: culture, employment, and the like."

One of the other places Carl Lindner goes is to Taft Broadcasting, which swallowed Charlie Keating's target, Gulf Broadcasting, during his hostile takeover/greenmailing effort in April 1985. Lindner, who had originally sold Keating the stock in Gulf, swallows Taft. Protests are made at the Federal Communications Commission because a Lindner subsidiary had recently been fined $690,000 by the Occupational Safety and Health Administration (OSHA) for covering up serious worker injuries, but Lindner prevails. Such charges and such fines and such contributions, of course, form a kind of white noise almost unnoticed in the daily din of U.S. government.

The same pattern of keen political interest is also characteristic of Michael Milken and his friends at Drexel. In the election cycle of 1985 and 1986, they make $391,000 in political contributions. In 1987, the firm also kicks in $49,500 to members of Congress for giving speeches. Individual employees also feel moved to give to the cause. Senator Alfonse D'Amato gets $40,000 for his 1985–1986 campaign. Senator D'Amato is a strong defender of the junk bond boom. For example, on December 6, 1985, the senator introduces a bill on junk bonds, but an earlier provision that would have limited thrift purchases of junk bonds has disappeared. When, a month later, the Federal Reserve considers putting limits on junk bonds, the senator writes them that this notion is "irresponsible."

When Senator Alan Cranston runs for reelection in 1986,

Milken and his fellow employees, plus a key client and the Drexel office on the East Coast, give $41,000. That same year, Cranston gives the welcoming address at the Predator's Ball. In 1986, when Senator Jake Garn is head of the Senate Banking Committee, he receives $25,000 from Milken friends at Columbia Savings (a voracious consumer of Milken's junk bonds) and the same day, as it happens, $17,000 from executives at Drexel. Garn happened to be the coauthor of the 1982 bill deregulating thrifts. Senator Tim Wirth of Colorado gets $20,000 from the folks at Drexel for his Senate race in 1986. Over a ten-year period Wirth gets $150,000 from the world of thrifts and junk bonds—a great deal of it for the 1986 race. In 1985, he attends the Predator's Ball. The list goes on and on and touches both sides of the aisle. Between 1985 and 1988 Drexel gives $122,000 to the Democratic Senatorial Campaign Committee.

Many point out that there is no simple connection between this generous giving and the actions of politicians. For instance, Charlie Keating gives large sums to Senator Alan Cranston. Cranston is proabortion, Keating is violently against abortion. These and other facts are often brought up to silence any suggestion that something inappropriate is going on.

Few can pronounce or remember their names because to American ears they all sound very similar. Nor can many people at ACC tell them apart because to American eyes they look alike—big, heavy men with dark skin and curly black hair. But even though there are over a hundred of them on his payroll, Charlie Keating knows every one of his employees. They are his groundskeepers—and his friends. Keating fires anyone who so much as dents a corporate vehicle (there are over two hundred), but the Tongans really wreck ACC machines—there are hardly any roads or cars on their home islands of Tonga. Once Chip Wischer gets a half-dozen insurance claims for collisions—all reporting accidents on the same day and about the same time at widely scattered sites around Phoenix. And in each case the driver has the same license number. He discovers that the Tongans have made copies of the one real driver's license in their possession and simply pasted their own photos on the document and written in their own names. When he tells Keating of the problem, Keating thinks it's great, it shows creativity.

They are very strong, and Keating likes to shadowbox with them. Two Tongans can wrestle an 800-pound tree into a hole. They work very hard. One day a contractor at Keating's Crescent Hotel sees a Tongan digging a hole for a tree when he hits a huge buried cable and is knocked over. The man gets up, returns to the hole, severs the smoldering cable, and plants the tree. But they tend to weigh a great deal, and their leader comes to Keating with an idea: he wants to give them extra money if they show up at, say, four in the morning and do exercises before work. None of them shows up; money is not that important to them. Then the leader has a second idea. He hires a very well built blond woman to lead exercises, and they all show up each morning.

They become a riddle to outsiders, a clue to Keating's desire to be king or adored. He is a man who commonly uses the word "nigger" in private conversations, and yet his closest friend seems to be a Tongan named Andy. He is a man who runs a rigidly structured company, a place where the dress code is strict, and where no voice may be raised, but the Tongans do not fit this profile. When they are sent to Estrella to help landscape the grounds, they catch rattlesnakes with their hands, then rip out the fangs and kill them. They seem to have a high pain threshold—one man has his foot so badly mangled by a piece of equipment that it is hanging from his leg by a few shreds. He continues working until the ambulance arrives. Andy is working up at Keating's house when a tooth bothers him. He goes into the garage, gets a pliers, and pulls out a molar. He goes back to work, but the pain still persists. He has plucked the wrong tooth. So he gets the pliers and pulls another one. Though they are not regular drinkers, when they do drink, they drink hard. They love to have a test of strength in saloons: they'll take turns hitting each other in the face to see who falls off the barstool first.

Sometimes ACC will buy up a block of houses to clear for a development and there will be a holdout who will not sell. They will pack the other houses with Tongans and maybe set up a soccer game fueled by a keg or two of beer, and soon the holdout will relent.

When ACC has a huge company celebration, the Tongans are there in tuxedos. The color of the company is white, the Tongans are dark, but this does not matter. When someone visits ACC headquarters, the first thing seen—before the spotless interiors and the stylish blond women—is a Tongan working the grounds.

They do not fit the image of Charlie Keating that Ed Gray and Bill Black are forming. Nor do they fit with the image of Keating held by the expensive law firms he retains or the mass of employees he dominates with his capricious rulings on order, tidiness, decorum. But they seem to fit with some need that is very real for Charlie Keating. They are a very loyal people, and Charlie Keating prizes loyalty.

The federal government is snooping around his business—a thing he hates, a thing he wished never to experience again after his humiliation by the SEC. His many investments must be closely watched; it is a dangerous world, and one cannot turn one's back when playing with junk bonds or hostile takeovers. Charlie Keating seems always to be surrounded by people, yet he has few if any close friends. His friends come from his deals, and as his deals change, so do his friends. He is very much alone.

He talks to Andy, something he seldom does with his closest executives. The Judy Wischers, the Robert Kieltys wait for his orders, hang on his words, but it does not seem quite the same. The people who work with him for years and watch him so very closely think that if he has any real friends they are people like Carol Kassick, a onetime cheerleader from Pittsburgh who is his personal secretary, or Andy from the island of Tonga. Andy is working hard, among other things caring for the grounds at Charlie's twenty-six-acre compound in Phoenix. He is buying new clothes, getting a car. He has a diamond embedded in a tooth. He is Charlie Keating's loyal friend in a world where they are hard to come by.

On the wall in the ACC lunchroom is a color photograph of the Tongans, a big photo nicely done. And the men, about seventy-five of them, are standing in three tiers, looking like sumo wrestlers with their shirts off, their dark bodies thickly muscled. A small brass plate is attached to the frame, and it says, "Lincoln Collection Team."

Things happen without plan or foresight. Chip Wischer begins having an affair. People begin to tell Judy about the affair, but she refuses to believe it. Whenever Kim is over at corporate headquarters on Camelback Road, Judy begins talking about how passionate and sexual her life is with Chip. She tells of their vacations together at Charlie's place in Cat Cay. Whenever Judy is out of town for the weekend on a business trip with Charlie, Kim stays over at the house with Chip and the children. Soon she is over at the house when Judy is there, doing things with Chip and the two daughters. They go out into the desert, they go hiking. She grows close to the girls. And Judy is very friendly too, telling Kim that her help with the children takes a responsibility off her, removes a load from her back. The Wischers own a condo, and as Kim's marriage falls apart, she rents it. Kim thinks Judy is "just so drippy-sweet nice." But sometimes Kim hears her over the speakerphone when she calls Chip at the office, and she is cold, she gives orders and hangs up. Increasingly, when Kim is over at ACC headquarters and runs into Judy, she has this desire, this deep desire, to say, "Oh, did you know I'm fucking your husband?"

Carl Lindner continues his patient march toward more and more money. He adheres to his love of debt. With his borrowed money, he has major stakes in United Brands, Penn Central, Circle K, Scripps-Howard, and many other corporations. His instincts, his apparent lack of fear, his inability to feel risk never falter. Victor Posner continues his controversial personal habits with his serial mistresses and corporate gambits and is always in court. Still, in 1986, Lindner loans him $55 million, and even though Posner eventually files Chapter 11, Lindner makes money on the loan. "You can strike a pretty good deal," one of his colleagues explains, "when somebody is as desperate as Posner."

Lindner continues to enhance his public image in Cincinnati. He now has assets of $6 to $8 billion (assets kept afloat by only a couple of hundred million dollars in equity), and he begins to move the corporate headquarters of his various acquisitions back to his hometown. Carl Lindner becomes possibly the single greatest force in protecting Cincinnati from the general decline of the Rust Belt. He also gives to things. The man who never finished high school tosses the University of Cincinnati much of the $9.6 million required to build a new College of Business Administration. They name the building after the man who hates normal corporate structure. The man who does little but pore over numbers and make deals also becomes the main money behind a $14 million restoration of Sawyer Point Park along the Ohio River. The adage on one of those little cards Carl Lindner loves to hand out says: "He likes to do his giving while he's living so he knows where it's going."

Of course, Charlie Keating's time cannot go solely to Tongans and congressmen and wars with regulators. He has a business to run, and it is so diverse and his appetite for cash so great that he can never waste a single day. For example, on January 1, 1984, just before he assumed ownership of Lincoln, Keating and his executives created something called American Continental Corporation and Affiliates Employee Stock Ownership Plan, which, being human, they shortened to ESOP. This creature is a typical employee stock plan in which workers can own and benefit from a piece of the company. Except that ACC's stock is very thinly traded, meaning that Keating, his family, and his executives control almost all of it and as a consequence can pretty much control its price. When the ACC people meet in July 1984 with the lawyers handling ESOP—Lee Henkel and his colleagues from Atlanta—the attorneys' notes make pretty clear what is desired: "Independent trustee [for the ESOP] will be o.k.—but how do we get independence and control?" If there is any question on this matter, Keating clears the air in a memorandum he writes on June 27, 1985:

[THE ESOP IS] THE MOST IMPORTANT ASSET WE HAVE,
I WANT TO BE POSITIVE:

(A) It is legally in perfect, up-to-date form and substance.
(B) It has excellent, detailed, accurate and current books and records.
(C) Appropriate minutes for its activities are kept.
(D) The ESOP committee (Our "Real" AMCC Committee) [Judy Wischer, C3, and others] meets monthly regarding same.
(E) The Formal Committee knows what is going on. Pay them fees.
(F) We keep it leveraged.

ESOP is the kind of corporate mumbo jumbo that gets lost in the grand scheme of things, the type of idea that in an audit of a business shows up in those irksome footnotes that plague accounting reports like acne scars. One of the key features of American business is that most people pay no attention and profess not to understand quite what is going on. ESOP works rather simply. For example, Charlie Keating makes interest-free loans to buy ACC stock or makes of ACC stock outright gifts to family members or key executives—one daughter and her husband get $1,540,000, another $1,132,000, a third $1,272,000, a fourth $2,070,000, and C3 receives $1,000,000. Judy and Chip Wischer get $100,000 in stock. When they want to sell these certificates to ESOP, the "real" committee that Keating carefully notes in his memorandum naturally decides when ESOP buys and who it buys from and at what price. Nobody pays much attention to matters like this at ACC or, for that matter, at a lot of other places in the United States.

From April through November 1985, as Charlie Keating and ACC gird up for combat with Ed Gray and the regulators, ESOP hums along. Keating himself sells ESOP 200,000 shares for $1,650,000; his wife, Mary Elaine, bags $1,162,500; his daughter Maureen, $689,896; his son-in-law Gary Hall makes $1,950,000; another son-in-law, Robert Hubbard ("You look like shit today," Kim Campbell is always telling him. "Don't you?"), makes $878,250; yet another receives $206,250; and so forth. All in all, in those months ESOP gives out $7,999,396 to eight people. Thanks to complicated, perhaps even brilliant accounting techniques, the money is formally taken from ACC but somehow guaranteed by Lincoln Savings and Loan. As Charlie Keating stressed in his memo, he wants to be positive it is perfectly legal in form and substance. He makes no secret of his dread of regulators.

William Schilling knows trouble when he sees it. He works for Ed Gray's bank board as the director of examinations and supervision; basically, he is the cop who decides whether a thrift is following the rules. Lincoln first pops up on his screen in May 1984, when the thrift requests permission to peddle $50 million in subordinated debentures. Schilling pounces on the request and tells Gray that FHLBB should grant it but only if Lincoln sticks to its business plan without any deviation. When Keating and his colleagues look at this demand, they drop the idea of issuing the bonds. Charlie Keating loathes being trapped in a business plan.

Next, Schilling recommends that Gray deny Lincoln's petition to be exempted from the new direct investment limit.

By July 1985, Schilling is getting alarmed by Charlie Keating's operation. He sends Gray a memo laying out his fears:

> [U]nder new management, Lincoln has engaged in several serious regulatory violations. Some of these violations, such as the overvaluation of real estate and failure to comply with Memorandum R-41(b) [the direct investment rollback], are the same type of violations that have led to some of the worst failures in FSLIC's history.

And Schilling has other worries. He knows the SEC is upset by Keating's tendency to make direct investment deals and then characterize them as simple loans. He thinks that Lincoln has a bunch of money in speculative land deals, securities, and commercial real estate. And he thinks, in the lingo of regulators, that as of May 31, 1985, Lincoln has negative tangible net worth—meaning it has hundreds of millions of dollars buried in what are called nonperforming assets, things like the model city of Estrella or the hotels that devour capital but cannot make any money for years. He suspects they fudge on their land appraisals. What's more, he figures they have exaggerated their assets and downplayed their liabilities to the tune of about $300 million so as to avoid the new rule on direct investment; also they are claiming that these deals fall under the earlier deregulated days of 1984, a practice called "grandfathering." Schilling just can't seem to stop telling Gray what is wrong with Lincoln: it doesn't follow its business plans, its books hide "substantial unrecognized losses," its income figures are "unreliable." Look, he explains, all the numbers seem fudged because Lincoln has bum appraisals, inadequate accounting techniques, and strange deals with insiders and affiliates. Besides, Charlie Keating, "who is not an officer and director of Lincoln, dominates its affairs without proper regard to corporate forms." He is spooked by the fact that Lincoln has at least 40 percent of its federally insured money in direct investments, meaning deals where there is no collateral because Lincoln is not loaning the money to someone but is itself the player. In two simple, blunt sentences, Schilling cuts loose with all the bureaucratic firepower he knows how to muster: "The survival of the institution will depend in a very large immediate sense, upon the success of these investments. . . . Lincoln proposes to embark on a high risk investment strategy with no tangible equity cushion, exposing it, and the FSLIC fund, to serious risk of loss." Basically, he gives Ed Gray a regulator's version of the set speech Charlie Keating is pounding congressmen over the head with on the Hill. Except that Keating does not see high risk, he sees high yield, he does not see violations, he sees innovations, he does not see crummy appraisals, he sees a player's feel for what land is really worth if it is backed with abundant capital. Schilling sees a gambler; Charlie Keating sees the man who is going to break the bank at Monte Carlo.

On January 27, 1986, a lawyer at Jones, Day, Reavis & Pogue, the nation's second largest law firm with headquarters in Cleveland, Ohio, writes to Keating's executives in Phoenix advising them that his firm has expertise in helping thrifts handle this new regulatory jungle. Four days later a squad of Jones, Day lawyers are in Phoenix having lunch with ACC people. The attorneys are alert—while pitching for business from what they hope will be their client, they take note of what seems to be an ACC appetite for good-looking, thin, well-built blondes. They also record that the only vote in this company that counts is Charlie Keating's. And the folks from Jones, Day have really prepared for this meeting—they've brought along one William Schilling, the same man who the previous year was working for the federal government and warning Ed Gray about what a menace Charlie Keating and Lincoln Savings and Loan posed to the government. Now he works for Jones, Day and is ready to do battle for Lincoln against the wily machinations of Ed Gray and the bank board.

Charlie Keating can handle shifting allegiances. He has a habit of hiring accountants from the same firms he has retained to make sure his company's numbers are on the up and up. He can handle a lot of things. No one ever really knows completely what is going on in his mind, in part because he can compartmentalize things, deal with a priest one moment, a real estate developer the next, then a grandchild, then a senator. But also there is the matter of velocity. Things happen very fast around Charlie Keating. Judy Wischer or Robert Kielty can watch someone go in to meet with Charlie, and twenty minutes later they suddenly discover that Lincoln has committed itself to a $70 million deal. Their job is to make it appear legal, make it profitable, make it happen. Because

Charlie will already be off, he will be looking up from his desk with a phone in his hand and talking to someone else, cutting yet another deal, whether it is with Mother Teresa for a slice of grace or with a congressman for a slice of power.

Between late January 1986, when the first overtures come in from Jones, Day saying they can help Lincoln deal with the regulators, and late February, Keating's calendar is crowded with meetings and deals. He reaches out again to Jamal Radwan and his Saudi-European Bank—backed by oil sheiks. "We want to help the Saudi-European Bank make money," he writes. The bank is in a bit of a bind, oil revenues are off as the price slides, and dividends to the bank's shareholders have not been forthcoming. In fact, back in 1985, Keating had written to his staff about their big investment in the bank: "Where's our 11.5–12 percent?" And Keating knows that Radwan is having trouble with some of the other investors and that his own holding is possibly big enough to be decisive in Radwan's survival as head of the bank. Besides, his friend John Connally is on the board. So he has a suggestion: he wants Saudi-European to "provide equity money . . . on deals we want to make but which give us regulatory problems in mechanics." In short, he wants the bank to front his deals by loaning his clients money so that they can cut deals with Lincoln and then Lincoln can, by using accounting techniques, book paper profits—in one deal $9 million, in another $37 million. And the bank cooperates. It is never clear, even to those working close to Charlie Keating, how many people in his company know on any given day what deal is going down, or, if they do know about the deal, it is not clear if they truly understand its mechanics. Or what exactly he means in his letter by "regulatory problems in mechanics." Nor is it obvious what exactly is in Charlie Keating's consciousness except the numbers and the feel of the deal. His employees will witness a transaction and then spend hours or days or months working on that deal, and it will seem like a major venture. But Charlie Keating will have moved on, the deal no more than the roar of money.

By February 1986, the deal is cut with Jones, Day and they come on board to help Lincoln prepare for a federal audit that will come down that spring.* Keating and others tell the law firm that

_____
*The following narrative is based on allegations in the Resolution Trust Corporation's RICO suit against Keating, Jones, Day, et al. Jones, Day is contesting the suit,

they expect the regulators to criticize Lincoln and they want help. Notes taken by Jones, Day people sketch out the problem: "Expect to find missing elements of prudence, due deliberation—e.g. appraisal *in file.* Regulations for land acquis . . . pretty inadequate. *Loans which* may *not be* loans. Conley D. Wolfswinkel Lee Henckel [sic]—watch out for his transactions [all emphases in original]."

A squad of twenty Jones, Day lawyers gets to work with Lincoln in early March 1986, and they keep at it day after day. They comb the deals for paperwork deficiencies, and when they find them they create what they call "To Do" lists highlighting problems missing documents. These are then given to an ACC commando squad operating under Judy Wischer called Judy's SWAT team. The SWAT team then creates documents that use an active verb tense and are undated and are designed to give the appearance of routine underwriting before the loan is approved. Sometimes documents are removed and given to a Jones, Day lawyer for safekeeping. Jones, Day asks, apparently as an act of legal hygiene, that its Things To Do lists be destroyed after the files are corrected. Judy Wischer instructs her team members to remove from the files any notes made by Charlie Keating and anything appearing in the loan files that links Charlie to a deal. On March 8, a letter arrives from the federal examiners announcing they will begin looking over Lincoln's books on March 17, St. Patrick's Day, as it happens. This sets off a red alert among the Lincoln personnel. Then, on March 10 and 11, the Jones, Day team discovers that board minutes and loan committee minutes contain wholesale forgery and backdating. They go to Robert Kielty and Mark Sauter and make a simple request: stop forging and backdating documents. Kielty and Sauter merely shrug. But Jones, Day, as the second largest law firm in the nation, is not without creativity. The ultimate ratification document that the team puts together for the Lincoln board contains grandfathers, meaning it forgives every decision and action taken since 1984. An emergency meeting is held on Sunday night, March 16, and Lincoln's board signs this new

and as we go to press the trial on the RICO charges is about to commence. While not admitting any guilt in the suit brought against them by ACC and Lincoln shareholders, Jones, Day settled for $24 million on March 31, 1992.

document. Keating and Kielty come to this meeting straight from the airport—they have been celebrating St. Patrick's Day in Los Angeles, where Lincoln has a float in the parade. The federal examiners arrive as scheduled on the seventeenth and the files, which are shipshape (the forged minutes are now forgiven by the board's ratification document), are handed over. The examination proceeds in the same building where Jones, Day's lawyers and Judy's SWAT team continue to audit the records.

All in all, it is tricky work. A handwritten memo by a Jones, Day team member on March 27, 1986, captures the delicacy of the task: "Nothing gets removed from a file unless it's misfiled—must consider whether it'll hurt more now or later if removal is discovered. Have GC [General Counsel] office review anything removed to confirm standard applied." In the margin, a Jones, Day lawyer adds, "If something is devastating, then consider it individually."

Carl Lindner is passionate about remaining anonymous. He senses that men in his kind of work can only reap trouble if they become famous, if they become celebrities—men like his onetime hero, James Ling. Michael Milken shares his belief. In February 1986, a writer, Connie Bruck, approaches him. She is writing a book about Drexel, and of course she knows the book will not be complete without Michael Milken and his remarkable department, which sells what he calls high-yield bonds. Milken says to her, "I don't want it done."

But he has a thought: "Why don't we pay you," he says, "the commitment fee that your publisher would have paid you, except we'll pay it to you to not write the book. Or why don't we pay you for all the copies you would have sold if you had written it?"* She declines.

Milken, like so many men, like Charlie Keating himself, has altered his habits now that big money has come his way. Where once he had grubbed food off paper plates at his desk (explaining to an SEC investigator in 1982, "which I eat in anywhere from one to five minutes"), now he dines on china. His unkempt appearance has vanished, and now he sports a new, expensive toupee,

---

*The book was written. (*The Predator's Ball: The Junk Bond Raiders and the Man Who Staked Them,* Simon & Schuster, New York, 1988.)

tailored suits, French cuffs. He comes to work in his chauffeured limousine, has hired a bodyguard, has bought a prestige aircraft, the Gulfstream IV. Where once he was obsessed with hiring people based on merit, now he is stuffing his office with childhood friends and relatives. One brother-in-law seems to do little but nap in his car down in the building's garage yet manages to take home $5 million in two years.

The world cannot simply stop because of federal examiners. On March 14, 1986, with the permission of the bank board's San Francisco office, ACC institutes a tax payment plan in which Lincoln upstreams its tax obligations to ACC on a quarterly basis with the assumption that ACC will hold the money in escrow until tax time comes. Keating and Lindner had set up a similar system with their regulated insurance subsidiaries back in the mid-seventies. No one pays much attention to this new plan, it is all done according to generally accepted accounting principles (GAAP). Since ACC has stockpiled more than $100 million in tax loss carryforwards from its home-building days, there is no real reason for it to pay any taxes at all. Nor does it. For the next two and a half years (the plan is instantly made retroactive to 1984), money will silently shift from Lincoln to ACC for this obligation, about $94 million, and hardly anyone will notice, including the federal auditors who spend months combing Lincoln's books.*

Charlie Keating is still plunging—he has just bought from Drexel a $100 million share in a new $660 million fund Ivan

---

*In September 1989, the tax scheme became the centerpiece of the government's RICO suit. Executives who worked at Lincoln or ACC at the time are almost uniform in not having sensed anything significant about the plan until this suit was filed. For example, Andrew Ligget was ACC's chief financial officer. In the Sporkin decision a series of memos from Ligget to Lincoln seeks, in the first quarter of 1987, an advance on the tax payment based on projected profits. This request hardly seems unusual or guarded practice since one of Ligget's memos ends "Thanks in advance." (Sporkin decision, p. 22, note 16.) Also, when Charlie Keating testified at the Sporkin hearing, he offhandedly touched on the tax-sharing plan: "First of all, we bought Lincoln and ACC the holding company. When I was unable to merge the two or however you'd say it, I still had the debt from the purchase in ACC. It wasn't specifically in my mind that these tax payments would cover that debt,but I had operational and debt situation in ACC that required servicing and just where the money was and where we got it was just a part of doing business. It wasn't related to the weakness of Lincoln." (Sporkin decision, p. 46, note 28.)

Boesky is putting together for stock speculation, hostile takeovers, and the like. Ivan Boesky is not a man others like. As his son once explained to one of his father's staff, "Seriously understand about my father. He is stark raving mad." Drexel has had a tough time floating the Boesky offering and has turned to Keating as a place to dump it. Keating now has trouble getting through to Milken (whose family net worth is reputedly reaching $3 billion) and increasingly has to satisfy himself with his assistant, Jim Dahl. When one of Keating's aides complains, he is told Keating has the wrong last name, that it is not Keatingstein. But such an affront is a small detail in a world devoted to harvesting wealth.

By 1986, Ed Gray's stomach is so bad he can barely keep down a piece of white toast and a cup of Campbell's Chunky Vegetable soup. Once a week he has breakfast in a private dining room with Paul Volcker, the head of the Federal Reserve, William Seidman, the head of the Federal Deposit Insurance Corporation, Robert Clarke, comptroller of currency, and George Gould, the under secretary of the Treasury. By 1986, this very private dining club agrees that the thrift industry is a disaster area. Gray tells them stories from the field: of a Texas thrift owner who built his own private overpass across a ten-lane freeway in Dallas; of thrifts that have invested in Arabian horse sperm banks, greenmail, windmill farms, and oil fields. He tells of the experiences of Gerald McQuarrie, who was picked by the bank board to take over busted Butterfield Savings and Loan in Santa Ana. His first day on the job, the phone rang, and a voice asked permission to take the company jet to the mountains for a holiday.

McQuarrie countered, "Who is this?"

The caller replied, "I'm your pilot."

"You're fired," McQuarrie responded.

Ed Gray has stories of thrifts spending money on whores, of a thrift dropping $1.3 million in two years on Halloween and Christmas parties—including $32,000 as payment for the bank owner's wife, who planned the good times.

Volcker, a huge, taciturn man, hears the tales and says, "Kamikaze banking."

Charlie Keating, on the other hand, is feeling pretty good. The audit of Lincoln, it is true, drags on and on, but he has his best people handling it. He suspects the auditors, who all come from the bank board's San Francisco office, are homosexuals—that, he thinks, is why they are so hostile to him. When one of the auditors combing Lincoln's books, a man Keating feels is sympathetic to him, disappears from the federal ranks, he senses foul play, perhaps a cabal against him by homosexuals. So he hires a private detective to track the man down. This operative gets into homes by claiming to be a movie producer and discovers the auditor has had a personal problem that has no bearing on Lincoln. But still, Charlie Keating thinks it does not hurt to be careful. That is why he is constantly pressuring Chip Wischer, who handles the insurance claims of all of his employees, for confidential information—who has the clap, who is boozing, who is doing drugs, who has AIDS. But Wischer will tell him nothing, and this makes Charlie Keating furious.

By July 3, 1986, Charlie Keating has had a bellyfull of the federal government. He bought an unregulated thrift, and now it is reneging on that deal. Some of his aides are advising caution, suggesting that maybe a regulated industry is just too much trouble for ACC and that they should sell Lincoln and get out. Others want to keep Lincoln but suggest Keating should stop being so hostile, so aggressive in his dealings with the regulators. Charlie Keating dismisses both ideas. He will not bend his knee to federal civil servants, he will not grovel. He will not give up his merchant bank. Fuck 'em.

On July 3, the federal regulators and Lincoln executives meet in Lincoln's conference room. Charlie Keating attends even though he holds no official position at Lincoln. The bank expects the occasion to be an exit conference where the federal regulators tell what they have concluded from the audit. They are seated at a table that is at least thirty feet long and eight feet wide, and Charlie Keating is at the head of the table. The federal and state examiners, about ten or so, take up one side of the table and face the window. The Lincoln and ACC staff fill the other three sides. Joe Kotrys, the federal examiner heading the inspection of Lincoln, does not see the meeting as a final accounting. He asks that no one make notes, and he requests that everyone in the room identify themselves. Kotrys goes back to what he considers the agenda, the continuing audit of Lincoln's books, and then Charlie Keating interrupts him.

"Who do you and these people work for?" he asks.

"For the Federal Home Loan Bank Board of San Francisco," Kotrys replies.

Well, Keating asks, under what authority is he operating, and when Kotrys says he does not understand the question, Keating pummels him with more questions such as who gets the numbers about Lincoln, where does the audit go, and so forth. Charlie Keating is getting angry, he feels that rage rise within him. The federal examiners try to explain to Keating that there is a "Chinese wall" in the bank board between the examiners and other parts of the agency and between the examiners and other parts of the government. For example, the man continues, he recently appeared before Congressman John Dingle and much of what he knew was confidential and was not brought out in the hearing.

Keating pounces. He too knows Congressman Dingle, he notes, and he will be seeing him again the next week. But that is not what bothers him. He brings up a memo dated June 24, 1986, written by the law firm retained by the board of directors of the Federal Home Loan Bank Board of San Francisco. This memo, Keating says, reaches the conclusion that regardless of operational successes, thrifts that are not operating consistently with the wishes of Ed Gray are being coerced into supervisory agreements or cease and desist orders. And he says this is wrong. The temperature in the meeting goes up: Charlie Keating is not simply questioning the examination, he is questioning the logic behind the examination, the right to make the examination at all.

He is hot. He bailed out a sinking thrift, and now it is making money and who are they to tell him how to run it? Charlie Keating knows what is really going on. Notes of the meeting record: "He stated that it was not possible, and certainly not factual, to say that Washington did not have a 'bone in its throat' for Lincoln. . . . Mr. Keating stated that in addition to Lincoln's economic loss [which he estimates at $5 million in management time for the examination], he walked around with a 'hollow feeling in the pit of his stomach' trying to run a profitable business, while the examination's direction from Washington and San Francisco constituted 'rank discrimination and harassment.' "

He goes on quoting from his annual reports, reviewing his deals. He is making money, and who in the hell are they to tell him what to do? By God, the results he is talking about did not come from luck but from "twenty hours a day of hard work by a real competent group of people whose lives are at stake in the business." "Don't they understand," he asks, "the world is deregulated and that is the way it is." Their rules can't change the world's need for junk bonds. And he is not taking risks; he personally knows the people running the companies he is investing in.

And then the question comes up: when will this examination end? The federal examiners do not know; it will take more time. Well, if that is the case, Charlie Keating says, the Federal Home Loan Bank Board is going to have a lot more problems with Lincoln. He asks, who do you think you're playing with, a bunch of kids? He resents the bank board creating problems by treating him like a fool. Don't you understand, he asks, we're not just dealing with large sums of money, we're dealing with our lives. Go ahead, just go ahead, Keating says, and do something and then we can take you to court and get this monkey off our backs. Lincoln, he wants them to understand, is not a tiger without teeth like some of the poor things the bank board has buried. He lives in a dangerous world, he is making money, and there is no one in the entire thrift agency who knows how to make so much as a nickel. Charlie Keating roars on and on, all of his frustrations pour out.

When the meeting finally adjourns, nothing has been decided. Except that Charlie and the federal government are now at war. His executives understand what they have just witnessed. There can be no possible accommodation reached with the regulators. Charlie Keating has gone too far for that. They realize that the meeting is a turning point, a kind of crossroads in the history of the company.

Keating has the lawyers, and now he lets slip their leashes. Kaye Scholer is a legal army of more than three hundred attorneys (beginning lawyers start at $77,000) with Peter Fishbein in command, and on July 15, 1986, twelve days after the meeting, the federal regulators are advised by Kaye Scholer that the examination has been an "extraordinary burden on officer and employee time" at Lincoln Savings and Loan. So, the letter continues, any further questions about Lincoln's loans or investments or practices should be addressed not to the federally insured thrift but to the New York office of Kaye Scholer, where such matters will be considered and decided. This is no small matter to the federal bank board people. William Black sees Kaye Scholer as "the biggest and baddest of them all." And now the federal government has been put on notice that it cannot enter a bank it insures and look at the books without first checking all its questions with a New York law firm.

Charlie Keating is prepared, he has been taking precautionary steps to protect himself from this gray horde of civil servants. Larry Taggart is California's savings and loan commissioner when Keating buys Lincoln in 1984, and he is a man dedicated to deregulation. When he retires on January 1, 1985, Keating immediately hires him as a consultant.* Pat Nolan is the California assemblyman who authored the 1982 bill that allowed state-chartered thrifts to plunge 100 percent into non–home mortgage investments. In 1985, he lobbies against an effort to reregulate the industry. He gets $35,000 in contributions from ACC company officials. Karl Samuelian is California governor George Deukmejian's chief fund-raiser. He is also ACC's lobbyist against reregulation in Sacramento. ACC gives Deukmejian $75,000. In 1985 and 1986, Charlie Keating, his family, and his executives pump almost $350,000 into California campaigns and into soft money political action groups. This is business as usual. Charlie Keating knows he does not live in a friendly world. He must protect himself. And after the meeting on July 3, 1986, there can be no turning back.

He goes to Washington and walks into the office of Treasury under secretary George Gould, Ed Gray's weekly breakfast partner. He wants to talk business, he tells him. "I have five senators,"

*The ways of American business seem to follow an invariable pattern. When Taggart resigns in December 1984, he joins TCS Financial, Inc. (later TCS Enterprises)—or rather emerges since the SEC later discovers that Taggart really joined TCS in November 1984, while still commissioner. TCS was less than two years old and almost broke—its equity on October 31, 1984, was down to $266,000, and if its current losses continued it would have been wiped out by the spring of 1985. In January 1985, Lincoln bought $2.89 million worth of TCS common stock, even though the prospectus warned in bold print THE COMMON STOCK OFFERED HEREBY INVOLVES A HIGH DEGREE OF RISK AND IMMEDIATE DILUTION. Because of this dilution in the stock it was buying, Lincoln instantly lost $2 million. What it got was Taggart's help in grandfathering investments to beat the December 10, 1984, limit set by Gray in his rule. What Taggart got was a $90,000 salary and an auto allowance—this from a company that at the time of Lincoln's cash infusion probably only had about $100,000 left.

Charlie Keating explains, "on both sides of the aisle who I'm very close to, who will listen carefully to what I say. You have legislation pending up there. I can be very helpful with your legislation if you like. Or I can really hurt you."

Gould is put off. He shows Keating the door and then tells his secretary not to let that man in again. Charlie Keating has crossed a line in the accepted culture of influence and legislation and money and power. Perhaps he knows this. Perhaps he does not care.

Charlie Keating is either fearless or foolish or both. He knows only two responses to any situation—either buy the person off or destroy that person. And he doesn't make an exception for something as cretinious in his eyes as the federal bureaucrats who want to police *his* bank. There will be no more nolo pleas in his life; he has never gotten the bad taste of his 1979 SEC settlement out of his mouth. He is about to become the Rambo of the savings and loan industry, a one-man war machine directing his fire at an army of civil servants. Beneath his quick mind lies his cunning, and beneath his cunning lie his feelings and beliefs, and beneath those things, deep down in the core of his being, lies the one lesson he has learned in this life: never give an inch, never back down from anyone, never live in fear, never, never be weak, so weak, say, your own son has to lift you out of bed in the morning and carry you out into the yard like a goddamn piece of furniture and plop you in a chair where you sit all day staring and feeding a squirrel and looking like some pink flamingo planted on the lawn.

In 1986, Charlie Keating will have at least sixty meetings or telephone conferences with politicians about his problems running Lincoln. And he will do other things as well. On July 31, 1986, twenty-eight days after his explosion with the regulators, Charlie Keating writes a letter to then congressman John McCain. He's mad, God, is he mad. What does he have to do to make people understand what those feds are trying to do to him and to the whole damn country?

Dear John,
    The FHLBB, under Ed Gray, is a "Mad Dog" turned loose in a police state effort . . .
    No wonder S&Ls are losing billions of dollars. No wonder their executives cringe in fear and terror—afraid to speak up.

The cost in dollars and lives, because of this horribly ignorant and misguided agency, is incomprehensible. . . .

Something begins to happen that is without precedent in the history of the generally ignored Federal Home Loan Bank Board. It is a slow, subtle process that is initiated after Charlie Keating's July harangue to the regulators. Ever since its creation in the 1930s, nothing seems ever to have leaked from the FHLBB. It is almost as if this tight-lipped history were an accident—nobody ever cared enough even to ask the flunkies in the FHLBB to give up a secret. The agency has all but lived in cobwebs on a Washington byway. It is a rocking chair agency, not a place an ambitious, power-hungry player would ever seek out. The agency is housed in a six-story architectural afterthought across from the Old Executive Office Building. The lobby is large enough to make a good tomb for a run-of-the-mill pharoah. It always seems lonely, with a rent-a-cop at the desk, the cold marble, and the portraits of the three bank board members on one wall with the smiling face of Ronald Reagan looming over them like a flag on a mast. The portrait is about as close to the president as anyone in the FHLBB ever gets. Ed Gray, the onetime gofer for Reagan back in California, now has no chance of seeing his hero or speaking with him. Often when he is in his office conversations will suddenly be buried under a roar when a fleet of six or seven presidential choppers (one for the president, one to serve as a decoy, the backup chopper, and so forth) sweeps over the bank board building as Reagan is ferried about on his official duties. At such moments Ed Gray will stand there in midsentence waiting out the *whomp, whomp, whomp* of the blades swirling over his office until he can return to explaining the savings and loan crisis to someone—the very points that he can never present to the smiling guy in the chopper. His office is close to the White House, but they have decided he is a dead man. David Stockman, the boy wonder of number crunching in the early years of the administration, never answered Gray's calls, never so much as agreed to a meeting with Ed Gray as the black hole of deregulated thrifts continued to suck in billions of dollars and make them disappear. Of course, why should Stockman or anyone talk to Ed Gray? As one of Stockman's aides announced to Gray's face one day in the White House mess, he is "off the reservation."

But now small gestures begin. Odd comments escape bank board employees. Piles of documents are pointed to and then described as part of the problem, part of what is going on—ah, those voices will say, they're about this guy Charlie Keating. But sorry, we can't let you look. But you take note, if you're human. And the documents concern a savings and loan in southern California called Lincoln. It is not really a concerted thing, a plan. It is a stop-and-start form of dribbling—sometimes a few words, sometimes a long conversation off the record. Sometimes a new thing altogether—actual internal bank board documents. It is as if the agency has spontaneously begun to leak, to fight back.

PART FOUR

ME AND THE DEVIL BLUES

Early this mornin'
* when you knocked upon my door*
Early this mornin', ooh
* when you knocked upon my door*
And I said, "Hello Satan,
* I believe it's time to go."*
Me and the Devil
* was walkin' side by side*
Me and the Devil, ooh,
* was walkin' side by side*
And I'm goin' to beat my woman
* until I get satisfied.*

        —Robert Johnson,
         Sunday, June 20, 1937,
         Dallas, Texas

In the summer of 1988, life has become a state of war for Charlie Keating. He has fought back in congressional hearings, fended off federal auditors and state auditors, and survived the hornetlike probes from the stray reporters who have stumbled upon his work. He has almost no time left for doing deals, it has gotten that crazy. For months, he has tried to stop a small magazine from writing about his deals. He knows they've gotten copies of the federal audits (from that bastard Binstein, no doubt), and by God, that's illegal, the audits are supposed to be absolutely confidential. Some goddamn fed has leaked them. They must be stopped from printing those documents. First, the little magazine gets a call from its libel insurer, and the editors are told that if they're thinking of writing about Charlie Keating their insurance is in jeopardy. Then fat letters ripe with threats and dark warnings begin to arrive from Kaye Scholer, one of a wolf pack of law firms retained by ACC and Charlie Keating's key legal muscle in New York. Then a New York public relations firm weighs in over the phone, stroking and threatening all in the same sentence. Finally, one day Charlie Keating picks up the phone and calls Bowden, the editor of the midget magazine. He says, "I've been thinking I need more presence down there, need more of a voice in the town, and I'd like to use your magazine." Bowden is a little stunned but says, "I'll have our ad people send you the rate card." Charlie pushes on, explaining, "No, no, I mean I'm thinking of buying the magazine." Bowden hesitates a moment—hey, maybe it's time to get off this treadmill of hundred-hour weeks, investors from hell, and maybe now his ship has come in!—and then says, "It doesn't work that way, Charlie." And Charlie Keating doesn't skip a beat, he says, "It never hurts to ask." And then he is gone.

BLIND
TRUST

After the July meeting Peter Fishbein of Kaye Scholer showers the bank board with more potential suits. Meetings are held with regulators to quarrel over possible leaks—Keating insists that the regulators have discussed a troubled deal in Louisiana and that this talk is threatening his credit lines with New York banks. The lobbying on the Hill escalates, the chats with congressmen grow more frequent. For example, three days after the disastrous meeting with the regulators in Irvine, California, Charlie Keating meets with Senator Paula Hawkins of Florida at a Phoenix hotel, loans her a limo for the day, and then speeds off to a lunch with Senator Dennis DeConcini at ACC headquarters. And the explosive growth of Lincoln does not stop—by late 1986 Keating has over three billion federally insured dollars in play, almost two billion of these in what the regulators decry as risky investments. For example, six days after the meeting with regulators, Charlie Keating is in New York exploring his investments in Sir James Goldsmith's fund for tackling Crown Zellerbach. That same day he finds time for Senator John Glenn. But there is a shift in Charlie Keating's life. The deal making is slowly being strangled, and he has entered a long-running regulatory war. Shortly after the July 3, 1986, meeting, the FHLBB reactivates its examination of Lincoln, and this look at the books will continue off and on into the spring of 1987.

Increasingly, he will fight to service the deals he has already made—the Pontchartrain hotel in Detroit, the Phoenician in Phoenix, Estrella, his city of the future, his heavy commitment to Sir James Goldsmith. But slowly he will cease to make new commitments. There will be no more brilliant raids against things like Gulf Broadcasting, lightning moves that shower ACC with $50 million paydays. Instead there will be new tactics. GFTA will become more and more important to Charlie Keating. With GFTA and the help of its owner, George Herrdum, he can sit in his computer room in Phoenix and with a flick of the keyboard make instant plays and instant profits, make them so fast the regulators will never be able to keep up with him. Also, the Saudi-European Bank, a treasure trove of Middle East oil money, will grow in importance because it is located in France, far beyond the rules of the FHLBB or SEC. And meetings with Toufic Aboukhater will also matter more and more since he and his sons are the gatekeepers of the Kuwaiti oil billions.

Starting early in 1986, the tax-sharing plan between Lincoln and ACC goes into play, and suddenly millions are flowing from the thrift vaults to Charlie Keating and his executives, money that is supposedly to be held in escrow until tax time but that really keeps his increasingly regulated business afloat with cash. He also has another plan: he will sell ACC junk bonds right out of Lincoln's branches, a move that is approved by the government and implemented in late 1986. But finally there is a more serious idea, one that cuts much more directly to the heart of what troubles Charlie Keating. He will take over the damn bank board. And he will destroy Edwin Gray, God willing.

Lee Henkel, Keating's old colleague from John Connally's* presidential campaign who through various partnerships has partaken in close to $100 million worth of loans from Lincoln and who has a personal $300,000 line of credit at the bank, flies to Washington, D.C., on June 23, 1986.** He meets with White House Chief of

---

*Connally and Barnes's Texas investments have been going sour, and in April 1986, a Lincoln subsidiary, AMCOR, forgives their obligation to make payments. When the federal regulators question this act of kindness in the fall of 1986, Bruce Dickson of ACC and Lincoln tells the government that it was "worth it" to be nice to Connally and Barnes because they could use their "political clout" in Texas against ACC if treated harshly.

**The passages that follow on Lee Henkel's relationship with ACC between June and December 1986 is based on allegations in the Resolution Trust's RICO complaint, which names Troutman, Sanders, a law firm in which Henkel was a partner, as a defendant. In November 1992, the Office of Thrift Supervision issued a consent order in which Henkel agreed to be banned from the banking industry, to be

Staff Donald Regan to talk about just who should be appointed to
the Federal Home Loan Bank Board. He does not come here without
his fans. Senator Dennis DeConcini has already written Regan recommending Henkel—in fact, while the White House is considering
Henkel's various merits DeConcini will call six times. Everyone
knows that Gray's term as head of the bank board will end in June
1987, and Charlie Keating wants Henkel positioned on the board to
become the next chairman. Regan, in the somnolence of Ronald
Reagan's presidency, calls the shots on such matters, and Lee
Henkel thinks he knows of a perfect candidate: himself. He assures
Regan that he has no involvement with any savings and loan institution. But the cost of this visit by Henkel and his law firm is billed
to ACC. One month later Henkel meets with Keating to talk about
his elevation to the bank board, and there are also discussions about
his holdings in Continental Southern, a large Lincoln investment.
ACC also pays for this visit.

Regan is as anxious to get right-wing Judge Daniel Manion on
the federal bench as Senator DeConcini is to get Henkel on the
bank board. The senator had planned to vote against Manion—
DeConcini, a former district attorney, is hard on law and order issues (he keeps popping up as a possible director of the FBI), but
even so, the judge is hard to swallow.

Manion is a forty-four-year-old John Birch Society sympathizer
whose legal briefs are written in borderline English. A pal of Indiana senator Dan Quayle, he has earned the almost uniform contempt of law professors, deans, and the American Bar Association.
The Senate Judiciary Committee has his nomination to the Seventh Circuit Court of Appeals sent to the floor with an unfavorable
vote. DeConcini and Regan have a chat on the phone. DeConcini
keeps saying that he really thinks Henkel would be a fine addition
to the bank board, and Regan keeps replying, "I really like Judge
Manion. What do you think about that?" DeConcini has a change
of heart in July, and his abstention during the vote puts the judge
onto the bench. Of course, a change of heart is normal cardiac
work for Dennis DeConcini—he originally ran for the Senate with
a pledge of serving only two terms, and here he is in 1986 raising
a war chest for his third run at six more years of public service.

debarred from practice before OTS, and to pay restitution of $50,000. He neither ad-
mitted to nor denied charges against him.

Regan has work begun on Henkel, but Robert Tuttle, the White House personnel director, stumbles on his many ties to Keating and tells Regan about them during a weekly staff meeting. William Ball, the president's assistant on legislative affairs, sweeps aside such quibbles by noting, "We owe DeConcini one."

On August 6, 1986, Michael Manning is in Washington, D.C., on business. He stops by the Federal Home Loan Bank Board and meets with a regulator named Bill Black who is busy waging a war against one Charles H. Keating, Jr. Manning knows nothing of Keating. He has come to lay out the Renda case (which involves savings and loans as well as commercial banks) for Black and explain to him how the bank board failed in its earlier review of Renda. Black grasps the intricate fraud instantly, and Manning is relieved. This is the first time he has met with a bank board official who immediately appreciates the need to chase Mario Renda and shut him down. The bank board soon joins the RICO suit against Renda and his colleagues.

Ed Gray can sense the danger in the air. He has no money, he has no friends. Freddy St. Germain, the darling of savings and loan lobbyists and the coauthor of the bill that launched deregulation, tells Gray one day, "My friend, you walk where angels fear to tread." The White House wants him out. He can barely hold down food. Because the insurance fund is almost gone, he cannot even shut down thrifts that are squandering fortunes and functionally bankrupt, and he cannot seem to get Congress to give him more money. He visits Ed Meese, his old friend from Reagan's governorship, and tries to get some support in order to stave off Don Regan's attack. But Meese is very noncommittal and speaks of how Don Regan now runs the White House and that there is very little he can do. It is a cool meeting, the kind of restrained conversation that tells a Washington player that he is in serious trouble.

In September 1986, Gray requests a meeting with House Majority Leader Jim Wright. He knows Wright will be the next Speaker of the House, and he needs to make a friend. Wright is in some ways a mysterious figure despite his decades on the Hill. He began in Texas as a messianic liberal, but when he lost his seat in the legislature, he decided to let his ideals live underground (much the same lesson another Texan who later rose to the speakership, Sam

Rayburn, learned when he was at first outspoken and subsequently ignored earlier in the century). Wright is a closet debt hater. He cannot abide it in his own life. Early in his career he paid off the mortgage on his house in four years, so ingrained was his belief that a man who owes other people money cannot be free. But he is a representative from Texas, where credit is a way of life. Besides, Jim Wright is possessed by a private vision: he will take over as Speaker of the House, and he will raise the House up to an equal standing with the presidency, and he will cut the imperial presidency off at the knees. He will restore government to the people, to that amorphous mass that should, in a proper world, find its true voice in the actions of the House of Representatives. He is not afraid of a fight. As a boy, he was a boxer, as was his father before him, and for decades, well into his fifties, Jim Wright continued to work out with the heavy bag. At one point he was going to participate in an exhibition match with the current world heavyweight champion, only to be dissuaded by the older bulls in the House, who felt it would tarnish the dignity of that chamber.

When Gray arrives at Wright's office, he is immediately lectured on how the bank board's regulators are "mistreating" thrift owners in Wright's home state of Texas by using "heavy-handed" and "Gestapo-like tactics." But there is more. In a later phone call Wright attacks a regulator named Joe Selby, a thirty-year career examiner with a reputation for shutting down bankrupt thrifts. The congressman raves that Selby is a homosexual leading a ring of homosexuals in a vendetta against Texans in the savings and loan industry.

Gray cannot ignore how desperate his situation is becoming. He sets up a second meeting with Wright, the one man who can forever bottle up the funds he needs in order to shut down runaway thrifts. And he goes to his office and for forty minutes walks Wright through the dimensions of what he sees as a crisis.

"I want to emphasize, Congressman," he adds, "that our remaining dwindling reserves stand behind more than eight hundred billion dollars in deposits."

"Would you repeat that?"

"There's two billion standing behind eight hundred billion in deposits."

And Wright says, "Hmm," and scribbles himself a note.

Later, Gray hears that Curtis Prinns, a supporter of Charlie

Keating who is an aide on the House Banking Committee, is offering people a very simple prediction about what the future holds for the bank board chairman, a prediction said to come from the lips of Jim Wright. Prinns is saying that when Ed Gray leaves office he will be "sleeping on heating grates."

Manning is in court in Los Angeles taking down Renda's associates one by one, working his way toward the center of the circle, where he knows Mr. X awaits. He prepares like an Olympic athlete in training, and as always, the night before the trial begins he is swept with fears—is there anything he has overlooked? Throughout the trial, he stops drinking altogether, eats in his hotel room lest a moment be wasted, pores over the evidence until after midnight, and then is up at four or five each morning.

As he stands at the podium and cross-examines a key participant on the first day, another defendant sits just behind him in the courtroom. Manning's body blocks the man from the judge's view, and the man rumbles in a voice barely audible to anyone but Manning, "You fucking liar, you son of a bitch, you lying bastard," in an effort to rattle his questioning. The judge cannot hear this stream of denunciations, and Manning cannot react. Again on the second day, the diatribe pours over him like sludge from a sewer, and then suddenly Manning pivots during the witness's answer, flips up his lapel so that only the audience can see the gesture and flashes a big button that says FAMOUS LAWYER. The heckler is rattled, he erupts in anger, and the judge's glare silences this inexplicable disruption. And Michael Manning feels better. He hates to lose.

Lincoln must be taken care of. There must be order, cleanliness, a proud and distinct bearing to the operation. On September 23, Keating dispatches his wife, Mary Elaine, his daughter Kathy Hubbard, and his personal secretary, Carol Kassick, to Los Angeles to tour the branches by helicopter. They leave a trail of memos: larger artwork, find an artist who works in pastel colors, lighter chairs in the safety deposit area, get rid of the pink cast in the wood. The women don't miss a trick: BRASS OR CHROME POTTING FOR PLANTERS, INSTEAD OF EXISTING WHITE. BRASS NOT RECOMMENDED FOR OTHER BRANCHES.

But not everything can be attended to simply by ordering some brass and chrome planters. Each quarter Lincoln must file a report of its earnings with the bank board, and these earnings must hit certain numbers to avoid trouble—for example, reserves must be kept at the legal level. And if they are not, Charlie Keating can be shut down. Also, for Lincoln to feed ACC with profits there must be profits, and Charlie Keating has been making the kind of long-term deals that do not pay off on ninety-day schedules. Charlie Keating is caught between his dreams and the niggling demands of regulators, so toward the end of each quarter he must flog his army of accountants to produce profit-making deals in order for earnings to be booked. During the summer and fall of 1986, the spread between Charlie Keating's dreams and Charlie Keating's deals continues to run at $10 million a month. Andy Niebling, one of his most important financial aides, has written a report demonstrating that they will all go bankrupt—a report an angry Charlie Keating has destroyed. And when his study is met with scorn by Keating, Niebling knows his career in this company is finished. Keating is facing the crunch that comes to all real players—the spread between immediate expenses and immediate returns, a problem summed up by one of Donald Trump's Atlantic City consultants, who in reference to Trump's large holdings there of mainly vacant lots, said, "It eats, but it don't shit." In Keating's search for money, a request is made to the bank board's San Francisco office to allow Lincoln to pay dividends to ACC, and this request is denied. By some accounting methods, ACC will lose $43 million in 1986. It borrows $60 million that year but pays down only $46 million of old debt.

The federally approved tax plan, whereby each quarter Lincoln pays ACC 40 percent of its profits to be held until payment is due the IRS, now seriously comes into play. So also does one C. V. Nalley, a partner of Lee Henkel in Continental Southern. Like Henkel, Nalley formed a relationship with Charlie Keating during John Connally's 1980 bid for the presidency. After Keating acquired Lincoln, Nalley and Henkel formed Continental with $25,000 borrowed from the thrift and took out an additional $750,000 credit line. In less than ten months, the partners (through Continental) had bought $12 million worth of raw land around Atlanta with Lincoln money. When Gray pushed through the direct investment rule in January 1985, Keating saw a way around it: he would use Continental Southern as his beard in deals by expanding its activities from simply buying raw land to land development, both residential and commercial. When Nalley balked at his new role, Keating considered buying out his stock in Continental Southern but hesitated when it was valued at $1.7 million.

As September 1986 draws to a close, Charlie Keating looks over the assets he has planted and decides it is time to harvest one, the Crowder Water Ranch, 13,542 acres ACC acquired for $11,727,372 in 1985 and 1986. The ranch is more than a hundred miles west of Phoenix, and it is part of a speculative wave sweeping the state where players buy land holding groundwater in the hopes that the growing and thirsty cities will in time pay a fortune for the resource: in short, a variation of the movie *Chinatown*. Keating has noticed this activity and, as is his custom, followed the lead of others and bought in.

Nalley pays $20 million for a one-third slice of the $11 million property, putting $5 million down and giving a promissory note for the rest. This simple act allows Lincoln to book a $15,070,000 profit and also enter on its books a $60 million value for the baked desert, an accounting touch that automatically makes the thrift look healthier. For Nalley, this investment has real attractions. For one thing, he is told that he will never actually have to pay the remaining $15 million owed on the debt. Also, his personal guarantee of Continental Southern's initial $750,000 of credit from Lincoln is wiped off the books and he is allowed to leave the company without any obligations. In addition, he never really has to put up a single dime of his own money. The only remaining problem is the $5 million down payment on the piece of Crowder Water Ranch. This is accomplished simply: a Lincoln subsidiary, Phoenician Financial Corporation, buys Nalley's Continental stock (stock Charlie Keating did not think was worth $1.7 million a few months earlier) for $3.5 million. Nalley never sees this money—it goes into the down payment. Then Nalley temporarily kicks in the remaining $1.5 million. With a $5 million down payment, the transaction meets generally accepted accounting principles for a bona fide deal. On the last day of 1986, Lincoln gives Nalley a $2.5 million credit line, of which he immediately pockets $1,575,000 and is made whole. He is told he never has to pay either the interest or the principal on this loan.

And that is how it is done. The transactions are very complex and, as far as Charlie Keating and his staff are concerned, are not linked. The buyer looks and, Charlie Keating insists, *is* real. The profits are booked, the 40 percent for the IRS upstreamed to ACC. But these taxes are never paid because ACC has such enormous carryforwards of tax losses from its home-building days that it can shelter over $100 million in profits. At the end of each quarter from late 1986 onward deals such as Nalley's blossom like flowers on the ACC and Lincoln books. Meticulous records are kept. Profits are booked, and cash, the lifeblood of ACC, flows into the veins of Charlie Keating's empire. In the next two years or so there will be $225 million worth of similar deals. For Charlie Keating this is how deals are done, especially with the hated regulators breathing down his neck. They are a way to keep alive his dreams of big hotels, new cities, corporate jets, lavish giving to charity. And most important, for Charlie Keating they can be defended as legal—they are all on the books in tidy rows of numbers. As one of his key aides explains, "lending money here, buying land there, money flowing here, money flowing there, accounting rules pressed right to the edge." The strange deals are the price Charlie Keating pays to keep his company alive until the real harvest, until the day, say, when the Phoenician is finished and worth, say, $600 million, or Estrella is truly moving and generating, say, $1 billion in profits. They are the way a player stays at the table until his luck turns.*

The Blessed Mother says, "Dear children! Today, I wish to invite you all to pray. . . . Dear Children, Satan is strong and is waiting to test each one of you. . . ."

But it is very difficult to hear her—she is beautiful, a wall of

---

*The full explanation by Keating's aide is as follows: "lending money here, buying land there, money flowing here, money flowing there, accounting rules pressed right to the edge. Your premise might be that he went a mile over the edge, Charlie's going to say, 'I didn't do anything without Arthur Young blessing it. Or Arthur Andersen, or whomever was up. Everything I did, they saw all sides of it, and they said okay.' And I think what the government's probably going to say is that maybe each isolated deal, you can, as an advocate, argue it's okay, but when you take them, when you take them all together you see this pattern. And the pattern is fraud. My view is what motivated that, which is really what's key for you, was the pressure to keep the thing alive, and Charlie always had this saying that you got to do what it takes to make you able to live another day, fight another fight. That was kind of his view. No, he didn't say it in the context of doing illegal things. . . ."

light, clothed like the sun—no one is prepared. We have all prepared for a different kind of world.

Charlie Keating is not idle on the political end of things. He meets with Vice President George Bush and is profoundly disappointed when Bush simply offers twenty minutes of jokes and smiles and then calls in a photographer to take their picture. The head of ACC has a very difficult time with the fact that the vice president of the United States is not an inspiring or even a very impressive figure. On October 20, Charlie Keating attends the meeting of the board of directors of Citizens for Decency Through Law. Three days later he is meeting with the German George Herrdum about his complicated system for playing stock and currency markets. And then on November 7, he must jet to Tokyo for a Drexel Burnham conference on Asia and the possibilities of junk.

That fall, while he is fending off the examiners who are prying into his books and inhibiting his operation, Charlie Keating grows indignant over the way Ivan Boesky is handling his $100 million investment. There have been no reports, none at all. So he calls him up on the phone and screams and eventually gets his money back—before Boesky cops a federal plea.* He continues to do business with Sir James Goldsmith in those offshore funds that alarm the bank examiners. For example, in November, Sir James makes a run at Goodyear Tire and Rubber with a $4.7 billion offer. When a congressman at a hearing asks him, "My question is: Who the hell are you?" Sir James responds that he hails from the "rough, tough world of competition." When two days later he backs off Goodyear, he leaves with a greenmail profit of $93 million.

---

*There is a complete record of the context for this call thanks to the federal government. On October 1, 1986, Ivan Boesky called Michael Milken at 5:30 A.M., and since Boesky had secretly cut a plea bargain with the government the call was recorded. Milken tells Boesky he will soon hear from Charlie Keating and the following conversation ensues:

"Who is Charlie Keating?" Boesky asks.
"You know, he purchased one hundred million of your debt—"
"Yes."
"And he bought it for his insurance company and his savings and loan."
"Right."
"And he needs an update for his due diligence standpoint."
Boesky bristles, "What kind of an update? I'm not inclined—"
(Jesse Kornbluth, *Highly Confident,* William Morrow, New York, 1992, pp. 13–14.)

For Charlie Keating, there is no time to waste. In 1986 Michael
Milken will pay himself $550 million, more than the take of the
entire firm of Drexel, which only cranks $522.5 million in profit.
His total income from his salary plus all his investments will hit
$714,850,538 (his federal and state taxes will come to $205.9
million). A competitor of Keating, Tom Spiegel at Columbia Savings and Loan in Los Angeles, has gotten his assets up to $10.4 bil-
lion and cut a paycheck for himself of $10 million, making him
the highest-paid thrift manager in the nation.

Charlie Keating does not wish to be second at anything.

Michael Manning finally meets Mario Renda in late 1986. He
has been waiting for this moment for years. He has studied his
background, his stabs at doing deals in Saudi Arabia in the seventies, his love of fine possessions. He finds a photograph of Renda's
office in the financial report of his company, First United Fund.
The desk sits on a pedestal two steps above the floor, the walls are
red and marble and gold gilt. Mario Renda is fat and about five
feet four inches tall. Manning stares at the photo and thinks that
this guy is gonna be a fun catch, that he's weak and insecure, that
if Manning threatens to pierce his veneer, he will panic.

Renda's lawyers try to prevent Manning from taking their client's deposition, telling the court Renda will take the Fifth Amendment. But Manning insists—he wants Renda to have to sit across
from him for hours, eyeball to eyeball. And he wants to ask him
detailed questions that will tell Mario Renda the entire case
against him. This is not normal procedure, but Manning wants
Renda to understand that he is cornered.

Manning borrows a room at the FDIC office in New York, a
small, cramped room with boxes of documents stacked from floor
to ceiling. Then he scouts out a narrow—less than three feet wide—
table so that he can get literally into Renda's face. For two and a
half days Mario Renda sits there, listening to questions that constitute an encyclopedia of the evidence against him, and for days he
exercises his Fifth Amendment rights.

("I wanted to disrobe him. I [didn't] want to do it in a New York
aggressive sort of way by shouting or screaming. But real quiet,
straightforward, hard charging, confident. I wanted him to know
that we'd put it together—that I know the motivations, the players,
the times, I know what he was saying, what others were say-

ing. He's a very emotional man, and I know that. Wild temper explosions.")

The room grows warm, and Renda takes off his expensive suit jacket. During a break, Manning fingers the jacket's label and exclaims, "Oh, Mr. Renda, I see you have your coat made by this tailor in Hong Kong, but you know you can't really get a Savile fabric and the right kind of fitting through this tailor." And then Manning, drawing on his Asian business trips, drops the name of a better tailor because he knows from his research that Renda prides himself on his dress and is obsessed with bargains.

Early on in the depositions, Renda's expensive New York attorney launches a strong attack on Manning and his colleagues. Manning starts swinging, beats the man back, and wins the point. And he believes he can see Renda thinking, hey, my lawyer can't beat up this guy from Kansas City like he is supposed to. And so it goes hour after hour. Renda is still powerful, he still has maybe $20 million, and he is not easily intimidated.

During breaks, Renda chats with Manning and his cocounsel. He says it is too bad they cannot clear up this matter with the FDIC because he could be very valuable as a consultant to the FDIC, as their resident expert in getting out of their current banking mess. Manning realizes there is a kind of truth to Renda's claim because he is brilliant. Michael Manning has no doubt that if Mario Renda went straight he would wind up as the CEO of a corporation.

At the end of the first day, Manning walks out of the FDIC building and it is pouring rain. Mario Renda's stretch limousine awaits him, and his chauffeur stands at the ready with an umbrella. Manning and his colleagues cluster on the street corner with their briefcases hoisted over their heads trying to hail a cab. Renda comes out, sees them soaked, smiles, and says, "Mr. Manning, I sure wish I could take you to your hotel. But I don't think there is room for all of you." And he laughs, gets in, and slams the door.

Manning feels very good. He knows now that he is getting to him.

Anticipating his bank board nomination, Lee Henkel wishes to hammer out just what his stock in Continental Southern is worth, and it is apparently not an easy task. Back in the spring of 1985,

Henkel had pegged his holding as worth maybe $300,000. But now, on August 7, 1986, he sees things differently: he thinks his holdings are worth $4.2 million or, if he discounts things a bit, $3.36 million. Pondering this matter, he writes a memo "in the event American Continental and/or Lincoln wishes to purchase the same." One week later, Henkel is back in Phoenix to see how interested ACC is in his stock (ACC pays for this trip), and a week later work begins on a blind trust for Henkel. Until the end of November rounds of haggling continue as ACC attempts to extricate Henkel from his Lincoln ties and also to enrich him as he moves toward the humble wages of a government servant. For example, because of his earlier guaranty of loans from Lincoln, Henkel is obligated to cough up around $8 million. But this is a small matter, easily adjusted by paying $125,000 to obliterate the burden for good.

In October 1986, George Gould, the under secretary of the Treasury who was so offended by Charlie Keating's brief social call in July, is watching C-SPAN in his office. A bill is before the U.S. Senate that will deliver the recapitalization of the bank board's insurance program so desperately desired by Ed Gray. In short, it will give the board more money so that it can shut down thrifts that are gushing losses before they have a chance to lose even more. Also, the bill carries a rider that will make Gray's temporary limit on risky investments for thrifts a permanent law. Suddenly an anonymous senator puts a hold on the bill, essentially killing it.

Alan Cranston is the anonymous senator. He is in a life-or-death struggle to retain his California seat in the November election, a fight that will cost him $13 million. Keating and his aides have already given his campaign $39,000, plus $85,000 to the California Democratic Party to help get out the vote. But just before the recapitalization bill goes to a vote, a Keating aide calls Cranston's office seeking his support against the measure. Joy Jacobson of the senator's staff, after hearing the ACC executive out, says, "Now I want to shift gears . . . and I want you to know this is totally unrelated." Then she asks for a $300,000 line of credit, money to be used in a last-ditch get-out-the-vote effort. A Lincoln employee flies from Phoenix to Los Angeles and meets with Cranston, his wife, and a lawyer in a limousine at the airport. The loan documents are signed as the limo speeds downtown.

Later, Democrats will calculate that the last minute get-out-the-vote drive brought an additional 160,000 loyal Democrats to the polls. Alan Cranston on election day beats his Republican opponent, Ed Zschau (who spends $15 million), by 115,033 votes. Alan Cranston is proabortion, and Charlie Keating's own daughters will not contribute a dime to him. But Charlie Keating lives in a different world, and he cannot afford such political purity.

On October 7, an aide to DeConcini writes him that the White House has called and said that Henkel's nomination is in the bag. The senator's staff calls Keating to share the good news. But there are delays, and on October 22, DeConcini's staff leaves this message with Regan's secretary: "Henkel appointment—wants it made." On November 7, 1986, Lee Henkel receives a presidential appointment to the FHLBB. Of course, his post must be confirmed by the Senate, but that can wait until it comes back into session. About a week after Henkel is appointed to the FHLBB, work begins on a conference scheduled for November 25 in Miami, a conference with Charlie Keating. At this meeting, Henkel's stock in Continental Southern is transferred to a Keating subsidiary for $3.7 million.

But the fight must continue on other fronts. On December 8, 1986, *The Washington Post* breaks a story that raises questions about Ed Gray's expense accounts. The night Ed Gray learned his father was dying in 1984, he hopped a corporate jet to California, a plane sympathetically offered by a thrift executive. This is now seen as an ethically questionable act. The time Ed Gray lost his billfold in Paris at a bank meeting and filed a claim for $794, that is also seen as possibly improper behavior. Ed Gray, who lives in a one-room apartment on borrowed money, voluntarily comes up with $26,000 when his attorneys advise him it is the best way to settle the matter politically with Congress. He also writes every member of the House and Senate banking committees a letter of apology.

Lee Henkel also has money concerns. The promised $3.7 million has not yet been placed in Henkel's blind trust. On December 18, 1986, he attends his first official bank board meeting with Ed Gray. The night before, in a session with Gray and his staff, Henkel had emphasized his belief that government should let business have its way. In the few weeks Lee Henkel has been at the bank board Ed Gray has taken note of the way he struts around the building and finds him "a sickening man." Henkel has told Gray, "I was sent over here to clean up this mess." He has brought along a proposal he has typed up. He wants to alter the direct investment rule, the rollback that Ed Gray pushed through that changed the amount an outfit like Lincoln could have in direct investments from 40 percent to 10 percent. Henkel wants to increase this ceiling dramatically, but he has written his proposal in such a fashion that later, so far as anyone can tell, it immediately benefits only one thrift in the entire United States, Lincoln Savings and Loan in Irvine, California, which is by the regulators' audit more than $600 million over the limit.

This first bank board meeting with Henkel as a member is a standing-room-only affair. As Gray puts it, "Everybody knew it was high noon." When Henkel puts forth his proposal, Bill Black attacks him, an act of ferocity that is highly unusual in the dull, dead ways of the FHLBB. When the meeting ends, Bill Black's staff checks and confirms his suspicion that Charlie Keating is about the only beneficiary of Lee Henkel's big idea. He tells Gray that this proposal will let Charlie Keating off the hook. On the same day Lee Henkel presents this idea to the bank board (but *after* he makes his proposal), a $3.7 million transfer is made to Lee Henkel's blind trust. And one day later, Lee Henkel withdraws $250,000 in cash.

The following day, December 19, the San Francisco office of the bank board decides to file what is called a 407 ordering an investigation of the alleged file stuffing and backdating uncovered in the audit of Lincoln in the spring of 1986 to see if a criminal referral to the Justice Department is in order.

Right after the meeting in which Henkel presents his new rule, Gray and Bill Black talk. Next, Black calls Ken McLean, a staff member of the Senate Banking Committee, and briefs him on Lee Henkel. A few days after that Ed Gray gets a call from *The Wall Street Journal* and puts the reporter on hold for three minutes while he huddles with Black and others about what he should say. Finally Black takes the call, and when the reporter runs some numbers by him on Charlie Keating's savings and loan, Bill Black confirms them. Six days after Lee Henkel's new idea meeting, a front-page story appears in *The Wall Street Journal* headlined:

"Bank Board's Henkel Proposed a Rule That Would Have Aided
S&L Tied to Him." The piece details his history of loans with
Keating and also contains numbers that have been recorded only
in the secret and confidential ongoing bank board audit. It also reports the audit's exact and confidential figures on just how far Lincoln is over the direct investment limit. Soon an even more
detailed story appears in the *Mesa Tribune*—right in Keating's
backyard.*

Charlie Keating knows he has taken a direct hit, and he is angry.
His investments all run on money, and these attacks are not helping him raise money from brokers and bankers. He can protest,
threaten lawsuits, shout, but he cannot make the news stories disappear. Ed Gray later says, "I don't know who called who, and I
don't ever want to know."

For Keating the debacle of the bank board meeting is merely one
problem among many. And then, at the end of 1986, the government changes the tax laws and ends the advantages of syndicating
limited partnerships as shelters. Developers begin to slowly stran-
gle and die, and Charlie Keating, who has planned all along to
syndicate his hotel empire (the Crescent, the Pontchartrain, and
the slowly emerging Phoenician), must think up a new strategy in
midstream. But he is a flexible man. In December 1986, with the
permission of the regulatory agencies, he begins selling subordinated debentures—junk bonds—of his American Continental Corporation in the Lincoln branches in southern California. He raised
money this way when he worked with Carl Lindner back in Ohio.
When he approaches one Arizona broker, Ernie Garcia, to handle
the sales, Garcia says no because he thinks no one can sell the
bonds under the circumstances. But Charlie Keating knows better,
and over the next two years, his staff will sell about a quarter of
a billion dollars' worth of bonds. Mainly to old people, as it turns
out.

You plant assets, then you harvest. But the whole strategy is
based on having funds to service the assets until they slowly grow

---

*According to a Keating aide, Charlie Keating viewed Black as operating on two
levels: regulatory and covert. On a regulatory level he hacked away at the estimates of
Lincoln's net worth because if he could get it to fail this standard by accounting techniques he could seize it and shut Keating down. On a covert level, Keating believed,
he leaked damaging material to the press. As a lawyer, he could appreciate the
beauty of this strategy.

and produce a return—those nonperforming things like Estrella or the Phoenician or the strange funds Sir James Goldsmith puts together. With deep pockets you can wait and harvest in the full ripeness of autumn. But Charlie Keating is facing that spread between his costs and his income of $10 million a month. And at the same time the regulations are slowly but surely cutting down his access to money. He will not accept this. On January 20, 1987, he flies Robin Symes and Ray Fidel, his two heads of Lincoln, over to Phoenix along with seventeen bond salesmen. There is no possible way to stop.

Three days later, he meets with Jim Dahl, Mike Milken's top man at Drexel. Two days after that, he takes everyone to the Super Bowl in L.A. There are many other meetings at that time, all to discuss who will replace Ed Gray when his term ends in June 1987. Plus one final thing: on the last day of the month there is a party for C3 and his wife, Krista. They are going to Zurich to study the computer techniques of George Herrdum. They are going to learn what Charlie Keating needs to know: how to take Herrdum's black box and make it pump a river of gold.

It is a new year, and by the time 1987 ends Charles H. Keating, Jr., through Lincoln Savings and Loan, will have driven his assets up above $4 billion. And his investments judged by the examiners to be risky will have risen to around $2,400,000,000. He has this plan, the one he told Keith Dickson back when he was one of his sons-in-law. He will be out of the savings and loan business by 1990. His empire will be freestanding, and he will be a rich man who has founded a dynasty. Or he has this plan, one he tells his key associate and the president of American Continental Corporation, Judy Wischer—he will increase Lincoln's assets (meaning deposits or money borrowed) from $8 billion to $10 billion, and with this he will build a safe and secure world for everyone around him.

He has no time, none at all.

The Mother of God says on January 1, 1987, "Dear children! Today I want to call you to live the messages I am giving you in the new year. Dear children, you know that for your sake I have remained so long to teach you how to walk on the road of holiness. . . ."

She is truly incredible; every day for years there has been this apparition seen and heard by six children. The authorities in Rome are cautious. They usually are—they have, perhaps, read their Dostoevsky.

On January 2, 1987, Senator Alan Cranston, who is looking forward to six more years of service, receives a memo from his aide Joy Jacobson stamped "confidential." Her message is quite simple: "Now that we [Senate Democrats] are back in the majority, there are a number of individuals who have been very helpful to you who have cases or legislative matters pending with our office who will rightfully expect some kind of resolution." Then she ticks off five, one of whom is Charlie Keating, who is continuing to have "problems with the Bank Board and Ed Gray."

One month later a Keating aide mails to Jacobson's home a copy of a petition that Lincoln has sent the bank board seeking the removal of Ed Gray from any votes on issues that involve Lincoln. A note explains, "Obviously this is a very sensitive, confidential matter . . . one in which we would appreciate . . . the Senator's review and notice." Keating begins pouring money into Cranston's project (one run by his son Kim) to register more voters in California, a contribution that will eventually total $850,000.

This is legal. It is how things are done.

By January 1987, Jim Wright has achieved his dream: he is the Speaker of the House. And one of the things he sets out to do is help a constituent named Don Dixon, who owns Vernon Savings and Loan, a thrift back in Texas. As it happens, Charlie Keating is a personal hero of Dixon's. Like his hero, Dixon has moved Vernon past stodgy and unprofitable home loans. For example, he has taken his wife and friends on a ten-day tour of Europe. They fly on a plane Vernon pays for and run up a $68,000 tab on what Don Dixon describes as a "flying house party." He has also invested Vernon's funds in a $2.6 million yacht and a California Rolls-Royce and Ferrari dealership. Naturally, in the normal run of business, he has had a few personal expenses—$561,874 for food and drink, stereos, televisions, mobile phones. And maid service. There are a few problems at his bank—96 percent of the loans are in default, and this means over a billion dollars is hanging out there. In the past four years, Dixon has paid himself $8.9 million and had the bank buy him a $2 million California home and maintain a corporate fleet of two jets, two propeller-driven aircraft, a chopper, and six pilots. He has also bought the twin of the presidential yacht and keeps it moored in Washington for entertaining politicians.

Wright has a simple goal for his constituent Don Dixon. He wants to keep Ed Gray from shutting him down. When Gray has dinner in a small Georgetown Italian restaurant with Paul Volcker and tells him of this peculiar Texas bank, Volcker snaps, "This whole thing could blow up at any time, and it's going to be the [White House's] fault." After dinner they walk home—with Volcker's security detail in tow—and continue talking about this disaster that each sees looming on the financial horizon, one hardly anyone in the administration or the Congress seems to notice.

From February 1 to February 5, Keating is in the UCLA medical center for prostate surgery. But even this unpleasantness cannot be allowed to interfere: while he is hospitalized he deals with Drexel and with Lincoln Savings and Loan. He reviews all his interest income and his expenses. Goes over deals with his chief legal counsel, Bob Kielty, checks in by phone with First Pacific in Hong Kong, examines the loans to his service corporations with Judy Wischer. Reviews all the titles of his executives—Charlie Keating continues to love changing executive titles so that all his people will be reminded that their rank is meaningless. Keep them on edge, otherwise they all go to hell, get soft, secure. Just look at this country, the Japanese are eating our lunch. After he gets out, he is in Cincinnati meeting with Carl Lindner. Then he moves on to planning a trip to Asia: he wants to meet all that Japanese money. On February 18, he is in Washington talking with Senator William Armstrong of Colorado, with Senator McCain, with Senator Terry Sanford, with Speaker Jim Wright. The next morning at 8 A.M. he is in the slums of New York at the school run by Father Brian, to which his corporation contributes heavily. He stays two hours. Black kids, Latinos, speaking that Greek, reading that Latin. And his company has paid for it.

Carl Lindner is nearing seventy, but he cannot back off the pace. He has parlayed a holding in U-Totem convenience stores into a big holding in a booming chain called Circle K. He has circled Taft Broadcasting (which ultimately beat Charlie Keating's play on Gulf in 1984-1985) and then swallowed it to forge something called Great American Communication Corporation (GACC). And this new thing, GACC, is made up of $1.4 billion of long-term debt riding on the slender surfboard of $247 million of net worth. The cash flow of the television and radio stations is not even adequate to service the debt load for the next three or four years. But Carl Lindner is not worried: he issues yet more debt to carry the costs. Besides, television stations should eventually be cash cows. Carl Lindner has analyzed the ones he has just bought, and he thinks they are undervalued. He is still, of course, in Penn Central. And he is now in United Fruit.

"He is like *Jaws* . . . ," says one Wall Street figure.

Bill Black has a name for the high-flying thrifts like Charlie Keating's that he sees as buried in bad investments and legally out of compliance with the regulations: "brain-dead thrifts." Such banks cannot be closed because there is not enough money in the federal insurance fund to pay off the depositors, and Ed Gray cannot get more money from Congress for the fund, in part because he is not taken seriously. But more important, if the insurance fund is refinanced, Ed Gray and his staff will begin shutting down brain-dead thrifts, and some congressmen live in districts dotted with such creatures. Speaker Jim Wright of Texas in particular has many supporters running banks that Ed Gray wants closed. Wright and his friends think there is no real problem, that with time the thrifts can grow out of their current bookkeeping situation.

In February, Bill Black is sent to a meeting with Jim Wright, one set up by Democratic power broker Robert Strauss of Texas as a way to make peace between the regulators and the thrift operators. Black sits in Wright's office as the Speaker accuses Ed Gray of being a liar. Bill Black offers that perhaps the Speaker is suffering from a "misimpression." Wright looks over at this civil servant from this agency he is growing to loathe, and he explodes, "Goddammit, goddammit, goddammit . . ."

Later, when Jim Wright talks to Charlie Keating, he says that Bill Black is "the most disrespectful government servant I've ever met."

Ed Gray is all but shunned. His closest friend in the jungle of government, his chief of staff, Shannon Fairbanks, is at him each and every day. She is saying, Ed Gray, you are finished in this city, they will never permit you to survive, and now you must look for a job. You must find the rest of your life, she suggests. But there is something in him that will not let go. Ed Gray knows he is finished, but he cannot accept this fact.

He seeks comfort, and so he starts dropping by the office of Senator Don Riegle of Michigan. Riegle is poised to become the next head of the Senate Banking Committee, replacing the retiring William Proxmire (and leapfrogging the more senior Alan Cranston, who will pass on the assignment). In the fall of 1986, Riegle wrote an article for the in-house publication of the bank board supporting Gray's position on the evils of direct investment. Since Gray is known to be a lame duck, there are not many senators who will waste their time talking to him. But Riegle is cordial, about the only senator who is. Riegle is concerned: he wants Ed Gray to stop smoking his two, three, four packs a day. The office is friendly, there are many soft couches, and it becomes Ed Gray's sanctuary.

Don Riegle is the kind of success that increasingly makes a home in the U.S. Senate. Public office has been about his only line of work. When he arrived in the House as a twenty-eight-year-old from Flint, Michigan, in 1966, he announced that he was following a fifteen-year plan that would make him president. By 1976, when he moved on to the Senate, he had built a Hill reputation based on two divorces, a sex scandal involving a congressional aide (she placed a tape recorder under her bed), and a peek-a-boo book about his life in the political arena, *O, Congress!* Now in the winter of 1986–1987, he is almost the last comfort Ed Gray has in Congress. He is the semblance of a friend.

On March 6, Ed Gray needs some more comfort, so he comes by Riegle's office to talk about the savings and loan crisis, almost the only possible subject for the obsessed bank board chairman. Riegle and his aides listen thoughtfully for an hour. And then the senator from Michigan dismisses his staff and says he wants to have a private chat.

"Some senators out West," Riegle begins, "are very concerned about the way the bank board is regulating Lincoln Savings. I think you ought to meet with them."

Ed Gray does not understand the words he is hearing. It is as if the months of conversation (which had helped keep Ed Gray alive) had never occurred.

"It's the same old baloney," Gray snaps. "People want to believe we're harassing Lincoln. I've been fighting this a long time, that I have a vendetta against Lincoln. It's wrong."

"I think you need to meet with the senators," Riegle offers soothingly. "You'll be getting a call."

"From whom? When?"

"You'll be getting a call."

"What do you mean?"

"You'll be getting a call."

There are so many calls in this city. On January 28, 1987, Charlie Keating and one of his lobbyists visit with Senator Don Riegle and his aide Kevin Gottlieb. They wish to help. Charlie Keating says he will raise up to $150,000 for Riegle's reelection campaign in 1988. Gottlieb functions, according to a fellow staffer on the Hill, as Riegle's "heat shield." He is a professor who originally joined the Senate as an intern dispatched by the American Association of Political Science, and he liked the political life and stayed. He has a good appetite for giving speeches at industrial meetings and a healthy appreciation of the ensuing honoraria.* As for his bank knowledge, one Senate aide offers, "What Kevin Gottlieb [knows] about the banking industry you could put on a deposit slip." On February 26, Riegle and Gottlieb meet again with Keating and his people. The next day Riegle and Gottlieb meet with one of Keating's accountants, Jack Atchison of the Big Eight firm of Arthur Young. There is so much to learn. Ed Gray does not know of these meetings as he talks and talks with Don Riegle in the sanctuary of his office during January and March 1987, as he sits and smokes and takes comfort in this last shred of an audience in Washington. Ed Gray does not know what Charlie Keating knows: that this is how the work of government gets done. He does not understand what Larry Flynt understood when they wheeled him out of the Supreme Court chamber in 1983 and he shouted, "Fuck this court!"

---

*For example, this account of Gottlieb in John L. Jackley, *Hill Rat: Blowing the Lid off Congress,* Regnery Gateway, Washington, D.C., 1992, p. 13: "Kevin Gottlieb, staff director of the Senate Banking Committee, made approximately thirty speeches at $600 apiece for an organization called Washington Campus. Gottlieb, in fact, earned more money in speaking fees in 1989 than U.S. senators were allowed to make. 'I'm not shortchanging the committee,' he told the *Washington Post.* 'I'm good at what I do.' "

*　　*　　*

The next day Senator Don Riegle of Michigan flies to Phoenix, Arizona, and is met at the airport by a limousine. He visits the headquarters of American Continental Corporation, tours the many projects the company has under way in Charlie Keating's helicopter. Keating is selling his vision. "Look at this," Keating says. "Look at my people. I'm proud to death of them. Look at the projects I've built. Why can't I get it across to the regulators that this is good. This is good public policy. Everyone who comes in here is impressed, but the regulators see the glass always half empty."

Riegle tells one of Keating's aides that he will talk to Ed Gray and that he thinks he can set up a meeting. Riegle's visit to Phoenix has required planning. Kevin Gottlieb has asked Earl Katz, a key fund-raiser for Senator Dennis DeConcini, for help raising money from Charlie Keating. Katz, who also borrows tens of millions of dollars from ACC and Lincoln, is Keating's liaison with DeConcini, the gofer who makes the calls to the senator asking for favors—landing rights at odd foreign airports, say, or immigration clearance for a foreign priest. It all takes planning. Riegle has a note on his schedule this March 7: "Earl Katz plans to take you to American Continental Corporation for an informal meeting of the principals there. No discussion of money. Earl will collect what needs to be collected later." Riegle has an additional note from his aide Gottlieb suggesting this visit to Phoenix will raise $10,000. When he leaves Charlie Keating, Don Riegle has $11,000 pledged to his coffers. He is given a limousine ride back to the airport.

Keating writes a letter to one of his subordinates explaining, "Senator Riegle will be the next chairman of the Senate Banking Committee, probably for the year 1988. Surely you know those who will support (from anywhere in the United States) this excellent senator in his reelection campaign. . . . This is extremely important. I need invitees. I need contributions." Keating also sends a letter to his employees—some as far away as Switzerland—recommending support for Senator Don Riegle of Michigan.

Upon his return to Washington, Don Riegle speaks to Dennis DeConcini about hosting a meeting with Ed Gray in the offices of the Arizona senator. DeConcini likes the idea. He talks to Keating constantly, and Keating has sent the senator a letter that says, look, I don't want to be unreasonable but I want a truce, I can't live with this weighing down on me. DeConcini is sympathetic to any real estate player—his family fortune has been made in Arizona dirt. "Charlie," he tells Keating, "you are a good man. I've seen your company, I've seen your people, and I will do everything in my power to help you."

On Thursday, March 19, he goes to John McCain's office to discuss the problems Charlie Keating is having with Ed Gray. At first, DeConcini suggests that he and McCain simply fly out to San Francisco and confront the regulators who are auditing Lincoln, but McCain is cool to this idea. Then DeConcini suggests having a meeting with Gray and McCain tells him he will think about it. After DeConcini leaves, McCain paces his office. He feels uncomfortable about the proposed meeting. McCain has checked with a Keating aide and asked, "Is this for Charlie? Is he going bankrupt?" The aide tells him yes, the company is right on the edge.

On the morning of Sunday, March 22, 1987, Charlie Keating holds a business meeting in Phoenix about the Hotel Pontchartrain. He is concerned about what the uniforms will look like, he is concerned about the lighting, about the quality of the restaurants, where the swimming pool will go, where the bars will be placed. At one in the afternoon he flies to Detroit, where he is the host at a gathering for Senator Don Riegle. The event at the Pontchartrain is a success. Don Riegle raises $78,250. Then Riegle receives a letter from Keating's accountant that lists a series of complaints about the Federal Home Loan Bank Board, a letter solicited by the senator.*

Tuesday morning at 9:30 Keating is in Washington with Dennis DeConcini. He is angry and goes into a long, rambling speech about how the government is going to destroy Lincoln and that such an act will destroy Arizona. He wonders if a meeting has been set up with Gray, and DeConcini tells him he senses some hesitation on McCain's part. "I will tell you," DeConcini continues, "John is very nervous about this. We're working on this together, I believe we should work together on this." Charlie Keating says, "McCain's a wimp. We'll go talk to him." But first, he must

---

*Riegle disputes this fact, although Keating's aide James Grogan testified at the Senate ethics hearings that Riegle solicited the letter.

visit with Senator Alan Cranston, and from 10:30 until noon they talk. While Charlie Keating goes about his business on the Hill, one of DeConcini's staffers calls an aide of McCain and relays the wimp remark. Keating arrives at McCain's office at one-thirty that afternoon.

Senator John McCain is furious. He all but orders Keating to sit down. He tells him he did not spend five and half years in a cage in Hanoi in order to have Charlie Keating question his courage. "One thing I'm not," he says, "is a coward." McCain's aides are very surprised. The senator almost never brings up his POW experience. And few senators ever berate major campaign contributors. Keating looks at McCain and tells him to calm down. He asks what he is talking about. McCain explains that he feels it is not appropriate for him to negotiate on Charlie Keating's behalf with a regulator. Keating cannot abide this remark and drifts off into a recital of all the wrongs he has suffered at the hands of Ed Gray and his staff. His face turns red, a vein throbs on his neck. He will not be lectured by a senator.

"Hey, John," he says, "I don't want you to go to the meeting! I'm sorry we even brought it up." And then he stands and begins to walk out of the office.

"No," McCain responds, "I'm going to the meeting. You're a constituent. It's the right thing to do. I'm going to go to the meeting. But I'm telling you, this guy Gray can cause me a lot of trouble, so we have to be sensible about this. I can look into something for you. I can help find out if you're being mistreated, but I can't go down there and in essence break arms and legs and do your business for you."

Charlie Keating will not tolerate having ethics explained to him by a U.S. senator, by a man who flies in his airplanes, stays at his home in the Bahamas, comes to his office for campaign contributions. He is very angry now. His ACC aide has seldom seen him this out of control.

"I don't need to sit here," he says, "and hear you preach to me. I don't want to ask you to do me any favors. I don't owe you anything, you don't owe me anything." And then Charlie Keating walks out the door. He knows he has destroyed a relationship he badly needs. But he will not give in. Later that day Charlie Keating makes a joke of the encounter and tells people that at least he got John McCain's attention.

*   *   *

There are 2,700 square miles of vacant land just west of Phoenix, and Charlie Keating's dream city of Estrella, at twenty-six square miles, is less than 1 percent of this land bank. It is March 31, 1987, and it is time to attend to this dream. Keating has bought the land for about $3,000 an acre, and on the last day of March he sells one thousand acres to West Continental Mortgage Investment Corporation (Wescon) for $14 million, or $14,000 an acre. Lincoln records a profit of $11.5 million on this deal. Wescon puts down $3.5 million cash and takes out a nonrecourse note of $10.5 million to cover the rest of the transaction. This is a remarkable feat for Wescon since it has a net worth of $30,000 and total assets of $87,000. But of course, the deal is not as simple as it at first appears.

A few days earlier, on March 25, an independent appraiser had told Lincoln that the thousand acres were worth only $8.5 million, about $5.5 million less than Wescon was happy to pay (the appraiser also noted on his report that he was assessing the land for one Ernest C. Garcia). Also on March 30, Lincoln loaned $30 million to a company owned by Ernie Garcia, and Garcia immediately drew $19.5 million of this sum as cash. That very day Garcia loaned $3.5 million to Wescon, precisely the amount of the down payment on the land in a portion of the Estrella project called Hidden Valley—which at the moment is a remote patch of desert linked to the outside world by a jeep trail. Garcia's loan to Wescon is a nonrecourse note, meaning if they don't pay it off, he can collect only by taking over the parcel of land in Hidden Valley. Out of this transaction Lincoln books a substantial profit of $11.1 million, and naturally, 40 percent of this amount must be sent to ACC for the escrow tax fund. Ernie Garcia himself gets the use of millions of dollars for his own ambitions. And so it goes, deal after deal, quarter after quarter.

The call for Ed Gray finally comes. He is to meet with the senators on the evening of April 2 in Dennis DeConcini's office. He wants to bring Bill Black—"the smartest person in the building"—along, but DeConcini insists he come alone. Usually an agency head brings staff, but sometimes meetings are more private.

Black senses a setup. Charlie Keating has accused Gray of having a vendetta and has filed a lawsuit demanding that Gray recuse himself from anything involving Lincoln. But Ed Gray thinks he has run out of options. The insurance fund propping up his trillion-dollar responsibility—the savings and loan industry—is almost out of money, and he cannot afford to anger members of Congress when he is seeking their aid. Then on April 1, the House Banking Committee guts the bill recapitalizing the insurance fund by cutting the monies from $15 billion to $5 billion and tagging onto this small sum all kinds of restrictions.

So at 6 P.M. on April 2, Ed Gray goes to Senator Dennis DeConcini's office alone.

Charlie Keating leaves Phoenix at noon on April 2—two o'clock Washington time—on his private jet. He is going to Los Angeles. It is the last day of Drexel's 1987 Predator's Ball. He goes to the Beverly Hills Hotel, an establishment owned by Ivan Boesky and the place where the previous October Boesky, as part of his then secret deal with the government, wore a wire in a meeting with Michael Milken, hoping to record incriminating statements about their business dealings. Boesky is now publicly disgraced as a confessed felon and is awaiting sentencing on various bits of insider trading. Government investigators are probing Drexel and grilling its staff.

As usual, there is an in-house video commercial put together by Drexel, one that ends with the slogan, "High-yield financing and Drexel Burnham Lambert—they help America work!" Then Milken himself gives one of his noted pep talks—this one on how junk bonds have pumped up medium-sized corporations and helped make the nation competitive.

At 8:30 P.M., Charlie Keating is back at the Los Angeles airport, and at 6 P.M. Washington time, he is in the air, approaching his headquarters in Phoenix, Arizona.

When Ed Gray enters DeConcini's office, he is stunned to see three more senators—Cranston, McCain, and Glenn—waiting. To the surprise of the other senators, Riegle does not attend. Senator Don Riegle has a very light touch. When he advised Gray to await a call, there was no one else present who could overhear his message. When Riegle and Keating spoke in Phoenix two days later, they were alone. When the call was made to set up the meeting, it came not from Riegle but from DeConcini. And when a member of DeConcini's staff became spooked by the fact that a senator from Michigan was pushing for a meeting about a man who lived in Arizona and called Riegle's office for an explanation, the answer came back that Senator Riegle was upset by the very question.

The meeting is designed to remain in the shadows. Ed Gray has no staff with him, the senators also are naked of any aides. This is that fine country called deniability (a situation described by one Senate staffer as "come upriver, keep your powder dry, and don't bring staff").

DeConcini barely begins to speak when McCain jumps in with "Mr. Chairman, we don't want to do anything that's improper."

Then DeConcini takes charge and speaks of "our friend" at Lincoln, referring to himself and the other senators as "we" and "us." He wants to uphold the Constitution of the United States—"We're concerned it [the direct investment regulation] is unconstitutional." He has a solution: Gray will withdraw his regulation cutting back direct investment from 40 percent of assets to 10 percent, or at least put a moratorium on it, and if he does this, Charlie Keating will return Lincoln to the home mortgage business with more enthusiasm. Ed Gray has never had a U.S. senator invite him into his private office and on behalf of a friend ask him to withdraw a regulation. He explains that he cannot repeal a regulation by himself, that it requires a vote of the entire three-person bank board. And he notes that it might be an inappropriate moment for such a vote since Charlie Keating is suing the entire board over the regulation. It is now a matter for the courts.

The senators have another question. Why is the examination of Lincoln—now more than a year long—taking so much time? Gray, who has been coached by Black, answers that the regulators in San Francisco would be best equipped to speak to that matter. Lincoln, he instructs the senators, is but one of thousands of banks he must oversee.

John Glenn points out angrily that Gray is the "chief regulator," and as such he should know about a case in which his people in San Francisco are said to be "running wild." The other senators share his disbelief that Ed Gray has so much to do all day that he knows little or nothing about Lincoln Savings and Loan.

Ed Gray, the former high school debating champion, fends off these inquiries with ease. "If my life depended on it," he tells the senators, "I could not tell you about the financial condition or regulation of Lincoln because I don't know and I don't believe I need to know these things."

He offers to set up a meeting between the senators and the regulators from San Francisco. DeConcini is not sure about such a meeting and tells Gray he will get back to him in a few days. The meeting winds down, there is little to say since Ed Gray professes no knowledge of Lincoln and the senators have apparently gathered to have a talk with the wrong person. A few days later, Ed Gray is informed that a second meeting is desired, this time with the San Francisco regulators. It is to begin in DeConcini's office on April 9 at 6 P.M.

The first week in April is a busy time. Charlie Keating is in Phoenix overseeing his properties and refinancing them. He has become fascinated by hotels for a very simple reason: if you build a house and sell it you make money once, but if you build a hotel room, you can sell it every night of the year, again and again. Still, he is trapped in long-term investments that do not pay off immediately.

To get some immediate profits and cash, he has just doubled a $40 million play in utility stocks, he has sat down with a representative of the Kuwaitis to talk about peddling all or part of the yet unfinished Phoenician, he has tossed $50 million into a Cooke Media junk bond deal. His hotel for business travelers, the Crescent, and his luxurious resort hotel, the Phoenician, are still swallowing millions of dollars and returning little or no revenue. Each quarter, his accountants scurry to create profits, and then a share of these profits goes from Lincoln to ACC under the government-approved tax-sharing plan. That week Lincoln has assets of $3.7 billion, and of this money 36 percent comes from brokered accounts, hot money. As Charlie Keating flies about inspecting his empire, he has put 3 percent of Lincoln's money into residential loans and 54 percent into risky investments, and for the first quarter of 1987, which has just ended, Lincoln has lost, in the eyes of some accountants, $15 million.

So he meets with the management of his savings and loan, he meets about a tax matter with one of the dozens of law firms he has on retainer, he squeezes in time for a representative of George Herrdum's GFTA—the German/Swiss outfit that markets that complicated computer system for playing markets, the black box he has just had his son, C3, master during an extended stay in Switzerland. He flies up to Colorado to look over some of those holdings, and in the plane is part of what it is all about for Charlie Keating—Charles H. Keating IV, C4, his young grandson, a new member of his family who by the nineties, he thinks, would be getting ready to run an empire, a veritable dynasty riding on a billion dollars or more when the time for the harvest comes.

That same week in Washington, D.C., the resignation of Lee Henkel from the bank board becomes official. Gray and Black and his other enemies within the agency have destroyed him—his interim appointment has no chance of surviving a Senate confirmation hearing after the articles that popped up in *The Wall Street Journal* and elsewhere about his ties to American Continental Corporation and Lincoln Savings and Loan. Keating says, "After the Henkel experience, I've given up trying to be responsible for who runs this country."

Ed Gray has a secret. In the lobby of the Federal Home Loan Bank Board building hang the portraits of the board members directing this trillion-dollar industry. He steals downstairs and takes Lee Henkel's portrait. His chief of staff, Shannon Fairbanks, is a by-the-books kind of person, and she tells Gray he cannot have the portrait, that it is federal property. Ed Gray has become more knowing about the real nature of government by April 1987. He puts the portrait in a place where Shannon Fairbanks will never discover it. And now every time he uses his private bathroom, he stares at the face of Lee Henkel.

Ed Gray calls the San Francisco office of the FHLBB to set up the next meeting with the senators and he talks to Michael Patriarcha, the head of the San Francisco region, a man Gray recruited in August 1986. The thirty-five-year-old Patriarcha has spent years keeping tabs on commercial banks for the Treasury Department—three as the chief regulator of the nation's eleven largest banks. Like Charles Keating, he has a hard view of the world. Lawsuits? He shrugs those off. Big Eight accounting firms like Arthur Young? Whores. It was during his watch at Treasury that Continental Illinois—the seventh largest bank in the country—floundered in 1984, costing the federal insurance fund $1 billion. He can never forget this failure. He refuses to be bound by regulations or technical compliance with the federal rules: "The typical response was, 'Hey, the regs say I can do this, or don't say I can't do this. . . .' And my answer was, 'I don't care what the regs say. Unless you can demonstrate that you've got the management with the [necessary] expertise . . . and [risk] controls in place . . . and capital proportionate to the risk . . . you ain't gonna do it.' "

Patriarcha is not some civil servant clinging to his metal desk. He is making $150,000 a year working for Ed Gray. He has been watching Lincoln for months and wondering, how can one savings and loan owner have so much clout? He answers this question with a hunch he always plays: follow the money. He knows Charlie Keating is a serious player. When Patriarcha begins poking into Lincoln's books, his wife, who worked for FHLBB as a lawyer, gets word that she might be able to land a high-paying job with a California thrift. She cools to the idea when she discovers that the offer comes from Lincoln Savings and Loan.

On the morning of April 9, the San Francisco delegation—Mike Patriarcha, Richard Sanchez, and James Cirona—huddles around a table at the agency's Washington headquarters planning strategy. Ed Gray is in Europe on official business. They are joined by Anne Sobol, a lawyer for the bank board, who tells them a criminal referral is going to the Justice Department recommending an examination of the evidence of file stuffing uncovered in the audit of Lincoln in the spring of 1986. There may also be criminal implications in the backdating of files and in possible fudging on direct investments. Sobol is particularly upset by the depositions she has taken of Lincoln's board of directors. When she shows them resolutions authorizing certain questioned direct investments, every single director denies that the signatures on the documents are actually his own. (Andy Neibling resigns when he discovers that his signature has been forged and goes back to Ohio.) Everyone at the meeting agrees to keep the fact of this criminal referral to the Justice Department a secret from the senators, whom they consider snitches for Charlie Keating. Patriarcha asks Sanchez how much longer it will take to wrap up the endless examination of Lincoln's books, and he is told two weeks. And then the men, along with Bill Black, depart for DeConcini's office for the six o'clock meeting.

DeConcini serves as master of ceremonies, and with him are Glenn, McCain, Don Riegle. Alan Cranston sticks his head in the doorway and says, "I just want to say that I share the concerns of the other senators on this subject." And then he is gone.

Riegle says, "I wasn't present at the last meeting." He explains that the other senators have invited him, especially DeConcini, who has written him a letter—one Riegle insisted he write. As Riegle speaks, Bill Black sits nearby taking notes. Ever since he was a champion debater in high school he has had this knack for taking exact notes. No one pays any attention to his scribbling.

The other senators explain their presence. DeConcini is there as the senator from Arizona, ACC's base, and he thinks Charlie Keating's offer to scale back on high-risk investments and move toward home mortgages is a good proposition. Also, he wants to make clear why Riegle is there: "I'm not on the banking committee, and I'm not familiar with how all this works. I asked Don Riegle to explain to me how the Federal Home Loan System works because he's on Senate Banking. He explained it to me, and that's why he's here."

McCain notes that part of his job as a senator is to help his constituents, but "I wouldn't want any special favors for them."

John Glenn explains his presence by saying, "Lincoln is an Ohio-chartered corporation."

Cirona interrupts and points out that Lincoln is a California institution, but Glenn is not fazed: "Well, Lincoln is wholly owned by ACC, and ACC is an Ohio-chartered corporation." This fact is also inaccurate.

Then Glenn makes a point: "You should charge them or get off their backs."

The examiners explain that Lincoln has made fifty-two real estate loans and there are no credit reports backing up a single one of them. "They're flying blind," Patriarcha says.

"What's wrong with this if they're willing to clean up their act?" asks DeConcini.

"This is a ticking time bomb," Cirona responds.

Riegle then pulls out a letter from Jack Atchison of Arthur Young, Keating's accounting firm. The letter, dated March 17, says the bank board is being "unusually antagonistic" and that this is "difficult to understand because Lincoln's strategies have thus far proved successful and have turned an association headed for failure into a strong and viable financial entity."

Now why, asks DeConcini, would Arthur Young say such a

thing if they did not believe it? "You believe," he continues, "they'd prostitute themselves for a client?"

"Absolutely," responds Patriarcha. "It happens all the time."

(In one year, Charlie Keating will hire Jack T. Atchison away from Arthur Young and pay him around $1 million a year.)*

There is a slight pause. And then the beat picks up.

"You can ask any lawyer you know," Patriarcha offers, "about these practices. They violate the law and regulations and common sense."

"Have you done anything about these violations of the law?" asks Glenn.

Patriarcha feels the room, smells the play. And fires.

"We're sending a criminal referral to the Department of Justice. . . . I cannot tell you strongly enough how serious it is."

John Glenn has one of Keating's aides waiting back in his office at that very moment for an instant report from the senator on what is said and done at this meeting.

"What can we say to Lincoln?" he asks.

Black pauses in his note taking and plunges in: "Nothing with regard to the criminal referral. They haven't and won't be told by us that we're making one. . . . Justice would skin us alive if we did."

The meeting is ending, and they have entered dangerous country without warning.

"I think," Patriarcha says, lest anyone leave without a clear picture of the problem, "my colleague Mr. Black put it right when he said that it's like those guys that put it all on sixteen black in roulette. Maybe they'll win, but I guarantee you that if an institution continues such behavior, it will eventually go bankrupt."

Glenn and Riegle walk away, muttering to each other, "What are we going to tell him?" There is that ACC executive . . . waiting in Glenn's office for a report.

Patriarcha, standing by the curbside waiting for a taxi, tells his colleagues, "These guys were all over us like sweat until we disclosed the criminal referral." He pauses and then likens the moment to "throwing holy water on a vampire."

---

*When Keating's own attorneys protest this hire as something that will look compromising in the eyes of the federal regulators, he snaps that his lawyers have never made him a nickel but his accountants have been money-makers.

Back at his office, John McCain has little he wishes to tell his staff. He raises his eyebrows, whistles through his teeth, and then says, "We've done everything we're going to do on this thing." McCain never spoke to Keating again.

At the bank board building, Black is busy transcribing his notes, which will be transmitted to Ed Gray that night.

Charlie Keating is at his home in Phoenix. He has just returned from Colorado, and when he gets the report of what his senators have done and not done he realizes that he has used up many cards. He has lobbied the House, reached into the selection of a member of the bank board, put five U.S. senators in a room to look after the interests of his savings and loan. And it is not enough. But he is not finished. The next morning he breaks his custom of keeping the press at bay—Charlie Keating does not like things he cannot control—and he allows a *Wall Street Journal* reporter to interview him for an hour about his business empire. He then sends the man off with his aides to view his many projects. If people will only take a look at his work, at his staff, then they will understand. He is convinced of this.

At times Charlie Keating can be candid about this system of making contributions to politicians.

"I've probably made some mistakes," Keating allows during an interview a year later. "The press coverage probably mainly comes from our contributions. That's seen as buying the council [he tossed in $80,000], buying the state. What do I think I'm buying? I don't think I'm buying a damn thing. I just should have never gotten into it. I supported the mayor of Scottsdale, and he voted against me every time. It wasn't a planned, deliberate, programmed thing. But in retrospect, we should have been a dropout in that ball game."

For him it began innocently, years ago. It was an almost unconscious thing, and then, magically, it grew. "I always raised money since the Connally thing for senators," he continues in his effort to explain. "Let's say it like this: senators run for election, and it's beyond comprehension. A senator will come to Phoenix strictly for a $15,000 luncheon or breakfast. When I was with Connally, the things we had to do to raise ten or twenty-five thousand dollars. . . . They come—the calls that I get, the letters, the pressure I get to contribute to guys in Nebraska, New York, New Jersey. In the beginning—remember now I was a lawyer—I was with another company that wasn't run by me, and then all of a sudden I had my own business. All of a sudden I made a lot of contributions and started a business. Then everybody and their brother—they don't want the notoriety, but they sure want the money. I wasn't good at saying no. I'm not going to try and sell that, but the whole thing basically comes from that, more than it does from an impulse to buy."

Yes, but what about those senators he drowns with money? What about Dennis DeConcini, John Glenn, Alan Cranston, Don Riegle, John McCain? Over a million dollars. And for what? To intervene in a bank audit being conducted by federal civil servants?

"Damn right," he snaps back. "I'm telling you, all I wanted then was to get it over with. . . . Hey, look, we're domiciled in Ohio, so we had Senator Glenn; we have a hotel in Michigan, so we had Senator Riegle; we operate out of California, so we had Senator Cranston; we live in Arizona where our headquarters are. Those were the senators. We went to them, and we said, 'Hey, look, we cannot survive anymore. We don't want you to go in and say anything but expedite.' Two years was more than a year longer than any examination we'd ever heard of before in history. Make a decision. The biggest problem a businessman has is cutting through, getting it done. Time is just critical. The cost of money.

"We don't do it anymore. We don't need our name in the paper, and we've withdrawn from contributing. I would say we're down, on a scale of one to ten, we're at a two—there's no point in it. If the politicians want laws that expose their contributors to ridicule and approbation, that's fine with me, it's their business. But they don't have me as a contributor. All these laws have really come in in the last ten years. It's a tough ball game out there today, they've buried themselves. The full effect of what they've done is twofold: one is that they've drummed out of the system the typical suppliers of their regular funds because you can't stand it, you just can't stand the scrutiny. The second thing they've done is, they have forced a situation where they'll end up charging the taxpayer at large the cost of the campaign. It is already crystal clear that the incumbent has ensconced himself in office by the draconian laws that publicize the contributors."

But what he insists on, what he always insists on, is that he did not initiate this way of running the United States, this custom of buying influence. He just recognizes how things are actually done in his country, and he does what he has to do. *

Ed Gray is more than a lame duck. He is broke, and no one in Washington, D.C., cares what happens to him. So when Senator Jake Garn of Utah—coauthor of the Garn–St. Germain bill, which launched three thousand thrifts into the new sea of deregulation—approaches him for help on lobbying a certain candidate as his successor, Ed Gray cooperates. He knows that Ronald Reagan will never reappoint him. He knows he needs to make powerful friends if he is to find a job. Garn has already met with Ronald Reagan in the Oval Office and pushed his own candidate—"called in all his chips," in the opinion of Gray. Garn has juice, and Ed Gray knows it.

Garn originally was a city commissioner in Salt Lake City, then he became mayor and then was elected to the Senate in 1975. Along the way he picked up a protégé, Melvin Danny Wall, the child of pious parents in Effington, South Dakota, where they ran a grocery store. Wall was an Eagle Scout toying with becoming a minister. Instead he became an urban planner, worked under Garn in Salt Lake City, and then followed him to the Senate, eventually becoming staff director for the Senate Banking Committee while his wife worked as Garn's personal secretary. Wall later described his role on the Garn–St. Germain bill as that of a "lab as-

---

*A glimpse of the political climate Keating operated in is provided by Stedino and Matera's *What's In It for Me?* pp. 121–122. A secretly taped conversation between Democratic politician George Stragalas and Stedino reviews the history of Keating's political donations to Terry Goddard, mayor of Phoenix in the eighties and eventually a defeated candidate for governor. The talk refers to Sam Goddard, Terry's father and a former governor, and Dennis DeConcini.

What happened was, Sam asked Dennis DeConcini—Dennis was his administrative assistant when he was governor . . . Dennis met with Sam and said, "I'll raise between $50,000 and $75,000 because Terry's runnin' for mayor." It's big money considering the limit is a quarter million. And Sam made the deal with Dennis. Dennis goes to Keating and Keating commits to the money and Keating says, "I wanna meet with Terry." Terry said, "No meeting. Let him put the money on the table. If he wants me, he wants me, that's what he's getting. He's not getting anything in return." So Keating says, "Fuck you!"

Okay, now . . . Terry calls Dennis and says, "Where's the money?" In Washington on the phone . . . three and a half hours on the phone this [U.S.] senator in his office talkin' to Terry, who's running for mayor. He [Terry Goddard] says, "Where's the money?" Dennis said, you know, "What kind of commitment" and so forth. [Terry said,] "No deals. This is a gift." Terry never got the money. The only politician that . . . stood up and said, "I'll tell you what. I didn't take money from Keating."

sistant." He is used to accommodating politicians, he is attracted to the pay and the feeling of power that come with being a Senate staffer. He has had a chance to meet many people over the years, including Charlie Keating.

Charlie Keating feels Wall is too much of a lightweight for the job, but he must be realistic since his own candidate, Lee Henkel, has been politically dead since that article in *The Wall Street Journal.* As for Gray, all Garn needs is his word not to oppose the nomination of Wall—even a dead or dying bank board chairman such as Gray can be an embarrassment if he voices opposition at a public hearing on his successor. And Gray complies, despite his low opinion of M. Danny Wall, because he has very few options left. So he pulls in what few favors he can still beg (one in a phone call to Ed Meese), and Wall is chosen. And then Garn cuts Gray dead.

In early May, the San Francisco office of the bank board finishes its one-year audit of Charlie Keating's empire and recommends it be seized at once—the technical term is "placed in conservatorship"—an act that historically has meant that the original operator never gets it back. It describes Lincoln as out of control, a financial disaster waiting to happen. But the long report goes nowhere. Not only is Gray a lame duck, but with Henkel's resignation the board lacks its full three members. Larry White, the other member of the board, tells Gray he will not act on any supervisory decision until a new chairman is sworn in. The only such supervisory matter before the board is Lincoln. And so Ed Gray calls no meeting, and there is no vote on this recommendation. His successor can deal with it, he thinks. He has had enough. At the same time Senator Dennis DeConcini pens Charlie Keating a note about the impending reign of Danny Wall at the bank board: "How thoughtful and insightful you have been in this area. Maybe things will change now that he [Ed Gray] is gone. I sure hope so."

Everything seems to be under control. Except that somehow the full audit—hundreds of pages of intimate financial details about Charlie Keating's empire, material that is supposed to be kept secret and protected by a fabled Chinese wall—falls into the hands of Jack Anderson's legman, Michael Binstein. And through talk and expressions of interest, he captures the help of Curtis Prinns, a House committee staffer and a supporter of Charlie Keating. Binstein does not tell Prinns about his horde of secret bank board documents. Instead he explains to him how fascinated he is by this unique entrepreneur, Charlie Keating. Prinns tells Charlie Keating he should talk to Binstein, that he will understand. That he will prove useful.

Binstein flies to Phoenix, and Charlie Keating talks to him at length. He sends Binstein out on the usual tour of his projects, he lets him wander through his headquarters and see the excellence of his staff. He will make another convert, he is sure. What he cannot seem to get across in Washington, he will get across by using the press.

Larry Flynt refuses to stop beating at the gates of American society. He keeps buying new magazines covering running, music, and whatnot, and he keeps making more and more money. He is hardly ever in the press except as a byword for filth, a kind of icon of what is beyond the bounds. In many ways Flynt, like Keating, has become addicted to lawsuits, and he is constantly in court or, on occasion, tossed into jail for contempt. *Hustler,* through service features like "Asshole of the Month," regularly harvests new litigation. And Flynt takes to these legal waters with gusto. He may be the only human being in the entire republic dedicated to exploring the deepest and darkest meaning of the First Amendment. He is given to comments: "Murder is a crime. Writing about it isn't. Sex is not a crime, but writing about it is. Why?"

In 1985, he prints a story on antipornography crusader Andrea Dworkin that contains sexually explicit photographs and some caricatures. Dworkin hires Gerry Spence of Karen Silkwood fame to defend her. Flynt then publishes a column about Spence that writes him off as a shyster who takes on clients simply out of greed. Spence sues Flynt for around $150 million. This does not seem to give Flynt pause. He likes to fight, and he is willing to fight with every means at his command.

And so, as Charlie Keating moves and countermoves to beat back the regulators' invasion of his business, Larry Flynt takes on more and more lawsuits. He can afford to do this because each and every day of the year he is probably making more money than Charlie Keating.

Keating is in Miami at his mansion on Indian Creek, then he's on to Cat Cay, then Cincinnati. He goes to Europe, stops off in

Monaco to check on the possibility of permanent residency. He meets with Toufic Aboukhater about getting more of that Kuwaiti money. He pauses in London to go over the design of a new motorboat for his retreat in Cat Cay and a satellite system to keep him in constant touch with the world and its markets when he is on a holiday. At the same time, he dispatches a large group of his executives to Asia for two weeks to scout out some of that Japanese financing. He declines to go himself because he feels his appointments are not with people of sufficient stature. He stops off in Dubrovnik, Yugoslavia, for a day to check out reports of a miracle that has occurred nearby.

It is a very crowded life. On June 23, he is in Zurich meeting with George Herrdum of GFTA about his mysterious black box and the wild pleasures of the currency market. The following afternoon he is back in Yugoslavia and goes to the Croatian village of Medjugorje where, since June 25, 1981, there have been reports that the Mother of God has appeared on a daily basis and given messages. Some of these communications are released, and their content is relayed to believers around the world within hours. While Keating is there, the Blessed Mother delivers this message: "Dear children! Today I thank you and want to invite you all to God's peace. I want to invite you to experience in your heart that peace that God gives. Today I want to bless all of you. I bless you with God's blessing. I beg you, dear children, to follow and to live my way. . . ."

At first the Communist authorities were hostile to these reports, but then they began to notice the enormous numbers of pilgrims and the money to be made off them. It is rumored that in Belgrade the Virgin is referred to as Our Lady of Hard Currency. Charlie Keating studies the possibilities of buying some land near the village church for a hotel. He visits with the priests and approves a movie to be made in the local language on the appearances of the Blessed Mother. He contributes $200,000 of ACC money toward this project. He stays with a peasant family, the mattress straw, the house small, a privy out back. He prays. And he does not touch a phone. But when his plane takes off for Zurich at 7 A.M. the next day, he is instantly placing calls. That evening he is in London with John Connally to attend the wedding of Toufic Aboukhater's son.

On June 30, Charlie Keating is back in Phoenix. Lincoln Savings and Loan now has $3.9 billion in assets, and its risky investments have edged up to 58 percent. Of course, there are those end-of-quarter deals that must be struck to book profits. For example, Ernie Garcia is down on the books for buying half of Lincoln and ACC's interest in one of Sir James Goldsmith's corporate war chests, plus a block of Memorex stock that Keating had picked up.* On June 30, Ed Gray ends his four-year term as chairman of the Federal Home Loan Bank Board. He goes home to his one-room apartment. He has no job. He is broke.

On July 1, 1987, M. Danny Wall is sworn in at a ceremony at FHLBB. He is wearing his trademark three-piece suit and ankle boots. As he waits with his friends and family for his oath of office to be administered, he receives an unexpected phone call.

"I'm sorry, sir," responds an agency secretary, "but he's with his family about to take the oath."

"I don't give a goddamn who in the hell he's talking to," the caller snaps. "I want him right now."

M. Danny Wall takes the call of Richard Hohlt, a lobbyist for the U.S. League of Savings Institutions, the main fist of the thrifts on Capitol Hill. Hohlt once explained, "When it comes to Danny Wall, he doesn't take a piss unless I give him permission." But then, Wall is a man of the Hill—he likes to describe himself as a "child of the Senate." He has already made a courtesy call on Jim Wright and been told to fire Bill Black.

---

*To fully understand the world Charlie Keating moved in and to realize that his machinations were not unique, it is worthwhile to take a look at the way Sir James Goldsmith created his funds for corporate raids. For example, on April 10, one of his entities, CZC Acquisition Corporation, made a fourteen- to nineteen-million-share buy order on the New York Stock Exchange for the stock of Crown Zellerbach. CZC had been incorporated one week before in Delaware and was a wholly owned subsidiary of GOSL Acquisition Corporation, which had also been born in Delaware a week before. GOSL, in turn, was a wholly owned subsidiary of General Oriental Securities Limited Partnership (GOSLP), which had come into being in Hamilton, Bermuda, six days earlier. The big player in GOSLP was General Oriental Investments Limited (GOIL), an entity created six months earlier in the Cayman Islands. Chunks of the Crown Zellerbach stock were bought by GOIL from Dia Investment Antilles, N.V., a Netherlands Antilles corporation, from Cavenham Holdings, Inc., a Delaware subsidiary of Goldsmith's Générale Occidentale holding company, which was based in France. The biggest piece of GOIL itself was owned by Campania Financiera Lido out of Panama, and most of Lido was owned by Enderbury Financial Inc., also out of Panama and sharing the same office. All of Enderbury was owned by the Frunneria Foundation, based in Liechtenstein and described as a charity. Sir James Goldsmith was the chairman of all of these entities. (See Dennis B. Levine with William Hoffer, *Inside Out,* G. P. Putnam's Sons, New York, 1991, p. 195.)

A few days before Wall's swearing-in, Ed Gray had received a postcard in the mail, an impersonal invitation to the ceremony. Normally, in government, when one agency head gives way to the next, there is a ritual appearance together. But this is not to be for Ed Gray. He goes down to the agency's headquarters anyway, and he stands in the back of the crowded auditorium as Danny Wall is sworn in as the new chairman. Gray's name is not mentioned in the speeches. No one recognizes him as he stands against the back wall alone.

Ed Gray goes home to his tiny apartment and lies down on the floor. He begins to sob uncontrollably. He is alone, there is no one he can talk to about what has happened, about what he has seen and what he senses is yet to come. He is the man who was once the butt of the press corps when he served on Governor Ronald Reagan's staff. Mr. Ed, the talking horse, the dolt. He calls out, What has happened to me? What have I done? And thoughts of suicide flutter across his consciousness.

While Ed Gray falls apart in his apartment, Danny Wall begins to make changes at the bank board. For instance, the furniture in his office does not project the proper image, so it is replaced. Then he notices that the phone doesn't match the color of his new furniture, so it too is replaced. He enjoys sitting at his desk and drawing new organization charts. Also, he inspects the entire building with engineers and finds many things to change because it is very important to "get things going in sprucing up things so that it [is] a more businesslike environment." He notes that some letters have fallen off the agency's sign out in front of the building, and he fusses over this matter because a new sign will tell others "things are happening." As he attends to these things, the thrift industry is bleeding $1 billion a month. M. Danny Wall sees a different meaning in the numbers. He announces that his "agency, this system and this industry are standing on the threshold of a new and brighter future." In July 1987, there is a 1,200-page monthly report on his desk from his staff at the bank board that notes that 383 savings and loans under his care are in danger of going bankrupt due to bad loans, bad management, speculation, and fraud. Danny Wall works and works on his new organization charts.

Charlie Keating is not idle, either. He writes Jim Grogan, an ACC aide, on July 15 about a piece of old business: "Highest priority—Get Black. Good Grief—if you can't get [Jim] Wright and

Congress to get Black—kill him dead—you ought to retire." Black had already left the Washington office on the eve of Gray's departure for a better-paying job at the bank board's San Francisco office. A few weeks after taking office Wall and his staff have Black on the speakerphone during a conference about yet another California thrift, and when arguments erupt, Bill Black says, "Jesus Christ!" Wall cannot abide such a comment—he once planned to be a preacher, for heaven's sake—and says, "I do not see any reason to invoke the name of the deity in this discussion." Thereafter, whenever Black is on the phone during a conference call with the staff in San Francisco, Wall will turn to his aides and mumble, "Why did they put this asshole on?"

That same summer Wall's chief of staff, James Boland, tries to explain reality to Michael Patriarcha. "There are things you don't understand," Boland says while at the same time hinting that the treatment of Lincoln and Charlie Keating is about to change. "We are doing this for your own good. These guys are so well connected they can get you in ways where you will never know you've been gotten."

Of course, Wall must deal with the unpleasant audit report turned in by the San Francisco office, the one that says Lincoln should be seized by the federal government at once. On July 23, 1987, William L. Robertson, the chief of examiners of the bank board, writes Wall a memo: "Since ACC's acquisition of Lincoln Savings, the supervisory history of the association reveals a pattern of management misrepresentations, speculative investments, flagrant and recurring violations, and an overall lack of respect for safety and soundness. . . . ACC acquired Lincoln Savings, and its FSLIC charter, only by misrepresenting its intentions as to how it was going to operate the association once acquired, and has since operated the association with little apparent regard for FSLIC regulations or safe and sound practices. Instead of operating as a community based lender, it has totally ignored the lending needs of its community, and has instead invested savings deposits acquired under the insurance coverage of FSLIC to engage in such risky ventures as takeover speculation, land speculation and junk bonds. In so doing, it has invested enormous sums of money without adequate safeguards or procedures to properly document the safety or soundness of its investments."

The eighteen-page document also recommends that Chairman

Danny Wall and the Federal Home Loan Bank Board put Lincoln Savings and Loan into receivership—a place from which the Charlie Keatings of the world never return. Wall reads this memo and knows precisely what to do. That same day Robertson is demoted and a man named Darrell Dochow is put in charge of examinations by the FHLBB. That same day the staff of the FHLBB meets with Lincoln concerning the threat of a lawsuit by Lincoln over leaks. Also, on July 23, ACC issues its eighth placement of junk bonds through Lincoln's branches, this one for $10 million. Five days later, the people at the bank board's headquarters in Washington, D.C., people like Rosemary Stewart, decide that a conservatorship of Lincoln is not viable.

Ed Gray needs a job desperately. There are no offers, and then a possible Florida position comes his way. He lacks the money to fly down, so he takes the train. He is embarrassed—he used to be a deputy to the president of these United States. He stays at a very cheap motel, but no one must know this, not ever. He manages to have his host and possible employer pick him up at a more fashionable place downtown. He tells him he flew in the night before. After the interview, he insists on being dropped off in downtown Miami—there is business he must attend to, he explains, you know how it is, the demands on your time just never seem to stop. And then he catches a bus to the train station. No one must know what has happened to Ed Gray.

In July, an article appears in the influential Washington, D.C., business magazine *Regardie's,* a publication named after its owner, Bill Regardie, whose slogan is MONEY POWER GREED. The piece is by Michael Binstein, and it is about a reckless savings and loan owner, a wild man who is squandering federally insured dollars. The 1987 audit (which has never been publicly released) forms the core of the account, which notes the fifty-two real estate deals done without a credit check, the real estate appraisals that federal examiners find grossly inflated, the $100 million blank check to Ivan Boesky, the hundreds of millions of dollars of junk bonds, the private air force of lavish corporate planes.

The story reads like a retelling of some kind of economic pornography.

Charlie Keating sits in his office and reads it and tells an aide, this could kill us, this could destroy my family. He's been fucked, and he knows it. The press has done it again. He cannot believe the lies, the misunderstandings in the piece. He wants to sue *Regardie's,* he wants to crush this Michael Binstein. He has been betrayed, he trusted this man. But his lawyers tell him this would not be wise—*Regardie's* is Washington based, and the suit must be filed there also. The capital is much too populated by media people, and Binstein would get sympathetic coverage. So Charlie Keating backs off.

Then his friend John Connally begins to die of the disease called bankruptcy. Connally tries one last desperate act to save his empire—he seeks money from a very shaky bank on the island of Tonga (a bank whose founder will be discovered dead in a Las Vegas motel room a year later). Keating himself can feel the squeeze as his long-term investments grow but his immediate income does not. He is increasingly cash short.

So he calls in Connally's loans, and his friend phones and says, "Charlie, I really need you to let up on me."

Keating says, "I can't, and I hope you understand that this is a business deal and we have to foreclose."

"I'm asking you as a friend. I need some more time."

"John, as a businessman I can't. It's a regulated company. I've done everything I can for you."

On July 31, 1987, John Connally declares bankruptcy. He places his debts at $93 million. He tells the press, "The people who came to Goliad and who came to the Alamo took a few risks, and for what? For what they thought was right. If you hope to achieve anything in life, you have to take a few risks."

Charlie Keating admires John Connally, and he wonders if he is man enough to bear such a burden of failure.

Two days after Robertson writes his memo detailing the sins and failings of Lincoln Savings and Loan, Charlie Keating is in Nice, France, to meet yet again with Toufic Aboukhater about the Kuwaitis and their money. Then he is in Zurich talking with George Herrdum—Keating is going to move all his black box bets with GFTA back to Phoenix. In fact, he will put the box right down the hall from his own office, and there he will work all hours of the day and night making various plays in the currency markets of the planet. That same day in Medjugorje, the Blessed Mother states, "Dear children! I beseech you to take up the way of holiness and to begin today. I love you, and therefore, want you to be holy. I do not want Satan to block the way. Dear children, pray and accept all that God is offering you and realize that the way is going to be bitter. . . ."

On August 1, two days after John Connally goes bust, Keating is in Paris, exploring the Ritz—his Phoenician must be the finest hotel in the world. That morning he meets with some people from GFTA again about a proposed $50 million investment in a company yet unnamed or even formed, one that will plunge into various rates, commodities, and futures and will do these things globally.

For six months he's been playing the currency markets on Herrdum's little black box, and hardly anybody in the company knows exactly what he is doing or appreciates the strain of it all. By the end of June, when he finally sends Ed Gray, that federal fool, down the government shitter, he has lost $13.5 million. As Danny Wall, that other Washington dummy, moves into position and putters around picking furniture for his office, well, Charlie Keating is following his hunches, hitting on that black box, doubling down those old bets, and for the third quarter of 1987, his losses add up to a total of $20 million. Finally the bank board slips a recapitalization bill through Congress, and President Ronald Reagan signs it on August 10, 1987, but Charlie Keating knows the new law is largely toothless—the funding is limited to $3.75 billion in any twelve-month period, which means the hated feds cannot seize and shut down thrifts wholesale. Still, he's got to find someone who can sell all that dirt out at Estrella, get those lots moving, pump up the cash flow. Then, there's the Phoenician Hotel, he's got to get on that baby, he can't let those architects and those contractors run wild out there. He's got to get that thing finished, open, and making money.

There's a lot to do, not just tend the black box. Though God knows, the black box is a bitch—in the fourth quarter he gets the feel, yes, he gets the feel, and he cranks a $5 million profit. But this leaves him $34.5 million short on a year of currency plays. Nobody knows these facts. They wouldn't understand.

He is a cameraman for a local television station in Phoenix, Arizona, and brushes up against Charlie Keating's world a couple of times. Once he is at the Phoenician right after the glittery resort opens, and he sees this tall man sweep past, surrounded by an entourage. Then, in March 1989, ACC hires his television station to shoot some promotional footage of its major development, Estrella. He is struck by the chopper—an interior like a limousine and a refrigerator stocked with champagne.

The second time he sees Charlie Keating is in December 1989, after the bankruptcy, after the federal seizure of Lincoln and of the Phoenician resort, after the filing of the racketeering charges. The cameraman and another guy from the station have been out in L.A. all day doing an interview with movie actor Martin Sheen. They catch the last flight back to Phoenix at 10 P.M. on America West, a discount operation with no amenities or first-class seating. After they're airborne, the cameraman notices Charlie Keating wedged into a coach seat three rows ahead of them. The guy traveling with him asks, "Is that Charlie Keating?" and the cameraman nods yep, that's him. So the guy gets up and walks down the aisle and stands over Keating, who then gets up, sticks out his hand, and says, "Charlie Keating." The stranger blurts out, "How can you live with yourself? Don't you feel sorry for all the people you ripped off?" Keating snaps his head back for a moment as if he has just been slapped and replies, "Don't make your judgments on me until the trial is over. And don't believe what you see in the newspapers and media. You just wait, and I think you'll be surprised."

THE
WATER
SLIDE

John Boyce remembers how upset his dad got when he found a stash of girlie magazines in his room. He was only twelve or thirteen, and he couldn't for the life of him figure out why his collection of naked ladies was such a big deal. His dad told him, "My God, John, we've got a good friend who's fighting this stuff." That was back in Cincinnati, and Boyce still carries a vivid memory of the first time he saw Charlie Keating. Boyce couldn't have been more than five or six. He can see that evening clearly in his mind. His dad had invited Charlie and Mary Elaine over to play bridge and right off the bat was giving them a tour of the house, and Boyce, still a tot, looked up and saw this guy with a bright smile and a shock of blondish hair and, well, what stunned him was Charlie Keating's height and he thought it must be wonderful to be so big that you had to worry about bumping your head on the ceiling.

But that was a long time ago, and now it is almost spring of 1987, and John Boyce is no longer five but thirty-eight. And he is a failure. He's botched up his job at the post office and has a lawsuit cooking against the government. He's overweight, he likes to drink, he's a chain-smoker. He generally sticks around Cincinnati and hits the bottle, but suddenly he is in Phoenix, Arizona, waiting to see Charlie Keating. The visit has come about accidentally. He can remember his mother musing over the years, wondering out loud just how the Keatings were making out since they moved to Phoenix. When she is out there visiting her other son, she always thinks of calling them but she can never remember the name of Keating's new company and so she never does. Then out of the blue came an invitation to the marriage of Keating's youngest daughter, and naturally she went—they'd been such good friends when her husband was alive and they were all young couples just starting out—and Charlie was chatting with her and then he asked, what's John up to these days? And she'd almost broken down and just told Charlie the truth: "He never finished college. He has a helluva drinking problem. He got fired from the post office. But he's okay now." Keating looked at her and said, "Have him give me a call. I owe you one."

Boyce's mother called him from Phoenix and told him about the conversation. And so he called Charlie Keating (it wasn't easy to reach him, he could never seem to catch up with Keating and his whirlwind schedule). Charlie pummeled him with questions: "What do you look like? Did you ever get married? Do you have any girlfriends? You aren't queer, are you? Why don't you have any girlfriends?" Boyce wanted to say "Not no, but fuck no," but he bit his tongue and was polite. So Keating said, "I want to give you a break."

That's how John Boyce wound up in Phoenix this day in early 1987. He is very nervous. He's wearing a brand-new suit, and this is the first time he's worn one in years. He walks into the ACC building and knows he does not fit—everyone seems so young and handsome and energetic. All too soon he is in Charlie Keating's office and Bobby Wurzelbacher—Charlie's son-in-law—is there and Boyce remembers that Wurzelbacher once dated his sister. Cincinnati is such a small world, he thinks. Keating has only about ten minutes, there's a plane he has to catch, so he gets right to the point: "As I said on the phone, I really want to do something to help you out. I want to give you a job. What I want you to do is come out here and get your health back and do yourself some good."

Boyce is taken aback—he's still in therapy with a psychologist over his post office trauma and has a hard time making decisions. All he really wants to do is get out of Keating's office and check out an ad he saw in the paper about a '67 VW Beetle for sale in nearby Mesa. He loves Beetles, he's wrecked two of them already. But Keating takes control.

"If you work four hours," he explains, "it doesn't matter. I just want you to get your health back. Just think of me as your dad for a while."

"Can I have thirty to sixty days to think about it?" Boyce offers.
"What are you going to do," Keating asks, "die in a mail sack in Cincinnati? What have you got going back there—a health claim with the postal service?"

Boyce stands there nervous and upset because he has made Charlie Keating angry. After five seconds of silence, he cannot take any more, and he says, "You're right. Okay."

Charlie Keating brightens, he has gotten through. He calls in a secretary and says, "I want you to meet John Boyce. Put him on the payroll for $30,000. Give him a $2,500 bonus."

Boyce stands there and feels his whole world, his whole idea of a world, going up in flames before his eyes. He likes his little apartment in Cincinnati. He likes his lawsuit against the post office. But Keating is moving much too fast for John Boyce to do anything about it.

They decide to make him a construction inspector, and they have him back on the plane to Cincinnati that afternoon with a ticket bought by ACC. He is told to report for work the following Monday. Once he is back in his small apartment in Cincinnati, Boyce recovers his bearings and calls and gets permission for a two-week delay before he reports for his new job.

When Boyce tries to recall his chance at a new life, the magical opportunity his father's old friend offered him, he still sounds bleak and can hardly weld the words together into a coherent sentence. "I was there to no purpose," he concludes, "but only to suit his purpose, whatever that was, maybe to see me succeed. . . . If there was one guy in the world I would have trusted enough to give up the situation I had to go out there because of the charisma . . ." And then he drifts off again, he cannot really finish the thought. John Boyce has one of those IQs that bump way up on the chart. He's a baby-faced guy hiding behind large-frame glasses, an overweight guy with cast-off clothing, a pot belly, and a surprisingly clear, almost velvety, voice.

Boyce has been at his invented job now for a couple of weeks, maybe a month, when one day Charlie Keating comes sweeping into his work area with a reporter in tow, some guy named Michael Binstein. And suddenly Charlie stops right in front of Boyce, flicks his fingers against his belly, and says, "Tell 'im."

Boyce, the only guy in the entire corporation that day who is not wearing a necktie, knows exactly what is called for, and so he be-

gins to recite, "I was a drug addict, an alcoholic, and my life was
ruined, and Charlie Keating, he's such a loyal man, he saved my
life because Charlie Keating never forgot the fact that my father
was his best friend. And Charlie Keating came and saved me, and
I would be dead without Charlie Keating. He gave me a job, and
he restored my dignity. Now I am working for the first time in
years, and my family is proud of me again."

As Boyce's recitation pours out for perhaps a minute, Charlie
Keating stands there with a large smile on his face and says nothing, makes no interruption, just looms there, all six feet five
inches of him, and listens to this testament to his own virtue.
When Boyce finishes, Keating wheels without a word and walks
away with Binstein straggling along. And suddenly John Boyce has
one more thing to say.

"God bless you, Charlie Keating," he shouts.

But Keating does not turn back, he displays no reaction, and
then he is gone.

There are so many deals, and just one of them would keep an
average guy floundering for a year in an effort to put it together.
On September 30, 1987, for example, there's the deal with MDC
where they agree to buy 630 acres in Hidden Valley, a back-of-
beyond part of Estrella that, according to the plan, will not be developed for years and years. MDC plunks down $2,775,391 cash
(shows good faith, shows it is a bona fide buyer) and then kicks in
$8,266,174 from a loan. The profits from this transaction are
booked at $8,587,000. On that same day, MDC peddles to an ACC
subsidiary four parcels of land for $16,306,000, and ACC pays
cash. Also that same day, Lincoln extends a $75 million credit line
to MDC. Naturally, with more than an $8 million profit on the
deal, Lincoln upstreams money to ACC for the tax account.

Still, there are other things to consider. On September 9,
Keating has meetings about land deals, about financing, about
Lincoln, about buying some mosaics from the tile designers at the
Vatican. He dispatches his daughter and son-in-law and his secre-
tary and her husband to Medjugorje. They meet with Father
Svetozar Kraljevic and talk about funds from Charlie Keating for
the priest, about ACC money for the movie about Our Blessed
Mother ("Note: get detailed receipts; very itemized"). Also, the
priest must be given a copy of a script about Fatima (Charlie

Keating plans yet another movie to spread the word of Our Lady), and they are to make sure the Medjugorje film and the one on Fatima aren't too similar. There is more. A visa must be arranged for the priest so that he can come to Phoenix and speak, also a Father Tomislave must come. Set up a radio show for Phoenix that features the children who see and speak with the Mother of God each and every day. And then get the priests to elaborate on just what the Blessed Mother is saying, yes, get them to elaborate. Make tapes with the various priests in Medjugorje, yes, get the tapes, anything will help. And Charlie Keating has this idea: he wants to send thirty Phoenix kids (say five from each parish) to Medjugorje. He'll make a radio spot and hold a contest, and if this works, they'll expand the project to the public schools so that the message of the Mother of God may be heard. Make sure also that the ACC logo will appear on the film and tell them that Charlie Keating will come in October.

As his staff follows his orders in Medjugorje, Charlie Keating is tied up in Los Angeles visiting new branches of his bank, and then, of course, there is dinner at the Four Seasons. On September 21, Charlie Keating is talking with the Ford Motor Company in Detroit about possible joint ventures in real estate, especially about Ford buying a piece of the still-under-construction Phoenician. The Pontchartrain must also be considered—it never seems to stop swallowing money, why, on September 1 $400,000 was injected into the hotel's collapsing veins and in ten days another $450,000 will be shipped via Bankers Trust Company of New York to the National Bank of Detroit. That afternoon, Charlie Keating flies back to Phoenix, and a day later, he is up and gone again to Washington, D.C., to struggle once more with the federal regulators about the never-ending audit of Lincoln. He makes a note: "Bill Black-Wright; disclosure; 5 senators . . ." Then he hits the Hill (". . . meeting with Senator DeConcini . . . Discussed: FHLBB examination of Lincoln; Fr. Svetozar from Medjugorje. . . .").

The very next day the Mother of God speaks at Medjugorje, and she says, "Dear children! Today, I wish to invite you all to pray. Let prayer be life to you. Dear children, dedicate your time to Jesus and He will give you everything that you are seeking. He will avail Himself to you completely. Dear children, Satan is strong and waiting to test each one of you. . . ."

Besides the Mother of God, Charlie Keating must deal with Michael Binstein, who wrote that article in *Regardie's* last July. Now it's reprinted in a Phoenix business magazine, *Arizona Trends*. Keating sues for about $30 million. But the suit does not name Michael Binstein because there is a slight problem of legal ethics: Charlie Keating uses Kaye Scholer for the suit, and Kaye Scholer has for years represented Binstein's employer, Jack Anderson. Still, the suit is better than nothing. Binstein, though not named in the suit, is under a cloud, and for a free-lancer, being under a $30 million cloud is close to fatal. He feels as though he has just been found to be HIV positive. Who wants to print stories by a guy whose work produces million-dollar lawsuits? Binstein and Bowden begin to talk on the telephone now—they have not met yet, but they share a secret, an obsession with this guy named Charlie Keating. Bowden has done nothing about making Keating a story except talk to Binstein when—boom!—his libel insurer calls and announces that if the magazine is contemplating a story on Charles H. Keating, Jr., its insurance will be jeopardized. He is impressed: he didn't even know the name of his own insurer until the call came. Next, letters begin to arrive from Kaye Scholer, and the list of partners on the letterhead looks like the New York telephone directory.

Then he coaxes the horde of material out of Binstein, those secret bank board documents. Bowden sits up all night in his office reading and rereading the audits, and he is absolutely hooked. He has it all figured out: this is a Ponzi game, a giant fraud, a Mafia bust-out. And Charlie Keating is a goddamn crook. Then Binstein ships the transcript of the April 1987 meeting between the regulators and the five senators. Bowden has only one dream in life, getting that transcript into print. But Bowden's lawyers keep cautioning, if he sues . . .

And so Bowden spends that fall and winter talking to Binstein and he is crazed by now, he is a prisoner of Charlie Keating's world. He keeps the federal audits by his bed, rereading them. He must get these things into print.

He has never met Charlie Keating, he has never even seen a good picture of him. Charlie Keating is a phantom in his mind, a kind of horrible Daddy Warbucks skulking in Phoenix.

John Boyce is shipped out to be a construction inspector, a job where he follows another employee around and tries to make sure that the workers do a good job. He checks to see if materials are arriving on schedule, he sweeps up debris that blights the construction site. It is summer in Phoenix, and the heat is killing him. So he sends a message to Charlie Keating that he cannot hack his job, and an appointment is made for him to talk to his mentor.

When Boyce arrives in the office, Keating is there with one of his sons-in-law, and Boyce explains that maybe he should go back to Cincinnati, maybe he is not cut out for Arizona. Keating laughs, turns to his son-in-law, and says, "Boyce can't take it. What have you got for him?"

Then Keating begins to question Boyce on his work experience. Boyce tells him that he did some data processing while in the navy. So Charlie picks up the phone, calls his data processing manager, and tells him, "John's been down on his luck, and I want you to help him out." He becomes a gofer and goes around the corporate headquarters doing things like counting the telephones. But most of the time he just sits around and reads.

Boyce stumbles upon a mining property in Colorado, and he is convinced that if he sinks a hole into this ground he will become very rich. So one day he races across the parking lot at American Continental and catches Charlie Keating getting into his car. He blurts out his idea and how he only needs a half-million-dollar loan so that he can go out and discover the buried treasure. Charlie Keating looks at John Boyce and gives a one-word reply: "No."

Ever since Ivan Boesky fell into the hands of the federal government and copped a plea, things have not gone so well for Michael Milken. Government investigators are crawling all over his junk bond operation, interrogating his staff, and this activity slowly begins to jam Milken's ability to do deals. Charlie Keating would understand and sympathize since by the fall of 1987, he is basically finished as a deal maker, a rainmaker, and has to spend all his time propping up earlier deals and going to meetings with the regulators or congressmen.

But Milken has the kind of mind that never stops working, and he has become obsessed with Third World debt. He thinks it is a bargain, and so in August 1987 he flies to Mexico City and talks with businessmen. He is appalled when they pledge to pay off their bonds in full despite the fact that they're now trading at only three or four cents on the dollar. Why do that? he asks. Why not buy back your own debt while it is cheap? That is his big idea. Latin America is economically on its back, all its bonds are trading at a pittance, and he thinks they are a bargain because, well, how can a country go broke? Why not just buy up, say, the national debt of Nicaragua? Sandinistas, they come and go, but countries are pretty much forever.

Charlie Keating shares this new passion of Michael Milken's and begins using the same language, that it is time to move beyond "junk bonds" and into a new era of "junk countries." And being Charlie Keating, he can do nothing by half measures, so on October 8, 9, and 10, he hosts a meeting at Estrella of major players, flies out John Connally, who has just been bruised by his bankruptcy (within days he was on television in a commercial pitching a savings and loan), and, of course, Michael Milken, a guy Charlie Keating considers "the creative genius of the century, maybe the last ten centuries." The meeting almost turns into a disaster when one of Keating's staff introduces Milken (who is a relatively prudish man and one intensely proud of his Jewish heritage) by telling a joke where Moses goes back up the mountain to chat with God and says, let me get this straight, you want us to follow these ten rules, not eat pork and cut the end off what? Somehow it all comes off. Keating and Milken are absolutely serious about buying Third World debt (eventually Milken will set up a fund just like the ones he once put together for corporate takeovers, and this fund over the next few years will make huge annual returns). On October 19, the day of the stock market crash, Milken is meeting with some representatives of KKR, the takeover wizards, to finance a $400 million junk bond offering, but he suddenly starts rambling about what he sees in the Third World and says, "I've been looking into the Third World debt, there are great opportunities there. Take Mexico." And then he is rolling on about buying up all this debt, buying up entire countries, turning their economies around, feeding the hungry, helping the poor, and the guys from KKR stare at each other and wonder what in the hell is this about? Milken can't seem to think like other people—when he meets Mikhail Gorbachev in early December 1987, the Russian says he wants to sell cars in the United States and Milken counters with "What do the Russians do best?" and by God, he knows that their ace in the hole lies in retinal surgery and cancer research. Milken has checked up on this, so he tells the Soviet leader, "The thing to do is convert nonmilitary science into commercial activities through joint ventures with American pharmaceutical and medical companies."

Milken and Keating both pull out of the stock market just before the October 19 crash.* Keating is in Monte Carlo at the time with his good friend Toufic Aboukhater, and he is on the phone almost every hour with his people at ACC. He must prop up his business associates who have been burned in the market, or they will default and his books will run red. One in particular catches his attention, Ernie Garcia, a young player who has done some of those quarterly deals on Hidden Valley real estate that are so essential to Lincoln's and ACC's profit profile. Garcia has a brokerage firm, is heavily into the market on October 19, and he is going down. ACC makes big cash infusions to keep him alive, cuts a complicated deal involving loans, and Garcia winds up temporarily buying those precious investments in Sir James Goldsmith's offshore war chests. By the end of the week he is still breathing, and Lincoln and ACC have booked some more fabulous profits. All this action postpones Charlie Keating's real goal in Europe, one he has been plotting for weeks: to go to Medjugorje to pray to the Mother of God. On Wednesday, October 21, he makes time to visit a shipyard and go over plans for a yacht and on Friday he's still tied up with this stock market crash, so he sends his wife and daughters and sons-in-law ahead to Medjugorje while he tends to business. Finally, on Saturday, he flies to the village, goes directly to Mass, then drives off to visit a priest and while on the road listens to the tape made by an American believer in the Virgin who tells of the experience she has had in this holy spot. He stays until Monday noon, he prays, he goes over the film he is financing. Charlie Keating leaves for Rome on October 26. The day before, the Mother of God sent another message: "My dear children! Today, I wish to invite all of you to decide for paradise. The way is difficult for those who have not decided for God. Dear children, decide and believe that God is offering Himself to you in His fullness. . . . Pray, because in prayer each one of you will be able to achieve complete love. . . ."

Highly Confident, p. 165, reports that Milken woke up on Wednesday, October 14, and said, "I don't like the market. Let's close the fund by the end of the week." He thus left on Friday, and the crash was on Monday. Keating had also pulled out.

On Tuesday, October 27, Charlie Keating is in the Pope's private chapel in Rome. He examines the sacred relics. That night he also settles the deal with Ernie Garcia and saves him in a sense—now Ernie Garcia is in his pocket. He also does another deal with Conley Wolfswinkel—he must keep booking those profits. By Friday, October 30, Charlie Keating is back in Phoenix.

John Boyce tries very hard to succeed. He quits smoking to please Charlie Keating, but his weight balloons. One day he is delivering memos and Charlie Keating looks up from his desk, notices the bloom of flab on his body, and announces, "You're too good-looking a guy for this." He turns to his secretary, mentions a name, and tells her to set Boyce up with the guy. Suddenly John Boyce is working out three times a week with a weight trainer, at twenty bucks an hour. Keating picks up the tab and wants regular reports on Boyce's progress. For six months Boyce goes on a strict diet, pumps iron, loses sixty-five pounds.

Boyce feels like a fool much of the time. Charlie gives him a bonus so he can buy a decent car, and he buys an old Studebaker. When Charlie Keating sees it in the parking lot, he is appalled. Or Boyce will try to dress better and take his sweater out of mothballs and wear it to the office and everyone will smirk and complain about the odor. Or Boyce delivers a memo to Keating's office and he is wearing a baseball cap and a windbreaker. Keating looks up at him and snaps, "What is it, you've got a hot date?" and Boyce feels terribly embarrassed. So just before he walks out the door of the office, he blurts out, "I've been wanting to tell you this for a long time. I just want you to know how fortunate I feel that you are my friend. And how appreciative I am." And Boyce can see from the reaction on Charlie Keating's face that he is genuinely moved by his words.

No matter what John Boyce says or does or thinks, no matter how badly he feels about himself at times, he always realizes his deep attraction to Charlie Keating. Just to be around him is a tonic. He is mesmerized by his energy, his dynamic way of speaking (so much like the power his dad had when he talked), his periodic statements of, well, visions. Charlie Keating seems to be able to go to the top of the mountain and see into that distant country called the future. There is the day Carl Lindner stops by the office and Boyce steps forward and introduces himself because

Lindner knew Boyce's grandfather, and that is the special thing about working at ACC, you get to see the future, you are part of the big picture, and yet it is still a family thing. A guy like Lindner, who is worth hundreds of millions, can walk in, and he will know your grandfather. He remembers the day Jim Ryun, the great miler, came to lunch and Charlie had tents put up and had the whole thing catered, and then he started talking and soon he had drifted into that special territory that seemed so uniquely Charlie Keating's, that place halfway between a speech and a monologue. Keating announced that they were all entering a new era in which they would be a cash-rich company instead of a heavily leveraged one, one with endless opportunities. There was a new global market out there, a place without national borders, and they were all going to go into that new, dazzling future. Or there was the time at Christmas 1987 when Charlie Keating announced to everybody that insurance was the wave of the future, that the insurance industry had less of this obnoxious regulation than the thrift industry, and so they were going to leave the savings and loan jungle and move into insurance, the new promised land. His voice almost choked up as he spoke.

Charlie Keating is buying books about the appearance of Our Blessed Mother at Medjugorje and giving them away by the case, sending them to everyone he can think of, including many of the priests in Phoenix. Boyce senses how seriously Charlie Keating takes this matter because he knows about his intense belief in the Virgin Mary. One day when Boyce is out at the planned city of the future, Estrella, he looks up and sees the ACC chopper overhead, and there is Mother Teresa blessing the project with a crucifix.

Charlie Keating seems to be into everything. His agenda for July 1, 1987, has a detailed list of appointments, and Keating has scribbled a note in the margin for his secretary, Carol Kassick: "All Fridays in July & August are Casual Days. Only you & Libby can wear shorts and high heels. Shorts OK, if not pregnant."

They are all at dinner at the Crescent Hotel—John Boyce, his two brothers, his aunt, his mom, his sister, Tish—and Charlie Keating is feeling great. He's had a few belts but is nowhere near drunk. He goes around the table asking Boyce's family what they would like.

He gives Tish $10,000. Boyce's aunt has a bad septic system, and so Charlie has that fixed free of charge. One of Boyce's brothers gets a computer and about ten grand. Boyce's other brother is a special problem, he's an out-of-work CPA and Charlie is leery of him. He asks him how deeply he is in debt, and Boyce's brother answers about $25,000. Keating turns to Boyce and asks, "Do you think I can trust him?" Then Tish pipes up that maybe it would be better to give her brother the money a little at a time, and Charlie thinks about this and tells Boyce to go with his brother and sister to another table and thrash out a proposal. Finally the brother comes over to Keating and, out of Irish pride, tells him that his offer is generous and that what he will take is fifty cents on the dollar. His mother asks for a trip to Australia, and why not, it's a magical kind of night.

Keating funnels all the gifts through John's paycheck, and then John discovers the unpleasant fact that he has to pay the taxes on all this loot and the bill damn near busts his ass.

In October 1987, Chip Wischer gets a shot at a world that has long intrigued him. He flies to London and spends a couple of weeks syndicating some insurance with Lloyd's, the cutting edge of the insurance world. He is due for a break. He's working eighty hours a week at ACC, and he's unhappy. He recently bought a company that makes concrete blocks—he'd done construction in college and likes working outside. He was looking for a way to escape ACC. Judy initially was against the idea because "You couldn't wear a suit and tie then." Then she installed her brother-in-law at the block company because he needed a job. By the time Chip gets back from his business trip to London, she has plowed $1.2 million of their money into the business and what is in it for him?—he's not riding around in a pickup running his block company, he's still stuck at ACC.

He arrives back from London about 4 A.M., and when he gets home he plops down the presents he's bought his kids and then collapses into his bed, poleaxed by jet lag. When he wakes up toward evening, he finds his brother-in-law and sister-in-law sitting downstairs, and he is not pleased. They're running the business he wants to run, and they're doing it with his money. Chip is always alert to money; after all, he is living in a $1.3 million house for which he and Judy made a cash down payment of more than $900,000. Around 9 P.M. he looks around at his in-laws, decides he can't bear their company, and goes back upstairs to bed. Later, Judy comes up and wakes him up to tell him that his retiring early was incredibly rude. He gets angry. Goddammit, he's financing their block company. He tells Judy he wants her sister and brother-in-law out of the block company, that they can damn well find their own living arrangement. And he wants out of ACC.

Judy says, "If I have to choose between my sister and you, you can pack your bags." Fine, Chip thinks, and he gets up and starts packing. Suddenly he hears his wife screaming, "Your father's leaving us!" and rustling the kids out of their beds. Eventually he gets his daughters calmed down and back to sleep.

And then Chip Wischer strongarms his wife against the wall and says, don't you ever bring our children into our marital problems again.

Finally, a few days off. Charlie Keating is at his Indian Creek estate in Florida from November 21 through 24, 1987, trying to unwind, but he does not seem to know quite how. No one has ever really taught him. On Sunday he goes with the head of the Tongans out to Manuel Diaz's farm and inspects trees for the Phoenician and Estrella. By Monday, he cannot lollygag around anymore, so he gets down to business. Where is that secretary? Send a letter to Toufic Aboukhater's son Bassam about his two-year contract to work for an ACC subsidiary in London; then there is a call to Judy Wischer about the loan situation and what investments to make; tell Robin Symes at Lincoln that they will need separate ACC offices in order to continue peddling those bonds; here, send this stuff to my son-in-law in Phoenix; get me Carol Kassick, the Sabre Jet's schedule must be reviewed; and where are we at on that film about Medjugorje? How's the logo for the Crescent Hotel coming? And what about these news clippings, ah, yes, send this one on an economic revival in Arizona; and this one on that city council meeting in that hick town; now, what about the loan that guy has in default? Get my son-in-law on his case. Here, take a memo on how we can save on taxes in Arizona and Florida; mail this letter to Fouad Jafar of Kuwait Investment and be sure to include the photographs of the Phoenician and the discussion of the hotel's completion date. Get this damned photocopier repaired.

And it goes on like that, hour after hour, day after day.

*　　　*　　　*

Jim Parker—black hair, brown skin—is a Mexican American who spent his childhood on an Indian reservation in the Pacific Northwest. For a while, he felt a calling to serve God and studied hard in a seminary, but it turns out his true calling lies in sales. He's doing fine up in Seattle, got an office building, got deals. And he's been around, sold a lot of property down in Texas when it was really booming. Then a friend of his runs into Charlie Keating, and Charlie says, hey, I've got this big project going in Estrella and I need someone to sell it, and the guy tells Charlie about Parker. So Charlie calls, and Parker flies down from Seattle with his wife. And Parker loves Estrella, he can grasp the concept—22,000 acres, a master plan, in fact the largest landmass being developed as a planned community in the entire United States.

("I caught the same vision. I shouldn't say the same vision, it certainly wasn't on the same magnitude of Charlie investing two hundred million dollars into the acquisition and development, but the vision . . . and I've always said I'd rather have a project with good blue sky. . . . I'd always rather have that open blue sky. To even have a blue sky at all. You've heard of the relationship in the banking industry, if you have a good bank and as much goodwill, it's blue sky, I like that.")

Parker takes his wife to his interview with Charlie Keating because she's his partner. They have been married a long time, and they make decisions together. Right off the bat, Parker calls Keating "Charlie." Keating says, "Jimmy, come on in here." Parker says, "I hope you don't mind, I brought my wife with me, Jacqueline." And Keating says, "I'd be very disappointed if you hadn't, she's a lot prettier than you."

("Then we came in and sat down and began to talk about family things just a little bit, Charlie's a family man, and regardless of the press that he's getting, I believe a man of moral fiber and integrity. And we both began to get excited more and more as we talked about the potential, and finally he throws his hands up in the air like this, like a baseball coach when he says you're safe, and he says okay, he says, here's the deal. Then he got on the phone, called in his chief financial officer and C3 . . . and his personal secretary and his attorney. And we drafted a contract, in essence, right there. We were talking about a percentage of gross land sales, and in the contract, it was a rough draft and she was doing it in

shorthand, and the attorney was injecting a bit here and there, and this CFO was running the calculator on what the numbers could be, and he said you can do what you want to do. You run that project like you want to run it. You report directly to my son, C3, or to myself, which I did all the time that I worked with him, which was not only an honor, it was expeditious and somewhat of a privilege.")

Parker tears into his new job, and soon he is making $50,000 a month in commissions. One day a courier shows up out in the desert at the Estrella sales office and plunks down a stack of $175 tickets for the local pro football team, the Cardinals. All the courier says is "These are from Charlie and he said to give them to you personally and you would know what to do with them." Parker is pleased, kind of honored, because Charlie Keating trusts his judgment. And soon he is papering potential investors and bankers and mortgage people with the free tickets. This tactic works.

("He likes people who could sense the opportunity, who could smell it, rise to the occasion. . . . And I mean, I get it on, a hundred and ten percent. One thing about Charlie that I love dearly . . . he'd run out every ground ball, and he'd slide head first, and I did not disdain the fact at all. He's smart. He sent memos, I've got copies of them. Think! Use your head! Do what's logical! Don't do what the book says or what everybody . . . Think! So I related to that and I gave him my heart. . . . This [Estrella] was a big deal to Charlie, launching this thing. A big undertaking, a lot of money, big plans for the future, a couple of billion dollars profit. . . .")

But the scale of the project, thousands of acres, over 73,000 lots, the largest man-made lakes in the state built at a cost of $12 million, millions for an expressway linking this city of tomorrow to the freeway (one bridge cost $5 million), millions for other roads and sewers and underground utility lines, millions for the yacht club and for the band shell. Keating hires people from Walt Disney to do the overall design of the lakes and the parks around them. There's the industrial park, only a six-hour drive from Los Angeles. Keating is going to recruit companies like Rubbermaid that want out of the hassle and expense of L.A. but still wish to remain on the Pacific Rim. He's got a lock on an international airport for Estrella. People can boat and fish on the lakes (the water is stocked, and there are six-, seven-pound fish), go sailboating, windsurfing, canoeing. Or just sit on the man-made beaches. Plus tennis, basketball, racquetball.

One day Charlie walks into his computer room with someone— he's giving a visitor one of his patented tours of his operation—and there is John Boyce reading a newspaper and Keating snaps, "You have to look important." Boyce is taken aback, reverts to his naval training and says, "Attention on deck!" Charlie Keating is not amused. A few days later Boyce finds a memo on his desk from Charlie and learns he is being shipped up to Colorado to work at an ACC subdivision there. Boyce works there for a few months just filing paperwork, and then in December, when he is back in Phoenix, he walks up to Keating and asks, "Do you think you have a minute to talk about what I am going to be doing now?" Keating snaps, "I've already decided that. I don't have any more time to listen to your crazy ideas." Later that month at the Christmas party, Keating reveals his new plan for John Boyce: real estate.

Estrella spooks Boyce; it's way out in the desert, there's snakes, it's hot. But he drives there every day and tries to sell the lots. C3 is sort of in charge, and he's got no time for Boyce and refers to him as one of his dad's pet projects. One night in Phoenix, Keating invites Boyce into his office. He tells him he's given him the chance of a lifetime and that he ought to make $200,000 a year out at Estrella. He starts touting Boyce to others as a great schoolboy swimmer (Boyce had been a star back at St. Francis Xavier in Cincinnati), and this makes him feel good, makes him think he really can master his new job.

Charlie is hot to make Estrella work, and Boyce knows this. A bad market? Keating will hear none of that talk. Boyce is working out there under a world-class salesman, a guy named Jim Parker. He thinks he's doing fine, and he spins into 1988 selling dirt. Then one day he is told to see Charlie, and he makes an appointment for 7 A.M. on a Saturday.

When he knocks on the office door, Charlie opens it himself and flashes an ear-to-ear grin. He's wearing shorts and a sport shirt and, though friendly, seems kind of distracted (Boyce will later learn that C3's wife is having a baby and there is a fear that the child may not make it).

"How would you like to go back to Cincinnati?" Charlie asks, and Boyce is caught off guard. He says he'd rather stay and work at Estrella since his brother has just had a heart attack and is filing for bankruptcy.

Charlie counters with "How would you like to go to Cincinnati and go to school for a year?" Keating apologizes for not being able to help Boyce's brother, but this is 1988 and ACC is having financial problems.

"What would you like to study, John?"

Boyce reveals his secret wish. "Actually, I'd like to study biblical prophesy in terms of world events."

Keating falls silent and looks at him with a puzzled face. Then he says, "You'd better not do that, because if you don't get into a course of study per se, you'll likely get sidetracked."

But Boyce presses on, says he wants to study with Hal Lindsay (author of *The Late Great Planet Earth*) in California. Keating will have none of this, tells him to go to the University of Cincinnati, and then picks up the phone and calls his brother, Bill, who is a provost there. He tells Bill that he's got John Boyce in his office, and he's indecisive and so just go ahead and enroll him. And John Boyce caves in. He asks only that this not be "sayonara," and Keating looks at him blankly and says, "I don't know what that means."

Ramona Jacobs lives with grief. On June 17, 1987, her twenty-three-year-old daughter, Michelle, was in a car accident and suffered catastrophic brain damage. There was an insurance settlement—Michelle spent eleven months in the hospital before she could come home and needs care for the rest of her life. In August 1987, Mrs. Jacobs opened a joint savings account at a branch of Lincoln in her and her daughter's names. It's her neighborhood bank.

In early January 1988, while she's at the teller's window, she asks for advice on a good investment for Michelle's settlement checks. The teller hands Ramona Jacobs a brochure that explains some bonds being issued by the American Continental Corporation and refers her to an ACC representative who has a desk right there in the bank. The bond salesman tells her that these securities are just what she is looking for, that they are very solid and pay very well and she will have no cause to worry. She slides the legal form that makes her the conservator of her daughter's estate across the desk to him. And then, as the year continues, she keeps pumping more of Michelle's settlement money into the bonds. The folks at the bank keep calling her and recommending them. Now she's got $11,000 of Michelle's money in the bonds. She really needs the interest they pay. Michelle gets $674 from Social Security and $368.72 in disability from her former employer, but even with medical insurance, she must shell out an additional $600 a month for therapy and other medical costs. The money that Ramona Jacobs can make off the bonds will go for a kind of dream: a van that Michelle can get in and out of, a van that can take her to special things, like recreational outings. A van that can give her daughter back a tiny piece of that world she has lost.

On January 25, 1988, the Mother of God once again speaks in Medjugorje, and, as always, her message is disseminated to believers, people like Charlie Keating, who are scattered around the world and get her divine words within hours: "Dear children! Today, again, I am calling you to complete conversion, which is difficult for those who have not chosen God. . . . But you seek God only when sickness, problems, and difficulties come to you, and you think God is far from you and is not listening and does not hear your prayers. No, dear children, this is not the truth. . . ."

("Charlie was a religious person. . . . He knows I am a motivational, promotional type of guy. . . . Well, one day I was sitting here, and Charlie and I conversed just briefly along the surface pretty much on topics of a spiritual nature. One afternoon, I'm out here running the show and a courier shows up . . . and he had a stack of books. I've got them in my library at the house. And I want to say this with all respect, yes, and a number of others related, similar topics and things like that, and probably if things would have continued on and I was amenable to it, I would have probably made one of those trips with him to Europe. . . .)

Kim Campbell can't tell exactly what is going on anymore. Her marriage is ending and here it's January 1989 and she's at Chip Wischer's fortieth birthday party. The year before they held a party for him at Insurance West and Kim told Judy about it and Judy said, "I don't have time for stupid shit like that." But this one somehow is different since Judy has called Kim and said, "I'm having a party for Chip, would you come?" So she does, after all she's living in a condo they own, is in love with Judy's husband, and is growing closer and closer to their kids.

At the party everything seems to be okay, and then the two kids are out on the dance floor and Judy does not like this and gets on them for such behavior. One of the girls runs over to Kim and says, "Kim, Mom hurt me." Judy just about loses it. Kim remembers that once the girls asked Chip, "Do you love Kim more than you love Mommy?"

After that party, Chip starts drinking heavily.

Charlie Keating has all these ideas about how to salvage his situation with the federal government. One is to escape the talons of the Federal Home Loan Bank Board office in San Francisco—he's convinced they're all homosexuals, how else can anyone explain their hatred of his operation? Finally he bullies Danny Wall and the rest of the Washington brass into letting him shop around for a thrift in another region. He will buy it, and then, presto, he will not have to deal with the San Francisco bank people. That is why on February 19, 1988, Charlie Keating and a lot of his staff are meeting in Seattle with bank board officials of the Twelfth District. Charlie Keating wants to buy a small, distressed thrift in the Pacific Northwest. He tells the bank officials that anything looks like a bargain to him since he's already dropped $50 million fighting the San Francisco regulators.

The Seattle officials are a little puzzled. They look at Lincoln's list of officers and they can't find the name Charlie Keating. Why isn't he an officer of his own bank, or at least one of its directors? Because, he says with a laugh, he doesn't trust the damn regulators and he does not want to go to jail. And now Charlie can't stop, he rolls into one of his monologues about how he hails from a poor family back in Cincinnati and how by hard work he's risen to ramrod a multi-billion-dollar corporation that delivers a helluva lot of benefit to the citizens of Arizona and California and how when deregulation became the law he'd gone out and bought Lincoln and ran it according to the rules as he and his advisors could best understand them, and then the government came crashing into his world and he was not about to let a bunch of civil servants destroy what he, Charlie Keating, had created for his family. The official meeting breaks up, but a member of the Seattle branch of the FHLBB tells Keating about a small, troubled thrift in Oregon, one that has $25 million in assets and can be had for, say, $10 million and Charlie turns to his staff and asks, how much would that cost us a year? $800,000. No problem, Charlie Keating says, he'll write out a check for it right now. The bank official is appalled—don't you want to go and see it, you know, do some due dilligence, comb the books? Nope, Charlie Keating says, that won't be necessary.

Because Charlie Keating knows his numbers—it's not cheap having seventy-seven law firms on retainer, paying for a herd of accountants, financing fifteen lobbyists on the Hill, contributing to politicians. No, it's not cheap. But the deal never goes through, the Seattle people decide they do not want Charlie Keating operating in their bailiwick. After all, they have met him, they have heard him speak. And no doubt they have gotten a sense of what they might be dealing with.

•

The Mother of God reports punctually, and on May 25 she says, "Dear children! I am inviting you to a complete surrender to God. Pray, little children, that Satan may not carry you about like branches in the wind. Be strong in God. . . . Never cease praying so that Satan cannot take advantage of you. . . ."

Bowden is losing, and he does not like losing. Charlie Keating has become his obsession. First, Keating's lawyers terrorize him with the fire and brimstone of potential lawsuits if he ever publishes a word written by Michael Binstein about Charlie Keating, and Bowden hates this kind of talk because he hates anyone telling him what to do. Besides, he doesn't think Binstein has done anything wrong. Still, that leaves all those secret audits, plus the transcript of the five senators meeting with the regulators. Hell, he'll print those. But when the lawyers get through with him, he can't quite operate freely—his goddamn legal geniuses have been maumaued by those shysters from Kaye Scholer. They say, sure you can go ahead and be a Peter Zenger, but "If Kaye Scholer comes down on you with all four feet, you will have our entire staff of 120 lawyers working full time at $120 per hour." He discovers that his magazine's investors feel their hearts grow still at the mention of Charlie Keating and are not keen on losing their fortunes defending the First Amendment. It seems he can't do anything, but he knows in his bones Charlie Keating is a crook, a fraud sitting up there in Phoenix running a giant Ponzi game.

He has a long talk with his partner at the magazine, Dick Vonier, who has an idea: they'll cut a deal with Keating, tell him out of the goodness of their hearts they won't publish the government documents about his empire. They'll do all this if Charlie will give them unlimited access to talk to him about anything in the world except the stuff in the secret government reports. Charlie Keating takes the deal. So on Friday morning, May 27, 1988, Bowden and Vonier are rolling through Phoenix traffic on their way to a 9 A.M. appointment with Charlie Keating. At precisely 9 A.M. they walk past a huge Tongan who is bending from the waist to pick a single leaf off the lawn and into the corporate headquarters of ACC.

Charlie Keating cannot see them right away—they catch a glimpse of this tall guy slouched in the glass-walled computer room, and he seems stoned on whatever is flashing on the screen in front of him. Bowden notices nobody is wearing a necktie. Bowden looks around the room and sees attractive women, and they do not seem to be dressed like nuns. Then, boom! just like that Charlie Keating is free, and they go into his office and sit down around the coffee table. Bowden searches for clues and sees a stack of new books Charlie Keating must be handing out that week: *How to Swim with the Sharks Without Being Eaten*.

Charlie Keating leans forward and asks, just what would you like to know? And Bowden plays a hunch and says, "I want to know, what does it feel like to get out of bed every morning with a couple of billion dollars in your britches?" Keating pauses, kinds of cocks one eye, and then he begins to answer. He talks for hours and hours; that night at dinner he is still talking. He shows them around his company, but he never seems to stop talking in that slow, almost drawling way. When his wife asks him why he is speaking to reporters, he tells her, "They blackmailed me." He introduces them to Judy Wischer, who's having a meeting in her office, and says, well, she's doing pretty good for a broad, isn't she? He'd done the same thing with his wife—patted her on the ass, announced she was the official decorator of the Phoenician Hotel, and hell, that's a pretty good job for an old broad, isn't it? His grandkids are constantly wandering in as he talks, or his daughters stop by. At those moments everything else comes to a halt and Charlie Keating gives them his full attention.

Charlie Keating seems willing to talk about anything except

those secret audits. Whenever Bowden drifts into those numbers, when the deals outlined and damned by the federal regulators slip from his mouth, Charlie Keating looks over with a slight smile and says, "You read too much."

Keating is feeling fine—he's just beaten back the regulators, gotten that MOU (Memorandum of Understanding) that shifts his next audit from San Francisco (adios, Bill Black) to Washington, D.C., a triumph unprecedented in the history of the FHLBB. And the way the MOU is written, it seems to grandfather, essentially forgives, everything that ACC and Charlie Keating have done in the past, all those funny transactions out at Hidden Valley, all that money flowing month after month to the Pontchartrain, even that bad number that keeps popping up that indicates that Lincoln is more than $600 million over the direct investment limit. All this, apparently, is forgiven.

Bowden discovers he likes Charlie Keating. He's so alive. He can roll with the punches. He starts drilling him on his obsession with pornography, he says it doesn't make any sense, and Charlie Keating says, I know, I know, and then Bowden asks, what is it, some kind of front, are you one of those guys who really likes to fuck little kids, and Charlie Keating does one of those pauses again and then says, I know that's what a lot of people must think, but no, I just hate the stuff and I'm not sure why, maybe my Catholic upbringing. He never skips a beat, and yet he doesn't have a pat answer, he seems to be spiraling on and on as if he were really trying to figure it out himself.

Keating can tell he's making a sale, can smell it in the air. Keating barks to his secretary to get some buttons, and she comes flying in with two big yellow jobs the size of a small pizza that say, I LIKE CHARLIE KEATING. Bowden and Vonier each get one. And then Charlie is barking again and the secretary shows up with a camera, and then suddenly C3 is there, and snap, snap, snap, there's a bunch of shots of the four of them. Charlie smiles and says, "Now I can blackmail you."

The end of June is like the end of any quarter for Charlie Keating, a very busy time. That March he had plopped $50 million into another one of Sir James Goldsmith's funds, GUAC, and the time has come to harvest some profits. So Charlie Keating is in Florida meeting with David Paul, the head of Centrust, a big local thrift. Paul is a man with the appetite of a monarch—the $233,000 sailboat, the waterfront mansion, the lavish meals (he once dropped $122,726 to fly chefs in from France to cook for fifty-six guests), the $29 million worth of paintings, the $30,000 dropped for gifts at Tiffany's, the $22,000 for imported table linen—and everything seems paid for by his savings and loans and characterized on the books as investments or business expenses. Now on June 17, one of Lincoln's subsidiaries sells half its interest in GUAC for $30 million, which allows Keating to book a profit of $24.5 million for Lincoln. At the same time, another Lincoln subsidiary, American Founders Life Insurance Company, buys 2,735,000 shares of Playtex stock from Centrust, which come to $24.6 million. Of course, deals are never that simple. After all the negotiating, one issue still remains to be settled between Charlie Keating and David Paul: who will fund his end of the deal first? They flip a coin, and Charlie Keating loses.

Then it is off to Europe to test some Italian restaurants with the family to see whether the food might work on the menus at the Phoenician. Finally, on June 25, 1988, he is in Medjugorje for the seventh anniversary of the initial appearance of the Blessed Mother. He can't seem to get enough of the place. ("Dear children! . . . Surrender yourself to God so that he may heal you, console you, and forgive everything inside of you that is a hindrance on the way of love.")

The black hair is full and of medium length, the face fine-boned, the eyes brown, the makeup reserved—the kind of look men once called class. Patricia Johnson is in her early thirties, a Phoenix native and divorced mother of three, an active Democrat, former girlfriend of the city's mayor, Terry Goddard. She has a $39,000-a-year city job, but because of the collapsing Arizona real estate market, she lives in a modest repossessed house snapped up at a bargain, a home crowded with memorabilia (original drawings of editorial cartoons and the like) marking her years in local Democratic politics. In June 1988, she is shepherding around twenty or thirty people from Ireland as part of her job on the Sister City Commission. Charlie Keating has thrown a free banquet for the group at his Crescent Hotel. She cuts across the room toward Keating out of curiosity—she wonders what the strange billionaire, the Republican Party big contributor, is like. She knows he has this thing about pornography, and, from her time with Goddard, she pegs him as a right-wing Republican.

So she walks up to Keating and his wife, Mary Elaine, and drops a few lines of party talk, and Keating looks her over and says, "I'd like to talk to you. Give me a call," and then turns and walks away. What's this? She is not used to men walking away from her. When he returns a few moments later, he adds, "By the way, what's your name?" *He doesn't even know my name.* Then he does something that really captures her attention. He goes into the Crescent gift shop, scoops up $80–$90 ties for the men and $150–$500 turquoise bracelets for the women and hands them out to the delegation.

Johnson waits to phone Keating—*must not show one's hand*—and then finally Charlie's secretary calls and says, "What about the meeting you promised, it's important." Two weeks after the banquet she steals time from her one-hour lunch break and goes to Keating's office. The whole thing intrigues her. All her local ties are liberal and Democratic, and here she is at the headquarters of this notoriously conservative force in Phoenix. She waits thirty minutes. *Who does he think he is?* Finally Charlie Keating pops out of the conference room, shouts, "Tell that woman I won't be long." *He still doesn't even know my name.* Johnson begins to boil. Then he is free, but he does not talk about a job at first. Charlie Keating has finally learned that you can ask a person almost anything if you don't make it a job interview. Johnson has prepared for this moment, and she dutifully rattles on for ten minutes about her background, work experience, and the like. He asks, are you married, and she says no, I'm divorced. Then he asks, how much do you weigh, and how tall are you? *How much do I weigh?* Keating considers this new vital information and then looks over at his secretary and asks her what she weighs. He moves on immediately to what he needs: a free-lance writer to help with brochures for the hotel he is building, the Phoenician. Can she do it? She says part-time work is impossible with her city schedule. Without skipping a beat, Keating continues; well, how about working for me full time? How much do you want? She says $45,000, and Charlie Keating says, how about $50,000? But Johnson is tired of feeling off balance with this man (*My weight? I've produced television shows, written for magazines, I am a professional person*), so she insists on her figure of $45,000. *I must get control of this situation.* Keating calls to a son-in-law who is passing the office and asks him what he thinks of hiring Johnson, and he allows that it seems like a fine idea. And that's it. She will begin in three weeks when her job with the city ends. They shake hands.

But Keating is not yet finished with her. He dips into his pocket—"you're gonna think I'm silly"—and pulls out a crucifix with a piece of the True Cross, the one given to him by Mother Teresa. Johnson, a lapsed Catholic, is once again off balance, and yet she is moved, she can feel herself genuinely moved by this tall guy standing there with a little crucifix in his big hand. She is attracted to Charlie Keating and not quite sure why. It's not sexual, that's for sure. She just can't feel any sexual energy coming off the guy, and she is used to that feeling, used to being desired by men. In fact, that is something that often bothers her. She's got a good head on her shoulders and is weary of men looking at her like she's some bimbo. She receives the standard present given to new employees, a silver-and-turquoise angel.

How much do you weigh?

("Hell, we had the Phoenix Symphony at Estrella, Fourth of July, 1988, seventy-two-piece orchestra on the beach, the entire Phoenix Symphony. He got up and made a speech before they started and they had been kind of, you know . . . you haven't contributed anything to the Phoenix Symphony yet. He made some comment about . . . pay them that night. And a shelter over them because we didn't want moisture to get in the instruments and $40,000 of fireworks display put on by the Pyromaniacs out of Washington, D.C.—they did the bicentennial celebration in D.C. The same people. It lasted ten minutes. The most spectacular fireworks display I've ever seen. . . . I mean, the place was jammed, people just came to see the Phoenix Symphony and fireworks display, Fourth of July evening. And we were all there selling real estate, we had developers and we had people, all night long parties, beer, wine, whatever you wanted free. . . . And Charlie had his helicopter. . . . He flew in there and it was nighttime, and he got up there and the band, they were playing these patriotic themes, and it was incredible. He spent forty grand on the fireworks. And then when the whole event ended, Charlie says enjoy yourselves. . . . Charlie's ready to go, and he flew out over the lakes real low and they had

*those lights on the water . . . and everybody was looking, so he
goes out, he's got these two pilots, across the lake like that and they
go almost straight up, and they turn like this, and then he does a
nosedive. Took him just like this down over the lake, coming back
this way, and headed east back to Phoenix. And . . . right down
over there, and like you were . . . the enemy. Of course, he got
everybody's attention, everybody, it was the only thing in the sky
after the fireworks display. . . . And the water was blowing like this
on the lake, and they had the lights coming down in front of the
helicopter, so it was just a spectacular aerial icing on the cake, after the whole thing was done, drinking and eating and fireworks
display and the Phoenix Symphony, he gave it an aerial display of
absolute crudeness, straight up in the air and then he left, and after that I said, Boy, that's Charlie.")*

Patricia Johnson is in Ireland right after the Fourth of July as
the final part of her final Sister City duties, and Charlie Keating
and his family are staying near her in County Clare. Keating often
stops by here on his way to Medjugorje, and he is living it up in
the bar at the Dromoland Castle when Johnson finds him. He impulsively tells the sixteen Irish people sitting at his table that he'll
fly them to Phoenix on his jets for a two-week stay at the soon-to-
be-completed Phoenician.

When Johnson returns to Phoenix, she starts her duties at
ACC. Soon she knows many things—nothing can be on her desk
top, she must dress very nicely. She learns never to put anything
down on paper if she can avoid it and never to create files if at all
possible—Charlie Keating tells her this himself. There is a tension
about the place. Patricia Johnson calls out to her secretary in the
bullpen, and the woman leaps up and races into her office with a
fearful expression on her face. When Johnson tells her never to do
that again, the woman looks not relieved but confused. There is
one executive who does a lot of the firing, and he keeps a picture
of the Grim Reaper taped to the bottom of his desk drawer.

One word does keep seeping into her consciousness: a cult, and
Charlie Keating is the Jim Jones of this outfit. Instead of deadly
Kool-Aid, he hands out money. A kid who handles zoning permits
downtown—hell, give him a Porsche. Charlie's secretary, Carol
Kassick, is working real hard; give her a Porsche too. Charlie
Keating pays Kassick $70,000 a year, Johnson hears, and he's al-

ways turning to her when a visitor is present and saying, "Tell 'im how much you make."

There is a small fire at the Phoenician that summer, and Patricia Johnson goes out to handle the press and gets her new shoes soiled walking through the puddles of water and soot. Charlie Keating walks up and says, "Well, at least let me buy you some shoes, won't you?" And she thinks sure, they only cost $29.95. He hands her five grand. She is in a meeting where they are considering publicity photographs for the Phoenician, and Charlie asks, "Well, what do you think?" Everyone says the pictures are just fine. Except Patricia Johnson, who says they're very poor. Keating says, come over here and sit by me and help me pick the right photograph, and she does. But another time she is in a meeting with about two hundred people and Charlie goes around the room and asks each department head to report and finally one guy pipes up and presents what he thinks is a better, cheaper, more efficient way to do something. He has found a way to save the company money. When he finishes, Charlie Keating rips him apart for twenty minutes—you've had this idea for a week and just now you mention it and you mean to tell me you haven't even implemented it yet? Johnson still argues with Keating, and she thinks he appreciates her for this. But an executive from the Phoenician takes her aside and warns her, "You're the only one who talks back to him, and that's not a good idea. Those of us who survive don't talk back to him. You think you're winning, but you're losing."

She and Carol Kassick are in New York with Charlie Keating, and they stay at the Helmsley Palace. They have breakfast with Father Bruce Ritter of Covenant House, and Charlie starts talking about Medjugorje and how he has been there three times to pray to the Mother of God and Father Bruce says, "Charlie, that's ridiculous, the visitations are not even recognized by the church." Charlie Keating gets angry and says that is the trouble with the clergy, they're always jumping on the laity in areas where they don't know any more than the average guy. "You have no right to say that," Keating snaps. Ritter backs off instantly, Keating just as suddenly calms down, and then the conversation shifts. Keating has been reading the newspaper and notices that Geraldine Ferraro's son has recently been busted for coke, and he thinks the kid deserves a break. He asks Father Ritter to look into it, see how the kid is—why, he can have a job out in Phoenix at ACC "for good money." Father Bruce tries to ignore this request and stares down at his plate as if hoping it will go away. Then Charlie asks Johnson if she wants to go to Europe the next day, and she says no, that will not be necessary. Well, Keating wonders, just how much money does she have for her stay in New York? And Johnson says thirty bucks. Here, take this, and he stuffs a wad of bills into her hand. When she gets to her room and counts it out, she finds she has a thousand dollars' worth of cash.

The Phoenician has to be perfect, a monument, a one-of-a-kind thing. Phoenix is clogged with four-star resorts. The solution is simple: build a palace for that 1 or 2 percent of people on the planet who can pay any amount for luxury, make the hotel not just the best in Phoenix but one of the top ten on earth. The financing is solved in part by getting Kuwaiti backing, they're not so anxious about immediate returns. Their thing is finding a safe place to park their money. Normally a hotel has to charge 1 percent of its room cost to break even, which in the case of the Phoenician would mean $500 or $600 a night. But the Kuwaitis can wait, they don't need a return every day, and hotels, once they're successful, can have incredible resale value. The Phoenician, if done right, should be worth, say, $600 million after a year or two. But there are headaches. When the Kuwaitis invest, they have one demand. The rooms must have bidets—they've got this thing about their women. It costs a fortune to retrofit them into a bunch of the suites.

Keating gets more directly involved at the beginning of 1988, and when the MOU comes down in May 1988, that does it. He eventually takes a suite and lives there. The thing must open on time, on October 1, because he has already sold all the rooms.

He loves explaining things, so why did he build this fancy hotel? Simple. "The space that you rent for shelter," Charlie notes, "will always keep pace with inflation because you get tomorrow's rent rate, you don't lease for five years, and you don't have options. So a hotel to me is a perfect inflation hedge. Particularly if you're in the building business—shelter is shelter for my money. The first thing that happened was that I was dead wrong because inflation abated, not only abated but almost went into the deep freeze. And then the law changed, and I couldn't syndicate. So I ended up in the hotel business without the right reasons. I thought we were heroes because we managed to be flexible enough to change in midstream. We had a decision to make, we could have either joined the Holiday Inn or Marriot group with the Crescent, or we could have joined the Hilton Resort–type hotel with the Phoenician. Or we could go to the upper one percent—I'm stupid, but I'm not so stupid that I don't know that that's generally where everybody breaks their lance. The biggest number of failures is the guy who builds the imperial palace and then it gets resold twice, and it finally gets down to the guy who pays the right price to make it work."

Making it work becomes an obsession for Charlie Keating and his wife, Mary Elaine, though she is not always such a help since she is what the contractors call "blueprint blind." The cost of the hotel is now running around $300 million, against an estimate of $150 million. There have been more than three thousand changes since the blueprints were approved and construction began. There are supposed to be steel canopies at the entrances to the bar, Charlie Charlie's, but Mary Elaine doesn't like the welds. So they regrind them, repaint them. Then she comes through and they have to do it again, three times. And then it still isn't right so all the metal is covered with wood—takes two solid days.

The whole thing has a seat-of-the-pants quality. When they started pouring concrete it was for a 400-room hotel, now it's a 600-room hotel. Then Charlie adds on a golf clubhouse, casitas, a health spa, an underground parking garage for 1,200 cars, a tennis complex, a pool island restaurant. The rooms go from white oak to red oak and back to white oak. "We had a very active owner," one contractor confesses. "You know that there's heart and soul in that building, you can look at it, everything in that building is of the utmost quality.

"Nothing was off the rack," the contractor continues. "Every item that you look at in the Phoenician you'll notice has no brand names on it, no exposed fasteners with the exception of hinges on the doors. Okay, this room is fine, we'll go to the next one. I think there are fifty-six different varieties of rooms. Holiday Inn has one. Fifteen in a luxury hotel is maybe reasonable, not even that much. They went through consultants like water."

Changes keep occurring that Charlie Keating can't control. The state slips through a new water law and slams down a deadline on using drinking water for huge pools and ponds of January 1,

1987. So the pools are thrown together, filled, certified. And then drained. The hotel doesn't exist yet, but the empty pools do. Costs a lot of money to do it that way. The Phoenician sits on the side of a mountain—they blast out 50,000 tons of rock.

He is down there in a suit and tie, or it's the weekend and he's got on boots, shorts, and a T-shirt. A guy is working, hears an odd sound, looks down, and there is Charlie Keating with a dustpan and a broom, whisk, whisk, whisk. Five-thirty in the morning, it's still dark, and Keating is there alone, walking through his hotel. ("He slept maybe four hours a night. He had all this business that he had to take care of, he'd be on his computer from one to three in the morning, then he'd come on site from three to whatever. . . . Do you go after a three-hundred-million-dollar project that is near-ing completion, or do you deal with your five-billion-dollar savings institution? He went after the three-hundred-million decision.") He'd say, move that wall, move it three inches, move it six inches, and they'd try to explain you can't just do that, there's a concrete column there that's holding up the damn building. But you moved the wall. And Mary Elaine was even harder to deal with. ("She would wait for Charlie on some stuff, but there were certain things that she knew she wanted and she'd let Charlie know. They got go-ing at each other a few times, but she would finally say I just can't accept it like that. And that was normally the end of the conversa-tion. It'd change. You were gonna hear about it for the rest of your life, so which is it going to be? You make the change.")

Charlie Keating decides to fire up his troops, those hundreds of people swinging hammers and pouring concrete at his hotel. It's late Friday afternoon, he has lots of cold beer, and he gets up in front of eight hundred construction workers and lays it on the line. "We're paying you guys too much money for too long," he begins, and the line draws big laughs. "This is really the best hotel in the world. That damn pool is the only problem. You guys must think it's a head." They laugh again, he's got them. It's hotter than hell, the beer sure tastes good, and Charlie Keating knows he can reach this crowd, own them. Motivate them.

"The problem is that due to some problems in the beginning with guys that ain't here anymore, like a few architects and some designers, we went through five designers; one of them died of AIDS, we didn't fire him. That's the truth. But we had five big-name designers, and every one of them was a catastrophe. I'll bet not one of the SOBs asked you guys—and I'm dead serious—what to do, how to do it. Nobody. They've got no humility.

"It's my own fault for not paying attention sooner. And so the problem is my fault. But I've got a problem. We went through a bunch of architects, and it's a disaster. We probably have millions in this—I was going to say dump, but it really isn't, it's gorgeous. Besides that, there might be press here. I don't know where the hell they come from, but when I'm around opening my big mouth, they sure hear it."

He can feel them coming to him, he can feel the distance between him disappearing—he is standing on an elevator platform—and this crowd of sweaty, dirty people. He'll go for broke, he motions toward the hulk of the unfinished Phoenician.

"This is the kind of a mausoleum idiots build, and then they can't make it work—and I'm dead serious now—and they sell it to the next—you know, they go bankrupt—and they sell it to the next guy down the line. He goes bankrupt. And they sell it to the next guy down the line. He goes bankrupt. The third guy finally gets it at a price he can make it work."

There, right out in the open, being taken out by the third guy. Charlie Keating is the first guy—too late now to get another place in the line—and he can see his doom. That's why he keeps telling people about this particular nightmare.

"I gotta make it work. One of the only ways I can make it work, and this is the one reason I got you here today, is I beg you, I gotta have it finished October first, because if I don't hit that fall season, I'm dead.

"You know what? I'm sixty-four years old. I'm a powder puff and I'm a wimp, but I could walk through that whole gang of you calling you all kinds of names and I won't have to worry a bit, 'cause there would be twenty Tongans around me at all times.

"And if all of you will put your name—somebody get a list—put your name, address, and phone number down, I'll put it on a plaque. And I'll put it somewhere on the grounds, so when you come back and this is the finest hotel in the world starting in 1989, they'll know who built it."

Then he comes off his platform. He hands out hundred-dollar bills, cases of beer, free pro football tickets. The drinking gets good. Fights break out among the various trades. He's done it. He owns them now.

As opening day draws closer, Charlie drags more and more of his executives over and puts them to work. Jack Atchison may be knocking down almost a million a year, but now people see him sweeping the driveway at the Phoenician. He floods the place with his people, has them wearing white T-shirts that say GUINEA PIGS in green ink. College kids are hired to run through a checklist to make sure all the construction is done right. These kids walk through a room and come out with four hundred flaws (fix the putty holes! paint the bottom of the sink bowl!).

The ballroom is 22,000 square feet and holds 2,500 people, the golf club takes up 47,000 square feet, the health club 17,000. When the golf course plays a little slow, Keating has it torn up, dumps another $4.5 million, and gets faster play. The first tee is up on the mountain, a guy wings that first shot out from a stone perch looking down on an endless green. The swimming pools cover more than an acre. Big numbers everywhere. Make a four-foot-wide sidewalk out of the concrete in the Phoenician, and it will stretch 600 miles.

His butt is on the line this time. But he's been pulling things out of the fire for decades, always been able to engineer a miracle. He'll do it again. Just needs a little time. Get the hotel open, get Estrella rolling, make a killing on those deals with Sir James Goldsmith. It'll work out. Just need some breathing room. The feds, they've started a new audit this July and it has to be done by December. Get a clean bill of health from them, and then, well, everything'll be fine. Why not? The MOU grandfathers everything else he's ever done with Lincoln. Go into the new year, hotel'll be open, harvest those assets. Pay off those bondholders, yeah, he's gotta do that, he's promised them. Yes, it can be done. He never stops planning, looking, he's ready for opportunity.

It all adds up after a while. Back in early 1988, when Judy was gone for eight, ten, twelve weeks or so, out there with Charlie trying to peddle Lincoln and get out from this regulatory stranglehold, that's the period when Kim and Chip and the girls spent so much time together. He can hardly remember when things felt so damn good. Maybe that's part of his problem: he can't remember feeling good. Besides, ACC doesn't seem the same anymore, he can sense that, well, there's stuff that's going wrong. Rumors flutter up and down the corridors of Charlie Keating's world, rumors that the government is going to take them down, that the cash flow has stopped and the paychecks may end, that Estrella is devouring money, that the Phoenician is not going to pump money, that the magic may be over.

So Chip Wischer makes a move. In August 1988, he files for divorce. And then his wife, Judy, counters with a petition for an annulment. Chip is scared, he does not know if he can live without all that money. After all, this is the kid who had stashed away $15,000 from summer jobs before he graduated from college, the kid who had an ulcer by the age of four. In December, he rescinds the divorce papers. Let's not get crazy here. Besides, he's a good Catholic, and divorce does not feel natural to him. Judy tells him they had better have a swell Christmas because the way things look this might be the last one for a long time. Chip listens hard. Judy never really talks business at home. And now Judy is saying this and she must know, she's with Charlie every day.

Patricia Johnson is in a glass-walled meeting room at the Phoenician. It is late September 1988, and the $300 million hotel will open in less than two weeks. She is living in the hotel with her three children and, along with thirty or forty other ACC employees, testing the facility for last-minute flaws. Keating is running a luncheon meeting, and his voice is even and crisp as they all plod through the agenda when Keating looks over and sees two construction workers walk past outside. He turns to a secretary and without pause or emphasis says, "Go out there and fire those guys." The woman darts out of the room, and for a few moments everyone can see her talking with the two men. Their faces show no expression, and then she returns and the meeting continues. Patricia Johnson thinks, "If that can happen to them, that can happen to me." She is suddenly feeling a kind of rush from being on the inside, from being with the boss, the feeling of heat rising off naked power. And then she understands how powerful and pleasant this feeling is. It is a wonderful drug. Charlie, she senses, is not angry. She has almost never seen him truly angry, just flickers of frustration. The firings, those she will see again and again. And she thinks she may understand a little better the deep attraction she feels to being so close to power. "Charlie," she thinks, "has such a short attention span. He likes chaos." Likes to stir things up. And, oh, the rush. She is sitting there watching through the glass as the two men are fired. But she is on the inside.

September is details, nothing but details—a huge hotel to finish and open. Still, there's lots of other stuff to keep in mind. Get ahold of Jamal Radwan about restructuring the Saudi-European Bank. Talk to Toufic Aboukhater about the shortfall of money with the Crescent Hotel—make this note: "Kuwait cash." And what about Japanese long bonds? Fly to San Francisco, receive that swimming award, give a ten- to thirty-minute speech on how the sport has influenced your life. Good God, it's already September 9—tell Mary Elaine that Perpetual Adoration starts today, and she should arrange a meeting between Charlie and the priest. Fly to Paris and go to Sir James Goldsmith's office to straighten all those raiding funds nesting in the Cayman Islands.

Charlie Keating pauses in New York for a sitdown with his accountants at Arthur Young. They can't seem to comprehend his deals. Why must he keep educating accountants? There is that deal at the end of June where ACC books a $5.4 million profit, but it does not look right to Arthur Young's people. And this other matter, involving a $50 million profit in September—why, to the accountants it looks simply like an exchange between two outfits of "dissimilar assets," a wash. Charlie Keating has had it with this nitpicking. Since Jack Atchison left Arthur Young in the spring of 1988 (how could he stay when Charlie offered him almost $1 million a year to work for ACC?) the account has been handled by Janice I. Vincent, and she is the problem in Keating's eyes.

"Lady," he says, "you have just lost the job."

The hell with Arthur Young. Big Eight accounting firms are all alike. So Charlie Keating buys a different bunch of watchdogs to reconcile his books—Touche Ross. On September 30, 1988, Lincoln has assets of $5.3 billion, with 65 percent in risk assets. Thirty-four percent of the deposits are brokered, the hot money of the jumbos. And thanks to those twits in Accounting, the losses for the quarter run to $20 million.

The hotel is going to open—on time!—and once again he has pulled it off. He'll be sixty-five years old in December, but he has not lost his touch. He feels so good, let's have a party. They gather down by the pools and the water slide, a huge, winding snake of a thing that runs down the side of the hill from an upper pool to a blue eye of water below. It ends next to the mother-of-pearl swimming pool that is surrounded by cabanas that are wired for computers. A guy can sit there and watch the kids splash around and still be able to work. The girls look terrific, too. Hey, he'll give any one of those babes a hundred bucks to go down that slide with her clothes on. Carol Kassick goes, then another, then another. What, some are hesitating? Hell, no, this is his party. And so he throws them down the slide—ready or not!

It's too good, just too damn good. Over $300 million, it's ready, the finest hotel in the world, and he knows it. Three thousand changes, the best of everything, a fistful of restaurants, one for red wine, one for white, and so forth. Fifteen hundred palm trees brought in from Florida. A couple of million dollars' worth of statues of American Indians standing here and there. A great cactus garden—you should have seen the botanist's face when she was choppered from nursery to nursery picking the finest specimens. He's done it all his way. These professional hotel managers, he's seen them, they'll ruin anything. So he has a better idea. He hires an ex-navy guy who for years ran an aircraft carrier—the captain, the guy who actually makes it all work, makes sure the men eat, the laundry gets done, the supplies never run out, everything stays shipshape. What is the difference between a hotel and an aircraft carrier except that one bobs on the water? He makes the guy the general manager of the Phoenician, and, by God, he does a helluva job. He puts one of his former pilots in charge of Mary Elaine's, the gourmet restaurant. Installs an engineer as his beverage manager. Good move, the guy doesn't steal, and all you need is someone who can keep track of the booze—big profit item, you know.

It's evening, the hotel will open within hours. Charlie Keating is in a suit and tie, he's wearing his expensive watch, his soft leather shoes, his pocket is stuffed with hundred-dollar bills. He cannot resist the moment. He scoops up a nearby grandkid, leaps onto the water slide—the thing is white walled and sweeps around and around back under itself through a jungle of plants, and you can't see where the thing is going or where it ends and the surface is so slick and wet no one can sit upright and so you wind up flat on your ass with the water coursing over you, hear that grandchild squeal!—and they streak down and down and down and into the warm blue waters of the waiting pool.

*　　　*　　　*

He tracks Bowden down. What the hell does he want? When Bowden picks up the phone, he hears his frantic, angry voice: Charlie Keating is pissed. That very afternoon, two days before his $300 million hotel opens, the afternoon Phoenix *Gazette* has come out with a huge spread ridiculing his hotel, calling it a fiasco and a piece of financial idiocy. They're quoting other hotel owners in Phoenix, and these guys—the competition, for Chrissake—they all think the new kid on the block is a real dog.

Charlie Keating can't understand such treatment—I had this reporter out here, I fed her meals, great meals, he shouts—and all he's trying to do is make a buck, give people jobs, build something that will make Phoenix proud of itself, and now this. And then after a few minutes of ranting—he is on a cellular phone, and Bowden can hear him barking asides to staff members stupid enough to come within sight of him as he storms around the hotel—he gets to the point: he says, hey, you're in media, what should I do to turn this around? And Bowden—why is he doing this?—tells him exactly what to do. Invite everybody out the night before the opening, all of the print press, all of television, all of radio. Ply them with free food and booze, say, hey, I'm not a rocket scientist but I did the best I could on this hotel and why don't you all wander around and see what you think. And get a good local PR person. Bowden gives Charlie the name of the woman who once salvaged Phoenix developer Del Webb's reputation from that unfortunate contract on the visionary hotel Bugsy Siegel built in the sands outside Las Vegas. Charlie Keating listens hard, says thank you, and then he is gone.

Of course, he never does any of the things Bowden suggests. He won't grovel.

Fuck 'em.

The night the Phoenician Hotel opens to the public, C3 meets one of the cocktail waitresses. When he goes home that night he walks past the bedroom he shared with his wife, Krista, continues on down the hall past his children's rooms, and sleeps in a guest bedroom. He does not join his wife in bed for the next eighteen months.

Things happen, but somehow no one seems to notice. The savings and loan crisis continues to spiral downward, the projected red ink mushrooms, but hardly a word is said. Michael Dukakis, the Democratic nominee for president, makes one speech attacking the Reagan administration for deregulating thrifts, and Vice President George Bush attacks the Democratic Congress for being the true parents of the problem, and then . . . silence. No one seems very interested in ferreting out the truth of the matter—so many politicians on both sides of the aisle have been players in this particular episode; Charlie Keating has dumped over $50 million fighting the feds, and there are not a lot of clean hands up on the Hill. No one wants to talk about this eight-hundred-pound gorilla sitting in the republic's living room. Fernand St. Germain loses his seat in the House of Representatives when his daily feedings by the U.S. League of Savings Institutions becomes a brief issue with his constituents back in Rhode Island—and he is only narrowly defeated.

Charlie Keating, through bundling, pumps at least $100,000 into George Bush's campaign. True, he doesn't think much of Bush, what a lightweight, but he hates Dukakis. The guy looks like he wants to be the king of the regulators. What with the new hotel open, Keating's got to do everything he can think of to make it all work. On October 10, he offers up about $20 million more of those ACC junk bonds he's peddling out in southern California. That ought to do it, but it's not enough. So on October 27, he offers another $20 million. Okay, now call Jerry Falwell and tell him this: the Phoenician has no cable television and so—and this is important—no one staying there can ever watch dirty movies. Get those born-again Christians in here spending money.

Everyone hears rumors that the company is going down. Even at the annual bash and pep talk for all the Lincoln clerks and tellers in Los Angeles, the theme is the creative destruction of capitalism. What are the bosses trying to tell them? On November 28, ACC offers another $20 million in junk bonds. People keep buying them. The sales folks use big photographs of the Phoenician in their pitch. You think a company that owns this baby is going to go broke? Just look at these rich color photographs.

Leaving takes time, everything takes time for John Boyce. He has to sign termination papers, and they spook him because he suddenly feels he is being cut loose from the company, abandoned by his friend. So he seeks out Bob Kielty, Charlie's legal advisor and a guy who has worked for him since he was a kid, and he asks if there are going to be bad feelings in terms of his father's memory. And Kielty says no, there is no problem, and that at some time in the future they will surely work together again.

Then Charlie calls him into his office, and when Boyce arrives there's a very attractive woman there. She's a tour guide for pilgrimages to Medjugorje, and Boyce thinks to himself, "Oh, my God, here it comes." He realizes he must be honest and truthful with his friend.

"You know," he begins, "I have had a great burden on my heart for you about this."

Charlie looks at him with a sheepish smile and says, "You're a Catholic, aren't you?"

"No."

"What about all your religious training?" Good God, the kid went to St. Xavier, his own alma mater.

Boyce tries to explain, to tell Charlie how years before he had come to believe in Jesus but that in this process of learning to love Christ he had discarded the Catholic Church.

Charlie Keating says flatly, "The Mother of God is appearing at Medjugorje."

"Well," Boyce replies, "you can't really call her the Mother of God."

The woman standing by gasps audibly.

"What do you think, that I'm stupid?" Keating roars back.

"I don't think you're stupid."

"Well, you inferred it."

Boyce wants to say so much to his friend, to explain that he is deceived, that he is a good man who has been misled into false doctrine, and so he starts quoting scripture.

"All this Bible stuff, I don't want to hear it. What about Cardinal Newman?" Charlie Keating turns to the woman and says by way of apology, "I really missed this one." Then John comes back to life and says he'd be willing to debate about Cardinal Newman.

The woman tries to ease the situation and says, "Well, Mr. Keating, some of our our biggest doubters have been some of our biggest converts once they've been over." And John grasps at this straw—his friend!—and offers to go to Medjugorje and take a look. But it is too late, much too late to reach an accommodation with Charlie Keating, who is angry.

He turns to Boyce and snaps, "Well, what do you want to do?"
And Boyce tries to explain to his friend how logically the Son cannot preexist the Mother. But Charlie Keating does not want to hear
this. Finally, Boyce says all he really wants to do is stay on and sell
land at Estrella. To be near his friend. Just then a secretary pops
her head in the doorway and asks Keating what kind of wine he
wants served with dinner. Boyce seizes upon this interruption as a
chance to steer this conversation from its disastrous course.

"Oh, by the way," he asks, "do you think we could get mother
her trip to Australia?"

"Haven't I done enough for your family?"

John Boyce will never have the opportunity to speak with Charlie Keating again, with his friend, the man who has been like tonic
in his life. But then, Charlie Keating is pretty damn busy. On December 13, ACC puts another $100 million in junk bonds out on
the market. The next day it offers another $30 million while Char-
lie has a nice lunch with Senator Alan Cranston.

There are Christmas decorations everywhere. Charlie Keating
needs help if he's going to peddle Lincoln. Someone has to stop
the regulators from tying his hands. Cranston, who has gotten
about a million bucks from ACC, slaps him on the back and says,
"Ah, the mutual aid society."

At first he is buoyant when the new auditors arrive in July. He
is convinced that if they just give him a fair shake, they'll see how
beautiful his operation is. After all, he's the one who insisted that
the audit be finished by December. And why? So he can get on
with his life. He feels in his bones that this time, what with the
regulators being dispatched from Washington instead of that
snake pit of queers in San Francisco, he'll come out just fine. But
still, he's got this other feeling. In September the California savings and loan commissioner orders him to stop selling ACC junk
bonds out of the thrift's branches. This isn't going to make it
easier. Never hurts to explore other options. In September, he is in
Florida talking with David Paul of Centrust about maybe doing
some joint ventures or even merging Lincoln and Centrust. That
fall, he's busy meeting in New York and Europe with the Saudi-
European Bank, of which he is now part owner. They can't be
touched by the regulators, they're in France. He talks with
Kuwaitis—endless supplies of money there. Keeps up contact with

Sir James Goldsmith because those offshore funds of which Charlie owns a fat slice are going to make him hundreds of millions of
dollars. Slowly, a second-level plan evolves in Charlie Keating's
mind. If the regulators prove impossible, he'll dump Lincoln, sell
it to someone, and retain only a few key assets. Estrella (gonna
make him a billion dollars, given time), the Crescent (a great hotel
for the businessmen), the Phoenician (it'll be worth $600 million
easy in a few years), and of course those various funds headed by
Sir James. That's it. Shed everything else, dump most of the staff,
settle back into what he always has dreamed of being, a merchant
banker, just sit in his glass room playing the currency markets
with his computer, just him and his family and a small staff. Go
private just like Carl Lindner.

Still, the examination must be faced. Through the summer and
fall, Charlie Keating tries to explain to the federal regulators
crawling all over his shop just what is at stake. They seem to think
they can examine ACC, the holding company, as well as Lincoln,
and he will have to set them straight. At a meeting on November 7, Charlie Keating tells the regulators, if you take Lincoln out
of my hands you'll lose at least $2 billion. They are stunned.

And why is he, it seems to them, blocking their every effort to
get at the books and find out what is going on? He keeps repeat-
ing: you people take me over, and you'll lose a couple of billion
dollars. You can't possibly work out this situation. You don't know
junk bonds, you don't know Kuwaitis, you don't know the hotel
business. Basically, you don't know much of anything except your
little guidelines.

Two billion dollars in red ink. Tell that to Danny Wall. He dares
them. He starts telling his executives that buying Lincoln was the
biggest mistake of his life, biggest mistake of all.

He hits the road constantly. He is trying to line up buyers for
Lincoln. This is not an insane notion. Under purchase accounting,
a new buyer can write down the books, simply wipe out bad loans,
and then the books will look fine, the net worth will be in line, everything will be street legal. And then, on the twentieth of December, the new examination appears, and it is devastating. Lincoln is
out of control, it will default, it has broken every rule and should
be seized. Lincoln is ordered to stop upstreaming tax money to
ACC. Now Charlie Keating faces a real chokehold.

Charlie Keating does what comes naturally to him. He flies to

Los Angeles with a bishop from Indonesia in tow, he gathers his Lincoln people together in a room. He begins to speak, he rambles, suddenly he is back in World War II flying a Hellcat, "Cherry" is playing on the radio, it is night, he's got a hot blonde waiting at the bar, but, oh God, he's landing with his wheels up. *("I'm not rich anymore. They've managed to get me down where it's very close for me, and I probably don't have the same financial base as you do at this point. I'm very much at risk. But I don't see how, and I know I can't, I can't walk away from the bondholders. I can't walk away from the people who have put deposits in here. I have a tremendous obligation.")*

He calls on Senator Dennis DeConcini. He wants him to get Danny Wall to delay the formal issuance of the new examination report so its damaging information (not a bit of it true, goddammit) will not interfere with selling Lincoln. But DeConcini balks—he's already been hammering Wall, at Keating's request, to finish the examination in a hurry. So when the exam finally works its way through all those federal desks and on December 20 officially goes to the bank board, well, Dennis DeConcini doesn't see how he logically can ask them to sit on the thing. Time's up. But Keating will not be stopped, he has never been stopped. He pitches a group of buyers who will plunk down $50 million for Lincoln. This gives the board pause—what government agency wants to own a $2 billion default? But the group fails to pass muster with the regulators. Keating says he's got other buyers. The delay continues.

A fire breaks out in the Los Angeles office of the California State Banking Department and burns, well, mainly ACC/Lincoln records. As the press relations person, Patricia Johnson must handle the story. She is told by Keating's aides that the fire was accidental and that she should keep it out of the Phoenix papers. She calls in old favors and does just that. Then she happens to bully her way through to the L.A. fire chief and finds out it was arson. Three reporters covering Keating in Phoenix have their cars broken into.

Bonds, gotta sell the bonds, keep the thing alive. Keating flies two squads of his sales force in from Los Angeles, delivers a speech—that'll pep 'em up—shows them the Phoenician, it looks so great. One salesman asks, "What else can you do to this hotel? It's so beautiful now. What else can you possibly do?"

"I can put a bond office in front of it and sell bonds."

He takes them all to Mary Elaine's—$21 shrimp cocktails, that'll buck 'em up—they go back to Los Angeles ready to sell. That month ACC issues another $50 million in junk bonds.

It's the twenty-fifth day of January, the year of Our Lord nineteen hundred and eighty-nine, and the Mother of God has a message: "Dear children! Today I am calling you to the way of holiness. Pray that you may comprehend the beauty and greatness of this way where God reveals Himself to you in a special way. . . ."

Charlie Keating moves on. He is now a prisoner of the East Coast, of regulators, of trying to find a buyer who will meet their standards. And he's got a lot else on his mind. That month he officially loses $11 million playing currency markets on the black box—that runs his marker up over $100 million. Doubling down, the regulators call it. He starts sending memos—shift cars from ACC to Phoenician, move the garage out there, get a place for the mechanic.

It all gets to be a blur. It is February 3, 1989, and George Bush is the new president of the United States. The technical problem that has been lurking in the savings and loan industry now begins to creep out into the light of day. Danny Wall is sitting in the West Wing of the White House with William Seidman, the head of the FDIC. Bush's new administration has a plan now that the elections are over. Bush will wipe out the FSLIC, the bankrupt insurance fund behind the thrifts, and give this task to the FDIC. The Federal Home Loan Bank Board will become two new entities, the Resolution Trust Corporation and the Office of Thrift Supervision. Everyone now agrees there are a lot of sick thrifts. Wall and Seidman have been beckoned to the White House to put some finishing touches on this scheme and give it their blessings. This looks good unless you are Danny Wall, since the plan basically wipes out his agency.

Seidman has a head like a ballistic missile. He's a New Mexico rancher, getting up on seventy, and he has a relaxed, no-bullshit manner. He is an old Washington player, a hardball inside-the-beltway kind of guy. He also loathes Danny Wall as a kind of regulatory wimp. Wall, meanwhile, sees Seidman as not a team player.

The White House officials calmly tell Wall of their new plans for his agency, gut him like a fish, and leave him flopping on the floor,

very nicely dressed but still gutted. Danny Wall whips around toward Seidman and explodes, "My God, I wish I was as smart as
you are! You schemed to get me. Your scheme worked. You sunk
us. It was your plot. It was your purpose from the beginning, and
you were so clever to have planned it that way. I wish I'd been
smart enough to outscheme you. You were so clever to blame us
for everything so your own problems could be concealed."

Seidman can barely mask his disdain for this sniveling punk.
"Okay, are you done now, Danny? Because if you say anything more,
we're going to have it out right now. I heard your message. I think
you're wrong. And I'm not going to listen anymore. So shut up."

There's a ghost in the White House that day, Charlie Keating.
He did not drop a reputed $55 million fighting the federal govern-
ment for nothing. He is now a symbol of what went wrong. It
seems so very long ago that Bill Black sat up straight at his desk
at the Federal Home Loan Bank Board and asked himself, just
who is this asshole Charlie Keating? This guy out in nowhere Arizona who is suddenly hiring the likes of Kaye Scholer? Ed Gray
noticed in December 1984 that Alan Greenspan—Christ, I was just
a chauffeur to him—was working for some guy with a savings and
loan, guy by the name of Charlie Keating—that seems like such a
long time ago.

In February, while Wall discovers that as a "child of the Senate"
he is suddenly an orphan of the federal government, Keating
meets with the regulators in Phoenix. The night before, Mother
Teresa called him and he was touched and said, sure, use my corporate plane. A living saint, he is convinced of it. The regulators
want yet another peek at his books. He tells them they are "Na-
zis." On February 7 one of his aides meets with a Cranston aide
to discuss the sale of Lincoln. Over the next two months, Cranston
calls Danny Wall four times, pushing for bank board approval of
the sale. His aide threatens bank board officials with congressional
hearings if they even think about shutting down Lincoln. But democracy can't run simply on love. Cranston's fund-raiser Joy Jacobson lets it be known that another $100,000 contribution would
be nice. Keating's aide says fine, you get the sale of Lincoln
through, and it's a deal.*

*During the Senate Ethics Hearings Jacobson allowed that "In retrospect, I think
there was a link there."

Keating keeps rolling, no long face for him. *People are lucky to be born.* The deals still have to be done to book that quarterly profit. It is almost on automatic pilot now. One Phoenix developer is called in to participate in one of these ritual transactions where Lincoln essentially loans all the money that makes the deal possible, agrees to a nonrecourse note, and then magically books a profit out of this accounting witchcraft. Charlie Keating is so confident of his customers now that when the developer comes into his office he finds all the closing papers laid out on a table for him to sign—papers for a deal he has never heard of until this instant. And, of course, he signs because Charlie Keating has him totally leveraged. In early February Keating tells Patricia Johnson he is going to get out of thrifts, just too much hassle, get into hotels. Why, if the sale goes through, "we'll be fine." He keeps trying to find new squads of buyers, keeps up the pressure on his staff. One night they stay up until 3 A.M. hammering out a deal, and when it looks like its done they break out the champagne. But it falls through—are the feds sabotaging him? Is that it?

Keating keeps calling the regulators, he's got to make them understand. They write tidy cover-my-ass memos of what Charlie Keating is saying. "He will give us the keys to Lincoln"; "from this moment on we are completely at your disposal." Finally, on February 27, he has a meeting with Darrell Dochow at the bank board, over the speakerphone. Keating is worn.

"We have no cash," he says, "and no ability to make a deal. Our people are leaving us. . . . If I don't do something this week, I don't know what I can do. . . ."

"I don't know how you're going to get a sale in a week," offers Dochow.

What? Don't these people understand anything? They've reregulated, they've changed the tax law to end limited partnerships, they've shut down the upstreaming of money from Lincoln to ACC for taxes, they've all but strangled ACC's ability to sell bonds.

"We can't get put behind bars," Keating continues, and for God's sake he's "not willing to sign Lincoln's death now. . . . I wish somebody would listen to me on that. I am not doing what you are thinking—running Lincoln in a reckless manner."

But, Dochow says, you never want to comply with the rules that the agency asks you to comply with.

"If you're worried about FSLIC insurance when you take Lincoln down, you're going to hurt the U.S. League [the major lobbying group for thrifts], hurt the guys leaking information, mess up Wall and everybody. . . . We're an honest bunch of guys, and there are plenty of people who believe that. I'm not trying to screw you or anybody else. There is not much time left for screwing around. There are a lot of people that are going to listen. The courts will hear two sides, and it is not something that any of us want. I am so weak I can't even fight."

He calls Johnson into his office and says, "The media's killing us. What can we do?" How about a press release, she offers. Fine, great idea. Let's say the sale of Lincoln is imminent. She shows the release to Keating's key lawyer, but he is on the phone and brushes her off. She goes back to Keating for approval. He writes in a few changes—anything can be improved—and then Johnson gives it to Dow Jones and a little while later she and Charlie sit in the glass-walled computer room and watch it come scrolling across the screen. But somebody out there is selling ACC stock short, and Charlie Keating is furious. A bunch of his old friends back in Cincinnati own ACC stock. Good heavens, a whole convent full of nuns has a fortune in ACC stock. How can he let them down? Besides what good is ESOP, the company's stock option plan, as a cash cow for Charlie Keating if the stock is lying there like a road kill?

He manages to pump through a few little hits from ESOP: $82,600 on January 23; $69,881.25 on February 21; $69,662.50 on March 21. The day after the press release the world caves in. Keating's in-house and out-of-house legal counsel are furious. The release had a flaw—the sale of Lincoln is not imminent. This could bring the SEC breathing down their necks. Charlie will not be lectured. He screams he is tired of being flogged in the press. Then the Kaye Scholer attorneys explode through the phone, and Charlie seems to sink into the background.

When he tells Darrell Dochow that he's just too weak to get up from his stool at the bell and go back into the ring, well, Charlie Keating is misreading his own heart. What Charlie Keating really knows how to do is fight, so he never really stops. But the signs are not good this month—in March, Michael Milken is indicted on ninety-eight counts of racketeering and securities fraud and faces a possible 520 years in prison. Keating continues to hunt for another set of buyers. But a new group of investors also fails to make the grade, and he is without a deal. So he goes to Dallas and talks. Then to Washington and talks. There must be a buyer out there. Back to Texas—prop up that deal—but it is a strain. It is March 3, and Charlie Keating is eating with his aides at the Mansion on Turtle Creek in Dallas. Judy Wischer is late, where is she? She enters the dining room wearing convict stripes and carrying a ball and chain. They all laugh, great, the rented costume helps cut the tension, rolls back the stress level. Then New York. Still, he can find nothing, so it's back to Washington and then New York again. Talk to the Saudi-European Bank people, meet with Sir James Goldsmith, take in a night of theater, *Phantom of the Opera.* It is March 21, Charlie Keating looks up from his dinner at Le Cirque, sees Robin Leach of the television program *Lifestyles of the Rich and Famous,* and sends Carol Kassick over to his table with brochures touting the Phoenician.

The world is moving in. The FHLBB officially completes yet another examination of Lincoln, notifies the bank that it has to increase its reserves, and also calls in outside lawyers to talk about seizing the bank. On March 29, Charlie Keating flies to Spain. He must meet with Sir James Goldsmith at his estate in Marbella, must ensure his hold on those shares of GOIL, gonna be worth millions in time. Then, late on the night of March 30, off to Düsseldorf and the next day he talks with George Herrdum, the black-box man, one right play and you can be back. On that date, Lincoln Savings and Loan of California has assets of $5.3 billion and has placed 2 percent of this money in home loans and 63 percent in risk assets, has gotten 33 percent of its money from brokered jumbos, and has lost in the past 120 days about $29 million. At 5:30 P.M. on April 4 his plane touches down in Phoenix and he does not have a deal, he does not have more money, and now the FHLBB wants at least $50 million pumped into Lincoln to shore it up. He sends a note to Senator Alan Cranston, a pleading note that says "some politically important person has got to lay it on the line to Danny Wall and Jake Garn that they inescapably and must decisively approve this deal. They must do it in such a way that the forcefulness cannot be misunderstood." (Wall is still technically alive since the bill gutting his agency has not yet cleared Congress.) Lincoln must be sold, it is the only way out for Charlie Keating and the federal government. Otherwise, if the bank is seized, there will be a shortfall of billions of dollars. Six days later, Keating and ·Cranston talk, and for the first time the senator discovers that if Lincoln is seized then ACC will have to declare bankruptcy and if ACC goes bust it will default on over $200 million worth of bonds, securities owned mainly by people who live in southern California. Keating tells him there may be fifty thousand such people. Cranston can understand what this means. He accepts a memo provided by Lincoln officials headed "Talking points for conversation with Danny Wall," and then he calls Wall, urging him to move forward on the sale of Lincoln. At 11 P.M. on April 12, Cranston calls bank board member Roger Martin on his unlisted home phone. At 5:30 A.M., Martin's phone rings again and Dennis DeConcini is on the line. He explains he got the number from Cranston. Martin is unhinged by all this attention. He calls his office and has his staff send a message to the senator's offices: stop calling him.

Executives start shedding their positions at ACC—one of Keating's sons-in-law bails out in early April. Still, some have hope. One Keating executive mortgages his home and buys a bigger position in ACC. Keating snorts out his contempt for such a stupid move.

Keating calls Patricia Johnson into his office. She has been ill at ease lately. She must field the calls from anxious bondholders, and she has taken to taping them and then playing the tapes to others in the corporation. What really bothers her is that the callers who are worried about their bonds all sound like very old people.

"I like you," he begins. "I realize you are a single parent with three kids, and you have done great work for the company. But I've been instructed to let you go." He's been instructed? She thinks, someone is ordering Charlie Keating around? He tells her he is going to have to let a lot of people go, no severance pay, no vacation pay. The till is empty, Charlie Keating says. She stands up and says, "You'll be in my prayers." As she walks out of the office, the last thing she notices is the glass Madonna standing on the corner of his desk.

On the night of April 13, Keating senses that the federal agents are very near. He has lawyers standing by in Washington and Phoenix—he has always pulled it out in the past—and late that night a bank board lawyer who is in Phoenix gets a call from an ACC bankruptcy lawyer who explains that if Lincoln is seized

Charlie Keating will take ACC into the fortress of Chapter 11, build a legal wall between his assets and the federal government. So at 2:30 A.M. the bank board lawyer calls Bill Black. That night American Continental Corporation goes into Chapter 11—taking eleven of Lincoln's subsidiaries into this legal tent with it.

On April 14, the federal regulators seize Lincoln Savings and Loan. Bill Black calls up Danny Wall to brief him on the strange events of the night before and explains that ACC's last-minute efforts were inadequate to prevent the government's takeover of Lincoln. But he does want to pass along a message from ACC: "The only thing, frankly, that they said to our counsel was that there was at least one senator in Arizona and California—and they wanted us to pass this on to you—who would be supportive of reaching a resolution with them, and that these senators were important to the agency."

Charlie Keating is not surprised. The federal agents poised for the seizure had booked blocks of rooms at his Crescent Hotel. These people think they can run a business? Charlie Keating has the knack of finding out what he needs to know. When the regulators take over Lincoln they discover listening devices in the room where their examiners had worked. On April 17, the bank board ships criminal referrals to U.S. attorneys and to the FBI in Phoenix, New York City, and Los Angeles. And that old file on Charlie Keating leaps back to life. The next day an ACC security guard is caught by surprised federal agents inside the Lincoln Savings and Loan office.

Robert Kielty, Keating's chief legal counsel who mowed his lawn as a kid back in Cincinnati, is worried. He paces his floor. He does not want to go to jail, and yet he thinks there will be a massive criminal investigation of the company. That is the way the government operates, he thinks, they must get some scalps so that they can explain what has happened and how nothing that happened is their fault. He should know; in the early seventies he was a U.S. attorney back in Cincinnati. But maybe they'll spare him, he tells others. After all, he's been careful to avoid looking too rich, too greedy. Why, he's always driven an old station wagon to work. Yes, that will help. And then he keeps pacing the floor.

It's the twenty-fifth day of April, the year of Our Lord nineteen hundred and eighty-nine. "Dear children! I am calling upon you to a complete surrender to God. Let everything you possess be in the hands of God. Only in that way will you have joy in your heart. . . ."

How long can a person wait? Kim tells Chip that something more solid has to come of their relationship, that she isn't simply going to be his "fuck buddy." And Chip, well, he's been moving like a glacier toward some sort of decision—but the money, all that wonderful money, can he give it up?—and in April 1989, he reaches a conclusion. Judy has hardly been around for months, what with flying all over hell and creation with Charlie trying to find a buyer for Lincoln that the federal government will accept, and he's drifted into life with Kim, stays over at the condo a lot, has a more peaceful kind of life. So on a Friday night that month, as ACC slides into Chapter 11 and Lincoln is seized by the federal government, he tells Judy he's been having an affair with Kim and that he wants a divorce so he can marry her. Kim's been out drinking all night with her friends, partying, and Christ, she's still drunk when the sun comes up. The phone rings, and as she picks it up half in a daze, she hears "Kim, this is Judy Wischer. I want you to stay away from my husband." Kim fires back, "Judy, I think you need to tell Chip to stay away from me. He doesn't love you, he doesn't want anything to do with you." But Judy isn't buying this line, and she says, "He has me, and that's all he needs." Kim is coming awake now, her brain is burning off that booze, and she says, "That's obviously not what he needs, or he wouldn't be coming to me all the time." Judy sounds angry to Kim when she says, "You better do what I tell you to do or else." Or else? So Kim says, "Or else what?"

Kim remembers it all so clearly, that crazy time when Chip finally faced up to the fact that he was unhappy and asked for a divorce. "All this shit's happening. The first was when they punched my radiator out with an ice pick. On my message machine there'd be disguised voices saying, 'You bitch, you whore, we're going to get you, you're messing with the wrong people.' I started carrying a gun. Then they shot out the driver's-side window, they pulled an electrical connection underneath, it could have caused an electrical fire. Then they loosened the lug nuts on my tires. Then they broke in a couple of times and stole stuff—a radar detector. They wrote SUCKS on my Beamer, knocked in the gas cap, took a key and scratched it all over."

On the weekends when Chip is back with Judy and the kids, Kim parties with a girlfriend she knows from a local bar, and the girlfriend knows everything that is going on in her life. Later she learns that her girlfriend is spying on her for money. She is certain of this fact: her girlfriend finally confesses to her. It is a crazy time.

Ramona Jacobs can't believe what she is hearing. Some family members tell her they've heard there is some kind of problem with Lincoln Savings and Loan and American Continental Corporation. Suddenly she thinks back to what a teller had told her that January. The teller had been very cautious, had said she wasn't supposed to say anything but she just had to tell her that the bonds were not insured and that she should be very careful. And Ramona Jacobs had replied, "Are you serious?" and the teller had said yes, she was serious. She'd then gone to the bond salesman— they were no longer in the branch but down the street in a little office, and that seemed strange—and he'd assured her that her bonds were a real good deal and perfectly safe, and so she rolled over a $2,000 bond that had matured. Ramona Jacobs thinks about all that as she hastens down to the local branch of Lincoln Savings and Loan and when she gets there she finds the building packed with people and a long line trailing down the sidewalk outside. She approaches a guy in uniform—turns out he is a security officer of the Federal Reserve—and he says he can't tell her much about the situation but that the bank is going to close in half an hour and that maybe she should come back the next week. She returns on Tuesday and is told that she cannot get her bond money at the moment. She is handed a two-page question-and-answer document on the bottom of which is a toll-free number for anyone who has more questions. Ramona Jacobs calls and speaks to a woman, but she does not seem to know any more than Ramona. She tells the woman that to her this whole situation seems to be a farce and the woman laughs, and they both hang up. And the mother of Michelle Marie Miller does not feel very good at all. Of course, she is not alone—there are somewhere between 17,000 and 23,000 people just like her who together have lost around a quarter of a billion dollars.

("I'll tell you something on that particular point, speaking of Charlie's stature, physical, and about body language. Charlie

didn't put on anything. Most of the time you'd see his sleeves rolled up literally to the elbow at his desk working and his tie loosened. That's the way Charlie was. He didn't have a drinking problem or anything like that, but mentally and emotionally he could let . . . blow the steam valve without blowing the boiler, you know what I'm saying? Blow it off and stay relaxed internally. I was in his office three weeks after Chapter 11, and I mean there was a lot of dust in the air. Everybody suing everybody, billion-dollar suits, and this and that, and I was studying his body language, and he literally was relaxed. He was standing and he was talking to his head attorney. And he was standing like this and he was standing and holding himself in such a way as to be as relaxed as possible at that particular moment, and I think that was an outward expression of where his head was.")

PART FIVE

OLD PAINT

I ride an old paint
I lead an old dam
I'm going to Montana
To throw a hoolīhan
They feed in the coolies
They water in the draw
Their tails are all matted
Their backs are all raw

Ride around
Ride around real slow
The fiery 'n snuffy are raring to go

Old Bill Brown
Had a daughter and a son
One went to Denver
And the other went wrong
His wife she died in a poolroom fight
And still he keeps singing
From morning 'til night

Well, when I die
Take my saddle from the wall
Put it on my pony
And lead him from his stall
Tie my bones to his back
Turn our faces to the West
And we'll ride the prairie
That we like the best

—traditional

It is February 1992, about two months before the sentencing of Charles H. Keating, Jr., in a California superior court. A man in his thirties races down the street on his way to a conference about dance when suddenly he collides with this tall, gangly fellow. They collect themselves, and then the man looks up, has a flicker of recognition, and says, "You're Charles Keating." The tall, lean fellow sticks out his hand and says, "Charlie Keating." They shake, and then Keating lopes off down the street. He suddenly stops, turns, and shouts back to the stranger, "Don't believe everything you read about me in the newspapers. It's not true."

YO,
YOU KNOW

As the plane comes into National Airport in Washington around 9 P.M. on April 10, Mike Manning is at the end of a long day. He spent most of it in Kansas City for Mario Renda's guilty plea and then grabbed the last flight out to the capital at 5:50 P.M. After takeoff, he worked on the final documents of the case, but these matters are housekeeping details. He downs two scotches and is sipping a third when he realizes that he doesn't need to rush around anymore, this thing is over, it's done. People have been saying to him, "Where will you find another rush like Renda?" He's constantly put this question out of his mind, but now he cannot, and what he thinks is, Jesus Christ, I have nothing in my credenza that doesn't rhyme with Renda, I have nothing to do as a lawyer. He has been making some plans to spend time with his family after essentially being absent for four years. To reacquaint himself with his friends. To be a normal person—he's just bought season tickets to Wolf Trap in suburban Virginia.

Tuesday he keeps himself busy at his office, but by Wednesday, April 12, he has absolutely nothing to do. Then a call comes from the FDIC, and Thursday night, April 13, he is having dinner with government people at Mr. K's. They talk to him about Charlie Keating. Manning has paid some attention to Keating, seen his name in newspapers, heard some dark mutterings during his visits to the FDIC on the Renda case, but basically the man is a blank to him—some savings and loan operator out in California. Now the FDIC wants him to take the case, see if there is anything wrong with Charlie Keating's operation. See if the FHLBB regulators are right in their claims or if Keating is correct in charging they have a vendetta against him. Manning listens, but he is already planning. He makes phone calls from the restaurant, getting associates out of bed in Washington and Kansas City and instructing them to fly to Phoenix at daybreak. As he leaves the restaurant, he is outlining the case in his head ("Was Charlie operating on the edge of the envelope but not outside it? Was he the victim of childish and petulant bureaucrats?"), plotting his new drawing of concentric rings, contemplating early flips from ACC staff, peering ahead to a trial with a magical zoom lens. At the center of his drawing is a small circle, and this time Manning writes in that circle, Mr. K. While Manning plots his strategy, ACC slides relentlessly into Chapter 11. The next morning Lincoln will be seized by the regulators.

Mike Manning has found salvation. He is thirty-nine years old, and he is finally facing the fact that he cannot honestly make social commitments—good-bye, Wolf Trap. And he is confessing to himself that he cannot keep his most recent promise to his wife—after Renda, he has told her, he will return to a normal practice, a normal life. He has been telling her this since their marriage in August 1970 and failing in this effort for most of the last nineteen years. She is inexplicably patient and supportive, and Manning is ultimately baffled by her acceptance of his obsessions. Most of all, as Manning walks out of Mr. K's and into the Washington night, he finally faces who and what he really is. He is a junkie, and he must have his drug, his fix. ("But I can tell you, it was something that frightened me and frightens me now even today about myself. When I heard about the Keating case, all the postpartum depression that I was feeling even two days after Renda was over with was gone. It was the Holy Grail, it was a Mission. The adrenaline started pumping again.")

He flies into Phoenix on April 17 and drives a rent-a-car into the ACC parking lot in Phoenix. Before he can get both feet out of the car, a security guard is on him, demanding "Who are you?" Manning politely explains that he is part of an FDIC team that is taking over Lincoln Savings and Loan. The security guard is not impressed: "You have to get this car out of this lot immediately."

Manning asks—after all, he's new in town—if this isn't the Lincoln building.

"Yes, it is, but this is ACC property, and if you don't get this car out of here, I'm going to have you towed out of here."

So Manning finds a parking space on the Lincoln side of the lot. The first thing he does is have the records checked to see if Mario Renda has penetrated Lincoln. He discovers he has not. Soon Renda's lawyer calls and offers Manning his client's help. Renda is in prison, and he would like to talk with Manning about Charlie Keating. Renda has said, come out and see me, I'll teach you how to catch the guy, I'll be your coach. But Manning never makes that meeting. Like everyone else who enters into the world of Charlie Keating, he is soon overwhelmed by the scale of things, by the enormity of the records. And Charlie Keating is making Manning play on *his* field, according to *his* game clock. Manning intends to change that reality fast. He will not be home until sometime in 1993. He is hooked.

The ACC building is humming with activity. Lincoln, across the small driveway, is a dead zone. The ground between the two is called the DMZ. The desks are empty, as are the file cabinets. Manning opens a drawer—not so much as a paper clip or a rubber band. All of Lincoln's books seem to have crossed to the ACC building, where shredding machines are running day and night.

One of Keating's lawyers arranges an introduction between Manning and Charlie. Manning says, "Good morning, Mr. Keating. Mike Manning. It's nice to meet you."

Keating does not speak. Then he grabs Manning's hand and gives it a bone-crunching squeeze. He stares into his eyes, he will not break eye contact. Manning stares back and smiles.

Several months later, they meet again.

"How are you?" offers Manning.

"Not very well, you bastard."

Without the loan files, the government is facing chaos in dealing with Lincoln's customers. Charlie Keating turns a deaf ear to the federal request—let them sue for the damn files. But in his haste to gut the Lincoln building, Keating left behind some original artwork, family stuff that really mattered to him. Keating's lawyers offer Manning a deal, the artwork for the files. And so Charlie Keating does one more deal. Manning and his team take a group of offices in the back corner of the Lincoln building, and then Manning carefully tapes over the windows so that no one can see in. The upper ranks of Lincoln have been fired or have quit. Manning does not trust anyone who worked for Lincoln. They do not respond to orders with any evident pleasure. So he becomes very careful about what is on his desk and what he says out loud. He and his colleagues soon learn that holdovers from Lincoln are briefing ACC personnel on the regulators' every move.

Seven days after the seizure, Charlie Keating goes public. He holds a press conference at the Biltmore Hotel. The press is there, and they are very hungry. Charlie Keating has rarely talked to the press. He considers them beneath contempt.

The family is there, of course. They all seem relaxed. Charlie Keating enters the packed room with his wife. As he moves toward the stage, he bumps into an old friend from Cincinnati, Garrett Fry. Their families have been close for half a century, and without warning Fry has flown out for the press conference. Charlie Keating looks at his old friend and says, "What are you doing here?"

But Garrett Fry does not tell him because he has come to Phoenix for a simple reason. For the first time in his life he is not sure who Charlie Keating is. ACC may go bankrupt? The stock, the shares held by so many friends in Cincinnati, by nuns, for God's sake, now possibly worthless? The bondholders, old people he hears, now wiped out? Fry wonders if he really ever knew his friend. Has he missed something? The day before, back in Cincinnati, Fry heard that ACC might move from the holding action of Chapter 11 into the total death of actual bankruptcy, and this has disturbed him very much. He is a stockbroker, and for years he has almost specialized in ACC securities. He has sold them to friends all over town. He has sold them to the good sisters in the convent. He has made a fortune on ACC stock. And why not?"*
He knew Charlie Keating. Before Fry left for Phoenix, his dying mother asked him, "Why does he need it all?" On the long flight, Fry turned that question over in his mind again and again. He has known Charlie Keating since they were boys. In the summer of 1986, he drove his twenty-seven-foot motor home out west and stopped by ACC headquarters for a brief hello. He announced himself to a secretary, but Keating recognized his voice and

---

*About one thousand residents of Cincinnati and a half-dozen local companies had serious holdings in ACC stock. Thirty of ACC's hundred largest shareholders were from Cincinnati, as were more than half of ACC's forty biggest shareholders of preferred stock. The *Cincinnati Post* estimated that the failure of ACC would cost people in Cincinnati more than $10 million.

boomed out, "Garrett, what in the hell are you doing here?" He booked Fry's family into a hotel, took them all out to eat at Tomaso's, and good God, Charlie seemed to know every waiter, cook, busboy, and guest at the restaurant. Lee Henkel was there that evening, and Charlie gushed to Henkel about how nobody in his entire life had ever done more for him than his friend Garrett Fry.

The press conference is hosted by John Connally's son, Mark. He works for ACC, he is an old family friend, and he knows the feel of bankruptcy. Of course, his father has recovered, he is a tough man. Besides, he has kept his huge ranch house—homesteaded it against his creditors. And his various federal and state pensions keep him off the street, they pay John Connally $300,000 a year. Mark Connally makes a few remarks, his face is very solemn. Then the room darkens and images of great beauty, great power, great wealth flash across the screen: the lakes at Estrella, the dark green of the golf course at the Phoenician, developments scattered about the United States—all of it the fruit of the labor of American Continental Corporation. This is not some fly-by-night firm, the images say, this is not a gang of rip-off artists. This is a sound business, the kind of operation that makes America a better place to live in. And then Charlie Keating steps forward.

The standing ovation lasts for a solid minute, the thunderous approval, the upturned faces of handsome young men and women—his employees. Keating puts the pages of his statement down on the podium—there is a tremor in his hands—and begins to read. The speech begins with an anecdote from Abraham Lincoln. Charlie Keating swiftly moves to the heart of his case: he has been taken down by a federal government that for years has been dedicated to his destruction. The senators, all those politicians he gave money to. Was he trying to influence them, to buy their support? Charlie Keating says: "I want to say in the most forceful way I can, I certainly hope so."

One of his key ACC lawyers is standing in the back of the room as Charlie Keating says this, and a cold feeling grips his spine. How can he stop the press from pouncing on this statement? Then it comes to him—he'll buttonhole reporters on their way out, explain to them that it was a typo in the text, that Charlie Keating really meant to say "I certainly hope not." But this tactic will never work. Because there is no typo, and Charlie Keating has just said exactly what he means and feels. And then Charlie Keating has finished speaking and walks off the stage and right out of the room. There will be no questions.

Keating has his people fired up. At ACC Judy Wischer calls a staff meeting after Chapter 11, after Lincoln is seized, and she says, "We have to work with the federal regulators now, but they are all faggots." Someone in the back of the room shouts, "Can we quote you on that?" And Judy Wischer says, "Yes."

Charlie Keating flies to Medjugorje in late June to pray to the Blessed Mother, and from the twenty-second until the twenty-sixth he stays with a peasant family and attends to his God. But there is much to do, lawsuits to launch against the government, employees to keep on their toes. On June 27, Charlie Keating is back in Phoenix and addresses five hundred of his employees at Charlie Charlie's in the Phoenician. He gives them one of his patented, rambling, off-the-cuff inspirational addresses (his official logs note it as " 'Pep Rally' Go Get 'Em.") He will not give in, and the press cannot quite believe what they are seeing. Could Charlie Keating actually be right, could he really be the victim of vindictive federal regulators?

On the twenty-fifth day of June in the year of Our Lord nineteen hundred and eighty-nine, the Mother of God says, "Dear children! Today I call you to live the messages that I have been giving you during the past eight years. This is the time of grace and I desire the grace of God be great for every single one of you. I am blessing you, and I love you with a special love. Thank you for having responded to my call."

Fame, notoriety, that kind of thing can always kill you, and Carl Lindner knows this very well. Just look at his old partner, Charlie Keating. In the spring of 1989, Lindner is forced into the public eye by an egomaniac who goes on television plugging his work. Al Neuharth's *Confessions of an S.O.B.*, with its half-accurate title, covers Lindner in a section entitled "Skinning Sharks." Neuharth, a man who has swallowed a hundred dailies whole and launched a national newspaper, *USA Today*, drags into the bright light one of Lindner's back pages, a little move he made in 1985. Neuharth is everything Carl Henry Lindner, Jr., cannot be and fears to be—a flashy man, given to enormous personal publicity, gray and black clothing as a trademark and a reputation for appreciating young blond women and white wine. He also is a man who beats Lindner at his own game and, what is even worse, brags of it in cold black type.

Just as Lindner is getting to that moment in life when he starts endowing buildings at universities and appearing shyly in the press as a kind of elder statesman of the corporate world and the backbone of those family values the Republican Party professes to worship, the book hits the stores in a roar of flack-generated huzzahs. "I was ready for the guy who tried to steal my company," Neuharth purrs. "Cincinnati billionaire Carl Lindner is a shark in sheep's clothing."

Back in 1979, Lindner had become the second largest shareholder in Neuharth's company, Gannett, and this immediately aroused suspicion. Neuharth had Lindner's m.o. down cold: "He buys his way into companies as a substantial shareholder, courts management, then increases his holdings, maneuvers his way on the board, and ultimately takes control." In 1985, Lindner is ready to make his move, and when he is rebuffed by Gannett in his search for shares—"I'd pay a premium over the market price. How much of a premium would it take?"—he goes into the market. Neuharth immediately hires the best antitakeover law firm, changes the corporate by-laws to thwart his new wannabe partner, and then, on May 21, Lindner files with the SEC about his holdings and ambitions.

Lindner is not happy when he learns of the by-laws (which stagger the terms of directors and jack up the price for bagging shares).

"Al," he says over the phone, "I'm shocked. I can't believe you're doing this to me. I can't believe you didn't ask me about it first. We've got to sit down and talk. Can you come to Cincinnati?"

Neuharth, keen on turf, says he's all tied up in meetings, but if Lindner wishes he can haul himself to Washington. That same afternoon Lindner calls Neuharth from the lobby of Gannett's corporate headquarters in D.C. He's got an idea—Gannett can buy him out. Neuharth offers $228 million. Lindner has a different idea of what is fair and just, say about $278 million. Neuharth turns to him with a smirk and says, "Carl, isn't that something I keep reading about called 'greenmail'?"

This Lindner cannot abide, cannot tolerate saying that word out loud: "I'm sorry to hear you use that word. We don't do greenmail."

Neuharth has a low tolerance for this kind of guff—after all, he's an S.O.B.—and besides, his take on Lindner is very simple: "Lindner is straitlaced, soft-spoken, slow-talking. He doesn't smoke or drink. He shuns publicity. He's a devout churchgoing Baptist. But the dollar is his almighty God."

They go into a proxy fight and have a lot of expensive dinners with Neuharth drinking glasses of vodka disguised as ice water. Lindner confesses he has a dream in which Gannett appears as a nice media company that one of his sons is running. And then, at a board meeting, Neuharth utterly destroys Lindner's efforts. But this is not enough for a real S.O.B., and Neuharth is the genuine article. He buys full-page ads in *The New York Times, The Wall Street Journal, The Washington Post,* the *Chicago Tribune,* the *Los Angeles Times,* and *USA Today* that attack "funny money financiers," junk bonds, and mergers. No names are mentioned—who needs names in this tight little shark pond?

The phone rings at Gannett headquarters.

"Al, how could you say terrible things like that about me?"

"Why, Carl, I didn't even mention your name. But if you keep up this bullshit about a big buyback bonus again, I may have to."

Lindner unloads his stock at no profit. And then, in Charlie Keating's time of troubles, this new book comes out and Carl Lindner, Jr., is in stores everywhere and people can see his name looming up from the page: "The shark was eager to swim away from me."

On September 9, 1989, Charlie Keating is again in Medjugorje staying with peasants. He prays to the Mother of God for three days. Then, on September 15, Michael Manning files his RICO complaint and the walls truly begin to tumble down. It is the largest bank fraud case ever presented by the United States government and charges Charlie Keating, his family, and his key officers with bleeding over a billion dollars of federally insured deposits out of Lincoln through various stratagems. The names rattle down the page: Charlie Keating, his son, C3, Judy Wischer, Robert Kielty, sons-in-law Robert Wurzelbacher and Robert Hubbard, ACC executive Andrew Ligget.

The suit also provides the press with the first simple scenario of what took place within the walls of ACC. It is what everyone is hungry for—a plot that will kill off all those nagging questions. Manning understands the press's deep need for a story line on which to base their accounts. He views his role as an educational one as much as a legal one. And besides, he is now officially playing offense, and that is the only time you can score in any real game. Contrary to a basic law school axiom about preparing a complaint, he has poured enormous detail into this one, almost mind-numbing detail because . . . he seeks two additional results. One, he wants everyone who worked around Charlie Keating to realize that Manning and his team are onto what they did so that someone will flip to the government side. And two, Manning wants the ACC and Lincoln brass to know that things went on that even the biggest executives were not really aware of, he wants them to finally understand just what kind of corporation they worked for when they joined Charlie Keating's world. In the complaint, the cast is listed up front just like in the program for a Broadway show, and then the straw buyers, sham land sales, inside stock deals, upstreaming of money, and fraudulent loans are laid out. There are delicious little details buried in the numbing and lawyerly prose. One odd transaction—what does one call it, a sweetheart deal?—involves a $30 million loan to a home-building company owned by R. A. Ober, Senator Dennis DeConcini's campaign manager in his successful race for a third term in 1988. The local papers haul out their largest type for the headlines. At the Phoenician, the newspapers are not available for guests that day.

One thing the public devours are tales of great wealth and great spending. Charlie Keating and his family paid themselves $34 million in salary, bonuses, and stock options (the ESOP sales). Charlie Keating spent more than $35 million on the care and feeding of his pilots and aircraft. Charlie Keating has a house worth more than $2 million in Phoenix, a place in Florida priced at close to $5 million, a fabled retreat in the Bahamas. Charlie Keating gave money away like a drunken sailor, the millions in loans to Father Ritter, the million or more to Mother Teresa. The United States has been wallowing in a culture of money, the lifestyles of the rich and famous have become the national pornography. But with the collapse of people like Charlie Keating, with the stagnation of the economy, a morning-after feeling replaces the new-morning feeling. That is the mood of the nation as Charlie Keating slowly slides toward the courtroom. Within three years, this new mood will grow fiercer and the unheard-of notion of taking a hard look at just what corporations are stuffing into the pay envelopes of the country's various CEOs will finally surface. The head of Coca-Cola took home an estimated $78 million last year? For peddling soda pop? The SEC will rumble about fuller disclosure of corporate perks—no mean feat since the Big Eight accountants have developed bookkeeping techniques that are about as secretive as the doings of the CIA or KGB.* Charlie Keating is ill prepared for this new scrutiny. He does not see what is wrong with the way he has lived, and in the big scheme of running a multi-billion-dollar operation, he cannot grasp the importance of a few tens of millions. He sees his basic identity as the same as Joe Six-pack's, and from time to time he says just that to the amazement of his listeners.

In Washington, an effort is mounted to deal with this new problem called the savings and loan crisis.** Politicians start mumbling about maybe giving back the money they received from Charlie Keating, but Senator Alan Cranston, for one, has spent his. And then he hears reports that the FBI is looking into his

*See Graef S. Crystal, *In Search of Excess: The Overcompensation of American Executives,* W. W. Norton & Co., New York, 1991, a Veblen-like study of what the big guys take home by a former compensation consultant. On its cover the book touts a simple fact: "In the last twenty years the pay of American workers has gone nowhere, while American CEOs have increased their own pay 400%. This is how they've done it."

**The government never really finds a handle on the crisis for a very simple reason. On June 14, 1990, the Democratic leadership in the House has a meeting in which they grope for some sort of position. One representative says that the party should "nail the Republicans and bring Neil Bush to the witness panel [over the billion-dollar collapse of Silverado in Denver]." But Speaker Thomas Foley points out a little problem with this notion: "We will not be able to avoid being called into this imbroglio. The record will include both sides of the political aisle. Those calling for a special investigation like Iran-contra should remember that Iran-contra was only a question of the actions of a Republican president and his staff. . . . The S and L crisis affects both parties." Five days later the Democratic National Committee publishes a statement by Chairman Ron Brown headlined "Democrats Call for More Investigators—Demand Prosecution of S&L Crooks." But this bold demand contains within it the warning, *"We strongly urge you to work closely with your campaign staffers to undertake a comprehensive review of your potential exposure on the thrift issue* [italics in original]." (John L. Jackley, *Hill Rat: Blowing the Lid off Congress,* Regnery Gateway, Washington, D.C., 1992, pp. 18–20.)

son's voter registration project, the one that saved his seat in the fall of 1986, the one to which Charlie Keating gave a last-minute infusion of $300,000 when it looked like Cranston might lose and when Charlie Keating needed Ed Gray's bill put on hold in the Senate. Cranston denounces this effort to "smear my son and drag him into the mud." In a *Los Angeles Times* poll 80 percent of the voters in California do not think Cranston should have taken money from Charlie Keating while he was pleading his case with federal regulators. It is as if somehow the rules have suddenly changed, as if politics were going through some awful season of reregulation. Cranston has been single for seven months, and at seventy-five he plans to marry a forty-nine-year-old campaign worker on Christmas Eve—he's already got the license. But because he is in "the middle of a stressful situation" he cancels the ceremony.

The senator's stress level is not helped by some of his colleagues in Washington. The House Banking Committee has spent much of the eighties as a kind of amiable lapdog for the banking industry. This is not too surprising since Fernand St. Germain chaired the committee. When his own investigators came to him in 1987 requesting that he hold a hearing on this man named Charles H. Keating, Jr., he was cool to the idea. One of Keating's lobbyists on the Hill, Dave Evans (a former congressman himself and veteran of the banking committee) attended to St. Germain on a daily basis. He would be there every morning to make sure the congressman had someone to take him to lunch—and pick up the tab. In 1988, Evans flew to Washington, walked into the offices of the House Banking Committee, and announced that he'd just spent quite a bit of time with their boss and maybe they should lay off this notion of a hearing about Charlie Keating. At that moment the notion seemed to die.

With St. Germain's defeat, Henry Gonzalez, a Mexican American from Texas, inherits the chair of the House Banking Committee. Gonzalez, a big man and a former boxer, is considered eccentric by many on the Hill. He is given to the occasional bizarre statement, and some people seriously question his intelligence. He has one other little quirk—he may be the last real populist on the Hill. He schedules hearings on Lincoln Savings and Loan for October and November, and the five senators who pleaded Keating's case, the corporation officials who did his work, the regulators who agreed to that Memorandum of Understanding back in May

1988, and many other people begin to wonder just what this loose cannon named Henry Gonzalez might do.

On October 26, 1989, they start to get a pretty good idea. Bill Black sits down to testify, and he seems to have remembered everything that was ever said and kept every memo that ever passed his way. For a day or two he's been working like a man possessed, preparing his statement—not a simple task, since a major earthquake rocked San Francisco while he was in the midst of writing it. He tells of homely little events he has noticed in the past few years, things like the bugging of phones at Lincoln so that the federal examiners could be overheard, the constant delays in Lincoln's audit that were condoned by his superiors back in Washington. He is not a man to waste time seeking delicate phrases. He says the bank board's staff was "shot in the back" by the bank board's administrators. He is the civil servant from central casting, the man who kept the public trust. He is clinical, he is lethal, he is on fire, and he dominates the room with both his passion and his odd calm, his precision in his charges and facts. Ghosts reappear to decry their fates, people like Ed Gray, who comes back from the dead to throw a few hundred stones. Danny Wall appears, of course, and escapes with his life but not much else. He resigns from his post as head of the bank board in December 1989. Kenneth Laventhol, an outside accountant hired by the federal government, gives a clear picture of the numbers: "Congressmen, seldom in our experience as accountants have we encountered a more egregious example of the misapplication of generally accepted accounting principles. . . . Lincoln was manufacturing profits by giving its money away."

As the hearings roll on, Charlie Keating is certified as a new national punching bag. As Congressman Charles Schumer, a Democrat from New York, puts it, "I've had people come to me and tell me about their older friends and relatives who were sold subordinated debt [junk bonds] which ended up being virtually worthless. Their life savings gone because of one unscrupulous son of a gun at the top of the heap—Keating. But now that we find that Washington knew that this subordinated debt in all probability was worthless and did nothing to stop the sale of subordinated debt, this is even more outrageous."

Charles Schumer has touched the raw nerve in Charlie Keating's world: the bondholders, the twenty thousand or so people like Ramona Jacobs, who now hold worthless paper. The public cannot forget the stories, or the faces, of these elderly Americans who went down to their neighborhood savings and loan, entrusted their life savings to the bank's staff, and then found out that the bond they'd bought was suddenly worthless. And the man who wiped them out, this Charlie Keating, he lives in a big house, he flew in a private jet, he had it made. The complexity of financial markets, of banking regulations, of government agencies, all these things may be more than people watching television can grasp. But not the faces of the bondholders. The one thing that seems to haunt Charlie Keating as a deep failure of personal responsibility is his obligation to pay back those bonds. But it is too late. The bank is gone. The corporation is dying.

In August 1989, the federal government passes a new law, the Financial Institutions Reform, Recovery, and Enforcement Act (FIRREA) and then rolls out its substitutes for the FHLBB—the Resolution Trust Corporation and the Office of Thrift Supervision. A flowchart designed to explain the new arrangement looks like the diagram for the boards in a computer. At the same time, it tells insured thrifts that they will have to dump most of their junk bond holdings by 1994. The thrift operators staring into the savage faces of born-again regulators do not wait. They dump their junk bonds wholesale, and by October 1989, the junk bond market has crashed. Among the broken players is Drexel, which limps along until February 1990 (living just long enough to pay out huge bonuses to its partners at the end of 1989) and then slides into bankruptcy. Mike Milken himself, Keating knows, is also a symbol now. A man obscenely rich ($714 million in income for one year), a funny-looking guy with a toupee who somehow hijacked the entire U.S. economy and ruined it. People begin to whisper a word they heard from their parents, a word that stood for a lost decade: Depression. And someone must be responsible for this situation.

On November 16, 1989, in the predawn hours, fifty federal thrift managers, FBI agents, private security guards, and an antiterrorism specialist seize the Phoenician. They tell the employees grinding through the graveyard shift that the U.S. government is now in charge. They instantly begin changing locks and securing sensitive files, and they produce a hit list of employees who are either relatives of Charlie Keating or too close to him and fire them

on the spot. (Those fired—in a move so reminiscent of Charlie
Keating's best style—later sue and collect handsomely from the
government.) Keating receives word at his hotel room in New
York—"We're being raided." John Akins, an events organizer at
the Phoenician, is told that the "Bastille" is being stormed and
goes down to the hotel. It is still dark, and he finds the grounds
dotted with Budget rental vans. He peers inside one and sees tired
men with earphones running a command post. One woman is captured before she escapes with operational documents, but two
vans stuffed with paperwork manage to flee into the night.

The government, with its FBI agents, antiterrorist specialists,
rent-a-cops, and electronic command center, has managed to assault an image that Charlie Keating has spent a lifetime creating,
that sense of self that is larger than life—there he is leaping from
a flaming Hellcat and "Cherry" is playing, blazing down the lane
to a Pan Am gold, storming to the top of AFC in Cincinnati,
launching a national campaign against pornography, building this
huge hotel, a place that is already being consistently listed as one
of the ten best on the surface of the earth. It is almost as if they
seek to exorcise some kind of demon. For months they have
wanted to take the Phoenician, but their hand was stayed by the
45 percent Kuwaiti interest. Keating initially convinced the Kuwaitis to resist partnership with the government—his opponents
began calling him "Charlie of Arabia"—but finally the Kuwaitis are
persuaded and the federal SWAT team moves in. They waste no
time ridding their hotel of the ghost of Charlie Keating. One of the
first moves is to put *Playboy* on sale in the gift shop.

On Tuesday, November 21, Charlie Keating is scheduled to appear before the Gonzalez committee. He is a torn man. Just as a
year before he was warning the regulators that if they took over
Lincoln they would lose two or three billion dollars, now he is telling the public that before the savings and loan crisis ends, the cost
will run a good $500 billion, which is well over the commonly
touted figure. Charlie Keating wants to go before the committee
and give them hell. His lawyers want him to keep his mouth shut
and take the Fifth. He is facing all these lawsuits, they warn. His
friend Pat Buchanan, the conservative commentator and bulldog,
tells him to speak out.

Charlie Keating gives thought to his appearance. He rents a

Chevy Caprice—no limo to be commented on by those bastards in the press. He strides into the hearing room surrounded by a squad of lawyers and aides. And then, as if by instinct, he reaches for control. He asks the committee to invoke a House rule that bans television, still cameras, and media microphones. Photographers, madly seeking to beat their banishment, begin clicking. And Charlie Keating wins this tiny victory.

Then he makes his statement: "I have no testimony to give today" and takes the Fifth. It is over in less than thirty minutes, police clear the halls, and Keating emerges. Photographers desperate to get some kind of shot of him shout out, "Hey, shithead!" hoping he will turn toward them. Then Charlie is in his black Chevy Caprice and speeding back to his hotel. The press reports he left in a limo. He is very tired now, and he naps. But he is hardly finished. He dictates some legal notes to his secretary: "Review failures of all government lending programs (also all programs of FSLIC and FHLBB, . . . Wall, Stewart, Dochow, Keating, questions." And there is one more note that floats there without attribution or explanation: "I am not Niagara Falls, I am a drop of water."

Chip Wischer starts the long slide. When Lincoln is seized and ACC goes into Chapter 11, he has this dream of buying his subsidiary, Insurance West, and going into business for himself. But this proves impossible, perhaps because he is tainted by his long association with Keating. No one in government will sanction his purchase. The drinking gets heavier. By Thanksgiving of 1989, he pretty much just stays at Kim's condo and drinks. He stays for days, calling his wife from time to time and telling her he is holed up in a motel down on Van Buren in Phoenix. Judy goes out at night with friends searching for Chip in the various dives that line the street, she never checks for him at the condo Kim has leased from her and Chip.

He tells Kim he is going to leave Judy, he is going to get that divorce, he's got a lawyer, he is going to start his life anew, but at Christmas he goes back to his wife. He spends the entire holiday drunk and hardly even gets out of bed. Around New Year's he shows up at Kim's condo again, and they go to Las Vegas. He calls up his folks back in Kentucky and tells them he is leaving Judy. A few days after they return to Phoenix, Kim gets a call on her car phone while on her way home from work. It is Chip, but he is not in the condo. He says, hi, how are you doing, and by the way I've moved back in with Judy. Kim thinks, why do I keep doing this to myself?

Chip stays with his wife for about a week and Kim keeps calling and calling, but there is no answer except when Judy or the children pick up the phone and they immediately hang up on her. Kim knows Chip is home alone all day, drinking, and she is worried that he will kill himself. He has talked a lot about suicide lately. She had planned to take him to Aspen for his birthday and meet some friends of his from Kentucky. Chip has told her where a house key is hidden, so she goes over, and just as she is about to go in, three guys from ACC show up. A neighbor called Judy and said, someone is trying to get into the house. They find Chip in bed. He is drunk, he has not bathed, he has not brushed his teeth. One of the ACC men says, "Kim, can I talk to you outside?" There he says to her, "Look what you have done. You've destroyed this family, you're destroying this man. You leave now. Kim, you're nothing but a fuck for him."

Kim grabs the man by the collar and says, "Lemme tell you something, don't you ever interfere in my life or Chip's life again." Then she shoves him away. After they leave, Chip says, "Kim, stay." He tells her that Judy has moved out and taken the kids.

They make love, and afterward Kim hears a woman's voice coming up out of the garage and saying, "Where is she? Where is she?" And that is how Judy Wischer finds Kim and Chip in bed.

Judy says, "Get out of my house."

"She's not going anywhere," Chip answers.

"If you'd put as much into this marriage," Judy replies, "as you have into this affair, this would have never happened."

Judy rips a gold brooch off her dress and flips it to Kim, saying, "Here, you can have this."

"Why would I want it?" Kim asks and tosses the brooch on a bedside table.

"I hope you're proud of yourself. I'll pray for your soul, Kim. You're going to be burning in hell. I'll spend many hours praying for you."

As she walks down the stairs, Kim says, "Hey, Judy, I'll pray for your soul, too."

Kim and Chip fly up to Aspen for his birthday celebration.

While they are there, Kim hears Chip on the phone saying, Judy, I love you. He is drinking more and more, and one of his friends from Kentucky, a doctor, tells Chip he must get some help. When they get back to Phoenix, Chip moves into the condo with Kim. One day he calls Kim up at work and tells her he is stopping off on his way home to see a doctor. After that, he explains, he must go by Judy's house because his daughters are having a slumber party and he has to be there. He says he'll call the next day.

But Kim does not hear from Chip the next day and no one answers the phone when she calls. So she goes over and finds his car in the garage, but the place is empty. And she cannot find him anywhere. On this fine Saturday in January 1990, he has simply disappeared.

Charlie Keating hates Stanley Sporkin, the man who will now judge him. Back in 1979, Sporkin ramrodded through the SEC case against Keating. Now, in the spring of 1990, Charlie Keating is in Washington, D.C., to harvest one of his new assets, a lawsuit. He is suing the Office of Thrift Supervision and Danny Wall, contending they had no right to take his bank away and he wants it back. The case will take up the next six months. This is the moment Charlie Keating has been waiting for, a courtroom, a level playing field, and he eagerly takes the stand. (On January 14, on *Meet the Press,* Keating says the "trial is now on and the truth will come out in the courtroom. . . . And the government's just plain wrong, and the accounting documents will prove it.") And he can afford lawyers; the sky is the limit. Chip Wischer, in his dedication to his job as the insurance man for ACC, got Charlie Keating a legal policy that has no cap on civil actions in it.

On the stand Charlie Keating is a friendly, helpful person. He tells Sporkin that he ran a loose shop in some ways, that he can't even remember what his salary was, that he didn't keep that close a watch on all of his businesses or the finances. He presents himself as a big-picture kind of guy. Sporkin listens with interest, and soon it is as if he and Charlie Keating are working together to get to the bottom of this government interference.

"The allegation that is being made here," Sporkin says, "let me see if I can restate it. The allegation that is being made and one that as you can see would be of concern to the board was that really Lincoln was being utilized for the sole purpose—well, as a piggy bank for you and ACC. . . ."

And Charlie Keating jumps right in and says, "With all my heart and soul I want you to know that I categorically—and I understand the consequences of this testimony—deny that. I had no concept related to that."

Keating and his lawyers feel that they are winning, and they think Sporkin—who they have tried to remove from the case—is listening and understanding their side. The energy flows back into Charlie Keating.

Chairman William Seidman of the FDIC is worried that the government is blowing its case. On Good Friday, Manning and his supervising attorney get a call from Seidman. He wants his FDIC legal team to help the bank board try the case. Manning goes to work with his team immediately. Easter weekend with his kids is canceled—they prepare Friday and Saturday and arrive in Washington on Easter Sunday. Monday he is in Seidman's office for a meeting. The head of the FDIC is bristling because he hates to lose. He tells Manning, "The lawyers are getting beaten up. I want the FDIC to fix that. Don't fail on this one." The next day Manning is in court. He is eager for a shot at proving to Judge Sporkin that Keating looted Lincoln. Keating himself seems imperturbable. In fact, that is what has Seidman so upset—every time he goes to a Washington party, people tell him Charlie Keating is winning the case. Manning and his team deliver evidence on insider deals, the shredding of Lincoln's files, the accounting gimmickry in Lincoln's books, and the looting of the thrift. By the time Manning is finished with Keating ACC has had its wake-up call.

One month later, Manning is called back to Washington to help with the conclusion of the trial. This time, though, he has a shot at cross-examining Keating. Manning patiently leads him through a series of transactions, and everything seems to be flowing along smoothly when he zings him with two areas that previously had not been introduced. One is that the night before Lincoln was seized, Keating took ACC and a fistful of its subsidiaries into Chapter 11, essentially making off with the assets while failing to maintain the net worth of Lincoln. Keating notices that Sporkin is surprised and troubled by this evidence. The other is driving home that Keating's high estimate of the Phoenician Hotel's market value was baseless. And briefly, Charlie Keating is uncomfortable. Mike Manning is satisfied, he feels he has disrupted Charlie Keating's momentum with Sporkin and put him on notice, that Manning and his team know how to unravel what he has done.

During a break in the examination, Keating clusters with a group of reporters in the back of the courtroom and he is in fine spirits regaling them with his stories about incompetent federal bureaucrats. Manning does not like watching this—Are they buying this line of malarky? Or are they just playing along with Charlie?—and after Keating finishes with his press feeding, he strolls over and starts talking to the reporters himself. Out of the corner of his eye, he can see Keating staring, and then Charlie starts coming toward him and Manning instantly changes what he is telling the press and suddenly announces, "And since the government seized the Phoenician Hotel, it is being run more efficiently than it ever was under Charlie Keating, and it is making more money than it ever did under Charlie Keating." Manning has figures in his hand to back up his charge. Suddenly Keating is in Manning's face, thumps on his chest with a finger, and says, "You're a goddamn liar, you're a goddamn liar, you're a goddamn liar, you guys will make my hotel a Howard Johnson's." Michael Manning is relieved. He has found a hot button. He has shaken this guy and made him lose his composure in front of reporters he had just charmed five minutes before. And in his gut, he now thinks he can take him out—especially if Sporkin does the right thing. Manning realizes that he enjoys this kind of head butting. One of the FDIC lawyers has recently accused him of being a "stimulation junkie."

While Sporkin is probing the merits of the case against the regulators and listening to weeks of testimony, Keating gives a deposition in another case, one he has filed against Ed Gray and Bill Black for allegedly maliciously leaking private bank documents about Lincoln to the press. Bill Black is there for this moment. He has never seen Charlie Keating, for years he has been fighting a phantom. When Keating walks into the room, Black is struck by his size and bearing—tall, thin, muscular, blue eyed and tough looking. This man is in his late sixties?

Keating sees him in the corner and says, "Black" with some force and revulsion. Black extends his hand but Keating will have none of it and says, "Not me, buddy."

While the attorneys quiz Keating, he keeps his gaze fixed on Black. He boxes playfully with the lawyers—"The Phoenician was the greatest hotel in the world until the government turned it into a Howard Johnson's."

Finally the long session ends, and Keating stands to leave, then looks over at Black and says, "Lots of damage done, Mr. Black. Lots of damage done."

"That's the one thing we can agree on, Mr. Keating."

But Bill Black is a detail in Charlie Keating's world, old business. New business is what matters to him now. He senses he is going to get his bank back, going to beat the federal government. He is on a roll, and he knows that feeling so well. On the final day of the Sporkin hearings, Keating says, "We'll be fighting until the day I'm dead. I have no intention of being raped by the U.S. government."

He takes to the road. He begins giving speeches. The man who once logged 200,000 miles in a single year denouncing pornography from public platforms has found a new form of decay to attack: the regulators, the heavy hand of government that is killing the nation and strangling the ingenuity of the American people. He stays in four-star hotels, eats in the finest restaurants, and never shuts up. He takes on the entire government, hits television—*Face the Nation,* Larry King—holds press conferences. And awaits the decision of Judge Stanley Sporkin.

By May 1990, C3 is thirty-four years old, has declared personal bankruptcy under Chapter 11, has debts of about $2.9 million, and is named in seventeen separate lawsuits. He has not slept with his wife, Krista, for eighteen months. The children, she thinks, should be enough to make him be home more, to be more of a father.

Finally one night, around three in the morning Krista calls Charlie Keating and Mary Elaine and says, your son is not home, something is wrong here. And within minutes Charlie and his wife are over there.

They hardly seem inside the door when C3 arrives. So Charlie asks his son what is going on and his son says he wants a divorce, he is in love with another woman. Mary Elaine starts swinging her large purse at his head, beating it against him again and again and again. Then Charlie drags him out into the hallway and throws him against the wall time after time after time. Krista thinks it will never end. Charlie Keating says, "You can't do this to me! You can't do this to me!"

It all comes tumbling out: the woman he met, the cocktail waitress at the Phoenician.

Rumors of what has happened float through the small world that once was the American Continental Corporation. After Lincoln, some of Charlie Keating's aides thought he was only a tenth the man he had once been, that something vital had been taken from him. But this thing with his son is much more severe. He will be standing with them and suddenly blurt out, "My son! My son! My only son!" and they will not ask what he means because they know—and because they sense it is an area too sensitive for anyone to enter. It seems to some of them that he all but ceases to exist in a business sense. He is concerned with only one thing, saving his son's marriage.

He pens his daughter-in-law a long note after that evening. He insists that the marriage must be saved for religious reasons, for the children. And he tells how, recommends the rosary, reading books together . . . page after page, a new kind of agenda written by Charlie Keating, one aimed at salvation.

There are those cases to prepare for: the SEC, the IRS, the RTC's RICO, the California criminal case. Someday soon the federal criminal case will surely come down on his head. And there are the bondholders' civil suits, so many cases. But Charlie Keating is busy.

The son moves out and lives in an apartment over the garage of a sister and brother-in-law. He paints houses.

Late in the afternoon of Chip's disappearance, Kim impulsively calls the house one more time and Judy answers. She says, "Just so you know, Chip has checked himself into a detox center and it's out of the state. I repeat, out of the state. And Chip told me to tell you that he didn't want anything more to do with you."

Kim thinks for a second and says, "Well, detox is thirty days, and when he gets out he can let me know what is going on."

That evening a man calls and says he must come by the condo and pick up some luggage that Judy needs for a trip back to Washington, D.C. Kim tells him fine, I'll leave it on the porch. Later, she is watching television when she hears a knock at the door, but she does not answer it. The house is very well protected. Chip, insurance expert that he is, has had an alarm system installed and added a series of special locks on the inside of the door that permit it to be opened a few inches yet remain secure. Kim hears a key turn in the lock and then sees a hand reach in with a tiny screwdriver and proceed to unscrew the binding locks. She knows the man and is not sure what to do. She thinks, I'm sitting here watching him do this, what's he planning to do when he gets in here? Do I let him come in and then shoot him? Do I call the cops? Okay, I call the cops and say, yeah, I'm having an affair with her husband and . . . do I get involved in that shit? Naw, I'm going to take care of this myself.

She gets up and goes over and kicks the door shut, crushing his trapped hand. The man is screaming. She brings her gun up and opens the door and says, "Don't you ever come back here again or I'll shoot you." The man leaves.

The next morning Kim calls her mother in Las Vegas and tells her she is coming up. When she arrives the phone rings and Kim picks it up and hears a voice say, "You were smart."

It is getting too crazy, and Kim wonders if she is going to wind up dead.

Ernie Garcia is driving Bowden around Phoenix in his Mercedes in May 1990 when Bowden drops the question on him: Did Charlie Keating deliberately issue bonds that would fail? He answers without hesitation, "Charlie knew these things were no good, but he had an ego big enough that he believed he was going to pull it off."

He remembers so much about Charlie now. And a lot of it is painful. He has pled, he will have to do some time for those deals, those things the government calls sham transactions. He is now one of their official straw buyers. But he thinks back to the gifts—a case of Dom Perignon, countless free certificates for holidays at the Crescent. None of these gifts had any context Ernie can remember now, they just happened—"all the time, it's just out of the blue."

"He had style," Ernie reflects, "charisma, great presence. In hindsight, he knows how to read people. I felt he was brilliant. He was in big deals, he had a high IQ. I liked him, and I thought he liked me."

Ernie is driving, and this opportunity to look straight out the windshield and speak as if to no one, as if alone, this seems to help him talk. He is the cocky business guy who got gulled, and this is not an easy thing for him to remember or admit. "Charlie," he sighs, "was a deal junkie. I know because when I was twenty-nine or thirty, I was a deal junkie. He just wanted to do deals, to be in the game. He was more susceptible to a pitch than anybody. He wanted to be like Milken. Charlie's a bigot. He'd go out of his way to be nice to, say, a gardener, to convince other people he was not a bigot. Then he started talking—he continually referred to blacks as niggers—and he watched to see how you reacted. I didn't react, so he'd play the safe route and tell about a good nigger friend of his. He hated Jews, too. I think that's why he could never make it into the big leagues, because Milken and those guys were Jews. Charlie would try to hide his feelings, but they could sense it and they wouldn't let him in, I think."

Ernie Garcia got a crash course in Charlie Keating, and that experience may never leave him. He thinks back to it again and again. By the summer of 1988, Garcia is over a barrel and he knows he can't pull his company out or meet his note with Charlie. And so does Keating. The inevitable meeting takes place at ACC with Judy Wischer and Charlie and some executives. Charlie puts his offer out—the debt will be forgiven, ACC will swallow what assets Garcia & Co. still has, Ernie will come to ACC for a big job. This is the price of the stock market crash of October 19, 1987. Ernie got caught in the market. Charlie Keating did not.

"I think you're really bright," Charlie says. "You've got to marry cash. We've got cash."

There is one more detail to the deal: Garcia has to can Bill Martin, his partner and best friend. He is to start work the next morning. Ernie says he has to think it over, that he has to talk to his wife—a woman Charlie likes. Keating says, "Call your wife. I've always found if I listen to my wife, I do best." Garcia says, "I'll be in at 6 A.M. to see you."

That night Garcia goes out and drinks with Bill Martin.

At 6 A.M. sharp, Garcia is at Keating's office. Charlie is alone. Garcia tells him no deal. He can see Keating is not prepared for this answer, that he's been positive Ernie will take the deal. And Garcia has seriously thought about it, thought, well, I'll work there for maybe three months, wipe out the debt, build a bankroll, then reunite with Martin and start over. As he speaks to Keating, Garcia can "see the shock in his face." Keating gets up and starts rolling down the blinds, his voice tightens with anger, and then he asks, "Then what are you going to do?" He is rude, cold, and curt, and he continues, "I can't believe you're not taking this. I'm giving you the opportunity of a lifetime." Garcia replies, "What do you want?" Keating says, "Come back at eleven." And then Keating cuts off the meeting, and there is this air of get-out-of-my-office. That morning, about 9 A.M., Bowden happens to call Keating, and when he mentions Ernie, Charlie says in that mellow, avuncular voice of his, "You know, he just left here and he didn't look too good."

At 11 A.M. Garcia's answer is still no. Okay, Keating says, I want everything you've got plus $15 million. Garcia says no to that deal too. What Garcia calls "the dark days" begin now. Judy Wischer and the ACC staff go over his holdings with a fine-tooth comb. They want his house, his car. They leave the fate of his staff up in the air—Will they handle the Garcia properties for ACC? Will they be fired? Garcia can't find out. "They were being cruel. I'd be out driving and get so upset my eyes would tear up and I'd want to beat the shit out of someone. Keating was this father-type mentor I'd liked, and all of a sudden I see all of this cruelty and I was mad at myself for being so goddamn blind." When he places calls to Charlie that summer, they never seem to get through. That fall Ernie and his wife get free tickets to the December 1988 Children's Ball, Keating's big fund-raiser for his campaign against child pornography. Garcia does not respond. Charlie's secretary calls three times and says, "Charlie wants you there." But Garcia puts her off. Finally, he and his wife go to the ball at the newly opened Phoenician. Charlie comes up and breaks into idle chitchat with them as if they had no past. Then suddenly, Keating says, "You know, hell, you never know what's going to happen. I could be broke next week." And later Garcia realizes that Charlie knew at that moment that he was going to be ruined.

"I will have gotten more out of this Keating affair," he says, "than anyone. He loved to do deals—that's me. I wanted to buy a savings and loan to get cash, too. Today I'm different. I want operating cash flow, not borrowing."

Now he's standing in a parking lot with Bowden. They have been talking for hours, drinking beers, eating fajitas. One thing that still bothers Ernie Garcia is that he felt this, well, affection for Charlie Keating, felt this deep attraction. Of course, now he feels anger, perhaps even rage, at Charlie Keating. His life has been derailed because he did deals with this man, and Ernie Garcia is not the kind of person who expected failure in his life or finds it easy to live with. Given this fact, this ruin that has descended upon him, why does he still think about Charlie, and when those moments come, why does he sometimes smile, sometimes have warm memories? Has he missed something, or is there something missing in him? Charlie Keating has put him into courtrooms, has put him under indictment, has dragged him down into the mud. But he still refers to him not as that man Keating, but as Charlie, with its ring of an old friend.

"You know, Ernie," Bowden offers, "the trouble is that you and I have learned a lot from dealing with Charlie but we're never going to meet another guy like him again. We can't use what we know."

"I know, I know," he says calmly.

He starts across the parking lot, then stops, turns back, and shouts, "I lied to you just then. I will meet another Charlie. And when I do, I'll clean him out."

Charlie Keating is going to tell the world, so in early August 1990, he is at the annual meeting of the International Platform Association, the booking forum for the nation's lecture halls. Speaker after speaker addresses the audience of agents at Washington's Mayflower Hotel. Michael Binstein is there. He wants to catch Keating's performance and approach him about an interview. To date, Charlie Keating has not answered his phone calls. Since that piece appeared in *Regardie's* in July 1987, one of Keating's certainties is that Michael Binstein has helped to ruin him and is the enemy. As Binstein walks along a corridor to the ballroom, Charlie Keating strides up with a son-in-law, Carol Kassick, and a hotel employee in tow and he and Binstein all but collide. They each stand there and do a double-take. Keating is as angry as Binstein has ever seen him, he seems to be quivering with rage, and a colleague of Binstein tenses because he thinks Charlie Keating is going to start swinging.

Binstein instinctively offers his hand and says, "How are you, Mr. Keating?"

Keating automatically extends his hand. Then, suddenly, he re-coils and says, "How would you be, you lying bastard, after what you did to me and my family?"

But Binstein presses on—if you just keep talking, eventually they all come around—and asks, "Why won't you talk to me?"

This is more than Charlie Keating can bear. He begins walking toward Binstein, seems to be climbing into his face, and suddenly their noses are almost touching. Charlie Keating answers, "I wouldn't talk to you, you lying bastard, if you were the last person on earth."

The hotel employee guiding Keating around is a woman less than five feet tall who probably weighs about eighty pounds. At first, she thought the two must be old friends, but now she senses trouble in the air and she gets between the two men, grabs Keating by the arm, and begins leading him away to the ballroom where he must give a sample of his proposed public lecture.

As the woman shepherds Keating toward the stage, Binstein stands quietly at the very back of the ballroom. But Charlie Keating spots him and suddenly begins gliding to where his hated enemy—Binstein, that goddamn lying reporter—is watching. He fi-nally comes to rest parallel with his target and then locks his eyes on him, that famous laserlike glare that kept his employees in line for years, and Binstein stands there as Charlie Keating gives him the treatment for five full minutes. He is astounded by his physical reaction. His chest has this deep burning sensation. He has never felt so intimidated in his life.

Then Charlie Keating goes up on the stage and delivers an an-gry, yet entertaining, account of how the federal government has destroyed him and the industry he belongs to and how it will de-stroy the American people next.

On August 22, 1990, Judge Stanley Sporkin announces his decision. He finds the regulators "fully justified" in taking over Lincoln. He describes Charlie Keating's treatment of Lincoln as like that of "an adult taking candy from a helpless child." He also takes a few shots at the accountants and law firms that worked for Keating: "What is difficult to understand is that with all the pro-fessional talent involved, why at least one professional would not have blown the whistle."

Charlie Keating ceases his speeches, his television appearances, his press conferences. He becomes almost a recluse. He is facing a very strange world. The federal government, in its effort to resolve its obligations to federally insured thrifts, has devised some interesting solutions. Buyers—often very rich, like the Bass brothers of Texas—are given incredible terms. The transactions are essentially subsidized much as they were for the buyers Keating found for Lincoln's deals, which now form the core of the many civil suits hanging over Keating's head. In many ways, the government is dumping savings and loans to enhance its books. Also, the government has kept the cost of resolving the savings and loan problems off its ledgers. The hundreds of billions it will cost are not part of the official federal budget, a tactic that would give pause even to the Big Eight accounting firms Charlie Keating once hired.

Within days of the Sporkin decision a letter goes out to family friends under the signature of the Keating children. They explain, "We must try to share with you what our United States government has done to our family. . . . During the 1980s, Congress encouraged successful entrepreneurs to help revitalize the savings and loan industry and bring it out of the dinosaur age. Our families invested all of their resources in this newly restructured industry. . . . An aggressive team of highly qualified employees guided by the management of our father, Charles H. Keating, Jr., nursed Lincoln into health and prosperity. It was an exciting challenge. Long hours, exhaustive travel and excruciating work paid off as he turned investments into profits for our companies and our security holders. . . . Now, we are being inundated with lawsuits. The media relentlessly disseminated only the government's side of the story to the public. In the process, our credibility has been wrongfully destroyed. Our father is constantly attacked from all sides. He is being tried and convicted without being given a full and fair trial where his side of the story can be told and where he can be judged on the evidence, not rumor and innuendo. . . .

"Unfortunately, the legal costs associated with defending ourselves are monumental. We lost all of our money when the government seized our companies. We are writing because we need your help. We desperately need your gifts to help defray our father's legal expenses.

"Please make your check payable to: CHARLES H. KEATING, JR. LEGAL DEFENSE FUND."

A classified ad appears in a Phoenix newspaper saying, "We are now in business to remodel, repair, or custom-build your residential or commercial property," and Charlie Keating is behind it. He sets up his favorite chef in a Scottsdale restaurant—he can see a chain of hundreds, all this within three months, he figures—but no investors come forward and the restaurant closes after a month or so.

On September 19, 1990, Charlie Keating is booked into the Los Angeles County Jail. He has just been indicted by a California grand jury on forty-two counts of criminal fraud in connection with the sale of $200 million worth of ACC junk bonds. Judy Wischer is indicted also, as are two officials from Lincoln. Keating's bond is set at $5 million. He sits in a cell because he cannot make bail. A photo of him in handcuffs and jailhouse clothes is printed in newspapers everywhere. He is sixty-six years old.

On the twenty-first day of Charlie Keating's stay in jail, a letter by his wife appears in the *Los Angeles Times*:

"To think that our court system is allowed to keep an untried, non-threatening man in a 'holding cell' runs counter to everything I always believed in the Constitution and civil liberties in America. . . . Our government has effectively silenced all savings and loan executives by what they have done and are doing to my husband. . . . Los Angeles County Dist. Atty. Ira Reiner said my husband's photo should be hung in every board room in America to warn executives not to be like him. Try to tell me that Charlie is not being used as a weapon of fear? Try to convince me that he is not being treated as a convicted felon?

"Yes, corporate America is scared. Do you blame them? Everyone told us, 'Never fight the government.' My husband, however, still believes he is right. Because of his beliefs, he has earned shackles and chains. He is lied about and mocked in the press and media. . . .

"He spends every day in a tiny concrete cell with an iron door. Except for court appearances, he does not see daylight. He is chained and shackled . . . when he is escorted to the attorney room to meet with his lawyers. He is allowed one visit per day, which consists of talking on a phone through a plexiglass wall while he is chained to a chair and guarded. Life is difficult. We are strong and we are together as a family. We must get him out!"

On the thirty-third day the judge lowers his bail to $300,000 and he is released. His family scrambles to find him clothing—the suit he was wearing when he was booked has been stolen.

It has not been easy for John Boyce since he left Phoenix and his friend Charlie Keating. In the summer of 1990, he spends a few months homeless on the streets of Cincinnati. He has just gotten out of the VA hospital for mental problems, and he cannot seem to cope with things like finding a place to live. He has spent the $30,000 in severance pay Charlie gave him in the late fall of 1988, when he was sent home to Cincinnati and a college program. He thinks back to his days at Estrella selling dirt with Jim Parker, when he had it so good. His salary after taxes was $1,600 a month, he had a lot of vacations, he had bonuses, and he had a friend. He knows he did not really earn his wages, that he never really produced for the company.

He still thinks about Charlie Keating. And he keeps working on his own problems. By the summer of 1992, he feels somewhat better. He is taking 900 milligrams of lithium a day, plus an antidepressant. He still figures the post office owes him $4,200 in back pay, but he cannot get them to settle. Still, he is okay. His disability pay from the government runs to $1,438 a month, almost as much as he made at ACC. He hears things about Charlie from time to time. His brother still lives in Phoenix, and he mails John Boyce each and every news clipping. Eight or nine months earlier, Mary Elaine was back in Cincinnati and popped in on his mother and told her that Charlie had been treated unfairly and that a man such as her husband should never have to go to jail. And John Boyce agrees.

John Boyce thinks he understands what happened to his friend Charlie Keating. He has a hard time explaining his thoughts on this matter to others because they involve many biblical quotations, an understanding of the importance of having a personal relationship with Jesus Christ, an understanding of the errors of the Catholic Church—the Pope, for example, is a fraud. He can clarify little things, like the fact that Charlie was so devoted to the Virgin Mary and the visitations of the Mother of God at Medjugorje because, well, because Charlie Keating had always had such a close relationship with his own mom.

"He's the kind of guy," he says, "who would do anything he felt he had to do to keep his ass going to fight for his life and his family. What was basically an honorable career—hypocrisy and the big salaries aside—when he got down to that one point, when his life was passing before him and he couldn't raise the money, then he did what he had to do. He thought he was getting screwed by the government. He didn't find any support in the community, and he put everything he had, put all his faith in the bonds. Charlie never intended to default on anything. In Catholicism, as in any religion, it says you can do illegal stuff if it's for the good of the church. The Pope has massacred hundreds of thousands of people over the years, Protestants and others, and that's been the whole attitude. I don't have any doubt in my mind that Charlie did what he thought he had to do. He never intended to fuck anyone."

One thing keeps coming back to him: once in a while, when John Boyce was at ACC, Charlie would say, "Stick around for two or three years. I have something really special in mind for you." But he never told John Boyce exactly what that was.

Still, John Boyce is all right. True, he has these problems, these things that rumble about his head and break his quiet. But he can handle that. He has the medication. But Charlie Keating is sitting in a California cell.

"I'm sitting here," John Boyce says. "I'm getting my checks. I'm free."

On March 3, 1991, four Los Angeles police officers pulled over a driver named Rodney G. King at 12:30 A.M. and beat him with their batons for eighty-one seconds. A passerby's video camera taped the incident. On April 29, 1992, a jury found the officers not guilty of all charges except one count of excessive force against one officer.

Then the fires started, more than a thousand fires, and they burned for days. Then the killings started, and continued for days, dozens and dozens of killings. The National Guard moved in. The U.S. Army moved in. The media moved in. The property damage topped a billion dollars. It was almost as though another savings and loan collapsed in Los Angeles.

It is Friday night, the first day of May, and Ted Koppel is broadcasting a *Nightline* program on Los Angeles, on the killings, on the burnings, on the verdict, on the race war, on the riot, on the rebellion, on whatever label anyone wants to give it. This evening's broadcast is entitled "Stop the Madness."

Two black men, a Blood named Bone and a Crip named Little Monster, are standing in an alley—great visuals. Ted Koppel probes their thoughts; he clearly wishes to understand what is happening.

"One of you," Koppel notes, "I don't know which it was, told one of my colleagues that this is sort of like the S and L scandal. Who was that? Was that you?"

And Bone dives in, "Yeah, that's me."

Little Monster adds, "Yo, you know what? Let me say this. I don't know what city official allowed this, but in the midst of this violence that was going on within L.A. they closed eighty-five schools in south central L.A. Where are these kids going? They put these kids right on the street. You got eight-year-old kids in and out of buildings."

"Yeah," Bone says.

"Where's the logic?" Little Monster wants to know.

"You know," Bone continues, "the United States government cost—cost them, what, $500 million to save the S and Ls, how much was that money they—$500 billion to save the S and L scandals? You mean to tell me they can't open up a recreational hall? . . . They rather spend the money on saving Ivan Boesky and the other guy ripped off all those old people and S and L scandals, you know."

"Keating," Little Monster cuts in.

"And people," Bone rolls on. "Look at this, and you got the working-class guy who says, 'Well, shit, they ripping off the S and Ls for five hundred billion dollars, why shouldn't I go get that VCR?' Or 'Why shouldn't I go get that fruit or Coke, you know. I work hard, I deserve it, you know.' . . . You see the—on the tapes, you know. These people don't look like thugs. They're like family. They're going in with their whole families. . . ."

Keating is assigned to a prison cell. It is not a country club. There are no country clubs in the California state prison system. Who knows, maybe he's watching Koppel with some Bloods and Crips? There is so much to do, all those cases coming up where Charlie Keating will have to defend himself against so many versions of reality—bondholder versions, federal criminal versions, racketeering versions, IRS versions, SEC versions, Saudi-European Bank versions.

Charlie Keating is a multipurpose solution now. He can be the bad apple, an aberration in the normal course of the nation's life, and when he is locked up, the problem is solved. Or he can be a verbal shorthand for Bone and Little Monster when they point out the injustice of the rich ripping everyone off and the poor being left with so very little.

In April 1992, *Playboy* runs a feature on Charlie Keating. The article, "Profit Without Honor," is in the same issue with Cady Cantrell, who weighs 118 pounds, stands five feet seven inches tall, is blond (at least her head is), has a waist of twenty-four inches, hips of thirty-six inches, and a bust of thirty-six inches *("Look at those hidden assets!")*. Her role models are Julia Roberts and Barbara Bush, and she wants to thank God, her parents, and that *Playboy* scout who found her and her body. Charlie Keating is portrayed in a painting, fully clothed. He is wearing a pin-striped suit, a green tie, and a white shirt, and two little horns poke out of his forehead. Behind him are the tortured faces of people in some kind of blazing hell. The subhead on the story explains, "Charlie Keating professed to be a beacon of morality in a depraved world. He also flimflammed investors, bribed senators, and rained ruin on every taxpaper."

By the spring of 1992 Charlie Keating is on the face of a deck of playing cards marketed as "The Savings and Loan Scandal." Five senators are puppets on his fingers. Now they are known as "The Keating Five." Charlie himself has become so well known that he pops up as a throwaway reference in a television situation comedy, the line spoken by a child.

Kim stays in Las Vegas through January 1990. She is afraid to return to Phoenix, so she gets a job in accounting. Three weeks after Chip disappears into some unnamed detox center, he calls her. She greets him with "You son of a bitch. Maybe it is over between us if you haven't called me in three weeks." But Chip explains that his telephone privileges have been curtailed at the center and he'd constantly been getting into fights. Besides, there is a two-minute phone call limit and the mail is censored. He calls again and announces, "I'm real confused, but I'm going to call you tomorrow and tell you that it is over because the counselors have told me that's how to get out." And Kim says okay. So the next day he calls and he does say it is over and Kim believes him. But she adds, if you'll move out and leave her, I'll come back to you.

The weekend before Chip is to be released from detox, Kim

drives to Phoenix to get her stuff out of the condo and then returns to Las Vegas. Two days later Chip Wischer is free, dry, and in Phoenix. His wife, Judy, is in Washington testifying at the Sporkin hearing (she will be on the stand four solid days and create over a thousand pages of testimony). Chip goes to the condo and finds it has been stripped. He searches for Kim in a bar she often used as a hangout. When none of her friends there will tell Chip anything, he does what comes naturally to him; he tries to pick a fight. No one will take him up on it and one guy finally says, "Hey, you're fucked up, get out of here." So he goes back to the condo and starts drinking. He keeps calling Las Vegas, but Kim's mother does not tell her about the messages. Kim is not doing real well herself. She also begins to drink heavily. Then she idly calls a friend in Phoenix who tells her that Chip has been looking for her.

She reaches him on his car phone. He is very drunk and rolling around Phoenix and he says we've really got to talk and then she hears a loud sound and the phone goes dead. She calls for days, but no one ever answers—it is March 1990 now. Chip is back drinking heavily. He sits around Judy's house with a bottle and then pitches the furniture out the window. Judy finally calls the police and Chip picks a fight with the largest cop. When he is released, he comes back to the house, tries to break in, and the cops return for him. This time they are prepared and bring along an ambulance and a straitjacket. As they tie him down, he says, "If I can't have Kim, I'm going to commit suicide." At the hospital, they throw him into isolation. They have very little choice. When he is admitted, his blood alcohol level indicates he is medically dead. It takes nine or ten days in isolation to bring him down sufficiently for detox therapy.

Chip scribbles letters to Kim from his new detox center, but she is trying to back away. She is in a seminar on how to deal with hurt, "how to get over it and all this kind of shit and the therapist says to write a letter to the person." So she does, but Chip never gets the letter. Finally she gets Chip on the phone, and he says he is going to move back with Judy after detox and make a go of his marriage.

By June 1990, Kim is still in Las Vegas and Chip is calling, calling, calling. And they talk. He's dry, he's started his own insurance business, and they begin to talk on the phone every day. In August, they arrange to meet on neutral ground—Laughlin, Nevada. Kim has a simple message; "Chip, you leave Judy, fine, come back to me. You let me know when you've got your shit together." A few weeks later, they vacation at little bed-and-breakfast inns in the wine country of the Sonoma Valley. Kim traveled with him when ACC was flourishing (that week in New York, those five days in San Antonio), but this is a new experience. For one thing, Chip was usually drunk in those days. She can remember the times she would literally pin him to the bed until he passed out. But now he is not drinking and they actually talk, and she is learning who he might really be.

Then in October Chip feels a big pain in his stomach, and he goes to the doctor who puts him in the hospital for bleeding ulcers. He is operated on and then lies there for seven days. When he gets out, he files for divorce, rents a house, and invites Kim down to see it—this is going to be our home, he says. Back in April 1989, Kim had gotten divorced. And what with all the lawsuits from the government and the bondholders, it seems someone is always parked across from their new home, watching them and taking photographs of them.

For Chip it is a whole new world—so this is what it looks like when you're sober? For Kim it is Chip. They both carry guns all the time. And then in February 1991 they get a horse and then another and another and another. And then a dog, rabbits, guinea pigs, goats. The house becomes a zoo, the kids are over on the weekends. Kim wants to find a small farm out in the country. They have survived ACC, they think, they have gotten past their days with Charlie Keating. They are new people. And all the money is gone.

In the spring of 1992 Judy Wischer must make a decision. She has stood by Charlie Keating for twenty years, and he has been the center of her life. And now he is in a California prison and a federal criminal trial is coming up in a few months. She has two young children and is possibly facing decades in prison. She does not understand why. She tells her lawyers, just let me talk to the federal prosecutors, let me explain it to them, and they will understand, and her lawyers shake their heads as if they are dealing with an addled child. But she must make a decision. She grants Chip a divorce. She becomes a government witness and begins to talk and talk. She does not really attack Charlie Keating, she does not denounce him, but she supplies one key element in the case.

She says the transactions in those strange deals where buyers got huge loans from Lincoln and then used them to do deals with Lincoln and then the profits were booked, she says those transactions were linked. And this makes the buyers straw buyers, not real buyers, and this makes the deals a felony.

All these actions—the plea bargains, the settlements with creditors, the pink houses, the horses, the divorces and custody agreements—are supposed to settle things and then people can get on with their lives. But it never really seems to work that way in the world of Charlie Keating. In the summer of 1992, an old lawsuit looms—one tied to some of those strange deals connected with the Hotel Pontchartrain in Detroit—and there is no reason to hope there will not be more suits. Chip Wischer starts to feel dizzy. And then his head explodes with migraines. He goes to a doctor, who gives him a checkup and finds he is hemorrhaging massive amounts of blood. His ulcers are bleeding again. So he lies in his room at home, his head pounding, his body wracked by pain, and tries to convince himself that he'll get past this and get on to a new country. He can look at some old framed photos: there he is with Judy and George and Barbara Bush, and goodness, how they are all smiling.

He has this plan, this outline of how he will behave when he gets back on his financial feet. It is very simple: he will try to never make more than $100,000 a year. He thinks this may protect him, because he now believes bad things can happen to him when the money gets too good. He thinks that the big money can make him forget what life is really all about. He's married now to Kim, he's sober, and he's taking care of his kids.

Father Bruce Ritter is accused by a young male of using him for sex, and then other accusations percolate up from the wards he has rescued from the temptations of the street. Other questions are raised about his handling of Covenant House, charges of high salaries and special deals, particularly for relatives. It is suggested that perhaps Father Bruce should seek therapy at one of the church's facilities for troubled priests. But there is another option, one he prefers. Father Bruce accepts an assignment serving the faithful in India.

Carl Lindner has some bumpy moments—he is always so highly leveraged, so unafraid of debt—but he continues to persist with his genius for juggling companies and accounts. He gives extraordinary amounts to the Republican Party; at times he is the largest single donor in the nation. When Charlie Keating sits in his Los Angeles County Jail cell without bail, Carl Lindner does not come to his aid. He has a huge interest in the Circle K Corporation before it slides into Chapter 11. His broadcasting empire is at risk in this age of cable competition. In April 1992, when Charlie Keating is sitting in a California prison, Carl Lindner is having dinner with President George Bush, along with 4,300 other people. James Elliott of Illinois—convicted of bank fraud involving a savings and loan—is supposed to be here, but alas, he couldn't make it. He is shopping for a presidential pardon, and he has sold a wad of tickets (at $1,500 a shot), partly by allegedly coercing eighty-five employees at his Cherry Payment, Inc. He denies the charge, but the resulting lawsuit has detained him. But Michael Kojima is sitting right at the president's table. Nobody is quite sure who he is, but no one really cares since he has kicked in $400,000 for his plate of chow. Later they will discover his office address is a front, his voting address a fantasy, and his business unlisted with the state of California. But this is not alarming. As Marlin Fitzwater, President Bush's spokesman, explains, "It's access to the system, yes. That's what political parties and the political operation are all about."

The dinner, like most, has a kind of menu: a plate of food for $1,500; a table, $20,000; a photo with the president, $92,000. Carl Lindner is not into haggling over the prices. His company has tossed $250,000 for the meal, second only to the mysterious Mr. Kojima. But such costs are not really a problem. Last year Carl Lindner's take-home pay was about $8.6 million, or $23,432 a day. His son Keith, 32, who runs Chiquita Brands for him, received $4 million in salary and bonuses, plus an additional $6.3 million in dividends and variations on stock options. His two other sons made do with about $9 million each. The money all flows from AFC, that strange beast Lindner helped create with Charlie Keating, and in 1991 Lindner cuts its debt load from around $3 billion to about $2 billion, though revenues fall from $7.8 billion to $5.3 billion. He has been holding a kind of fire sale of his assets for the last few years to get out from under his mountain of debt. There have been the normal little frictions of corporate life: in 1988, OSHA fined one of Lindner's many outfits, John

Morrell the meat packer, $4.3 million for violations. This set the national record at the time. Not too much is really known about Carl Lindner's world. Since he took his company private in the early eighties, he does not have to tell anyone much of anything. For example, he does not have to explain to anyone why, when his old friend Charlie Keating could not make bail, he did not kick in the bucks to spring him.

Sir James Goldsmith also continues to thrive. He is a man who somehow manages to keep his balance. He seems able to maintain the deep loyalties of friends and the respect of enemies. When Charlie Keating lost his bank and then his corporation and fortune, Sir James still took his calls. Perhaps this trait of Goldsmith's is best displayed by the feelings of Olivier Todd, who in 1981 edited *L'Express* in France for Sir James. He was fired that year for running an unflattering cover photo of President Valéry Giscard d'Estaing. Yet, five years later, the fired editor said, "If I rang him up from darkest Africa saying I was deathly ill, he'd send a plane for me, I'm sure. My friends say I'm crazy to believe this, but I do."

Like Milken and Keating, Goldsmith seemed to sense the stock collapse of October 19, 1987, and was out of the market when it fell. He attributes some of this to his penchant for gambling, which he says, "is useful because as a gambler you know that luck goes and comes." By 1989, he is back in Britain making a run at a $23 billion corporation. And then he all but drops from sight. He gives up corporate raiding and turns to . . . ecology. In early 1992, his private jet touches down in Hanoi. For an hour and a half, Vietnamese Prime Minister Vo Van Keit closets himself with Sir James Goldsmith, who sees Vietnam as possibly the next miracle economy of Asia.

Larry Flynt has also changed into a man with a low profile. His company continues to prosper. The lawsuits continue but in a kind of halfhearted way as an automatic function of *Hustler*'s monthly feature "Asshole of the Month," which regularly offends some American who does not share Larry Flynt's deep affection for the First Amendment. By all accounts, Flynt is not leveraged like Carl Lindner, nor is he in a prison cell like Charlie Keating. He is the one outsider from Ohio who seems to have avoided many problems. True, he cannot move his legs, he cannot feel from the waist down. That will never change. Also, he was not at President

Bush's fine dinner in April 1992, and thus there is no $92,000 photograph of him with the commander in chief. There has been some serious pain: his wife, Althea, died in 1987, and reports vary as to whether the death resulted from AIDS or a drug overdose or some other cause. But Flynt has managed to persist, and he will always be the man who told this nation's highest judicial tribunal, "Fuck this court."

The five senators finally face the Senate Ethics Committee. They must answer to a Senate driven by PAC contributions, by bundling—a practice that protects senators from money and influence about as successfully as Puritan bundling protected hot loins from each other—and they are duly judged. John Glenn and John McCain are found not to have violated the standards of the U.S. Senate—they are in essence exonerated and the case against them is tossed out. Don Riegle and Dennis DeConcini, while no action is taken against them, seem to land in some kind of ethical gray area in the testimony. Alan Cranston, who is getting up on eighty and has announced he will not run again, is judged to have let down the world's greatest deliberative body and is chastised. The senators return much of the money given by Keating, now that they are aware of just who and what they are dealing with.

In August 1992, things look for Ed Gray much as they did in the dark summer of 1987. Just three months earlier, he finally paid off his $140,000 line of credit from a bank in Washington, D.C. The huge personal debt had been created when he was the FHLBB chairman and trying to sustain his wife and his two daughters in college. In one sense he is closing off the Keating years by getting out of debt. He now works in Miami as CEO for the Chase Federal Bank (actually a savings and loan, but a few years before it changed its name to escape the stigma associated with being a thrift). He took the job quite naturally in September 1987 because no other financial institution in the United States would touch him. In fact, the owner of Chase was the only savings and loan man out of 3,200 who would even give Ed Gray an interview. Ed Gray tried to chase down every rumor of a job, but whenever he got so much as a nibble, word would swiftly come back that he was, well, too hot to handle.

At the Chase Bank, Ed Gray is paid $200,000 a year, but in many ways he has managed to recreate the miserable style of living he enjoyed at the Federal Home Loan Bank Board. For family reasons, his wife must remain in California, and that naturally raises his expenses. Also, paying off that $140,000 loan for the past five years has slashed into his income. So he is living in Florida in a small apartment, much like the cell he inhabited in Washington. And the bank has not been fun for him. He has come to an institution whose portfolio is stuffed with bad commercial real estate loans, nonperforming assets *("It eats, but it don't shit"),* and Ed Gray, the regulators' regulator, feels that commercial real estate loans are poison for savings and loans because they are too risky. This is not a unique point of view; the nation's streets are lined with empty office buildings. So for five years he has tried to steer the thrift to a safe harbor, and all this while the bank has failed to meet its net worth requirement and has been under intense scrutiny . . . from the federal regulators. He has lived with the constant fear that the government will take over his bank. He imagines the headlines about the man who couldn't practice what he preaches. His efforts to solve this problem have slowly but surely caused his estrangement from the bank's owner, and after a while Ed Gray began to slip into the black depression that hung over him like a cloud in 1986 and 1987. By the summer of 1991, he hit a real low being pounded into oblivion by Charlie Keating.

Still, he does not doubt that what he did then was right. There have been some quiet satisfactions. Don Regan, who tormented him as White House chief of staff, went down in ruins when he crossed Nancy Reagan (and possibly meddled with the mojo of her main advisor, a San Francisco astrologer). Jim Wright, the Speaker of the House, was forced to resign over questionable personal financial matters. The five senators have become a pop group called the Keating Five, and the surviving four now jockey to salvage their reputations and hang onto their seats. Danny Wall, who snubbed Gray at his swearing-in ceremony as chairman of the bank board, perished in the aftermath of the thrift industry's collapse. Freddy St. Germain is gone. George Bush gets testy when asked about one of his sons' business prowess in serving on the board of a busted savings and loan. The son is barred from the thrift industry for life. The people who mocked Gray have fallen, and this feels good and seems fitting.

And Ed Gray believes that what he is now doing is right—and he means right in some fundamental sense. As for Chase, he says, "I changed the mentality of this S and L. The problem with the institution was that inordinate risks were taken on too little net worth. We didn't have net worth to withstand bad loans. The thrift charter is great; the question is how you are going run the business."

As for reregulation, he still says, "I think I have been vindicated after being accused of being a dinosaur because those institutions that followed my creed are still there. In the year 2000, they will still be there."

Sometimes he thinks back to Charlie Keating and dark thoughts come into his mind: "When I think about Charlie Keating, I think about Lee Henkel. I think about some of the other folks who helped Charlie Keating. I'm thinking of people who are intimately involved in defeating the regulators—the accountants, the lawyers, the lobbyists. I don't think a lot of those people have gotten their just deserts. Many have gotten off very lightly. I don't find many of them in prison. The Lee Henkel story just curdles one's blood. It says so much about what was bad and corrupt about that time. It was well known when he was put on the board that he was Charlie's buddy. If I had left, he would have been at least the acting chairman."

In the summer of 1992, Ed Gray is waiting to find out if a buyer will take over his bank. This purchase, to his relief, will be, in the jargon of the regulatory world, "an unassisted buy" involving no government bail-out money. But this does not change the fact that the bank must be sold or it will fail because the Chase Federal Bank of Miami desperately needs a new infusion of capital. And if it sells, Ed Gray will be out of work by October 1. He has no money, no reserves, no savings. He plans to look for a job—maybe something back in California. Because Ed Gray must find work.

He has become in the eyes of some an elder statesman, a survivor of an entity now called the eighties. Haynes Johnson of *The Washington Post* is working on a book about what went wrong during those years, and he comes to interview Ed Gray as a man who might know. He asks, have we learned anything? Will we be wise enough to make sure this does not happen again? And Ed Gray says, no, no, no. There is a softness in his voice, a weariness as he makes this pronouncement.

Still, there is one thing Ed Gray looks forward to doing. In September 1992, Bill Black is going to leave government service and the world of the regulators, and Ed Gray has a present for him. For years he has carried that official bank board portrait of Lee Henkel with him. Come September, he will give it to Bill Black.

Mark Sauter, at one time Keating's legal expert on banking regulations, is now facing a different career. After the fall of Lincoln and the filing of suits, he is one of the first ex-ACC executives to become a cooperating witness. And he has much to tell of how Charlie Keating and his employees prepared for those awkward federal examinations and how they plotted to keep the regulators at bay and off balance. But even today, he cannot completely disguise his contempt for the government employees who swarmed over Lincoln's books—how they dressed poorly, lacked keen minds and first-class educations, looked like nerds. He almost grimaces at the memory.

Sauter's tales of Lincoln sit well with the government attorneys, and his future does not look too dim. He tells Manning and his colleagues that by late 1985 ACC and Lincoln were corporate cesspools, and this image of slime and corruption is surely enough to gladden the heart of any lawyer preparing to face a jury. But eventually it is discovered that Sauter embezzled over a million from Keating's company. Now he is most likely facing some prison time for this theft.

But the most striking thing about Sauter and other insiders whom Manning is now preparing for trial is that while they can admit to things that are crimes, they find it difficult to admit to being a criminal. Sometimes it even goes beyond that: they seem unable to recognize that their acts were anything more than "technical felonies." In September 1992, Manning is working with one of Charlie's former minions. During the interview, the executive retreats back into a comfortable cocoon where he is able to claim that incompetent regulators forced them into "technical noncompliance." From Manning's sixteenth-floor office, one can gaze out across Phoenix toward Keating's old headquarters on Camelback Road, and finally Manning loses his calm, points out the window, and says, "There is a two-and-a-half-billion-dollar black hole over there on Camelback Road. That didn't just happen because people at ACC forgot to dot *i*'s and cross *t*'s. That happened because of these deals—these frauds."

But the memory stays with Manning, and it bothers him. It

seems no matter how hard he works or how much evidence he compiles or how many confessions he hears, he moves far too slowly toward his goal. To get the Mark Sauters of the world to face that black hole. To get anyone to face that black hole. To have a general recognition that some things are plain wrong. Not just illegal, though that would be plenty. But wrong.

It is the twenty-fifth day of April in the year of Our Lord nineteen hundred and ninety-two, and the Mother of God speaks in the war-torn area of Medjugorje: "Dear children! Today I invite you to prayer. Only by prayer and fasting can war be stopped. Therefore, my dear little children, pray and by your life give witness that you are mine and that you belong to me, because Satan wishes in these turbulent days to seduce as many souls as possible. . . . I am with you, and your suffering is mine. . . ."

Charlie Keating can't come into Tomaso's restaurant in Phoenix anymore. He is sitting in a cell in California doing ten years. But it is still in a sense his place, the venue where he knew the name of every busboy and waiter and they all knew him. Mike Manning comes here to dine and—in a way that's hard to explain to anyone who is not similarly obsessed—commune. He has now spent almost four years studying Charlie Keating. He and his associates have built what is almost the primal case in their RICO complaint, and all the civil and criminal litigation against Keating and others at ACC seems to flow in good part from their research. In many ways, this fact has come into being because of a set of odd circumstances. After spending five years exposing Mario Renda, Manning is uniquely schooled in the techniques of modern bank fraud and how those complicated cases are won. Without the lessons Manning learned in the Renda case, whatever transpired at Lincoln and ACC could have remained hidden in the millions of documents. One of the other factors that has been to Manning's advantage is that as a fee attorney, a hired gun for the government, he can afford the staff necessary to plow through the mind-numbing details of financial transactions and build a case. Federal criminal attorneys often lack the resources to pursue such matters— a lesson Manning learned in the summer of 1984, when the U.S. Attorney in Kansas City passed on the Renda case. And so he and his associates have become a kind of warehouse of information, the guides through the wilderness of files, depositions, transactions.

Now all this is slowly coming to an end as the settlements come in, as the trial dates finally arrive and the convictions begin. But as Manning savors his Italian dinner in Tomaso's, there is still one little bit of unfinished business: understanding Charlie Keating himself. Manning is struck by how people can't seem to come to terms with Keating, how they persist in seeing him as simply greedy or as simply a crook. How they can't fathom his deeper drives. Mike Manning sees Charlie Keating as not that different from himself or many other people. So, as he works his way through the soup and pasta courses, he tries to explain what he sees.

"Charlie's motivation wasn't money. It was power and acceptance. He was earning his way into a club that he coveted—the Boesky, Milken, Lindner club—with Lincoln and what he was doing out here was his ticket into that club. One of the things that bothered him most was that he didn't occupy a position that others occupied at the Predator's Ball. Drove him crazy. At one Predator's Ball, the names of all of Milken's biggest clients and best contacts were printed on a plastic bag that people carried material in. Charlie was crestfallen that ACC's name wasn't on that bag. Charlie's quest for money really . . . it gave him a name in the streets, it made him stronger, more manly, and more powerful. Money, for money's sake, was not what pushed this guy. It was power and the seduction and control of people and events.

"If you look at how ACC was structured and how it was run and the kind of things Charlie liked to be involved in, it's almost as if he wanted to be an elected official or president of the United States. His jet, his entourage. He bought himself that kind of playground. Power to control people's lives, to be recognized nationwide as somebody who created markets, who created something out of nothing. One of the things that is very interesting about Charlie is Estrella. Charlie knew that that place under any population-absorption table that anybody would have done here in Phoenix was not going to be absorbed into the residential real estate community for thirty or forty years. But he was so sure of himself, so sure that he could create a market for homes where no one else could create it. He could create something special that couldn't be found in the charts and studies that made prisoners of the mediocre; couldn't be found or even dreamed of by most people. He could create something where nobody else could create it. That is why Charlie is unique and not so easily understood as those motivated by simple greed for money."

And here Manning pauses, as if he has almost misspoken. Manning a Keating apologist? Well, yes, in one sense. Charlie Keating believed in his deals. In his Estrella, his hotels, in his relationship with Sir James Goldsmith. He's a kind of dreamer, and he dreams big dreams. But Manning believes he abused his public trust and is also a criminal. Mike Manning is convinced he can prove it and prove also that this criminal activity involves bank fraud.

"There were usually two levels to his fraud. One level is the level of misrepresentation and fraud he employed to acquire an asset in pursuit of his dream of creating markets where other people couldn't create them. But then there's another level, which is triggered whenever that dream seems likely to fail. And Charlie can't afford the embarrassment of failure. It is that second level of a fraud when he sees the dream threatened or collapsing and he tries to buy his way out of it through a whole second series of compounding frauds. Even when I sit down and talk with friends or colleagues about this, they think of this guy as an evil wrongdoer from Jump Street, and he's not really. Bondholders? It's not that he would have done it honestly, but he would have found a way to pay them off. He would have done it with another con, he would have repaid them with someone else's money, but he'd have repaid them.

"What he always thought he could do is buy himself out of trouble with another deal. He wanted power and acceptance badly, it wasn't just the money. Charlie wasn't stingy."

And Manning stops again in his explication of Charlie Keating. It is now getting on midnight, the restaurant has closed, but the staff has not come near the table, not interrupted the flow of his words. The waiters are all standing by the bar, watching silently. The food was consumed hours ago. The cups of espresso are drained. The kitchen is closed. Michael Manning puts a capstone on his years of stalking Charlie Keating. "If tomorrow Keating is over, I'm going to be hungry for that next rush."

He pauses and says almost wistfully, "An amazing guy."

*   *   *

It is hard to say how Charlie Keating is doing. He is sixty-nine years old in December, but he does not look it. Everyone keeps trying to make him think he is old, to insist he is somehow failing, losing it. But it is not true. When he was booked into the California prison system, the photo identification card—complete with a haunting face in cheap color, a face that does not seem to understand what is happening—lists his height at six feet five inches, his age at sixty-eight, and his weight at 190 pounds. Still the athlete's body. He works in the mess hall as a busboy, getting items and cleaning up afterwards. When son-in-law Brad Boland is asked if his father-in-law has managed to fit in, he answers, "No way, he'll never fit in there, he'll never belong."

His friend Michael Milken is in a federal prison in northern California. Originally, he was serving ten years—when the sentence sank in on that day in November 1990, Milken collapsed as he and his wife shrieked like tortured animals. From time to time he appears in courtrooms to testify against his colleagues—part of his plea bargain—and this results in his sentence being reduced and by early 1993 he was in a halfway house awaiting his release. Whenever he appears in court, he's not allowed to wear a toupee—it is against prison regulations—and his appearance is always remarked upon. Since cameras are barred from the courtroom, sketch artists are dispatched to capture his portrait. These drawings are reproduced endlessly so that the American people can see him without . . . his disguise. He looks remarkably like any other bald-headed man. But he can never be simply that because he is Michael Milken.

Charlie Keating keeps up on things. He mails agendas to his family now, instead of dropping them on their desks. His secretary, Carol Kassick, still helps him. He's paying her $3,000 a month, plus $6,000 to cover expenses. There is a great deal he must do. He is preparing for those cases where he faces centuries of prison time and billions of dollars in fines. He wants to go to court now. There seems to be money. No one is quite sure where it comes from. And yet at times there does not seem to be money—twice before trial he had to sit in jail because he could not make bail.

But it is hard to break his spirit. After he failed to make bail on the federal criminal charges in December 1991, he was riding in a paddy wagon with his son, C3, and Judy Wischer and some other prisoners when he started talking to one con and suddenly he yelled to Judy at the front of the van, "Hey, Wischer, see this guy next to me? He is a bank robber and he is a gentleman bank robber." And then Charlie turned to the guy and asked, "How long did it take you to rob eight banks?" And the con answered, "Two minutes flat." Charlie yelled again to Judy and asks, "Hey, Wischer, how long did it take us to rob a bank?" And Judy Wischer knew it was a joke but, God, she thought, this is a scary joke.

His estate in Cat Cay somehow wound up in the hands of his friend Manuel Diaz. He no longer has his house in Phoenix— private creditors finally penetrated his defenses and seized the compound in August 1992. But the family had known of this threat and moved out months in advance. The federal prosecutors think they know where he has money, but it is unlikely they will ever get their hands on it. Their theory goes something like this: those deals in the last few months before Lincoln was seized were sham deals, efforts to park money. For example, they think Charlie Keating did not really lose $11 million playing the currency markets in January 1989, they believe those losses were fabricated and the money was parked. They have similar suspicions about some of his investments in the Cayman Islands, in those strange funds with odd names. One thing seems to happen from time to time. People will loan Charlie Keating's family pretty big chunks of money. And this money, being a loan, is of course not taxable as income. At first the authorities thought maybe he had parked $25 million—not billions, no, the billions were really spent on hotels, land, subdivisions, bonds that went south, and the like because how could a player stash it rather than put it into play where a guy can make a big killing? But now they whisper it may only be $12 million. Whatever it is, it is probably beyond reach, and the loans his family receives, those are, as noted, quite naturally not taxable. The government has Charlie Keating in jail, but the man has six children, a wife, twenty-two grandchildren, and he may still from time to time think of the federal government and say to himself, fuck 'em.

Of course, he has many other things to think about. He was tried in California courts in the summer and fall of 1991 for criminal fraud against the bondholders, and he looked very good.

There were nuisances, aged bondholders who attended the trial each day and stared holes into his back. One out-of-work entertainer walloped him with a powder puff to get some ink. Turned out he was not even a bondholder, just a guy down on his uppers who could use a fresh clip for his career. Charlie never talked to the press then, his lawyers had him muzzled. But when Senator John McCain testified against him, Keating looked so relaxed—the ease of his body language was so smooth and beautiful—and the senator looked so very uncomfortable. Charlie Keating never stopped staring at him. And then his lawyer felt they had the case in the bag—the prosecutors could never link Charlie with any false presentation of the bonds to customers, in fact, they seemed to turn up memos where he warned his salesmen never to do such a thing—and so he rested without presenting a defense. Turns out it was a big mistake. A poll of the jury taken later showed that a majority was for acquittal until that moment. But they were offended that no defense was presented and came back with a conviction. But then, arrogance has been a kind of Achilles' heel for Charlie.

Then in December the federal criminal charges finally came down—seventy-three counts—and Keating once again could not make bail and went to jail for a few weeks. But he went with style. Neil Bush, the president's son, had been on the board of directors of a Colorado savings and loan, Silverado. When the thrift went down with a billion dollars' worth of losses, well, nothing too bad happened to Neil Bush, even though he'd had a bunch of sweetheart deals with a guy who was borrowing millions of dollars from the bank. So when Charlie went to jail again, he said, there but by the grace of political clout goes Neil Bush. He shared a cell with his son, and almost immediately thirty-five FBI agents hit his Phoenix home with two choppers with searchlights circling overhead—they feared his wife and kids would make off with some, well, loot. All of this takes its toll. One four-year-old granddaughter pitches a coin into a fountain and wishes her grandfather could come home. An eight-year-old grandson comes home from school with a bunch of artwork and compositions all loaded with clues to his fear of being under surveillance.

Finally, in April 1992, the judge got around to sentencing Charlie on the California case and Keating showed up in court with his wife, kids, and grandkids. The judge threw the book at him, ten years, five before the possibility of parole. And Charlie took it on the chin, told his family to be calm, said he'd be all right, and handed over his watch and cuff links to them. He sure as hell wasn't going to be ripped off by jailhouse trusties again. And then he went out the door and into the paddy wagon—big photo of him in the newspapers smiling from the backseat, hands shackled. It seemed strange. Why would a guy who has money allegedly stashed overseas and connections with big guys in the Middle East and Europe, an old guy who isn't getting any younger, why would a guy like that show up for sentencing when it was certain they were going to send him to prison? But people around him always said, nobody understands Charlie Keating. Because he is not simple. Or he is so elemental the rest of us cannot hope to fathom him.

While he was sitting in his cell in California, another civil suit against him by the bondholders went to the jury. On July 11, 1992, the jury came back and fined Charlie Keating $3 billion (later reduced by the judge). They said they wanted to "send a message." In this same case, the insurance companies that backed some of Keating's accounting firms and law firms took heavy damage, with fines reaching up around $200 million. The law firms and Big Eight accounting firms have now become a key to the problem—they were derelict, it is believed, so a few good busts on the chops will shape up those professions in the future. Problem solved. Then a strange federal court case came down in August. It seems when the government rewrote the rule book in the summer of 1989 and created the Resolution Trust Corporation, it also changed the accounting procedures for the thrifts and made them drop things that had previously been legal, things that had helped their books, especially helped them meet net worth requirements. One thrift sued and said it had been illegally deprived of property, and the federal judge agreed. Now there are forty similar suits pending, and they all look remarkably like what Charlie was saying when Ed Gray reregulated and suddenly put Lincoln into violation.

By the summer of 1992, the Resolution Trust Corporation, having taken over the assets of the Charlie Keatings of the nation, now faces some of the same problems. It can't keep track of the property it has seized from failed or felonious thrift operators. It has spent $100 million on a computer system designed for this task, but the system is a bust. But the RTC announces that this is not a problem: "Instead of having a fully operational Cadillac, we can get the job done with a Chevette," spokesman Steve Katsanos says. But the current system does have a few kinks—a modest house in Phoenix appraised at $73,000 is on the RTC books at $79 million, a markup that would impress even Charlie Keating. Of 1,660 properties that have sold for $500,000 or more, 552 lack any appraised value or even a list price. The RTC also seems to be indulging in what some folks might call dumping, basically peddling stuff for just about anything to get those numbers right for their reports, a practice that has a touching similarity to the frenzy at ACC at the end of each quarter when the staff had to make the books look good. Some property is going for fifty cents on the dollar in order to make a quick sale. But the RTC people say they have little choice in this matter since they have a quota, as it were, of peddling $100 billion worth of repossessed property by September 30, 1992. And rumors float around the carcass of Lincoln Savings and Loan. The whispers suggest that since the regulators took it over, its total loss under their care has risen from $2.6 billion to maybe $3.2 billion. In the summer of 1992, another odd echo of the end of Lincoln Savings and Loan arises. The federal government is poised to take over Homefed Bank in San Diego but hesitates because of a small problem. If seized immediately, the bank could cost the federal government $4.5 billion to make it whole, but if left to bumble along and work out its problems, the government figures the loss will only run about $2 billion. So the doors stay open. All this sounds a lot like Charlie Keating, in the fall of 1988, warning the government auditors that if Lincoln is seized it will cost $2 or $3 billion to cover the losses but if he is allowed to work out the bank's problems everyone will be better off.

A lot of other things have turned out differently. The Kuwaitis finally bought all of the Phoenician and now have about $300 million in it, just about what it cost Charlie Keating to build it. The place is never empty, occupancy rides well over 70 percent. American Express featured it in its *Travel and Leisure* supplement, where it was rated number two among the top twenty mainland U.S. resorts.

Charlie Keating is not made to dwell on the past, to brood.

That's not his way. Besides, it would do no good. He may never get out of jail. He's old. And he's a symbol now, not a person. *("I am not Niagara Falls, I am a drop of water.")* By November 1992, he'd shed maybe twenty-five pounds off the 190 pounds of muscle he carried at his sentencing in April 1992. And what's crazy is that no one is exactly sure why he has lost all this weight. Is it stress from being in a cell? Or is it, as some prosecutors think, an effort on his part to look frail and elicit sympathy from judges and juries?

He is in a way what he always wanted to be: somebody. He's leaping forward, there is a slap as his body slams into the water, then lap after lap, going for the gold. You can become addicted to the applause. And he has his faith, his God. They can't ever take that away from him.

("The Mother of God is appearing at Medjugorje.")

As for the rest, he'll see them in court. Any court. A level playing field where regulators can't make up the rules. Listen, you're going to be surprised, wait until you hear it in court. Don't go by the newspapers.

("He always said, I'm not going to grovel for those regulators. People would come in and tell him to grovel, that he had to deal with these guys. Charlie won't, he won't do it for anybody. There was a side of him where he could be so charming but with people in power, regulators, he'd just say, fuck 'em.")

Because first, last, and always, Charlie Keating is a player. Hand over those bones, here's ten grand on the hard way, the clean green of the crap table, throw them.

("There isn't any point in not being a player—you're here.")

The verdicts can't change that fact. The press *("Hey, shithead!")* with its accounts can't touch that fact. The politicians *("I don't need to sit here and hear you preach to me")*, the judges, none of them can get near this fact. It is a thing, a sensation, a feeling—like a Hellcat roaring through the night over the ocean, the music washing against you softly—that most people never know, never know at all. Because they won't reach for it, won't take a chance *("A lot of business is luck, not skill")*.

He once tried to explain how he felt about life: "What I wanted when I was growing up? As I look back, I've enjoyed everything I've ever done. Even the crises. I never had a game plan for tomorrow. I never thought I ought to be this or that. I was a lawyer because my father wanted me to be a lawyer. I was a navy pilot because I thought that was great. I was a swimmer because people clapped when you won. I have thought about that often. I've really enjoyed it. Now, if you sat me down and said, what would you rather be doing, I could think of alternatives. People are lucky to be born."

EPILOGUE

CODE
BLUE

Charlie Keating built things, and, at some level that haunts anyone who looks over his records, he thought his schemes would work. He did not simply rob a bank. He broke a bank with his dreams. If he is simply a thief, why did he put the money into deals and projects instead of into his own pocket? If he is just a hardworking businessman simply trying to make a profit and create jobs, why the need for jets, fancy meals, big paychecks to his family? If he is such a devout communicant of his faith, why did he peddle hundreds of millions of dollars' worth of junk bonds to old people when he knew his empire was in serious jeopardy?

Is Charlie Keating guilty? Verdicts are not difficult to reach once the charges have been framed. Given a set of legal charges, the evidence plays out and the judgments come in. And such answers are the normal and proper result of the court system. But you cannot grasp Charlie Keating's real guilt or lack of guilt unless you entertain the notion of his innocence. Only when you imagine he believed in what he did can you understand what was wrong or right with his actions. And to decide what is *wrong* or *right* about Charlie Keating's world is to decide fundamentally who *you* really are.

Then you are still left with one more matter.

Who is Charlie Keating?

Two letters he wrote help illustrate the ideas Charlie Keating professed. On May 14, 1986, he wrote the San Francisco office of the Federal Home Loan Bank Board, the regulators, a long letter. Normally, his staff would intercept these effusions and rewrite them. In short, tone them down. But this letter is untouched by calmer hands and is almost an endless roar of rage. In its own way, it is remarkably candid. Imagine, for a moment, sending such a letter to an IRS agent who is demanding an audit of your income records. If there is to be a defense (although defense is hardly a word in his vocabulary) of Charlie Keating, it seems only fair that it be in his own words.

Since you refer to me in your letter of May 8, 1986, I will reply to same.

Your letter is yet another wave in a constant stream of harassment which underscores a regulator gone beserk.

From I.B.M. and General Motors to the least of your brethern and from the bulk of corporate America, the Hi Yield Bond [junk bond] to which you refer with disdain, is a common instrument of finance and, for the most part, profit. Every major investment handler in the United States verifies that statement by originating and/or market-ing some. Without Hi Yield Bonds, corporate America could not ex-ist, the economy would be in a shambles and only monopolies of the most prestigious and largest companies could obtain financing.

However, to argue the case with you ad nauseam as with virtually all other areas of your intrusion into our operations, as that of all others whom you regulate and harass and persecute, is fruitless. Accordingly, should you find a buyer for our well-managed and profitable association (by any standards) we will sell before you bankrupt us, as you have done to so many, and will continue to do by your blind pursuit of regulation for its own sake. Never have so many taxpayers and institutions suffered so much from so few.

First of all, your comment that we represented Lincoln would "extricate itself from speculative investments in junk bonds in the future" is untrue. We did not. Neither are the bonds speculative nor junk.

Over and above that, the investments are in complete conformity with all laws, all regulations and are prudent and profitable.

Next, your letter dated May 8 gives us only until May 23 to re-spond. With the constant stream of new regulations from the FHLB (provide "The Regulation a Week FHLB") and the need to comment and adjust to some; the requirements of time and money to cope with the maze of prior regulations; the attention of our top person-nel required by your current examination, now complicated at its conclusion by the late arrival of your overloaded appraiser on the scene; your stream of invectives and accusations and demands for volumes of information, 90% of which is useless; your misrepresentation of regulation and law; in a word, your continuous harassment makes the May 23 deadline ludicrous.

Beyond that, we *won't* [accept?] your authority to impose upon us the unusual requirements of your letter and in this regard our outside counsel will promptly be in touch with you. We consider your actions and those of various individuals at the FHLB in Washington to be without precedent or authority in the history of U.S. regulatory bodies. As such, we expect to hold you corporately and personally responsible in law.

Lincoln is extremely and conscientiously well run and profitable. When you find a buyer for us or when we do, as a result of your forcing us to do so or perish, we anticipate a loss in value which can only be laid at your doorstep. However, better a loss than joining all the other associations [thrifts] forced into bankruptcy by your harassment and blindness.

We bought a Savings and Loan in February 1984, well before the regulatory genie was let out of the bottle. We took what was a sure-to-fail S&L and made it profitable. Extremely so. This was done in complete conformance with all applicable laws and regulations. This has continued, in spite of your constant changing of the rules and regulations in complete opposition to the avowed doctrine and philosophy of the President of the United States.

We can no longer cope with you. We will get out. If you let us sell in an orderly manner, perhaps we can find a corporate giant who can pay the proper price and who will fit the mold of your driving the Savings and Loan business into the hands of a few giant corporations to the detriment of all American citizens. You are creating a cartel in the Savings and Loan business, right under the nose of the President who, heart and soul, eschews same. It is a tragic example of Regulators gone haywire.

We have several thoughts on how to sell Lincoln and, since your tactics make you a partner in everything we do (which is illegal and not your mandate), perhaps we should sit down with whoever has some final authority and try to find a way to get this done as painlessly as possible.

Meanwhile, give us another 30 days and we will, as usual, reply to your inappropriate and unwarranted demands of May 8, 1986.

If you will review our prior responses, written, verbal and in person, you will find we have always been courteous, prompt and specific. However, there is a limit. We have reached it. Your constant intervention, harassment, and vicious accusatory language have taken all heart and hope out of us. We have operated a clean, profitable S&L. There is little more we can do. Nothing satisfies. You continue to burn the house to roast the pig. Our forbearance is at an end. Contact by counsel, as I have said, will follow at once.

There is a temptation to see many of Charlie Keating's actions as deceptions, tricks to mask darker and more hidden motives. To see his whole life as a kind of business deal with a trail of documents obscuring what is really going on and his human relationships the equivalents of shell corporations. There is another letter written in his own hand that provides clues to who Charlie Keating is. It is written to his daughter-in-law, Krista, in the spring of 1990 when he is faced with the possible collapse of his son's marriage. His bank is gone, his fortune is largely gone, his planes are gone, his reputation is dying, and soon his corporation will be gone. He is facing an avalanche of lawsuits, and within months he will be in jail. But this letter is a document about other matters. He offers his thoughts as to how she and her husband can save their marriage. Is it the work of a hypocrite? A manipulator? A crook? An economic pornographer? A con man? A fool? A father? A devout Christian?

Or is it nothing more, nor less, than what it purports to be?

> If I were you.
> I'd write a list of ideas for a happy ever after preceeded by reasons to achieve same. e.g.
>
> Dear Krista,
> I return home with love for you and your children. . . . As you suggested I wrote a few notes, reasons and ideas. I hope they help. I come with love. . . .
>
> 1. We took a vow for better or worse: in good times and bad: in sickness and in health: till death we part.
> 2. Our Catholic faith which we consider the will of God expressed through his Church does not permit Divorce.
> 3. We are both good moral people. We have excellent children. Common sense does not permit Divorce.
> 4. We need each other. Our children need us. We love each other.
>
> Ideas
>
> 1. Forget the bad.
> 2. Family Rosary every day. Never miss.

3. Family dinner at home no later than 6 p.m. at least 4 nights a week.

4. Frequent guests at our house—our age and generally those with whom we work and do business. Small dinner parties and fun and conversation.

5. Sports and outdoors for entertainment. No T.V. No movies. No concerts. Reading of good books, Fiction and non.

6. Exercise together with kids. CIII a very disciplined individual program. Very heavy.

7. Individual religious reading ½ hour per day.

8. Families. Problem area. Need frank discussion without arguments to achieve a solution. Serious misconception re CIII family. Must ferret out reality, admit it and deal with it.

9. Husband head of house. Wife is heart. Absolute basis of successful marriage. True to nature. Read St. Paul on the subject.

10. Job responsibility must be met. Too late to walk away. Bankruptcy possible. Need each other. Gonna be tough.

11. No shrinks, no outside, us and kids.

12. Quiet time. Peace. Sacrifice.

13. Make love. Not war. CIII Life for Krista. Krista life for CIII. Turn this into one of the world's great loves.

SO SOMEDAY

Believe me if all those endearing young charms
Which I gaze at so fondly today
Were to fade in my arms
And flee from my sight
Like Fairy Gifts fading away
You would still be adored
As this moment you are
Let thy loveliness fall where it will
Around the dear ruin
Each wish of my heart
Would entwine itself
Verdantly still.

. . . Meet me at airport. Let's have a nice evening at home. Just you and me and [the children]. . . .

R.I.P.

On January 6 in the year of Our Lord nineteen hundred and ninety-three, the Dow rides at 3,305.16, the Yen rises against the dollar, the spot oil market slips nineteen cents, and bonds are steady. And in a federal courtroom in Los Angeles, California, the jury delivers its verdict against Charlie Keating and his son, C3. It takes the court twenty minutes to read the decision out loud. Keating, sixty-nine, is convicted on seventy-three counts of racketeering, fraud, and conspiracy and faces a possible fine of $265.5 million and sentence of 525 years. His son, thirty-seven, is convicted on sixty-four counts and faces a possible sentence of 475 years. The jurors tell reporters that the week-long testimony of Judy Wischer against Charlie Keating led them to their decision. Of course, there are other cases still pending, including a billion-dollar racketeering suit to be tried against the Keatings by Michael Manning.

When the verdict is announced, Judy Wischer is sitting in a room in a glass tower in Phoenix. For two days, Manning has been deposing her. During a break in the interrogation, he tells her the verdict. And Judy Wischer breaks down and weeps.

D.O.A.

On Monday, April 19, 1993, five minutes before Michael Manning is to begin presenting his racketeering case, Jones, Day, one of the largest law firms on the surface of the earth, enters into a *nolo* agreement with the federal government in which it admits to no wrongdoing and offers to pay $30.5 million in cash and $19.1 million in notes to settle the matter at hand. In a separate action, William Schilling, a former employee of the Federal Home Loan Bank Board once assigned to the audit of Lincoln Savings and Loan and subsequently an attorney with Jones, Day handling the Keating account, agrees to be barred for life from practicing law in the banking industry. Now the evidence assembled over the course of four years by Manning and his colleagues against Jones, Day will never be read out loud in an American court of law. In keeping with our customs, justice has been done.

ACKNOWLEDGMENTS

Long ago I learned that a reporter is only as good as his sources. Here are mine:

Jack Anderson, Dale Van Atta, and Joseph Spear were my muckraking mentors and close friends at the Washington Merry-Go-Round. They taught me everything I know about investigative reporting, but not everything they know.

If good editors have antennas then Joe Spear has a NASA-size satellite dish. He steered me to the banking beat back in 1983, putting me on a trail leading to Charles Keating. Dale Van Atta, one of the country's premier reporters and a Renaissance man, shared the secrets of the "K Mart" lecture with me. My partner Jack Anderson taught me to go against the grain and avoid press conferences.

Between 1986 and 1992, *Regardie's* magazine was my second professional home. The debt I owe former editor Brian Kelly for a dozen different articles and this book would be too embarrassing to ennumerate, even if I could. His brilliant editing and direction have turned sow's ears into silk purses. We both worked for a swashbuckler named William Regardie, of whom this can be said: He had guts.

I'd also like to note other friends and colleagues who collectively have served as a braintrust for this book.

Daryl Gibson was a miracle worker. Her editing of an earlier manuscript, done under crushing deadline pressure, paved the way for my collaboration with Charles Bowden.

Richard Vonier, editor of *Phoenix* magazine, served as a silent partner for me and Chuck. Miserable days spent sweating it out in the desert were relieved by the nights spent picking Vonier's brain at the Hollywood deli.

Everyone who is writing a book should have a good friend for conversation, commiseration, and cigar smoking; Jim Lynch was mine.

Jerry Kammer of the *Arizona Republic* blazed some of the earliest trails in the Keating story. His friendship never came with strings attached.

Peter Behr of *The Washington Post* is a class act and one of the best in the business. Together we deciphered the Keating Five transcript.

My agent, Gail Ross, and her former assistant, Elizabeth Outka, were the best allies an author could have.

Jean Calabro was always there with encouragement, editing, and exceptional secretarial skills. She's an inspiration.

Finally, thanks to Robert Sherman—without whom I'd still be a midnight security guard.

—MICHAEL BINSTEIN

In the world of Charlie Keating a lot of people will talk but no one wants to be named. Many of the people who contributed to this book still live in a kind of financial wilderness because of their former employment by Keating—the American version of a biblical curse. So to all those who helped me to understand, a big thank-you. The documents of ACC's and Lincoln's passage through the U.S. economy slumber now in a 30,000-square-foot archive in Phoenix and have proven invaluable, as have the various House and Senate hearings that monitored the salad days of deregulation in the 1980s.

Books on the eighties have provided either information or understanding. Among them are James Ring Adams, *The Big Fix: Inside the S&L Scandal,* John Wiley & Sons, Inc., 1990; John M. Barry, *The Ambition and the Power: A True Story of Washington,* Penguin Books, 1990; Connie Bruck, *The Predator's Ball: The Junk Bond Raiders and the Man Who Staked Them,* The American Lawyer/Simon & Schuster, 1988; Janice T. Connell, *The Visions of the Children: The Apparitions of the Blessed Mother at Medjugorje,* St. Martin's Press, 1992; Graef S. Crystal, *In Search of Excess: The Overcompensation of American Executives,* W. W. Norton & Co., 1991; Jesse Kornbluth, *Highly Confident: The Crime and Punishment of Michael Milken,* William Morrow and Company, 1992; Michael Lewis, *Liar's Poker,* Viking Penguin; David B. Levine with William Hoffer, *Inside Out: An Insider's Account of Wall Street,* G. P. Putnam's Sons, 1991; Stephen Pizzo, Mary Fricker, and Paul Muolo, *Inside Job: The Looting of America's Savings and Loans,* McGraw-Hill Publishing Co., 1988; James Stewart, *Den of Thieves,* Simon & Schuster, 1991; David A. Vise and Steve Coll, *Eagle on the Street,* Charles Scribner's Sons, 1991.

In addition, the facts and quotations in this book are based on numerous interviews, Senate and Congressional hearings, legal depositions, and that enormous archive of seized ACC records. Charles Keating's alleged actions are probably the most extensively documented crimes since the work of Richard Milhous Nixon.

To anyone who had to deal with me during the writing of this book, I would like to extend an apology. Insanity seems inevitable if you are foolish enough to enter the wonderland called modern American business, where everything is done by the numbers and the numbers can be baked, broiled, steamed, sautéed—cooked whatever way is desired. Thanks to these culinary skills, some folks wind up in cell blocks and some break bread with presidents. I would also like to thank Ruth Fecych, a tireless editor who helped carve a manuscript the size of a blue whale down to at least elephantine dimensions. And I should say a word for David Rosenthal, who bought the original idea and now can suffer accordingly.

—CHARLES BOWDEN

ABOUT THE AUTHORS

CHARLES BOWDEN has lived in the Southwest for thirty years and has squandered his time writing for newspapers and magazines and scribbling some books. He's devoted the best parts of his life in what is commonly called the natural world. In this magic garden, he stumbled upon Charles H. Keating, Jr. Unlike many creatures that fascinate Bowden, the Charles Keatings of this world will never become endangered species.

MICHAEL BINSTEIN is the co-author with Jack Anderson of the 60-year-old "Washington Merry-Go-Round," a nationally syndicated column appearing in 600 newspapers nationwide. He broke some of earliest stories about the savings and loan scandal, including the first exposés of Charles Keating and former house speaker Jim Wright. *The Washington Post* wrote in November 1992: "Just as two local reporters, not the White House press corps, broke the Watergate story, Binstein managed to barrel his way past the heavyweights from *The New York Times* and *Wall Street Journal.*" Binstein was formerly a contributing editor for *Regardies's*, the Washington-based political and business magazine, and has served as a consultant to ABC News and public television's *Frontline* series.